D1218056

WITHDRAWN

DEDUCTIVE REASONING
AND STRATEGIES

DEDUCTIVE REASONING AND STRATEGIES

Edited by

Walter Schaeken
University of Leuven

Gino De Vooght
André Vandierendonck
University of Ghent

Géry d'Ydewalle
University of Leuven

2000

LAWRENCE ERLBAUM ASSOCIATES, PUBLISHERS
Mahwah, New Jersey   London

The final camera copy for this work was prepared by the editors,
and therefore the publisher takes no responsibility for consistency
or correctness of typographical style. However, this arrangement
helps to make publication of this kind of scholarship possible.

Lawrence Erlbaum Associates, Inc., Publishers
10 Industrial Avenue
Mahwah, New Jersey 07430

Cover design by Kathryn Houghtaling Lacey

Library of Congress Cataloging-in-Publication Data

Deductive reasoning and strategies / edited by Walter Schaeken ... [et al.].
    p. cm
  Includes bibliographical references and indexes.
  ISBN 0-8058-3238-6 (cloth : alk. paper)
    1. Reasoning (Psychology) I. Schaeken, Walter.

  BF442.D43 1999
  153.4'3 21--dc21   99-043475

Books published by Lawrence Erlbaum Associates are printed on acid-free paper,
and their bindings are chosen for strength and durability.

Printed in the United States of America
10   9   8   7   6   5   4   3   2   1

List of Contributors

Monica Bucciarelli, Department of Psychology, University of Torino, Via Langrange 3, 10123 Torino, Italy

Ruth Byrne, Department of Psychology, Dublin University, Trinity College, Dublin 2, Ireland

Alison Capon, Department of Psychology, University of Plymouth, Drake Circus, Plymouth PL4 8AA, UK

Nuria Carriedo, Facultad de Psicologia, Universidad Nacional de Educación a Distancia, P.Box Apartado No. 50.487, Madrid 28071, Spain

Mathias Dekeyser, Laboratory of Experimental Psychology, University of Leuven, Tiensestraat 102, 3000 Leuven, Belgium

Ian Dennis, Department of Psychology, University of Plymouth, Drake Circus, Plymouth PL4 8AA, UK

Chris Desimpelaere, Department of Experimental Psychology, University of Ghent, Henri Dunantlaan 2, 9000 Gent, Belgium

Gino De Vooght, Department of Experimental Psychology, University of Ghent, Henri Dunantlaan 2, 9000 Gent, Belgium

Vicky Dierckx, Department of Experimental Psychology, University of Ghent, Henri Dunantlaan 2, 9000 Gent, Belgium

Maria Devetag, Scuolo Superiore S. Anna, Via Carducci 40, 56100 Pisa, Italy

Caroline Dupeyrat, LTC UMR CNRS 5551, Maison de la Recherche, University of Toulouse-Mirail, 5 Allées A. Machado, F-31058 Toulouse Cedex 1, France

Géry d'Ydewalle, Laboratory of Experimental Psychology, University of Leuven, Tiensestraat 102, 3000 Leuven, Belgium

Orlando Espino, Department of Cognitive Psychology, University of La Laguna, Campus de Guajara, 38205 Tenerife, Spain

Jonathan Evans, Centre for Thinking and Language, Department of Psychology, University of Plymouth, Plymouth PL4 8AA, UK

Neil Fairley, Division of Psychology, University of Wolverhampton, Wulfrana Street, Wolverhampton, WV1 1SB, UK

Juan Garcia Madruga, Facultad de Psicologia, Universidad Nacional de Educación a Distancia, P.Box Apartado No. 50.487, Madrid 28071, Spain

Merideth Gattis, Department of Psychology, University of Sheffield, S10 2TP Sheffield, UK

Vittorio Girotto, CREPCO, Université de Provence, 29 Av. R. Schuman, F-13621 Aix-en-Provence Cedex 1, France

Michel Gonzalez, CREPCO, Université de Provence, 29 Av. R. Schuman, F-13621 Aix-en-Provence Cedex 1, France

Francisco Gutiérrez, Facultad de Psicologia, Universidad Nacional de Educación a Distancia, P.Box Apartado No. 50.487, Madrid 28071, Spain

Simon Handley, Department of Psychology, University of Plymouth, Drake Circus, Plymouth PL4 8AA, UK

Philip Johnson-Laird, Department of Psychology, Princeton University, Princeton, NJ 08544, USA

Stephen Kilpatrick, Division of Psychology, University of Wolverhampton, Wulfrana Street, Wolverhampton, WV1 1SB, UK

Paolo Legrenzi, Institute of Psychology, State University of Milan, Via Larga 19, 20122 Milan, Italy

Ken Manktelow, Division of Psychology, University of Wolverhampton, Wulfrana Street, Wolverhampton, WV1 1SB, UK

Sergio Moreno, Facultad de Psicologia, Universidad Nacional de Educación a Distancia, P.Box Apartado No. 50.487, Madrid 28071, Spain

Thomas Ormerod, Department of Psychology, Lancaster University, Lancaster, LA1 4YF, UK

David Over, School of Social and International Studies, University of Sunderland, Chester Road, Sunderland, SR1 3SE, UK

Reinhold Rauh, Albert-Ludwigs-Universität Freiburg, Institut für Informatik and Gesellschaft, Abteilung Kognitionswissenschaft, D-79098 Freiburg i. Br., Germany

Maxwell Roberts, Department of Psychology, University of Essex, Wivenhoe Park, Colchester, Essex, CO4 3SQ, UK

Carlos Santamaria, Department of Cognitive Psychology, University of La Laguna, Campus de Guajara, 38205 Tenerife, Spain

Fabien Savary, 3040 Henri de Salieres #3, Montréal, Québec, Canada H1N 2Y2

Walter Schaeken, Laboratory of Experimental Psychology, University of Leuven, Tiensestraat 102, 3000 Leuven, Belgium

Walter Schroyens, Laboratory of Experimental Psychology, University of Leuven, Tiensestraat 102, 3000 Leuven, Belgium

Olaf Spittaels, Laboratory of Experimental Psychology, University of Leuven, Tiensestraat 102, 3000 Leuven, Belgium

André Vandierendonck, Department of Experimental Psychology, University of Ghent, Henri Dunantlaan 2, 9000 Gent, Belgium

Massimo Warglien, University of Venice, Department of Economics, Dorsoduro 175, 30123 Venice, Italy

Contents

To identify relations between dimensions   167
To identify polarity within a dimension   168
Constraints on spatial strategies   170
Limited forms of reasoning   170
Limited dimensions of space   171
Understanding strategies through general principles   172
References   173

9. **Strategies of Constructing Preferred Mental Models**   177
    in Spatial Relational Inference
    Reinhold Rauh

    Material from research on qualitative spatial reasoning   179
    Abstract model construction strategies   181
    Model construction strategies: Domain-unrelated   184
    or domain-specific?
    Conclusions   188
    References   189

10. **Model Construction and Elaboration in Spatial**   191
     Linear Syllogisms
     André Vandierendonck, Gino De Vooght,
     Chris Desimpelaere, and Vicky Dierckx

     Number of models and reasoning performance   194
     Accuracy   196
     Premise reading time   197
     Model elaboration   198
     Premise memory or model representation?   200
     Accuracy   201
     Problem representation   202
     Solution time   202
     Premise reading time   202
     Strategical issues   203
     Concluding remarks   204
     References   206

Preface

This book emerged from the Workshop on Deductive Reasoning and Strategies which took place at the Royal Academy of Science, in Brussels, Belgium, March 20-21 1998. The workshop was held under the auspices of the National Committee of Psychological Sciences, and was sponsored by the Fund for Scientific Research Flanders and the Federal research project IUAP/PAI P4/19.

We hope that this book will serve to direct the readers' attention to various trends in the psychology of reasoning and the way these trends connect to the role of strategies. Indeed, we hope to illustrate the diversity of research related to reasoning and strategies: There are chapters about syllogistic reasoning, spatial reasoning, propositional reasoning, statistical reasoning, and some additional meta-theoretical chapters. Moreover, the final collection includes the work of scientists from all over the world.

Because many of the contributions do not deal exclusively with one topic, they have not been explicitly placed into sections. However, the ordering of the chapters reflects the main issue addressed by each author. Reading the first version of the manuscripts for the book raised the question of what we would do with the presentation of the two major theories of deductive reasoning, that is, the mental model theory and the rule-based theories. Indeed, many of the authors gave an introduction to these theories. We decided that it would be best if the authors wrote their chapters to stand alone. As a result, each chapter is self-contained and can be read on its own. Some repetition of key theoretical issues therefore occurs. However, you will also notice that many of the authors refer to other chapters in the volume. This is, of course, a consequence of the fact that the book originates from a workshop, in which there was room for the participants to discuss their ideas. Because these discussions were one of the main goals of the workshop, we tried to include them in some form in the book. Instead of an introduction we opted for a final chapter to the book, in which we tried to formulate some conclusions based on our ideas, the ideas presented in the different chapters, and some aspects of the discussion sessions that took place during the workshop.

We owe much to Marleen Devijver. Her secretarial work for the workshop was invaluable. Moreover, she made a major contribution in preparing the manuscripts for publication. We also thank Walter Schroyens for his help in preparing the camera-ready copy for the book, and Kristien Dieussaert and Niki Verschueren for their help in checking the indices. We want to express our gratitude to Permanent Secretary Prof. N. Schamp of the Royal Academy of Science for his cooperation: He made it possible for our workshop to be held in the buildings of the Royal Academy of Science in Brussels. We also thank his secretary, Mr. Verdoodt. We are indebted to Prof. V. Dekeyzer of the University of Liege and to Prof. G. Lories of the University of Louvain for acting as chairpersons during the workshop. We gratefully acknowledge these individuals who contributed to planning and conducting the conference: Marjan Coene, Sara De Maeght, Vicky Dierckx, Kristien Dieussaert, Mathias Dekeyser, Nicolas Geeraert, Jan Lauwereyns, Walter Schroyens, and Niki Verschueren.

Finally, we want to thank all contributors for their enthusiastic cooperation in the realization of the workshop and of this book.

Walter Schaeken
Gino De Vooght
André Vandierendonck
Géry d'Ydewalle

1

What Could and Could Not Be
a Strategy in Reasoning

Jonathan St. B. T. Evans

The term "strategy" is discussed with reference to Evans and Over's (1996) distinction between implicit and explicit thought processes. A strategy is used to refer to processes which are relatively slow, goal-directed, systematic, and under explicit conscious control. The remainder of the chapter concerns the theoretical accounts that have been given of reasoning in three domains: transitive inference, syllogistic reasoning, and propositional reasoning. It is argued that many descriptions of the processes involved in reasoning refer to tacit processes which could not—by the above definition—be strategic. These include pragmatic comprehension processes and nonlogical heuristics. However, it is also argued that to reason deductively rather than inductively does require a conscious effort at deduction and only occurs in response to specific instructions. Thus deduction is seen as a strategy. An account of strategic deductive reasoning with the mental models framework is preferred.

To start with let us consider some examples of what we mean by the term *strategy* when we talk of people employing strategies in reasoning, problem solving, and decision making. It seems to me that we would not talk of strategies when people are making quick decisions with little time for conscious reflective thought. Thus we would not talk of a footballer employing a strategy when receiving and releasing the ball in a couple of seconds, but we might consider that a golfer could employ strategies in choosing the kind of shot to play. Similarly, we would not consider strategic thinking to be implicated in how a car driver reacts to a sudden emergency on the road, but might we believe that it is involved in how the manager of small company deals with a crisis in the company's performance.

Of course, the employment of slow thought processes is hardly sufficient to justify the term strategy. We might think that the golfer is playing mechanically without thinking about the best way to play the course, or that the manager is blundering along without any clear ideas about how to deal with her crisis. Thus another facet of the term strategy is that some kind of systematic planning or goal-directed thought is involved. Strategic thinking thus involves the development and application of methods. Still, this does not sufficiently define the term. For example, the skilled footballer has method in the quick decisions involved in passing the ball, developed by years of experience. One could analyze patterns of play and show that good players make more appropriate choices to the context, taking into account the state of the play when the ball is received. Experts refer to this as "vision."

Why should fast-process but nevertheless systematic and goal-directed decision making not appear to be strategic? Perhaps because it is intuitive or unconscious in nature. However, if we examine the notion of conscious thinking a little more carefully, we can see that it involves two important and distinct facets: awareness and intentionality. If a process is expert but implicit and the person concerned cannot verbalize the expertise in any clear way we may be reluctant to ascribe the expertise to a strategy. That is the awareness aspect. The intentionality aspect arises because we think that a person employing a strategy has some choice and conscious control over what is to be done. For example, we think that the person could try out one strategy and if it did not work, try another. Or we think that strategies are things that can be explicitly taught to people. Certainly, in cognitive psychology, researchers interested in strategies frequently manipulate their use by verbal instruction. This implies that strategies are methods that can be described and understood verbally and then adopted consciously.

In short, we use the term strategy to refer to thought processes that are elaborated in time, systematic, goal-directed, and under explicit conscious control. We also assume that strategic thinking is active and flexible: Individuals can choose to operate one strategy rather than another when faced with a given type of problem. They are not operating under the passive constraints of past learning. The nature of strategic thinking as defined earlier has close connections with what some researchers describe as explicit as opposed to implicit cognition. We examine this distinction before proceeding to consider reasoning strategies as such.

IMPLICIT AND EXPLICIT COGNITION

Dual Processes in Thinking

In the field of implicit learning, some researchers believe there is evidence for two distinct cognitive systems, one implicit and the other explicit (Berry & Dienes, 1993; Reber, 1993). I have discussed this work and its implications for the psychology of thinking elsewhere (Evans, 1995) and will describe it only briefly here. The implicit system is characterized as being evolutionarily primary, shared with other animals, inaccessible to verbal report, distributed and robust in the face of neurological insult. The explicit system on the other hand is uniquely human, associated with language and consciousness, and localized in the brain. Another important distinction is that knowledge acquired implicitly tends to be context specific whereas explicit knowledge can be transferred much more readily to contexts other than those in which it was acquired. Although this dichotomy makes perfect sense to me in the light of research on the psychology of thinking and reasoning, it should be noted that it is somewhat controversial in the current literature (see, e.g., Stevenson, 1997).

Evans and Over (1996) have elaborated a similar distinction as applied to human thinking, reasoning, and decision making. This is linked—though not one to one—with a distinction between two kinds of rationality as follows:

Rationality₁: *Thinking, speaking, reasoning, making a decision, or acting in a way that is generally reliable and efficient for achieving one's goals.*

Rationality₂: *Thinking, speaking, reasoning, making a decision, or acting when one has a reason for what one does sanctioned by a normative theory.*

This distinction was originally introduced by Evans (1993; a similar distinction between adaptive and normative rationality was proposed by Anderson, 1990) to account for a paradox in the psychology of thinking: Why is it that members of such an intelligent and well adapted species as human beings produce so many errors and fallacies in experimental studies of reasoning and judgement? The proposed answer is that normative theories such as logic and decision theory may not provide appropriate criteria for rational action in a complex world of poorly defined information, and that normally adaptive mechanisms may not easily be adapted to meet the instructional requirements of an artificial experiment. As an example of the latter, the belief bias effect in syllogistic reasoning may be cited as evidence of irrational₂ reasoning: This is the tendency to be influenced by the a priori believability of conclusions when assessing the validity of logical arguments (see Evans, Newstead, & Byrne, 1993, chap. 8 for a review). However, Evans and Over (1996) argue that it is adaptive in everyday life to reason from all relevant belief, and this tendency is automatically transferred to the syllogistic reasoning experiment, despite instructions to draw conclusions on the basis of the information given.

The distinction between implicit and explicit thought is critical to arguments such as the above. If the influence of belief in reasoning is "automatic" and resistant to instructions, then this implies the operation of implicit processes, beyond conscious control. On the other hand, as we see later, people can adapt their reasoning processes to an extent when instructed to base conclusions on necessity rather than belief (Evans et al., 1994; George, 1995; Stevenson & Over, 1995). This in turn implies the operation of an explicit thinking system. The two systems can almost be seen as competing with one another, as in the study of Evans, Barston, and Pollard (1983) where participants appeared to adopt an unstable mixture of logical and belief based reasoning.

Evans and Over (1996) developed a distinction between explicit and implicit thinking systems similar to that of implicit reasoning researchers, described earlier. They argued that much of our capacity to be rational$_1$ is derived from implicit processes either acquired by implicit learning or already present in innate modules. They further suggested that connectionist systems are appropriate for modeling these kinds of processes. To achieve rationality$_2$—for example to be able to formulate a mathematical proof, or more prosaically to understand how to fill in a tax form—generally requires use of the explicit system. This system is by contrast to the implicit system, slow, sequential, and limited in processing capacity. However, the access to language and reflective consciousness permits an important facility which Evans and Over described as *hypothetical thinking*. Hypothetical thinking allows us to represent (as mental models) possible states of the world. This in turn permits us to draw deductions, to make forecasts, and to base our decisions on analysis of future possibilities rather than simply responding on the basis of past success. It is important to realize, however, that no act of thought is purely explicit. At the very least, implicit pragmatic processes select information as relevant and determine the locus of attention of the explicit system. Thus biases in reasoning and judgment (judged by rational$_2$ criteria) often arise because the wrong information is encoded as relevant by the implicit system (Evans, 1989).

**Methodological Issues—Use of Verbal Reports
and Verbal Instruction**

How can we tell if a process is explicit and learn of its nature? I have been for many years—and remain—sceptical of the value of introspective reporting, but sympathetic to use of verbal protocol analysis (see Evans, 1989, chap. 5). Some authors treat these alike, although to me the distinction is critical. Asking someone to report their strategy is introspection and subject to all the dangers of that method famously identified by Nisbett and Wilson (1977). Introspection requires memory and interpretation of processes and can often give rise to self-theorizing or rationalization. To take one example of the problem, in a study by Evans, Harries, Dennis, and Dean (1995) a group of general practioners were asked to judge whether they would prescribe lipid lowering agents (to reduce blood cholesterol) for a series of hypothetical patients described by a computer program. The patients varied in a number of characteristics of medical relevance (e.g., weight, age, gender, family history of heart disease, history of diabetes, and so forth). When interviewed after the task most doctors claimed to have considered nearly all the relevant medical factors in making their decisions. Multiple regression analyses on the judgments actually made, however, revealed that typically only a subset of cues had an influence. The doctors were quite unable to tell which of the cues they described as relevant had actually influenced their choices.

The problem in the doctors' study is fairly typical. Doctors have been taught the theory at an explicit verbal level, and this is reflected in their interview data. However, the complex judgments involved in a multicue task, probably involved intuitive, that is implicit processes that are only able to take account of a limited number of cues. But people do not report use of intuition, they rather describe a "strategy" that they did not in fact use. Would introspections be valid when the process used is in fact an explicit one? There are two difficulties here. First, because introspections *can* be rationalizations of implicit processes, how would we know from the report if an explicit process was used on this occasion? Second, even if the process is explicit that is registered in verbal working memory at the time, it may be forgotten or misremembered and retrospective reports could still contain theorizing about one's own behavior as in the many examples discussed by Nisbett and Wilson (1977).

I agree, however, with Ericsson and Simon (1984) that use of think-aloud protocols is much more useful, and indeed have employed verbal protocol analysis a number of times in my own research work. Here, the participant is not asked to remember, report, describe, or interpret anything but merely to externalize explicit thought by verbalizing it. Protocol analysis is particularly useful for discovering the locus of attention, the goals that people are following, and the order in which subprocesses are applied. It is, however, the task of the psychologist, not the participant, to interpret the protocols and discover any strategies that they may contain. The obvious limitation of the method is that implicit processes—by definition—cannot be verbalized. Evans (1995) discussed the analysis of think-aloud protocols recorded when people were working on the Wason selection task. On this task, people have to decide which of four cards to turn over in order to decide whether a conditional rule is true or false. Their choices can be shown to be strongly influenced by "matching bias" (Evans, 1998; Evans & Lynch, 1973): That is, they tend to choose cards whose visible symbols are named in the rule, regardless of their logical significance. Of course, noone reports matching bias: Noone describes a strategy of picking matching cards.

What the verbal protocol analysis does reveal, in the case of the selection task, is that people focus their attention on the matching cards. It also shows that they focus on matching values when considering what could be on the hidden sides as well. Now, although we can use other measures of attentional preference to tell which visible values people are considering (e.g., by asking them to point at cards considered using a computer mouse—Evans, 1996) only by verbal protocol analysis could we discover which *hidden* values people are thinking about. If we ask people *why* they choose the cards they do, then we move into the realm of introspective reporting which as Wason and Evans (1975) demonstrated, can produce rationalizations of choices on the selection task. If instead we study think-aloud protocols and try to interpret them ourselves, we may form better theories of what is going on. For example, Evans (1995, 1996) has argued on the basis of the protocols and other evidence that people try on this task to justify the choice of cards with reference to the logic of the rule and instructions given. This is their explicit response to the explicit instructions. However, their attention is focused by preconscious implicit processes on to the matching cards which appear to be relevant, and the explicit processes in this case serve only to justify (often erroneously) the choice of these cards.

As is made clear by numerous examples discussed by Evans and Over (1996) I do believe that the Wason task is exceptional and that our choices and actions on other tasks often are determined by explicit reasoning. I have discussed this example mainly to show the difficulties involved in the interpretation of verbal reports. There is another method available for the study of explicit processes that is a little easier to work with, and that is use of verbal instruction. If behavior on a task is at least partially under explicit control, then it should be possible to influence it by the kind of instructions given. If you don't accept this premise, then you can't really work on deductive reasoning at all. A task is only deductive if participants are instructed to make judgments of necessity, that is, to produce or endorse conclusions that *must* follow from the premises given. Only by giving—and assuming comprehension—of verbal instructions to this effect can one hope to investigate people's ability to make deductions.

Let me attempt, then, a tighter definition of what I mean by an explicit thought process and how it can be measured. Such a process registers—at least fleetingly—in verbal working memory, and thus aspects of it can be externalized by concurrent verbal reporting. Explicit processes also involve conscious control and can thus be modified by appropriate verbal instructions. Indeed, the flexibility and controllability of explicit thinking is its major strength and the compensation it provides for its very slow and limited processing power when compared with the implicit system. I use the term *strategy* here to refer to a process that is explicit in these terms and that contains a method aimed at achievement of a goal. With these preliminaries now completed, we turn to the main question with which this chapter is concerned. Which of the various processes envisioned by theories of reasoning in the literature could be considered a strategy in reasoning and which could not?

THEORIES AND STUDIES OF DEDUCTIVE REASONING

Transitive Inference

Transitive inference is a form of relational reasoning in which objects are ordered on a single dimension. A relation is transitive whenever "*A is above B on the scale*" and "*B is above C*," then "*A must be above C.*" Many comparatives used in everyday language appear to convey this property of transitivity: for example "*better–worse*," "*taller–shorter*" or "*darker–lighter.*" The most popular paradigm used for studying transitive inference in the psychology of reasoning is the linear syllogism or three-term series problem, such as:

Mary is taller than Sue.
Sue is taller than Joan.
.: Mary is taller than Joan.

This argument is deductively sound, because its premises are only consistent with a state of affairs in which the conclusion holds. The following, however, is invalid:

Mary is taller than Sue.
Joan is taller than Sue.
.: Mary is taller than Joan.

Here, the premises are indeterminate. That is, they are consistent with two states of affairs, in only one of which the conclusion holds. Thus the conclusion, although possible, is not necessary given the premises. Most experimental work has concentrated on determinate premises pairs in which people are asked either to draw a conclusion or to answer a question such as "Who is tallest?" Because error rates tend to be low, analysis is often based on response times.

Transitive inference was a popular topic in the 1960s and 1970s and has been relatively neglected in the more recent literature (however, for examples in the spatial domain, see Rauh, chap. 9, this volume; Vandierendonck, De Vooght, Desimpelaere, & Dierckx, this volume). The early literature was dominated by a debate between the imagery theory of De Soto, London, and Handel (1965) and Huttenlocher (1968) on the one hand, the linguistic theory of Clark (1969) on the other. According to the imagery theory, people solve these problems by constructing visual images in which objects are placed one above the other. Thus, given the premise *"Mary is taller than Sue"* one sets up a spatial array as follows:

Mary
Sue

Then given the further premise *"Joan is shorter than Mary"* one adds the third terms as follows:

Mary
Sue
Joan

The image can now be inspected to answer questions such as *"Who is shortest?"* This theory led to (largely successful) predictions about problem difficulty based on principles such as preferred direction of working and end-anchoring of terms. Clark's theory on the other hand supposed that the information in the premises was encoded linguistically and only integrated when a question was asked. This theory also had principles such as lexical marking and congruence: It should be easier to process unmarked comparatives and adjectives (e.g., *tall* as opposed to *short*) and easier if the question is congruent with the form of the representations. For example, the foregoing syllogism would be encoded as:

> Mary is tall+, Sue is tall.
> Sue is tall+, Joan is tall.

With this representation, the question "*Who is tallest?*" would be congruent and hence faster to process than the question "*Who is shortest?*"

When I first looked at this literature in detail in order to review it (Evans, 1982, chap. 4), I was struck by the fact that although the theories were couched in very different terms, their principles entailed almost identical predictions about the relative difficulty of different kinds of linear syllogism and that both theories were well supported by the evidence. In order to try to separate the two, I then examined two further questions: Was there any direct evidence that a visual process was involved in solving these problems, and was there evidence that information was integrated prior to the question being asked as envisaged by the imagery but not the linguistic theory? The results of this survey surprised me at the time bearing in mind that Johnson-Laird's (1983) seminal work on mental models was as yet unknown. The answer to question (a) was that the evidence for visual images was almost entirely reliant on introspective report; evidence based on "converging operations" provided at best weak and ambiguous support for the operation of a visual process. The answer to (b), based on a variety of sources of information, was an unequivocal "yes." The conclusions were essentially supported by the updated review of Evans et al. (1993, chap. 6).

The reason I was surprised was that the imagery theory appeared to be correct in terms of integrated representations, but it was far from clear that images were responsible. We are, of course, nowadays accustomed to thinking in terms of information being represented in integrated mental models, and following the comments of Johnson-Laird (1983), cautious concerning the equation of images with models. The more important consideration for our current purposes, however, is that the two theories, so similar in predictions about problem difficulty, look very different when we ask if they describe something that could be a strategy. People report "using images" to solve the problems and this does indeed sound very much like a strategy. We could certainly advise people to manipulate spatial arrays of objects as a means of solving these problems. On the other hand, the linguistic theory describes processes that clearly could *not* be a strategy. Noone would suggest that we have conscious control or knowledge of the encoding of sentences.

Consider the finding that syllogisms phrased using "*taller*" (*better, stronger,* etc.) are easier than those phrased using "*shorter*" (*worse, weaker*). According to Clark, these are easier because the comparative is unmarked, that is used to refer to the dimension as a whole and not just one pole of it. This is explained on the grounds that unmarked comparatives and adjectives are faster and easier to retrieve from memory. According to the imagery theory, however, unmarked comparatives are placed at the top of a vertical spatial array and people prefer working top-down to bottom-up. Are these proposals psychologically incompatible? Although the imagery theory sounds strategy-like it may be that people have no *control* over their tendency to put unmarked comparatives at the top and then work top-down. They may simply be experiencing the phenomenological consequences of the kind of tacit linguistic processes that Clark has described. In other words, the two theories might not just be making equivalent predictions—they might be *describing the same process* in different terms.

I am led to consider this last possibility first by the similarity in predictions of the two accounts and second by the fact that one account is focused on conscious experience and the other on implicit (linguistic) processing. Actually we know, as mentioned earlier, that Clark was wrong in proposing that linguistic information is retained in the representation of premises and not integrated until a question is asked. However, his analysis of the linguistic factors affecting the difficulty of encoding information in the first place might well have been correct. Integrated mental models built on the basis of verbal premises clearly have to go through a linguistic encoding phase. The fact that the processing of these models may give rise to an experience of imagery might not be of any particular significance.

I hope that this discussion brings out clearly the point made in my introduction, namely that we cannot attribute use of a strategy simply on the basis of an introspective report. People may well have a mental experience when solving a problem which they can report. This experience may (or unfortunately, may not) in turn be linked to the underlying process. We must not, however, attribute the status of a strategy on this basis alone. It is only a strategy if it is flexible and controllable. This is the reason that Evans and Over (1996) gave so much weight to studies of people's ability to change their reasoning methods according to instruction, when discussing explicit aspects of reasoning. Unfortunately, most of the studies of "strategies" in transitive and relational reasoning to date have in fact relied heavily on introspective report (see Evans et al., 1993, pp. 206–208).

Syllogistic Reasoning

There is a considerable psychological literature on syllogistic reasoning despite the fact that this limited logical system, devised by Aristotle, is now of little more than historical interest to philosophers and logicians. A syllogism has two premises and a conclusion, which may or may not be determined by the premises. For example, the syllogism

Some B are C.
No A are B.
.: Some C are not A.   S1

is valid whereas the similar looking syllogism:

> *Some B are C.*
> *No A are B.*
> *.: Some A are not C.*   S2

is not valid. In order to be valid, the conclusion must hold in all possible states of affairs consistent with the premises. The conclusion to *S2* would hold in many cases. For example:

> *A = men*
> *B = mothers*
> *C = students*

Given our real world knowledge of these sets we might well argue as follows:

> *Some mothers are students.*
> *No men are mothers.*
> *.: Some men are not students.*

Although both the premises and the conclusion are true, the form of argument is nevertheless fallacious. This can easily be seen if we set *A* equal to *"male philosophy students."* Now, the argument reads:

> *Some mothers are students.*
> *No male philosophy students are mothers.*
> *.:Some male philosophy students are not students.*

where the premises are still true, but the conclusion evidently false. No such counterexample can be found for *S1* which is in fact logically valid. Of course, our participant populations—untutored in formal logic—may have difficulty in understanding what is meant by logical validity and its relation to truth. This is why deductive reasoning experiments always require instructions which define the nature of validity or logical necessity, for example, by saying that an argument is only valid if its conclusion *must* be true, given that its premises are true.

Two well established findings in the experimental literature on syllogistic reasoning are the following (see Evans et al., 1993). First, when the problem content is abstract or arbitrary, people endorse or generate many fallacious arguments. That is to say they approve as valid conclusions that *could* be true given their premises, but that do not have to be true—as in *S2* above. Thus despite the instructions given (of which more later), untrained participants are not good at ensuring the logical necessity of arguments. Second, this tendency to draw fallacious conclusions is greatly reduced when those conclusions are expressed in thematic terms that conflict with prior belief. For example, people would not endorse *S2* when expressed in the male philosophy student example shown before.

The latter effect is referred to in the literature as "belief bias" which is a misnomer, because it suggests that people are drawing conclusions because they are believable. The typical belief bias experiment compares valid syllogisms with plausible fallacies like *S2* and also compares performance on problems with believable and unbelievable conclusions (e.g., Evans et al., 1983). Typically people draw more believable conclusions, but this "belief bias" is largely restricted to invalid, fallacious arguments. Because such studies have generally lacked a control condition with neutral conclusions psychologists have fallen into the trap of believing that people are biased to endorse fallacious conclusions compatible with belief. In fact, those studies that have included neutral controls (e.g., Evans & Handley, 1997; Evans & Pollard, 1990; Newstead, Pollard, Evans, & Allen, 1992) have shown that fallacies are accepted as often when their conclusions are neutral or abstract as when they are believable. Thus the phenomenon is really a *debias* because unbelievable conclusions suppress fallacies. This finding has major theoretical importance as I demonstrate next.

A large number of theoretical accounts have been proposed to explain syllogistic reasoning data (see Evans et al., 1993, chap. 7). Most of these accounts are not at all strategy-like in nature. One tradition focuses on the interpretation of the premises, emphasizing linguistic and pragmatic influences. For example, the prevailing tendency to endorse fallacies might be due to people making illicit conversions of premises (for example reading *All A are B* to entail *All B are A*) or misreading premises due to Gricean implicatures (e.g., taking *Some A are B* to exclude *All A are B*). Such approaches involve proposals that enhance the semantic informativeness of the premises and thus legitimize conclusions that would otherwise be logically fallacious. This leaves undefined the issue of how people draw logical conclusions from their personalized representations. An exception is the Verbal Reasoning (VR) model proposed recently by Polk and Newell (1995) in which conclusions are derived directly from encoding and re-encoding the premises without any separate process of reasoning. Like the linguistic theory of transitive inference discussed earlier, however, all the interpretational approaches involve tacit processes which do not seem amenable to modification by conscious strategies.

Another tradition tries to account for syllogistic reasoning in terms of entirely noninferential mechanisms. The classical proposal of an atmosphere effect (Woodworth & Sells, 1935) in which people are supposed to endorse conclusions whose mood (universal–particular or affirmative–negative) is similar to the premises, is surprisingly well supported by the data (see Begg & Denny, 1969). This theory seems to have fallen from favor more due to its a priori implausibility than to its lack of empirical adequacy. There is clear evidence in the deductive reasoning literature as a whole that people do have a modest degree of deductive competence (see Evans & Over, 1996, 1997) which is ignored by this kind of theory. However, this has not deterred other authors from proposing noninferential theories, most recently that of Chater and Oaksford (1999) who argue that syllogistic data can be accounted for in terms of heuristic decision processes related to the information conveyed by the premises and conclusions. Again, these kinds of theory do not describe anything that sounds like a strategy.

One theory in this field stands out both as having an account of deductive competence and allowing scope for strategic thinking. This is the mental models theory of syllogistic inference (see Johnson-Laird & Bara, 1984; Johnson-Laird & Byrne, 1991; see also Johnson-Laird, Savary, & Bucciarelli, chap. 11, this volume). This theory proposes that people form mental models representing possible states of affairs consistent with the premises. Reasoning occurs by (a) deriving potential conclusions from these models and (b) attempting to validate them by a search for counterexample models in which the premises are true but the conclusions false. Thus there are three stages as follows:

1. Model formation:	The reasoner forms an initial model from the premises.
2. Conclusion formation:	The reasoner derives a putative conclusion from the model which is informative (e.g., not a repetition of a premise).
3. Conclusion validation:	The reasoner searches for a counterexample, that is a model in which the premises are true but the conclusion is false. If no such model is found the conclusion is valid.

The model theory can account for the limited deductive competence people show in syllogistic reasoning by postulation of the third, validation stage. However, it can also account for the strong tendency for people to endorse fallacies on the grounds that people's ability to search for counterexamples is limited by working memory capacity. An important piece of evidence in this regard is that people perform better when attempting *valid* syllogisms whose premises are consistent with only one mental model than when reasoning with multiple-model syllogisms (see Johnson-Laird & Bara, 1984, and for a recent replication, Evans & Handley, 1997). The point here is that if people were only responding on the basis of a single model then they should be equally happy to endorse valid multiple-model syllogisms as one-model problems, because any model of the premises will support the conclusion. It seems that some people at least are aware that other models exists and not confident that they have checked them all.

Recent evidence suggests that although people *can* search for alternative models, they do not necessarily do so without strong encouragement. In a recent large-scale study, Evans and Handley (1997, Experiment 2) presented participants with all possible premise pairs together with every possible conclusion for evaluation (The same experiments are discussed by Handley et al., chap. 12, this volume, for other purposes). The problems were classified a priori as Necessary (valid problems whose conclusion must follow), Impossible (invalid problems whose conclusions must be false, if the premises are true) and Possible (invalid problems whose conclusions may but do not have to be true). The last category was divided post hoc, on the basis of participants responses into commonly endorsed fallacies—Possible Strong, and rarely endorsed fallacies—Possible Weak. Examples of syllogisms in all four categories were then presented to a separate group of participants in an independent replication study (Experiment 3). The results for these selected syllogisms are shown in Fig. 1.1. The striking finding is that Possible Strong syllogisms are accepted as often as Necessary ones and Possible Weak almost as infrequently as Impossible ones. This finding only seems to make sense on the assumption that people are willing to make a validity judgment on the basis of the first model that they consider.

On the face of it, this seems to be a poor result for the model theory, since little validation appears to be taking place. (Recent evidence from Newstead, Handley, & Buck [in press], using a different methodology led to a similar conclusion.) However, Evans, Handley, Harper, and Johnson-Laird (in press) have discovered that the computer program implementation of the model theory (Johnson-Laird & Byrne, 1994) does generate models in a specific order which corresponds to our distinction. That is, the fallacies that people accept are the ones where the first model constructed supports the conclusion. Also, a rather different perspective emerges if we propose that this final stage of the model theory involves strategic thinking.

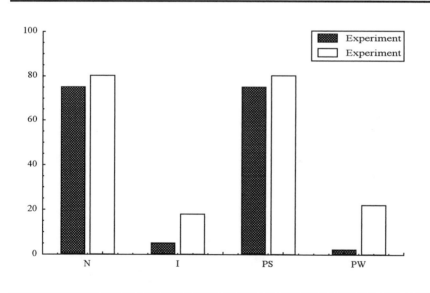

FIG. 1.1: Endorsement of conclusions of four kinds of syllogisms in the study of Evans and Handley (1997): Necessary (N), Impossible (I), Possible Strong (PS) and Possibly Weak (PW).

Evans and Over (1996) argued that the natural mode of thinking is inductive and not deductive, and that people make an effort at deduction only when given appropriate instructions. They also argue that the validation stage should involve an explicit process and take issue with some of Johnson-Laird and Byrne's comments in this regard (see Evans & Over, 1996, chap. 7).

The belief bias phenomenon supports the proposal that people can search for alternative models. As mentioned earlier, fallacies tend to be suppressed when their conclusions are unbelievable. The fallacious arguments used in these studies (e.g., Evans et al., 1983) are of the kind that Evans and Handley (1997) term Possible Strong, that is, ones that tend to produce fallacies when materials are neutral or abstract. Evans and Handley (1997, Experiment 5) investigated belief bias for Necessary (valid), Possible Strong, and Possible Weak syllogisms using a conclusion evaluation task. The results are shown in Fig. 1.2. In line with the literature there was a significant decrease in acceptance of Possible Strong arguments when the conclusion was unbelievable, but no increase relative to a neutral conclusion when it was believable. With Possible Weak syllogisms, however, there *was* a significant increase in the (normally low) acceptance rates when conclusions were believable. Thus it appears that people may have searched for a model they would not normally have considered when trying to prove a believable conclusion.

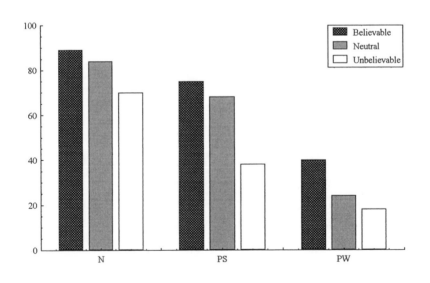

FIG. 1.2: Endorsement of three kinds of syllogisms as a function of believability in the study of Evans and Handley (1997, Experiment 5).

If the validation stage is strategic, then it should be possible to influence it by instructions. Specifically, instructions emphasizing the need to prove logical necessity should suppress fallacies. Standard instructions on deductive reasoning tasks do indicate the need to draw necessary conclusions—or else it is not a deductive reasoning task! However, they do not usually labor the point. Newstead et al. (1992, Experiment 5) and Evans, Allen, Newstead, and Pollard (1994) reported several experiments in which considerable emphasis on necessity was made compared with standard instructions, with belief of conclusions also manipulated. In general, the use of such instructions significantly suppressed both the rate of fallacies and the extent of the belief bias effect, although the belief bias was not eliminated. By contrast, some recent studies have looked at relaxation of strict logical reasoning instructions and found that belief based conclusions are made much more frequently as a result (George, 1995; Stevenson & Over, 1995).

In summary, I am proposing the following. People's normal mode of reasoning is inductive. That is, given some information they will construct a single mental model representing some state of affairs and base their inferences on that single model. The processes responsible for this are almost certainly implicit and beyond strategic control. However, people *can* make an effort at deduction when explicitly instructed to do so or motivated by their prior beliefs about the conclusions. This (weak) deductive competence is discussed in some detail by Evans and Over (1996, 1997) who consider it to be central to certain kinds of uniquely human intelligence that they describe as involving rationality$_2$ or impersonal, normative rationality. Evans and Over associate this kind of rationality with explicit thinking which connects clearly with the argument that I have just made. Note that my proposals here extend published accounts of the mental model theory of reasoning (e.g., Johnson-Laird & Byrne, 1991), which make no reference to the idea that an implicit comprehension stage may (or may not) be accompanied by an explicit effort at deduction.

Propositional Reasoning:
Models Versus Rules

I have argued earlier that *part* of what the model theory describes could be strategic and part could not. The same would apply to the versions of theory aimed at explaining data in propositional reasoning: mostly reasoning about conditional and disjunctive statements. In this domain, however, there is a powerful rival account in terms of mental logic (e.g., Braine & O'Brien, 1991; Rips, 1994). I suggest that although the model theory describes something that could, in part, be a strategy, the same is not true of the mental logic approach. Mental logics involve highly abstract sets of logical rules that can be applied to reasoning in all domains. The proponents argue that these rules are fundamental to all intelligent thought (Rips, 1994) and built in to the lexicon by which we access the meaning of words such as "if" (Braine & O'Brien, 1991). Thus mental logics appeared to be hard-wired and quite probably innate in origin.

Roberts (1993; see also Roberts, chap. 2, this volume) complains that both the mental models and mental logic theory are proposed as fundamental or universal reasoning mechanisms and as such disregard evidence for individual differences in reasoning and the operation of strategies. However, theorists of both persuasions add many auxiliary assumptions to account for all kinds of aspects of reasoning data, not just those to do with individual differences. For example, mental model theorists propose—but do not define—pragmatic influences on the formation of models. Mental logics are supplemented also by pragmatic systems, such as the pragmatic reasoning schemas proposed to account for facilitation effects on the Wason selection task (Cheng & Holyoak, 1985). For example, because Braine and O'Brien's system involves only valid rules of inference, they account for fallacies in terms of pragmatically invited inferences. The problem with all these supplementations, however, is that the system as a whole is lacking in testability (see Evans & Over, 1996, 1997).

There is more than one distinction to be made to understand all this. Implicit processes can originate in innate modules or from implicit learning. The core notion of a fixed universal reasoning mechanism in the mental logic approach seems to be an example of the former, but the supplementary pragmatic system seems to be an example of the latter. Both, however, are implicit rather than explicit in nature. Neither proposal seems strategic in nature or to connect with the conscious effort at deduction that I have described in relation to syllogistic reasoning. However, this does not mean that you cannot have rule-based strategies for reasoning. Certainly, you can in the case of domain specific rules. For example, a car mechanic can follow an explicit policy in diagnosing the reason for a car failing to start. Specific rules can be taught and applied for deciding whether the fault is electrical or fuel related, and if the former whether pre- or postignition, and so on. In similar fashion we can teach our students rule-based strategies for deciding which statistical tests should be applied when analyzing data sets, and so on. It is not the notion of rules which constrains application to strategic thinking. It is the idea of abstract, universal, and built in rules that creates this problem.

Let us leave the rules vs. models argument for a moment and ask the question: To what extent are responses to reasoning problems under conscious control? Earlier I referred to some work on the Wason selection task involving protocol analysis which shows that people's attention on this task is directed by pragmatic cues of which they are unaware. In fact, I have argued for many years that behavior on this task can be accounted for simply in terms of choosing what is pragmatically cued as relevant (e.g., Evans, 1989). More recently, I suggested that although people do also engage in explicit reasoning on this problem, this serves only to rationalize choices and not to alter them (e.g., Evans, 1995, 1996). I think my views on this are open to misunderstanding, however. Because I specifically propose that people's explicit deductive reasoning does affect their choices on other problems—such as the truth table task—there is no reason why such reasoning *cannot* affect selection task choices. It is just that it normally does not, for reasons I have discussed elsewhere.

A recent investigation of individual differences in selection task performance by Stanovich and West (1998) provides some interesting evidence in this regard. They found that measures of general intelligence or "g" are unrelated to performance on deontic and thematic versions of the selection task, which most people solve. However, the minority of participants who succeed in solving the much more difficult abstract and indicative selection task are significantly higher in g than unsuccessful participants. Stanovich and West explained the findings in relation to my own theoretical analysis of the task and specific recent proposals by Evans and Over (1996). They suggest that the implicit, pragmatic system is not related to g. Pragmatic responses to the selection task will lead people to correct choices on the deontic selection task which is why success on this version is not related to g. However, pragmatic responses lead to matching bias and incorrect responses on the indicative selection task. Hence, they suggest that the minority who succeed on this version are those who can suppress these pragmatic influences and solve the problem by explicit reasoning. Thus, although the majority may decide before they think (Evans, 1996), these individuals actually think before they decide.

The argument here suggests there are two different notions of intelligence. The first is universal and embedded in the implicit cognitive system. It enables us to achieve most everyday tasks without conscious thinking and corresponds to what Evans and Over (1996) have termed as rationality$_1$. The second involves the explicit reasoning system and corresponds to rationality$_2$. Rationality$_2$ involves individual differences in g, whereas rationality$_1$ does not. If we think about the kinds of activity that are rational$_2$—proving theorems, playing chess, understanding tax regulations, designing algorithms, and so on—then this relation to g seems to be correct. Hence, intelligence—in the sense of 'g'—depends on effective use of the explicit thinking system which some people are much better at than others.

Stanovich and West's work demonstrates that psychometric studies of intelligence may be much more relevant to cognitive theory than is often supposed. Let us follow the argument that rationality$_2$—including competence in deductive reasoning—requires use of the explicit system. It follows that deductive competence is *strategic*. Where could the strategy of deduction arise within the major theories of propositional reasoning? We have already argued when discussing the model theory of syllogistic reasoning that the strategic aspect is the effort at deduction arising in the attempt to validate conclusions by searching for alternative models. Johnson-Laird argued that the major factor which constrains this search is working memory capacity, although I have argued also that motivation arising from instructions or from unbelievable conclusions plays an important part. However, if competence—when motivated—is ultimately limited by working memory capacity then this links neatly with recent evidence that such capacity is itself highly loaded on g (Kyllonen & Christal, 1990).

What of the mental logic approach? Authors in this tradition also propose a relevant distinction. Braine and O'Brien distinguish between direct and indirect inference (Rips [1994] makes a similar distinction between forward and backward reasoning). Direct inferences, such as Modus Ponens, follow immediately from our stored set of rules. This part of the process might be seen as implicit or intuitive. Actually, these authors also propose the operation of pragmatic factors which may also be at this tacit level. More difficult inferences, however, such as Modus Tollens require indirect reasoning in which suppositions must be made and later refuted. This may be the part of the process that is strategic and related to general intelligence. One could argue that keeping track of suppositions requires working memory space and hence build a rule-based argument to explain the relationship of strategic reasoning to general intelligence.

So far as I know, neither mental model theorists nor mental logicians have proposed the idea that deduction arises from an explicit strategy which is related to general intelligence. Nor have they suggested the clear distinction between implicit and explicit processes in their own theories that I have indicated before. I should therefore make it clear that I am merely speculating on the manner in which these theories could be extended to embrace the ideas I am putting forward.

SUMMARY AND CONCLUSIONS

Strategies in reasoning involve explicit mental processes aimed at achieving a goal. They are under conscious control and can be varied according to instructions or the preference and experience of individuals. Some individuals are also more able than others—by virtue of higher general intelligence. However, theories of reasoning processes to be found in the psychological literature generally lack specification of which aspects of the processes they discuss are explicit or strategic and which are tacit. In this chapter I have examined a number of these proposals and tried to identify what could and could not be a reasoning strategy in these theoretical systems.

Throughout the three main paradigms we have considered—transitive inference, syllogistic, and propositional reasoning—we find theories that have no apparent strategic component at all. A number of theories emphasize linguistic and interpretational processes or noninferential mechanisms based on decision heuristics which appear to operate completely at the tacit level. There also appears to be a clear division between the two major accounts of deductive competence based on mental logic and mental models. The application of hardwired abstract logical rules provides little scope for strategic thinking, but the use of indirect suppositional reasoning may well do so. Similarly, although the interpretative stage of the model theory (modeling the premises and formulating a provisional conclusion) would appear to be an implicit process, I have argued that the validation stage is strategic in nature. People can be motivated to make more or less effort at deduction by instructions and other factors. This scope for strategic thinking does not, however, appear to reside in the model-based reasoning model of Polk and Newell (1995) which emphasizes interpretation at the expense of validation.

I will summarize my main claims in model theoretic terms, which I prefer for reasons discussed in detail elsewhere (Evans & Over, 1996, 1997). The natural mode of hypothetical thinking is inductive. That is, we tend to consider just one state of affairs (mental model) at a time and the model we consider is derived from tacit pragmatic processes. Providing such models seem satisfactory, we based our inferences upon them. This leads to generally effective, rational$_1$ decision making in most situations. Although processing of language and of tacit knowledge may in part be logically deductive at the implicit level, the solution of explicit deductive reasoning problems as presented to participants in typical experiments cannot be achieved by implicit process alone. Participants frequently apply default pragmatic reasoning processes that lead to the endorsement of fallacies and the influence of prior belief. To avoid biases and achieve deductive accuracy—in short, to be rational$_2$—on such problems requires explicit, strategic thinking—a conscious effort at deduction. As with all strategies, deduction is variable. Some people (high in g) are better at it than others; some experimental procedures and instructions are more likely to induce a deductive strategy than others.

A comment needs to be made concerning the automation of strategic thinking. It is a commonplace observation that the acquisition of physical skills, such as driving a car, requires conscious effort in the early stages but may become automatic with practice. Anderson (e.g., 1990) dedicated much research and argument to demonstrating that the same is true of many cognitive skills, which in his terminology become "compiled." In arguing that deduction requires strategic thinking, I am of course, referring to naive, untrained individuals. Those highly practiced in solving deductive reasoning problems such as logicians (and reasoning researchers!) might automate a schema for, say, Modus Tollens reasoning, so that to them this inference becomes almost as straightforward and easy as Modus Ponens. Such automation passes the deduction concerned from the realm of rationality$_2$ into that of rationality$_1$. That is, the reasoner is no longer necessarily conscious of the basis of the basis of their argument (while making it) and is instead using a well learned processes to achieve what (for them) is the personal goal of deductive accuracy. There is, of course, nothing peculiar to the logicians in this kind of transition. An experienced car mechanic, for example, will apply fault diagnosis procedures in a rapid, automatic way without the need for the conscious effort of the trainee. The only significant distinction between rational$_1$ processes like these acquired initially by explicit reasoning—as opposed to by implicit learning—is that the expert will generally be able to provide a rational$_2$ explanation of their reasoning is required.

In conclusion, Evans and Over (1996) favored a model-based approach to the explanation of hypothetical thinking of all kinds but placed no special emphasis on deduction. My discussion of reasoning strategies here is completely consistent with that framework. Although these distinctions could be applied in a rule-based approach, the current state of the model theory is more congenial with my proposals. Specifically, we can say that although people do not habitually seek to validate conclusions by seeking alternative models of the premises they can be induced to do so. Validation of conclusions in this way is the explicit process that underlies the effort of deduction—the strategy of deductive reasoning.

REFERENCES

Anderson, J. R. (1990). *The adaptive character of thought*. Hillsdale, NJ: Lawrence Erlbaum Associates.

Begg, I., & Denny, P. J. (1969). Empirical reconciliation of atmosphere and conversion interpretations of syllogistic reasoning errors. *Journal of Experimental Psychology, 81*, 351–354.

Berry, D. C., & Dienes, Z. (1993). *Implicit learning*. Hove, UK: Psychology Press.

Braine, M. D. S., & O'Brien, D. P. (1991). A theory of If: A lexical entry, reasoning program, and pragmatic principles. *Psychological Review, 98*, 182–203.

Chater, N., & Oaksford, M. (1999). The probability heuristics model of syllogistic reasoning. *Cognitive Psychology, 2*, 191–258.

Cheng, P. W., & Holyoak, K. J. (1985). Pragmatic reasoning schemas. *Cognitive Psychology, 17*, 391–416.

Clark, H. H. (1969). Linguistic processes in deductive reasoning. *Psychological Review, 76*, 387–404.

De Soto, L. B., London, M., & Handel, L. S. (1965). Social reasoning and spatial paralogic. *Journal of Personality and Social Psychology, 2*, 513–521.

Ericsson, K. A., & Simon, H. A. (1984). *Protocol analysis: Verbal reports as data*. Cambridge, MA: MIT Press.

Evans, J. St. B. T. (1982). *The psychology of deductive reasoning*. London: Routledge and Kegan Paul.

Evans, J. St. B. T. (1989). *Bias in human reasoning: Causes and consequences*. Hove, UK: Lawrence Erlbaum Associates.

Evans, J. St. B. T. (1993). Bias and rationality. In K. I. Manktelow & D. E. Over (Eds.), *Rationality* (pp. 6–30). London: Routledge and Kegan Paul.

Evans, J. St. B. T. (1995). Relevance and reasoning. In S. E. Newstead & J. St. B. T. Evans (Eds.), *Perspectives on thinking and reasoning* (pp. 147–172). Hove, UK: Lawrence Erlbaum Associates.

Evans, J. St. B. T. (1996). Deciding before you think: Relevance and reasoning in the selection task. *British Journal of Psychology, 87*, 223–240.

Evans, J. St. B. T. (1998). Matching bias in conditional reasoning: Do we understand it after 25 years? *Thinking & Reasoning, 4*, 45–82.

Evans, J. St. B. T., Allen, J. L., Newstead, S. E., & Pollard, P. (1994). Debiasing by instruction: The case of belief bias. *European Journal of Cognitive Psychology, 6*, 263–285.

Evans, J. St. B. T., Barston, J.L., & Pollard, P. (1983). On the conflict between logic and belief in syllogistic reasoning. *Memory and Cognition, 11*, 295–306.

Evans, J. St. B. T., Handley, S. J., Harper, C., & Johnson-Laird, P. N. (in press). Reasoning about necessity and possibility: A test of the mental model theory of deduction.

Journal of Experimental Psychology: Learning, Memory, and Cognition.

Evans, J. St. B. T., Harries, C. H., Dennis, I., & Dean, J. (1995). Tacit and explicit policies in general practioners' prescription of lipid lowering agents. *British Journal of General Practice, 45,* 15–18.

Evans, J. St. B. T., & Lynch, J. S. (1973). Matching bias in the selection task. *British Journal of Psychology, 64,* 391–397.

Evans, J. St. B. T., Newstead, S. E., & Byrne, R. M. J. (1993). *Human reasoning: The psychology of deduction.* Hove, UK: Lawrence Erlbaum Associates.

Evans, J. St. B. T., & Over, D. E. (1996). *Rationality and reasoning.* Hove, UK: Psychology Press.

Evans, J. St. B. T., & Over, D. E. (1997). Rationality in reasoning: The case of deductive competence. *Current Psychology of Cognition, 16,* 3–38.

Evans, J. St. B. T., & Pollard, P. (1990). Belief bias and problem complexity in deductive reasoning. In J. P. Caverni, J. M. Fabre, & M. Gonzales (Eds.), *Cognitive biases* (pp. 131–154). Amsterdam: North-Holland.

George, C. (1995). The endorsement of the premises: Assumption based or belief-based reasoning. *British Journal of Psychology, 86,* 93–113.

Huttenlocher, J. (1968). Constructing spatial images: A strategy in reasoning. *Psychological Review, 75,* 286–298.

Johnson-Laird, P. N. (1983). *Mental models.* Cambridge, UK: Cambridge University Press.

Johnson-Laird, P. N., & Bara, B. G. (1984). Syllogistic inference. *Cognition, 16,* 1–62.

Johnson-Laird, P. N., & Byrne, R. M. J. (1991). *Deduction.* Hove, UK: Lawrence Erlbaum Associates.

Johnson-Laird, P. N., & Byrne, R. M. J. (1994). Models, necessity and the search for counter-examples. A reply to Martin-Cordero & Gonzalez-Labra and to Smith. *Behavioral and Brain Sciences, 17,* 775–777.

Kyllonen, P. C., & Christal, R. E. (1990). Reasoning ability is (little more than) working memory capacity?! *Intelligence, 4,* 389–433.

Newstead, S. E., Handley, S. H., & Buck, E. (in press). Falsifying mental models: Testing the predictions of theories of syllogistic reasoning. *Memory & Cognition.*

Newstead, S. E., Pollard, P., Evans, J. St. B. T., & Allen, J. L. (1992). The source of belief bias in syllogistic reasoning. *Cognition 45,* 257–284.

Nisbett, R. E., & Wilson, T. D. (1977). Telling more than we can know: Verbal reports on mental processes. *Psychological Review, 84,* 231–295.

Polk, T. A., & Newell, A. (1995). Deduction as verbal reasoning. *Psychological Review, 102,* 533–566.

Reber, A. S. (1993). *Implicit learning and tacit knowledge.* Oxford: Oxford University Press.

Rips, L. J. (1994). *The psychology of proof.* Cambridge, MA: MIT Press.

Roberts, M. J. (1993). Human reasoning: Deduction rules or mental models or both. *Quarterly Journal of Experimental Psychology, 46A,* 569–590.

Stanovich, K. E., & West, R. F. (1998). Cognitive ability and variation in selection task performance. *Thinking and Reasoning, 4,* 193–230.

Stevenson, R. J. (1997). Deductive reasoning and the distinction between implicit and explicit processes. *Current Psychology of Cognition, 16,* 222–229.

Stevenson, R. J., & Over, D. E. (1995). Deduction from uncertain premises. *Quarterly*

Journal of Experimental Psychology, 48A, 613–643.

Wason, P. C., & Evans, J. St. B. T. (1975). Dual processes in reasoning? *Cognition, 3*, 141–154.

Woodworth, R. S., & Sells, S. B. (1935). An atmosphere effect in syllogistic reasoning. *Journal of Experimental Psychology, 18*, 451–460.

2

Individual Differences in Reasoning Strategies: A Problem to Solve or an Opportunity to Seize?

Maxwell J. Roberts

This chapter summarizes research into individual differences in the use of strategies for deduction tasks, and discusses its importance. It is divided into three sections. First, key terms are defined, and the major findings on strategy usage in the deduction literature are reviewed on a task-by-task basis. Second their importance with respect to the arguments of Roberts (1993) are discussed; it is suggested that deduction strategies are not just an interesting area to study, but that they also render the identification of fundamental reasoning processes somewhat difficult. Finally, four different approaches to the understanding of individual differences in strategy selection are discussed, and those most likely to yield interesting findings are identified.

The study of individual differences in the use of deductive reasoning strategies has been a minority interest for many years. However, the steady accumulation of findings means that not only can different strategy users be identified for many deduction tasks, but also that significant advances have been made in understanding why different strategies are chosen and how they develop. Although research into these issues may, on the surface, lack the glamour of the pursuit of fundamental reasoning processes (see, e.g., Johnson-Laird & Byrne, 1991; Rips, 1994a), these are nonetheless important topics for at least two reasons. First, given the overwhelming evidence that people can and do use different strategies for deduction tasks, any attempt to explain human deduction that ignores these must be incomplete. Second, researchers such as Siegler (e.g., Crowley, Shrager, & Siegler, 1997; Siegler, 1996; Siegler & Jenkins, 1989) suggest that cognitive development can be understood in terms of strategy selection and development, and hence any findings concerning these for deductive reasoning tasks will potentially be of interest to a far wider community.

INDIVIDUAL DIFFERENCES IN DEDUCTIVE REASONING STRATEGIES

There have been many attempts to define the term *strategy* over the years, but some common themes generally emerge. Siegler and Jenkins (1989) capture the

23

essentials thus: A strategy is *"any procedure that is nonobligatory and goal directed"* (p. 11). Hence a strategy is any set of cognitive processes which, in theory, could be modified or dispensed with. This definition sidesteps the issue of whether either knowledge of strategies, or the processes of determining which to use, are conscious. However, it may still be too strong for some researchers in the field because it reduces the status of hard-wired processes to strategies if they can be substituted for by other processes. Roberts (1993) thus suggests a weaker, and less contentious definition: A reasoning strategy is *"a set of cognitive processes which have been shown to be used for solving certain types of deductive reasoning tasks, but for which there is not sufficient evidence to assert that these processes themselves constitute all or part of the fundamental reasoning mechanism"* (p. 576). This suggests what might be a candidate for a strategy and, as shown later, in practice is identical to Siegler's definition. The majority of research into deduction strategies has been concerned simply with identifying these rather than explaining why people differ. It is relatively easy to classify the various strategies into a small number of categories, and these are described next. For a fuller description, the reader should consult Evans, Newstead, and Byrne (1993).

Spatial Strategies.   These have been proposed in various forms by many researchers (see, e.g., Gattis & Dupeyrat, chap. 8, this volume), but have in common the property that information is represented spatially, such that the configural information in the representation corresponds to the state of the affairs in the world. For example, the relative height of a set of objects might be represented as a linear array, with the tallest entity at the top and the shortest at the bottom. Thus, a spatial representation can be conceptualized as a mental diagram, although this need not take the form of a mental image. The mental models theory of Johnson-Laird and Byrne (1991) is the most highly developed theory that has the spatial representation of information as its basis.

Verbal Strategies.   These have also been proposed by many researchers in various contexts, and have in common the property that information is represented in the form of verbal or abstract propositions, and that various content/context-free syntactic rules enable new conclusions to be drawn from the represented information. The degree of abstractedness of the representation is an issue that is open to disagreement, but all theorists agree that these rule processes are either distinct from spatial strategies, or that verbal strategies are somehow fundamental to reasoning, and that spatial strategies either may be developed with practice (Rips, 1994b, p. 166) or are epiphenomenal to underlying propositional processes. Deduction rule theories of reasoning (e.g., Braine & O'Brien, 1997; Rips, 1994a) come into this category.

Task-Specific Shortcut Strategies.   When solving a deduction task, people may develop shortcut strategies that can result in massive gains in performance.

These strategies do not really fall into either of the previous categories. Usually, they are extremely task-specific, often they are even specific to certain presentation formats. Sometimes, detailed representations are dispensed with altogether, and people are able to obtain a solution directly from the problem statements. For this reason, these strategies are sometimes termed *representation-free strategies* or *perceptual strategies* (e.g., Quinton & Fellows, 1975). However, not all task-specific shortcut strategies are entirely representation free. For some, intermediate steps and running totals may nonetheless need to be stored, and to exclude these from this category would probably be a mistake. The nature of these strategies is discussed in detail under the specific tasks concerned.

The action of task-specific shortcut strategies may often resemble the action of simple rules (e.g., the *two-somes* rule for categorical syllogisms—see later) and it is important here to emphasize that they are distinct from verbal strategies. The sets of rules posited for a verbal strategy are generally taken to form a closed, coherent system which is domain-free and cannot easily be modified with practice. Hence, it is frequently asserted that whereas the Modus Ponens rule is a natural component of a rule system, the Modus Tollens rule is not possessed (e.g., Rips, 1994a) and cannot be added easily if at all. By contrast, task-specific shortcut strategies may be learned rapidly under the right circumstances with little or no practice. There are no obvious constraints on what can be learned or discovered, but these discoveries are likely to be very domain specific and hence difficult to generalize to other tasks.

The foregoing is not an exhaustive taxonomy of the ways in which deduction problems can be solved. When problems are phrased in terms of real-life situations, it is possible for people to apply their knowledge and beliefs, which may either interact with, or bypass their reasoning processes altogether. In addition, it has also been proposed that context dependent rules may be important determinants of performance (e.g., the pragmatic reasoning schemas advocated by Holyoak & Cheng, 1995). Finally, the action of preconscious heuristics may also have a role to play in determining solutions. These focus attention on aspects of a problem that warrant closer scrutiny, and it has been claimed that they can at the very least bias performance on certain tasks, and at other times can entirely account for performance (e.g., Evans & Over, 1996).

An ongoing feature of much deduction research has concerned the nature of the *fundamental reasoning mechanism*. This is a notional, hard-wired device that underlies all deductive reasoning. Much research is intended to show not just the primacy of one type of strategy over the rest, but also mutual exclusivity, such that a type of strategy is used for *all* deductive reasoning. Others draw back from the assertion of mutual exclusivity, but still wish to show primacy; hence the proposed processes are fundamental to deductive reasoning but are not always observed because of the use of reasoning strategies. These draw upon different and nonfundamental sets of processes hence overlaying and obscuring the fundamental mechanism. The major debate is currently between proponents of the mental models theory (e.g., Johnson-Laird & Byrne, 1991; Johnson-Laird, Byrne, & Schaeken, 1992, 1994; Oakhill & Garnham, 1996) and various deduction rule theories (e.g., Braine & O'Brien, 1997; Rips, 1989, 1994a) and has occasionally been very heated indeed. The issue of whether either camp has convincing evidence for their case is beyond the scope of this chapter, and Evans et al. (1993) should be consulted for a more in-depth comparison. This should also be referred to for further details of any of the following major reasoning tasks with which the reader is unfamiliar.

As is shown later, the existence of individual differences in the use of reasoning strategies—*qualitative* individual differences—has important implications for the resolution of the fundamental reasoning mechanism debate, and because of this, such differences are often ignored by researchers. Where they are mentioned, the reader should make a distinction between: *intrastrategic differences*, where all people use the same type of strategy in order to perform a task (e.g., all use mental models strategies) but differ in the exact processes used; and *interstrategic differences*, where people differ in the types of strategy used (e.g., some people use mental models, others use deduction rules). Interstrategic differences are the focus of this chapter. Hence, wherever individual differences are referred to, readers should assume that they are interstrategic unless informed otherwise.

Sentence–Picture Verification

For sentence–picture verification, people are typically given a series of trials in which simple sentences describing two objects (e.g., *the cross is above the star*, or *the star is not below the cross*) are each followed by a picture of a cross and a star, one above the other. The task is to determine whether each picture is a true depiction of its sentence. Although neglected by deduction researchers, the task fits with standard definitions of deduction, and has produced some of the most important findings in the strategies literature. Initially, Clark and Chase (1972) and Carpenter and Just (1975) asserted that all people use verbal–propositional processes to solve the task, so that each sentence is encoded verbally, and its picture is converted into a verbal proposition (e.g., *cross above star*) and the representations compared. However, MacLeod, Hunt, and Mathews (1978) found that approximately 25% of people fitted this model very poorly, and proposed that they were using a spatial strategy instead. For this, each sentence is converted into a spatial representation, and directly compared with the picture on the display. In support of this, they found that for people whose response times fitted the verbal strategy well, their verbal ability test score predicted performance, but not their spatial ability. The reverse was found for those fitted the verbal strategy poorly. These findings have been replicated by Coney (1988). Kroll and Corrigan (1981) have shown that changes in task format can derail the spatial strategy easily, causing spatial strategy users to change to the verbal strategy. This suggests that although the verbal strategy may be the *natural strategy* for this task (either used or known to be valid by the majority), the spatial strategy may be a task-specific shortcut. More recent work by Marquer and Pereira (1990) and Roberts, Wood, and Gilmore (1994) casts doubt on this overall analysis of the task. It is difficult to distinguish between the spatial strategy and a modified verbal strategy in which negatives are recoded into positives, so that for example, *"not above"* is recoded to *"below."* Despite this, there is no doubt that a variety of strategies is used for this task, the problem is one of accurately identifying them.

Categorical Syllogisms

A categorical syllogism traditionally consists of a pair of premises followed by a conclusion. The premises link two *end* terms via a *middle* term, the latter appearing in both premises. Hence, the first premise links two entities, A and B, with one of four possible quantifiers *"All, No, Some or Some ... Not."* The second premise links B with a further entity, C. The task is usually to generate or evaluate a conclusion linking C with A. For example, if *"All of the engineers are chess players"* and *"Some of the chess players are not chefs"*, then does it follow that *"Some of the chefs are engineers"*? Generally, where it is asserted that all people use the same fundamental processes, this has been spatial—mental models, or analogous Euler Circles or Venn Diagrams (see also Handley, Dennis, Evans, & Capon, chap. 12, this volume; Johnson-Laird, Savary, & Bucciarelli, chap. 11, this volume) – although propositional theories have also been proposed for this role (e.g., Rips, 1994a).

Explicit searches for strategy differences for this task are rare, but Ford (1994) presents a particularly interesting subject by item analysis, in which concurrent verbal protocols, and people's notes were used in order to identify strategies. The majority had a clear preference, with approximately one third relying on a spatial strategy. A further third appeared to be relying on a verbal strategy—analogous to the use of Modus Ponens and Modus Tollens rules—in order to determine the relationship between entities, and to substitute an end term from one premise for the middle term in another, with appropriate modifications to the quantifiers as a result.

Ford only presented valid syllogisms, and it is possible that had she used others, then other strategies might have been observed too. For instance, Gallotti, Baron, and Sabini (1986) found that some people spontaneously developed the *two-somes* rule, that is, for any syllogisms where the word *some* appears twice, there is never a valid conclusion. Although termed a *deduction rule* by Galotti et al., this is probably best categorized as a task-specific shortcut strategy, and its use will lead to massive gains in speed and accuracy for the items to which it can be applied. Different strategy users have also been identified by Gilhooly, Logie, Wetherick, and Wynn (1993) on the basis of expected errors for particular trials. For the *atmosphere* strategy, people base their conclusion on rules concerning the quantifiers of the premises, without fully considering their meaning. For example, if either or both quantifiers are particular (i.e., *some*, or *some ... not*), then the conclusion will likewise be particular (compare with the earlier *two-somes* rule: task-specific rules need not always be valid). Users of another task-specific strategy; *matching* were also identified. Here, the quantifier of the conclusion is chosen to match the most conservative quantifier of either premise, where *no* is the most conservative, followed by "some ... not," "some," and finally "all." Overall then, for categorical syllogisms, widespread individual differences in strategy choice can be identified if the data are analyzed at the level of the individual. However, on the basis of the small numbers of individual difference studies conducted so far, it is far from obvious whether there is a natural strategy for this task.

All of the earlier studies have used syllogisms with neutral premises and conclusions. Conclusions can also be devised such that they may conflict with, or be in line with people's beliefs (e.g., *all dogs are cats, all cats are mammals*). Framing syllogisms in this way tends to cause strong *belief bias* effects which are difficult to remove, particularly for invalid conclusions. Attempts to see whether some people are more likely to succumb to their beliefs than others have been largely unsuccessful. For example, Evans, Barston, and Pollard (1983) found that whether or not an individual succumbed to belief bias for one trial appeared not to be a predictor for other trials. This finding is surprising because it suggests that quantitative individual differences in the degree of belief bias are entirely due to random errors of measurement, that is, statistical noise, and hence further investigation of this topic is desirable before ruling out the existence of individual differences.

Linear Syllogisms
and Relational Reasoning

Linear syllogisms require people to make deductions about spatial relationships between entities. For example, *"Dave is taller than Peter, Tom is shorter than Peter, is Tom shorter than Dave"*? Universal theories have been proposed for this task from the outset, with De Soto, London, and Handel (1965) suggesting that all people used a spatial strategy, in which a mental ladder of the terms was constructed, whereas Clark (1969) suggested that any perceived spatial representation of information served no functional purpose, and that a verbal strategy accounted for the performance of all. Here, problem premises are represented as unintegrated propositions (e.g., *Dave is more tall, Peter is tall; Peter is less short, Tom is short*) and inferences made by locating the linking term and relating the propositions back to the question. Finally, Sternberg (1980) suggested that everyone uses a mixed strategy, in which people first represent the premises propositionally, and then use these to construct a spatial representation. However, in the same year, Sternberg and Weil (1980) also published an individual difference analysis of strategies, and this study should be regarded as definitive. Here, an initial and largely unsuccessful attempt was made to train people to use various strategies, but by using multiple regression on the response data of individuals, it was possible to classify people into one of four strategy groups: spatial, verbal, mixed, and algorithmic (i.e., a task-specific shortcut strategy). Group strategy classifications were then validated by the differential correlations between performance and scores at verbal and spatial ability tests (see also Shaver, Pierson, & Lang, 1985).

In addition to these strategies, there are many possible task-specific shortcut strategies that should be regarded as being distinct from the verbal strategy mentioned before. Examples may be found in Wood (1969, 1978), Johnson-Laird (1972), Wood, Shotter, and Godden (1974), Quinton and Fellows (1975), Sternberg and Weil (1980) and Ohlsson (1984). Strategies are usually detected via performance data—their use typically speeds performance and raises accuracy—although concurrent and retrospective protocols, psychometric test data, and eye-movements data have also been utilized. As one example, Wood presented extended syllogisms such as:

Who is taller, John or Ian, if ...
John is taller than Paul
Dave is taller than Paul
Tom is taller than Dave
Ian is taller than Tom
Dave is taller than John

This problem can be solved by scanning the two sides of the display. John and Ian both appear on the left, but only John appears on the right, and so Ian must be the taller. However, it is easy to devise problems that cannot be solved by this strategy, and for linear syllogisms, all task-specific shortcuts may be defeated by appropriately designed items, or by modified task formats—the shortcut strategies all rely on information being presented simultaneously, that is, *parallel presentation*. Where these strategies are encouraged, some practice is usually required before they can develop, their use being preceded by verbal or (more often) spatial strategies.

This prevalence of task-specific shortcut strategies has led seekers of the fundamental reasoning mechanism to modify the task in an attempt to eliminate them. *Serial presentation* is one possible solution—whether by presenting problem statements in writing one at a time, or verbally. In addition, Byrne and Johnson-Laird (1989) used problems in which two-dimensional spatial arrays had to be constructed. Even so, although the overall effect here is to make the spatial strategy predominate, the current author has found that typically, 10% of people still match the rival verbal strategy.

Conditional Reasoning
and the Four-Card Selection Task

For conditional reasoning tasks, people have to make deductions concerning "*if... then*" statements. For example, "*If Tom is in Paris, then Linda is in London, Linda is not in London, so what follows*"? Using negated terms, disjunctions, additional premises, and varying their believability all add to the diversity of problems that can be tested, and other conditional reasoning tasks such as truth-table evaluations and the notorious Wason four-card selection task are possible. However, unlike other reasoning tasks, evidence of interstrategic differences between individuals simply does not exist despite the diversity of responses that are observed. For example, there is considerable variation in the likelihood that the strictly illogical Denial of the Antecedent and Affirmation of the Consequent inferences will be made (see, e.g., Evans, Clibbens, & Rood, 1995; see also Byrne, Espino, & Santamaria, chap. 5, this volume). In addition, George (1995) has observed two modes of responding when the believability of the premises is manipulated: Some people never succumb to this manipulation, always making the valid Modus Ponens inference, whereas for the rest, the likelihood of this inference varies according to premise believability. However, all of these findings can be explained in terms of intrastrategic differences.

A closer look at the literature suggests a possible reason for this. It is often accepted that it is very difficult to produce distinct predictions which can distinguish between, say, mental model and deduction rule theories (e.g., Evans, Ellis, & Newstead, 1996; Johnson-Laird, Byrne, & Schaeken, 1994; see also Madruga, Moreno, Carriedo, & Gutiérez, chap. 3, this volume). Hence, debates among people seeking the fundamental reasoning mechanism often move to discussions of theoretical coherence, testability, generality, and psychological plausibility, and away from theoretical predictions and data. Put simply, both types of theory can account for the same patterns of data equally well, and this prevents the identification of the dominant strategy of an individual even more so than overall for a group. This is because strategy identification procedures require much more precision when applied to an individual than when determining the dominant strategy of a group. In addition, many of the rules suggested by deduction rule theorists are indistinguishable from task-specific shortcuts. For example, although deduction rule theorists hypothesize that all people posses the Modus Ponens rule, this could easily be explained in terms of a shortcut developed as a result of using mental models repeatedly to make this inference, rather than as a fundamental, innate rule. [After several years of teaching this topic, the current author believes that he has finally learned the Modus Tollens rule, which deduction rule theorists believe is not naturally present in the deduction rule repertoire.]

Turning to the four-card selection task, again there is little evidence for individual differences in strategy usage. This may be because, as suggested by

Evans (e.g., Evans & Over, 1996) this task simply does not elicit analytic reasoning processes for the vast majority. Hence, if people are not reasoning, we cannot expect differences in reasoning strategy. However, there appears to be a small minority who can consistently get the tasks correct, and Stanovich and West (1998a) suggested these people are successfully using analytic processes. Again, given both the difficulties with identifying individual differences in conditional reasoning strategies in general, and the requirement to test many hundreds of people before an adequate group of analytic reasoners could be assembled, this means that the effort entailed in determining which of these people are using either spatial or verbal strategies is unlikely to be rewarded.

To summarize, the various conditional reasoning tasks are unlikely to prove to be an interesting domain for those seeking individual differences in strategy usage, although the possibility of the development of improved techniques for investigation cannot be entirely ruled out. This would almost certainly depend on the radical developments in both mental models *and* deduction rules theories, or the application of new methodologies. This failure should be regarded an isolated phenomenon in the field of deduction; clear individual differences in strategy usage are observable elsewhere.

Other Deduction Tasks

Truth-Teller Problems.   These problems require a person to determine which of several characters either always tell the truth (traditionally known as *knights*) or always tell lies (known as *knaves*) from their statements. For example:

A: "I am a knight but B is a knave."
B: "I am a knight."

Rips (1989) suggested that fundamentally, deduction rules are used to solve these problems, whereas Byrne and Handley (1997) suggested that mental models are fundamental, but also identify several task-specific shortcut strategies that develop spontaneously while the task is being solved. This identification has so far been at the level of the group rather than the individual. Hence, as a whole, people tend to speed up with practice more on problems to which simplification strategies can be applied than on problems to which they cannot (but see also Schroyens, Schaeken, & d'Ydewalle, 1996). However, these short-cuts represent intrastrategic differences rather than interstrategic differences: They are variations in how mental models might be used to solve the task, rather than suggestions for strategies that replace mental models altogether. As such, these individual differences are outside of the scope of this chapter.

Family Relationship Problems.   These problems (e.g., Wood, 1978; Wood & Shotter, 1973) require people to make deductions along the lines of: "*What is the relationship of him to his father's brother*"? A spatial strategy appears to be the natural means of solution, in which a grid of relations is navigated. Some people are able to improve their performance at the task by generating task-specific shortcuts, their protocols indicating an awareness of certain patterns. For example, the term *fathers' father* always translates into moving up a grid twice, and this *up-up* operation always means *great*-something, while *up-across-down* always means cousin. Hence, rather than having to keep track of individual transitions, recurring patterns can be linked directly to solutions, thus considerably reducing the load on working memory and improving performance.

Compass Point Directions Tasks. These tasks (e.g., Roberts, Gilmore, & Wood, 1997; Wood, 1978) require participants to decide where a person taking a set of compass point directions (e.g., *one step east, one step north, one step west, one step north, one step east, one step south*) would end up in relation to a starting point. The natural strategy again appears to be spatial, with people representing the entire path and reading the bearing of the final location in relation to the start. The shortcut strategy of *cancellation* is discovered and reported by some people. Here, opposite steps are canceled, with those that remain constituting the correct answer. A running total of cancellations appears to be far less demanding on working memory than a spatial representation of the path, and the use of this strategy reduces both times and error rates dramatically.

Summary

Although studies into individual differences in deductive reasoning strategy usage are not numerous, clear patterns emerge. For some tasks, verbal and spatial strategy users can be identified relatively easily if care is taken, although the replication of some isolated studies would be desirable. Task-specific shortcut strategies appear to be widespread, usually enabling dramatic improvements in performance; only for categorical syllogisms do some shortcuts inevitably lead to errors. Even here, given the difficulty of some types of syllogism, it may well be the case that people who use the atmosphere or matching strategies are better off in any case. Finally, concerning the current mental model–deduction rule debate, a clear natural strategy appears to be identifiable for some tasks; verbal for sentence–picture verification and spatial for two-dimensional spatial relations, family relationships, and compass point directions tasks. For linear syllogisms, the natural strategy appears to be mixed, although the major mechanism of inference is a spatial array. Finally, for categorical syllogisms, conditional reasoning tasks, and truth-teller problems, there is no clear natural strategy.

THE PROBLEM OF INDIVIDUAL DIFFERENCES

Having summarized the major work on individual differences in deduction, the next step is to discuss whether this research is merely an interesting diversion, or whether it has deeper implications for the field in general. To this end, the arguments of Roberts (1993) concerning the problem of individual differences are still relevant. Hence, *"if a theory of reasoning is being proposed which is intended to describe the processes used by all people for all reasoning tasks, then what is the status of this theory if it is subsequently found that not all subjects [sic] are using the same processes?"* (p. 575). However, no distinction was previously made between verbal strategies (such as those based on deduction rules) and task-specific shortcuts. By making the distinction here, it is necessary to update some of the arguments.

The problem of individual differences affects any research intended to identify the fundamental reasoning mechanism. If it is to be proposed that mental models or deduction rules are fundamental to all deduction, then how does a discovery of a subset of people who use the wrong strategy affect the original assertion? Where this problem is acknowledged, it is usually claimed that reasoning strategies may occasionally overlay and obscure the fundamental processes. However, this assertion automatically leads to the question of how a fundamental process and an overlaid strategy may be distinguished by means of experimental data. The extent to which any experiment can distinguish between these is almost certainly being overestimated. Although data may be used to identify the processes that are used to perform a particular task by the majority of people, to conclude from this that these processes are somehow fundamental requires several assumptions. These include the following: (a) that there exists a fundamental reasoning device; (b) that there exist deduction tasks that provide a clear window through which these processes may be observed, unobscured by strategies; and (c) that it is possible to determine which task(s) fit the criterion for (b).

If the need to address these assumptions is ignored, it is easy to show that experimental data cannot be used to identify the fundamental reasoning mechanism. Suppose, first, that this really does exist, but its processes can be overlaid by reasoning strategies. What would we expect to observe? We might see people using a variety of strategies for a variety of deduction tasks, precisely the pattern shown in the previous review. Without knowing whether or which tasks provide a window through which the fundamental mechanism can be observed, how could we know where to look for it? Now suppose that there is no fundamental reasoning mechanism, no processes are privileged and all constitute reasoning strategies. We would expect to see exactly the same pattern of behavior, and now speculating on which task provides a window through which to observe the fundamental processes is a futile exercise.

In the years since Roberts (1993) was published, the only citations have been neutral—drawing readers' attention to the arguments—or being in full agreement with them. The citations that are at the very least neutral—and possibly receptive—are those of Evans et al. (1993); Evans, Newstead, Allan, and Pollard (1994); Falmagne and Gonsalves (1995); Evans, Clibbens, and Rood (1995); Vandierendonck and DeVooght (1997), Girotto, Mazzocco, and Tasso (1997) and

Doyle and Ford (1998). The citations that broadly agree with the arguments are those of Aronson (1997); Barrouillet (1997); George (1997), Yule (1997) and Stanovich and West (1998b). The current author has been unable to locate any attempt to resolve the problem of individual differences in print to date. Because there are no attempts for the current author to discuss, instead, let us assume that a fundamental reasoning mechanism does exist, and that tasks exist that enable its actions to be viewed directly. Given these, the remainder of this section considers several possible suggestions for identifying the fundamental reasoning mechanism. Unfortunately, even if these two assumptions are valid, the identification of the fundamental processes is still a virtual impossibility.

The Unanimous Verdict

The unanimous verdict is based on the premise that the strategy used by everyone for all deduction tasks must be fundamental to all deductive reasoning. Unfortunately, the numerous studies demonstrating individual differences in deduction strategies mean that this simply does not apply. However, coupled with following suggestions, a resurrection of the unanimous verdict might be possible.

Certain Tasks, Where a Mixture of Strategies Are Observed,
Are Outside the Scope of the Universal Reasoning Theory.

One possible solution is to reject tasks in which individual differences in strategy usage have been observed, hence assuming that only strategically pure tasks provide a clear window through which the basic processes of the fundamental reasoning mechanism can be observed (see, e.g., Byrne & Johnson-Laird, 1989, pp. 564–565). However, if we reject not just the tasks in which individual differences may be observed, but also, to be on the safe side, tasks where it is difficult to be certain whether or not there are individual differences in the use of reasoning strategies (conditional reasoning and truth-teller problems), this leaves no tasks at all.

A less stringent criterion would be to reject tasks without a clear dominant strategy, also leaving aside conditional reasoning and truth-teller problems because of the difficulties in identifying the dominant processes. The assumption here is that tasks with an obvious dominant strategy provide a clear window, free of strategic pollution, through which the fundamental processes may be observed. This leaves sentence–picture verification (verbal strategy dominant), linear syllogisms (mixed strategy dominant), and the two-dimensional relational inference, family relationship, and compass point directions tasks (all spatial strategy dominant). No winner can be declared on this basis, at least one of these tasks is overwhelmingly polluted by a reasoning strategy, and the foregoing assumption becomes false by definition. However, if there were a sound reason for rejecting sentence–picture verification, this would leave us with tasks having spatial representations as the dominant means of inference.

The exclusion of tasks, for whatever reason, is not a decision that should be taken lightly. Even if the earlier exercises had been completely successful, this would come at the price of reducing the scope, power, and interest of the winning theory. A full understanding of human deduction would still require that individual differences in the use of strategies, observed for the majority of tasks, be understood too. Excluding most tasks serves only to divert attention away from this major component of human deductive behavior, leaving it uninvestigated and unaccounted for. The outcome is therefore a universal theory of deduction which at the same time is too narrow.

Rival Strategies Have Not Been Identified Reliably.

Although different deduction strategies have been identified by many researchers in numerous studies, another possibility is to reject their conclusions on the basis that the various methodologies are unreliable. However, the dismissal of such a large body of knowledge should not be taken lightly. Just about every available method has been used in order to identify different strategies, and although it may be possible to criticize certain studies on specific points, to reject all of these on this basis would call into question much of the methodology of cognitive psychology.

Alternatively, it could be argued that minority strategies are merely the outcome of statistical noise, which has caused idiosyncratic patterns of data that masquerade as independent strategies. Hence, for example, for the potential verbal strategy users on the two-dimensional relational inference task, it is perfectly possible that these people are simply showing an unusual pattern of data caused by random errors of measurement. Unfortunately, statistical tests cannot detect the difference between these and qualitative individual differences in strategy usage on the basis of a single performance measure, and so others are necessary. However, it is very rare indeed for individual difference researchers to rely on one single analysis in order to identify individual strategy users; converging evidence is both essential and commonplace. On the other hand, even if minority strategies can be troublesome, in other situations such as for categorical syllogisms, neither the verbal nor the spatial strategies identified by Ford (1994) could fairly be said to be a small minority.

Rival Strategies Are Merely Variants of Operation of the Fundamental Reasoning Mechanism.

Rather than rejecting tasks or studies, the remaining possibilities consider various ways in which competing strategies may be rejected as candidates for the fundamental reasoning mechanism. The first suggestion is that rival strategies may draw upon identical processes to the proposed fundamental strategy. For example, Rips frequently argues that the use of mental models merely reflects the operation of underlying rules of inference. Alternatively, Johnson-Laird and Byrne (1991) suggested that under certain circumstances, the use of mental models may mimic the output of the atmosphere strategy applied to categorical syllogisms. However, to assert that all rival strategies reflect the use of, say, mental models is probably unreasonable. It is highly unlikely that either the *two-somes* rule for categorical syllogisms, or the various shortcut strategies for linear syllogisms, require representation and inference from mental models.

A further problem with this suggestion is that, if it is to be claimed that the wide diversity of strategies are all based on the same underlying processes, this must call into question the falsifiability of any universal theory of reasoning. Hence, to capitalize on the assertion that rival's theories reflect the operation of one's own mechanisms comes with a cost. Once a theory becomes too effective at accounting for everything then, paradoxically, it can become weaker.

Task-Specific Shortcut Strategies
Cannot Be Fundamental by Definition.

It can only be reasonable to insist that a fundamental strategy must also be a general strategy. For example, strategies such as atmosphere for categorical syllogisms cannot be applied to other deduction tasks, and some strategies for certain linear syllogism problems cannot even be applied to other linear syllogisms (consider the use of the words taller *and* shorter in the example syllogism given earlier). These strategies are unlikely to represent the action of a fundamental reasoning mechanism. However, not all observed strategies are task-specific, and for many reasoning tasks, both spatial and verbal strategies have been identified as well as shortcuts, and so a unanimous verdict is still not possible, although the removal of task-specific shortcuts from the running does simplify the options somewhat.

Rival Strategies Are Merely Task-Specific Shortcuts
Despite Their Apparent Generality.

A final way of attempting a unanimous verdict is to assert that *all* rival strategies are merely the manifestation of task-specific shortcuts. These therefore have developed according to task demands on an *ad hoc* basis, and do not reflect the operation of a coherent, fundamental mechanism. This was implied by Rips (1994b) when suggesting that spatial strategies for solving syllogisms may be learned. In addition, the Modus Ponens rule suggested by deduction rule theorists looks suspiciously like a rule that might be learned as a result of many attempts to make the Modus Ponens inference by the use of mental models. Certainly, given the range of task-specific shortcut strategies that have been learned, and their rule-like operation, there is no real reason to suggest that the basic deduction rules need be an innate, programmed set. Hence, if either theoretical camp could devise a set of criteria for distinguishing between fundamental and task-specific shortcut strategies, which could uniquely show that either deduction-rule or mental model strategies were inherently task-specific, then the debate would resolve itself without the need for further empirical work. Whether or not this is possible is a question for the rival camps to answer.

The Majority Verdict

If the fundamental reasoning mechanism cannot be identified by a unanimous verdict, then a majority verdict may be necessary instead, either explicitly, or implicitly via a statistical test. This is based on the premise that the strategy used by the majority for a given task or tasks is fundamental to all deductive reasoning. The problem with this verdict is that patterns of individual differences are highly related to task format, so that one particular task format may favor certain strategies whereas another may favor rival strategies. Hence, a majority strategy may only have this status because a particular presentation caused the particular strategy balance.

Research into linear syllogisms is particularly relevant here; different conclusions have reflected different task formats since the outset. Clark (1969) used parallel presentation and concluded that only verbal processes were used for solution, while Huttenlocher (1968) used serial presentation (auditory this case) and concluded that spatial processes were used. The use of the verbal strategy to solve linear syllogisms appears to be particularly demanding on working memory capacity, and so this is only effective with parallel presentation. When serial presentation is used, the higher demands made on working memory mean that the most effective strategy is to represent each newly presented piece of information on a spatial array before it is removed and new information is presented. Evidence for this comes from Potts and Scholz (1975) who found that spatial processes dominated when the premises were shown together and were removed before the question was shown, but that verbal processes dominated when question and premises were shown simultaneously. Ormrod (1979) and Newsome (1986) have also obtained similar findings, as has Coney (1988) for sentence–picture verification. Parallel presentation also favors task-specific shortcut strategies (e.g., for linear syllogisms and for the compass point directions task, see Roberts, 1991).

The relationship between task format and choice of reasoning strategy is also important when considering research into the two-dimensional spatial layout task. This has traditionally used serial presentation (e.g., Byrne & Johnson-Laird, 1989) and the majority of data are generally in line with the use of mental models rather than deduction rules (see also Rauh, chap. 9, this volume; Vandierendonck, De Vooght, Desimpelaere, & Dierckx, chap. 10, this volume). Hence, wherever it is reported that a particular strategy is used by a majority, if there is any possibility that this has been biased by task presentation, then there is a need to replicate the findings with the alternative presentation. However, it must be emphasized that the suggestion is *not* that all conclusions have been biased by task presentation, only that some care is required to ensure that this is *never* the case.

Suppose that the majority of people are found to use a particular strategy and there is no possibility that the task presentation has biased the study, can we now conclude that these processes are supported by the fundamental reasoning mechanism? Unfortunately, the answer to this is no, and the pointer toward this is the earlier task presentation results, which are clear evidence that different strategies have different memory demands. Hence, if a particular task is conducive to a particular strategy, then this may have dominated not because it is fundamental, but because it is the most suited to that particular task. Roberts (1993) therefore suggested that many reasoning tasks are *strategically* limited: Their demands mean either that only certain strategies are worthwhile, or are possible (other strategies going beyond people's abilities to execute them). A majority verdict is therefore also an untrustworthy means of determining the fundamental reasoning mechanism, and in any case majority strategies can exist even if there is no fundamental mechanism.

Summary

The problem of individual differences is very serious indeed, and few of the previous solutions are convincing. However, this does not rule out future developments from changing the situation. Until then, it is reasonable to conclude that the issue of whether the fundamental reasoning mechanism supports mental models or deduction rules has not and cannot be resolved empirically, whether by a unanimous verdict or by a majority verdict. We cannot currently distinguish between fundamental processes (if they exist) and overlaid strategies by observing patterns of performance. In addition, the intractability of this problem calls into question whether deduction tasks are a natural kind that could even be expected to be performed by a single, hard-wired device. Overall, the inevitable conclusion if the earlier arguments are accepted, is that further work devoted to the identification of the fundamental reasoning mechanism is superfluous. In the interim, perhaps the individual differences in the use of strategies themselves deserve more attention than has previously been the case.

APPROACHES TO STRATEGY SELECTION

So far, it has been suggested that an understanding of individual differences in strategy usage is a useful pursuit both in lieu of the outcome of the debate on the nature of the fundamental reasoning mechanism, and because a full account of human deduction must include all aspects of such behavior, including individual differences. However, suppose that a particularly clever piece of research has enabled the mental model–deduction rule debate to be resolved. Theoretically, this would be a major achievement, but what would its applications be? If the winning theory was mental models, we might decide to improve children's use of these processes, perhaps trying to accelerate their development, although if the use of mental models is natural and fundamental, it is not clear whether there is any need for this over and above day-to-day experience. On the other hand, the use of mental models is not always the best strategy, so perhaps children should also be taught to recognize this and develop improved strategies in these situations. If this teaching program were to be adopted, a full understanding of deductive reasoning strategies would be necessary *in addition to* an understanding of the fundamental reasoning mechanism. Alternatively, suppose that the winning theory turns out to be deduction rules. Should people be discouraged from using spatial strategies? Should we produce instructions for appliances without diagrams? Should computers only be designed with command-line interfaces, thus providing a direct link with the fundamental inference processes? Hardly. These thoughts suggest that even if we know the nature of the fundamental reasoning mechanism, there will be few implications for applied psychology without a full understanding of reasoning strategies as well. In addition, if there is no fundamental reasoning mechanism, then a full understanding of these is all that can be hoped for.

The first part of this chapter has focused on findings concerning the classification and identification of different deduction strategies. Differences are widespread even in simple, basic laboratory deduction tasks, and this must also be true in the real world, perhaps more so. Having identified the strategies, another observation is that the most effective are not necessarily used by everyone, so that inappropriate strategy selection is a genuine cause of poor performance for many people. This leads to further questions such as: *Why do people use different strategies? Is it possible to predict in advance who is going to choose a particular strategy?* and *Is it possible to improve people's ability to develop and select the most appropriate strategies?* There is a long way to go before we could hope to have full answers to any of these, but the remainder of this chapter reviews the different approaches to answering them.

Cost–Benefit Analysis

One suggestion for why people choose different strategies is that each person conducts an assessment of the relative merits of the available options, reaching a rational decision based on his or her available resources and the demands of each strategy, with a view to maximizing performance. Hence, people high in spatial ability will tend to find that spatial strategies have the advantage, and will be their best choice, whereas people low in spatial ability will tend to find that verbal strategies have the advantage for them, and avoid the use of spatial strategies. Overall, we should observe *direct aptitude-strategy relationships*, where the aptitude that predicts performance depends upon the resources necessary for performing the task. MacLeod et al. (1978) found results exactly in line with this prediction for the sentence–picture verification task (although findings by

Marquer & Pereira, 1990, and Roberts et al., 1994, mean that caution is required before accepting them).

The exact means by which such a mechanism operates, and whether it is open to conscious control, are both uncertain. There is an extensive literature on the role of metacognitive processes in monitoring and regulating performance (e.g., Brown, 1987; Schoenfeld, 1987). Others (e.g., Reder & Schunn, 1996; Siegler, 1996) suggest that the most appropriate strategy can be selected entirely by the action of low-level processes. However, it is easy to find evidence that the cost–benefit analysis approach is not enough by itself. The most effective strategies are rarely used by all, and may require considerable experience before they develop. Unless the cost–benefit analysis is particularly slow and faulty, this implies that not all strategies are available to all people, and that strategies may develop while a task is being performed, and hence that these development processes must be understood in addition.

Cognitive Styles

Cognitive styles represent tendencies to process information in certain ways (see Riding, Glass, & Douglas, 1993; Sternberg, 1997, for reviews). Many different styles have been proposed but of particular relevance to this chapter is the *visualizer–verbalizer* distinction: Some people may have a natural tendency to use verbal representations, whereas others may tend to use spatial representations. A plausible explanation for this behavior is that with time, people with low spatial ability assemble a repertoire of verbal strategies that enables them to avoid drawing upon deficient resources. High spatial ability people will assemble a repertoire of spatial strategies that enables them to make maximal use of superior resources. Such an approach would predict direct aptitude–strategy relationships, and thus the results of MacLeod et al. can also be explained by this approach.

Other evidence in support of cognitive styles is discussed by Roberts and Newton (1998). Often, people will persist with an inefficient strategy, which matches their stylistic preference, when far more efficient strategies are possible. However, Roberts et al. (1997) showed that the cognitive style approach is unable to give a general account of strategy selection. For the compass point directions task, the spatial strategy users tended to have much lower spatial ability than cancellation strategy users. Hence, people chose strategies inappropriate to their abilities, giving an *inverted aptitude–strategy relationship* (see also Cooper & Mumaw, 1985). The low spatial ability people were particularly penalized by their failure to adopt cancellation; the use of the spatial strategy is particularly demanding for them. It could be argued that an inappropriate stylistic dimension was chosen for predicting strategy selection at this task, but such an assertion only emphasizes the difficulty that this approach has in making falsifiable predictions. Overall, Roberts and Newton suggest that results supporting the notion of cognitive styles may be subsumed by the developmental approach discussed next.

The cognitive style and cost–benefit analysis approaches are primarily concerned with how people choose among strategies from two or more options. The issue of whether all strategies are available to all people is taken to be unimportant, and this is the reason why these approaches are limited and are unable to make general predictions concerning strategy selection. For highly efficient task-specific shortcut strategies, it appears that they are simply not available to all people. The next two approaches consider this issue directly.

Knowledge of Strategies

The knowledge-based approach suggests that for any given task, the people for whom the most efficient strategy is available are those who have learned about it from past experience. This knowledge is taken to be the only systematic way in which people who use the strategy differ from people who do not. This approach is grounded upon studies of expert–novice differences in highly specific domains (Ericsson & Charness, 1994). Experts are found to have a larger knowledgebase than novices, which enables them to choose the most appropriate strategy for a given problem in their domain of expertise. The leap of inference is to apply this retrospectively to other tasks. Hence, those people who choose the most effective strategy for any given task must have been the people with the greatest "expertise" in that domain. However, people who choose the more effective strategies for, say, linear syllogisms may not have had any obvious prior experience at this task, and in which case, to preserve the expertise explanation, it is necessary to assert that the relevant knowledge originated from experience gained and transferred from related tasks. General abilities such as spatial and verbal ability, and also intelligence, are generally held to be irrelevant to strategy use (Simon, 1990).

The knowledge-based approach has support from findings by Kyllonen, Lohman, and colleagues (Lohman & Kyllonen, 1983). They have observed that people who achieve high scores on spatial ability test type problems are those who use a larger range of strategies to solve them, and are more flexible, and hence are more likely to change strategy from trial to trial. However, this observation leads to two possible explanations, either that knowledge of a wide range of strategies leads to high spatial ability, or else that greater spatial ability leads to a wider range of strategies. The authors appear to favor the first of these. However, care must be taken not to overgeneralize knowledge explanations. At an extreme, this stance is both tautological and denies the existence of strategy discovery. A further problem arises from the phenomenon that expert knowledge tends to be highly domain specific, and transfers only with the greatest of difficulty, thus going against the earlier transfer explanation. Ultimately, the extreme knowledge-based stance is a rather static account of strategy possession. Novices do not possess effective strategies, whereas experts either do possess them, or otherwise the task of generating them is trivial for them. Clearly, knowing the correct strategy in any given situation will put a person at an advantage over someone who does not.

However, if people without the necessary knowledge can nevertheless derive an effective strategy, whereas others who do not obviously differ from them in terms of specific knowledge cannot, then expertise/knowledge-based approaches are not enough to give a general account of strategy selection. When knowledge fails a person, it may be necessary to attempt to develop strategies from scratch, and the development of strategies during problem solving is a genuine phenomenon observed in detail by several researchers (Siegler & Jenkins, 1989; Wood, 1969).

Developmental Approaches

In order to have a full account of individual differences in strategy usage, it is necessary to understand how strategies develop during problem solving, and why this occurs at different rates for different people. This approach considers what a person can learn about a task from the way in which information is encoded, represented, and manipulated. Hence, whereas strategies may be chosen on the basis of past experience, new strategies may also develop from current experience of solving problems. Although traditionally associated with children, adults develop new strategies too, and researchers such as Siegler (1996) suggested that the processes of development in general are identical for children and for adults. Hence a desire for a general understanding of strategy development from a developmental perspective need not exclude findings derived from experiments on adults.

The key events in the development of new, more effective strategies appear to be the identification and deletion of redundant steps. These enable inefficient but general strategies (whether verbal or spatial) to be converted into more task-specific shortcuts, for which the lack of generalizability to new tasks, or even new formats, is a risk worth taking for the gains in productivity on the current task. Several mechanisms to account for this have been proposed. For example, one possibility is that the move to more effective strategies is triggered out of necessity by a failure of the current strategy to work satisfactorily, as modeled by the impasse-based strategy modification system SOAR (Laird, Rosenbloom, & Newell, 1986; VanLehn, 1988). Others suggest that strategy development occurs as a result of repeated problem solving success with a current strategy (Siegler & Jenkins, 1989). In general, the results discussed by Siegler and colleagues go against impasses as the major drive of strategy development for children's arithmetic. Findings in the deduction literature not only confirm this, but also give an intriguing account of individual differences in strategy development.

Wood (1969, 1978) observed that for linear syllogisms, those people who developed task-specific shortcuts the fastest were those who were initially better able to solve them by using more general strategies. A related finding comes from Galotti et al. (1986) for categorical syllogisms. Here, those people who were more likely spontaneously to discover the *two-somes* rule were the more proficient at solving them before the rule was discovered. Finally, Roberts et al. (1997) found that people with high spatial ability were more likely to use the cancellation strategy for compass point directions tasks, and were also better able to reason by the use of a spatial strategy when given problems that inhibited the use of cancellation. These studies all show that the best performers at general strategies (either verbal or spatial) are also the more likely to develop task-specific shortcut strategies that will improve their performance still further. Hence, new strategies are developed by those who are successful at problem solving rather than those who fail, and this suggests the cruelest irony of all; that the worst performers at a task, who would benefit the most from the use of more effective strategies, are those who are least able to develop them. This general principle highlights the need to understand strategy development processes: The implications for everyday reasoning and problem solving are of profound importance.

Mechanisms for the deletion of redundant steps have been suggested by Wood (1978) who described these processes as *reflective abstraction*, and more recently by Crowley et al. (1997). Their exact details need not concern us here, but both have in common the deletion of redundant and repetitive problem-solving steps. The basis for individual differences is the necessary ability to perform a particular task, that is, the domain-general skill or skills necessary for the optimal execution of a strategy. This may include spatial ability, verbal ability, numerical ability, or intelligence depending on the strategy, the task, and its presentation. In general, high ability people are more likely to generate recognizable redundancies and regularities in their problem-solving representations. Low ability people are more likely to generate "noisy" representations in which regularities are less detectable. In addition, Roberts et al. (1997) suggested that the need to evaluate newly developed strategies for their validity may also lead to less frequent adoption by low ability people. This is because, where necessary, the only means of evaluation is to compare the output of a newly developed strategy with that of the general strategy currently in use, which is known to be valid. Even if the answers that are being generated by the new strategy are the more accurate, low ability people will be less likely to be able to execute a general strategy by definition. A persistent disagreement in answers between old and new strategies must inevitably lead to the rejection of the validity of the new strategy.

Summary

Of the four approaches to strategy selection, the cognitive styles approach is probably the least able to provide explanations and make useful predictions. The knowledge-based approach is trivially true: Those who know the best strategy are more likely to use it, but otherwise it must be an oversimplification. The developmental and cost–benefit analysis approaches together can give an account not only of how new strategies are discovered, but also of how they are evaluated and chosen, and why individuals differ. Hence, a cost–benefit analysis may determine which general strategy is likely to be selected by an individual, and then strategy development processes may or may not be able to add effective task-specific shortcuts to the strategy repertoire. Evaluation of a new strategy for validity may be required, with further cost–benefit analysis necessary in order to determine whether the new strategy is worthwhile.

The foregoing sketch provides one possible account of strategy selection. The next step is to determine whether this is adequate, and to flesh out the fine details of the processes, attempting to understand individual differences wherever they occur. One point to note is that the developmental processes described earlier may be characterized as *strategy reduction processes*, but sometimes the construction of new, *more elaborate* methods to solve problems may also take place (e.g., Kuhn & Pearsall, 1998). A further task would be to see whether the processes outlined earlier apply here too.

AFTERWORD: PROBLEMS AND OPPORTUNITIES

For those attempting to understand strategy selection and development processes, several problems and debates fade into the background and become irrelevant. These include the problem of individual differences, the deduction rules–mental models debate, and the issue of whether the mental models–deduction rules debate constitutes an attempt to resolve a false dichotomy. Although positive outcomes to these might have some bearing on strategy issues (e.g., by suggesting the strategy that a person is most likely to choose first), the lack of any answer will not hinder research into individual differences unduly.

Assuming that the reader has found something of interest in this chapter, why has this research been neglected over the years? One possibility is that it superficially appears to be less glamorous than research concerned with other topics. A more practical problem is that individual differences research is harder to do well. Considerably more people must be tested than for conventional research, and each person must be tested more intensively than is usually the case. To add to difficulties, the minority nature of this research means that the domain has not yet had the opportunity to develop a standard agreed nomenclature and taxonomy for methodology and phenomena, and this can only be off-putting to a potential researcher. It makes different studies harder to integrate, and leads to the feeling that each new piece of work requires the reinvention of the wheel. However the payoff is the potential for genuinely novel and important findings in a still relatively new area of psychology. This is truly an opportunity to be seized.

REFERENCES

Aronson, J. L. (1997). Mental models and deduction. *American Behavioral Scientist, 40,* 782–797.

Barrouillet, P. (1997). Modifying the representation of if … then sentences in adolescents by inducing a structure mapping strategy. *Current Psychology of Cognition, 16,* 609–637.

Braine, M. D. S., & O'Brien, D. P. (1997). *Mental Logic*. Mahwah, NJ: Lawrence Erlbaum Associates.

Brown, A. (1987). Metacognition, executive control, self-regulation and other more mysterious mechanisms. In F. E. Weinert & R. H. Kluwe (Eds.), *Metacognition, motivation and understanding* (pp. 65–116). Hillsdale, NJ: Lawrence Erlbaum Associates.

Byrne, R. M. J., & Handley, S. J. (1997). Reasoning strategies for suppositional deductions. *Cognition, 62,* 1–49.

Byrne, R. M. J., & Johnson-Laird, P. N. (1989). Spatial reasoning. *Journal of Memory and Language, 28,* 564–575.

Carpenter, P. A., & Just, M. A. (1975). Sentence comprehension: A psycholinguistic model of verification. *Psychological Review, 82,* 45–73.

Clark, H. H. (1969). Linguistic processes in deductive reasoning. *Psychological Review, 76,* 387–404.

Clark, H. H., & Chase, W. G. (1972). On the process of comparing sentences against pictures. *Cognitive Psychology, 3,* 472–517.

Coney, J. (1988). Individual differences and task format in sentence verification. *Current Psychological Research and Reviews, 7,* 122–135.

Cooper, L. A., & Mumaw, R. J. (1985). Spatial aptitude. In R. F. Dillon (Ed.), *Individual differences in cognition (Vol. 2),* (pp. 67–94). Orlando, FL: Academic Press.

Crowley, K., Shrager, J., & Siegler, R. S. (1997). Strategy discovery as a competitive negotiation between metacognitive and associative mechanisms. *Developmental Review, 17,* 462–489.

De Soto, C. B., London, M., & Handel, S. (1965). Social reasoning and spatial paralogic. *Journal of Personality and Social Psychology, 2,* 513–521.

Doyle, J. K., & Ford, D. N. (1998). Mental models concepts for system dynamics research. *System Dynamics Review, 14,* 3–29.

Ericsson, K. A., & Charness, N. (1994). Expert performance: its structure and acquisition. *American Psychologist, 49,* 725–747.

Evans, J. St B. T., Barston, J. L., & Pollard, P. (1983). On the conflict between logic and belief in syllogistic reasoning. *Memory and Cognition, 11,* 295–306.

Evans, J. St B. T., Clibbens, J., & Rood, B. (1995). Bias in conditional inference: implications for mental models and mental logic. *Quarterly Journal of Experimental Psychology, 48A,* 644–670.

Evans, J. St. B. T., Ellis, C. F., & Newstead, S. E. (1996). On the mental representation of conditional sentences. *Quarterly Journal of Experimental Psychology, 49A,* 1086–1114.

Evans, J. St. B. T., Newstead, S. E., Allen, J. L., & Pollard, P. (1994). Debiasing by instruction – the case of belief bias. *European Journal of Cognitive Psychology, 6,* 263–285.

Evans, J. St. B. T., Newstead, S. E., & Byrne, R. M. J. (1993). *Human reasoning: The psychology of deduction.* Hove, UK: Psychology Press.

Evans, J. St. B. T., & Over, D. E. (1996). *Rationality and reasoning.* Hove, UK: Psychology Press.

Falmagne, R. J., & Gonsalves, J. (1995). Deductive inference. *Annual Review of Psychology, 46,* 644–670.

Ford. M. (1994). Two models of mental representation and problem solving in syllogistic reasoning. *Cognition, 54,* 1–71.

Galotti, K. M., Baron, J., & Sabini, J. P. (1986). Individual differences in syllogistic reasoning: Deduction rules or mental models? *Journal of Experimental Psychology: General, 115,* 16–25.

George, C. (1995). The endorsement of the premises: Assumption based or belief-based reasoning. *British Journal of Psychology, 86,* 93–113.

George, C. (1997). Rationality in reasoning: the problem of deductive competence – commentary on Evans and Over. *Current Psychology of Cognition, 16,* 87–92.

Gilhooly, K. J., Logie, R. H., Wetherick, N. E., & Wynn, V. (1993). Working memory and strategies in syllogistic-reasoning tasks. *Memory and Cognition, 21,* 115–124.

Girotto, V., Mazzocco, A., & Tasso, A. (1997). The effect of premise order in conditional reasoning: A test of the mental model theory. *Cognition, 63,* 1–28.

Holyoak, K. J., & Cheng, P. W. (1995). Pragmatic reasoning with a point of view. *Thinking and Reasoning, 1,* 289–400.

Huttenlocher, J. (1968). Constructing spatial images: A strategy in reasoning. *Psychological Review, 75,* 550–560.

Johnson-Laird, P. N. (1972). The three term series problem. *Cognition, 1,* 58–82.

Johnson-Laird, P. N., & Byrne, R. M. J. (1991). *Deduction.* Hove, UK: Psychology press.

Johnson-Laird, P. N., Byrne, R. M. J., & Schaeken, W. (1992). Propositional reasoning by model. *Psychological Review, 99,* 418–439.

Johnson-Laird, P. N., Byrne, R. M. J., & Schaeken, W. (1994). Why models rather than rules give a better account of propositional reasoning: A reply to Bonatti, and to O'Brien, Braine, & Yang. *Psychological Review, 101,* 734–739.

Kroll, J. F., & Corrigan, A. (1981). Strategies in sentence-picture verification. The effect of an unexpected picture. *Journal of Verbal Learning and Verbal Behavior, 20,* 515–531.

Kuhn, D., & Pearsall, S. (1998). Relations between metastrategic knowledge and strategic performance. *Cognitive Development, 13,* 227–247.

Laird, J. E., Rosenbloom, P. S., & Newell, A. (1986). Chunking in Soar: The anatomy of a general learning mechanism. *Machine Learning, 1,* 11–46.

Lohman, D. F., & Kyllonen, P. C. (1983). Individual differences in solution strategy on spatial tasks. In R. F. Dillon & R. R. Schmeck (Eds.), *Individual differences in cognition (Vol. 1),* (pp. 105–135). New York: Academic Press.

MacLeod, C. M., Hunt, E. B., & Mathews, N. N. (1978). Individual differences in the verification of sentence-picture relationships. *Journal of Verbal Learning and Verbal Behavior, 17,* 493–507.

Marquer, J. M., & Pereira, M. (1990). Reaction times in the study of strategies in sentence-picture verification: A reconsideration. *Quarterly Journal of Experimental Psychology, 42A,* 147–168.

Newsome, G. L. (1986). The role of end anchoring and congruence in the solution of linear syllogisms. *Journal of Research and Development in Education, 20,* 52–58.

Oakhill, J., & Garnham, A. (1996). *Mental models in cognitive science: Essays in honour of Phil Johnson-Laird.* Hove, UK: Psychology Press.

Ohlsson, S. (1984). Induced strategy shifts in spatial reasoning. *Acta Psychologica, 57,* 47–67.

Ormrod, J. E. (1979). Cognitive processes in the solution of three-term series problems. *American Journal of Psychology, 92,* 235–255.

Potts, G. R., & Scholz, K. W. (1975). The internal representation of a three-term series problem. *Journal of Verbal Learning and Verbal Behavior, 14,* 439–452.

Quinton, G., & Fellows, B. J. (1975). 'Perceptual' strategies in the solving of three-term series problems. *British Journal of Psychology, 66,* 69–78.

Reder, L. M., & Schunn, C. D. (1996). Metacognition does not imply awareness: Strategy choice is governed by implicit learning and memory. In L. M. Reder (Ed.), *Implicit memory and metacognition* (pp. 45–77). Mahwah, NJ: Lawrence Erlbaum Associates.

Riding, R. J., Glass, A., & Douglas, G. (1993). Individual differences in thinking: Cognitive and neuropsychological perspectives. *Educational Psychology, 13,* 267–280.

Rips, L. J. (1989). The psychology of knights and knaves. *Cognition, 31,* 85–116.

Rips, L. J. (1994a). *The psychology of proof.* Cambridge, MA: MIT Press.

Rips, L. J. (1994b). Deduction and its cognitive basis. In R. J. Sternberg (Ed.), *Thinking and problem solving* (pp. 149–178). San Diego: Academic Press.

Roberts, M. J. (1991). *Individual differences and strategy selection in problem solving.* Unpublished doctoral dissertation, University of Nottingham.

Roberts, M. J. (1993). Human reasoning: deduction rules or mental models, or both? *Quarterly Journal of Experimental Psychology, 46A,* 569–589.

Roberts, M. J., Gilmore, D. J., & Wood, D. J. (1997). Individual differences and strategy selection in reasoning. *British Journal of Psychology, 88,* 473–492.

Roberts, M. J., & Newton, E. J. (1998). Understanding strategy selection. Manuscript submitted for review.

Roberts, M. J., Wood, D. J., & Gilmore, D. J. (1994). The sentence-picture verification task: Methodological and theoretical difficulties. *British Journal of Psychology, 85,* 413–432.

Schoenfeld, A. H. (1987). What's all the fuss about metacognition? In A. H. Schoenfeld (Ed.), *Cognitive science and mathematics education* (pp. 189–215). Hillsdale, NJ: Lawrence Erlbaum Associates.

Schroyens, W., Schaeken, W., & d'Ydewalle, G. (1996). Meta-logical reasoning with knight-knave problems: The importance of being hypothesised. *Psychologica Belgica, 36,* 145–170.

Shaver, P., Pierson, L., & Lang, S. (1985). Converging evidence for the functional significance of imagery in problem solving. *Cognition, 3,* 359–375.

Siegler, R. S. (1996). *Emerging minds: The process of change in children's thinking.* New York: Oxford University Press.

Siegler, R. S., & Jenkins, E. A. (1989). *How children discover new strategies.* Hillsdale, NJ: Lawrence Erlbaum Associates.

Simon, H. A. (1990). Invariants of human behavior. *Annual Review of Psychology, 41,* 1–21.

Stanovich, K. E., & West, R. F. (1998a). Cognitive ability and variation in selection task performance. *Thinking and Reasoning, 4,* 193–230.

Stanovich, K. E., & West, R. F. (1998b). Individual differences in rational thought. *Journal of Experimental Psychology: General, 127,* 161–188.

Sternberg, R. J. (1980). Representation and process in linear syllogistic reasoning. *Journal of Experimental Psychology: General, 109,* 119–159.

Sternberg, R. J. (1997). Are cognitive styles still in style. *American Psychologist, 52,* 700–712.

Sternberg, R. J., & Weil, E. M. (1980). An aptitude x strategy interaction in linear syllogistic reasoning. *Journal of Educational Psychology, 72,* 226–239.

Vandierendonck, A., & DeVooght, G. (1997). Working memory constraints on linear reasoning with spatial and temporal contents. *Quarterly Journal of Experimental Psychology, 50A,* 803–820.

VanLehn, K. (1988). Towards a theory of impasse driven learning. In H. Mandl & A. Lesgold (Eds.), *Learning issues for intelligent tutoring systems* (pp. 19–41). New York: Springer-Verlag.

Wood, D. J. (1969). *The nature and development of problem solving strategies.* Unpublished doctoral thesis, University of Nottingham.

Wood, D. J. (1978). Problem solving—the nature and development of strategies. In G. Underwood (Ed.), *Strategies in information processing* (pp. 329–356). London: Academic Press.

Wood, D. J., & Shotter, J. (1973). A preliminary study of distinctive features in problem solving. *Quarterly Journal of Experimental Psychology, 25,* 504–510.

Wood, D. J., Shotter, J., & Godden, D. (1974). An investigation of the relationships between problem solving strategies, representation and memory. *Quarterly Journal of Experimental Psychology, 26,* 252–257.

Yule, P. (1997). Deductive competence: Mental models or task-specific strategies— Commentary on Evans & Over. *Current Psychology of Cognition, 16,* 87–92.

3

Task, Premise Order, and Strategies in Rips's Conjunction-Disjunction and Conditionals Problems

Juan A. García Madruga
Sergio Moreno
Nuria Carriedo
Francisco Gutiérrez

Rips (1994) presented a study in which he used three-premise problems: a conjunction or a disjunction in the first premise, followed by two conditionals. Although the mental model theory predicts that conjunction problems (one-model) will be easier than disjunctive ones (multiple model), Rips did not find significant differences. We present four experiments on the effect of the kind of task, the order of premises, as well as people's strategies and metaknowledge of the problems' difficulty. Conjunctive problems were easier than disjunctive ones when using a construction task and changing the order of premises. Likewise, reasoners used different strategies with conjunctive and disjunctive arguments and they are conscious of the greater difficulty of disjunction problems. The results confirm the mental model theory.

One of the most outstanding characteristics of the human mind is its capacity to draw valid inferences from verbally expressed statements. This deductive component of human thought (Wason & Johnson-Laird, 1972) is best illustrated by the competent behavior of those who by the analysis of formal reasoning have made logic a science. However, this capacity is also to be found in those who, though having not received formal training, are nevertheless up to solving deductive problems according to the principles of logic (albeit perhaps only in certain, determined circumstances). There are then two circumstances that allow us to speak of a human capacity for deductive thought, one that we could identify with logic itself and its 2000 years old traditions; and another, which has more to do with the acts of the untrained as studied in the psychology of reasoning (which has but a mere 100 years to its name). It is no wonder then that the first, logic, has been and still is of great importance in the development of psychological theories that seek to explain those mechanisms that underlie human deductive behavior.

There are two major and differing approaches to the study of the psychology of reasoning, namely the formal rules theory and the mental models one, both being founded on concepts in logic. The formal rules theories share the syntactic conceptions of logic that defend and use proof-theoretic methods, based on deriving valid conclusions by means of rules of inference. The mental models theory, for its part, offers a semantic focus upon logic, basing itself on model-theoretic methods using truth tables to specify the meaning of connective propositions and, thus, the validity of any inferences to be drawn (see Johnson-Laird, 1993).

Formal rules theorists maintain that the human being has within the mind a set of rules or inferential schemes similar to those of logic, upon which answers to the deductive problems are derived. From a conjunctive statement of the type:

Raquel is in León and William is in Oviedo.

it is held that any of its components can be drawn as conclusion. If we are asked either if Raquel is in León or William in Oviedo, in both cases the answer will be yes. According to the mental rules theorists, this is due to human beings enjoying the use of a $A\&B$, $\therefore A$ mental rule.

Another rule would work upon a disjunctive proposition of the type:

A or B,
not A
$\therefore B.$

The following valid conclusion could be drawn:

Raquel is in León or William is in Oviedo.
Raquel is not in León
$\therefore$ *William is in Oviedo.*

Both these rules have their place in the current mental rules theories (Braine, 1990; Braine, Reiser, & Rumain, 1984; O'Brien, Braine, & Yang, 1994; Rips, 1983, 1994). The reasoner's task can here be broken down into three distinct phases: discovering the abstract form of the statements, applying the formal rules that lead to a valid conclusion, and re-translating the conclusion into a specific problem-content (Evans, Newstead, & Byrne, 1993). The key to such theories is to be found in the middle stage of the operation: applying of the rules or inference schemes. The larger the process of deriving a conclusion, the greater the problem's difficulty. The rules theory's fundamental prediction is thus drawn from the number of rules or intermediate steps required for reaching a conclusion. If this is so, then the two examples would present a similar kind of challenge as each calls for using a single rule, despite the fact that in the second example there was a second premise. If the disjunctive rule was to be applied, the second example called for coordinating two premises, a thing that would make it more difficult.

The mental model theory, on the other hand, approaches reasoning in a clearly distinct way. There are three stages of deduction according to the model theory: *comprehension* (i.e., reasoners apply their knowledge to constructing models that represent the state of affairs described in the premises), *description* (reasoners try to formulate a parsimonious conclusion that accounts for the models constructed in the prior stage), and *validation* (they now try to falsify their previous conclusion by searching for alternative models or counterexamples; see Johnson-Laird & Byrne, 1991). A prime assumption of the mental model theory is that given the limited nature of human working memory resources, people try to represent explicitly as little information as possible: The more information represented explicitly, the greater the load on the working memory. Therefore, human reasoners make most of daily inferences from the initial and incomplete representation or models of the premises. The distinction between initial and totally explicit representation is applicable to connectives that require more than one model, such as disjunction and conditionals. In the case of conjunction, given that this connective demands only one model, initial and explicit representations are the same (Johnson-Laird, Byrne, & Schaeken, 1992). Let us see how this theory would be applied to the previous examples.

In the first of the two, the representation for a conjunction statement such as "*Raquel is in León and William is in Oviedo*" would be a single model such as this one:

L   O

From this representation it is obvious to conclude that either of the statement's two components (*Raquel is in León, William is in Oviedo*) is valid.

The second example is somewhat more complicated. The first disjunctive proposition, *Raquel is in León or William is in Oviedo* would be represented initially by the two models set out on different lines:

L

    O

However, such an initial representation does not capture the whole sense of the disjunction which could be either inclusive or exclusive. Consequently, the reasoner needs to create a more precise representation building up more explicit models like these:

Inclusive		*Exclusive*	
L	O	L	¬O
L	¬O	¬L	O
¬L	O		

Whereas the first representation includes the possibility that both components of the conjunction are true, the second excludes this.

Going back to the initial disjunctive representation, we can now see that solving the second problem did not require a complete explicit representation. The information in the second premise of the problem, *"Raquel in not in León,"* (¬L), contradicts and hence eliminates the first model of the initial representation. It can be incorporated within the second model thus creating a new one (¬L   O) which also already forms part of the final and explicit representation of both disjunctions. From this model the valid conclusion *"William is in Oviedo"* can already be directly reached.

As we can see, according to the mental model theory the solution to this second example would be harder than in the first example as a second model would be called for. This greater difficulty should be apparent from the smaller number of correct answers to the problem, the larger amount of time to reach a conclusion, and the rating of the difficulty of the problems.

We have tried not only to describe through examples just how both theories are applied in practice but also to make clear the problems they give rise to when it comes down to choosing and designing experiments that would allow to discern them. According to the rules theories, both problems call for a direct and immediate applying of a single rule in each case, although in the second example, this single rule would needs be somewhat less manageable because of the supplementary statement. For the mental models theory, the difference between the two problems goes in the same direction than the one predicted by rules theories. In short, there is only a nuance difference in the prediction of both theories. Moreover, both theories are armored with a protective belt modifiable at will which allows them to accommodate new results without having to alter the hard core of the theory itself, a phenomenon that has led some authors to doubt the possibility to decide for either of these theoretical approaches. Thus Evans and Over (1997) hold that *"If neither approach is fully and precisely defined in itself, then the issue of which is 'correct' is going to be hard to decide on empirical grounds"* (p. 27). We share the doubts as to whether or not crucial experiments could ever be designed that would allow to really distinguish between the merits of the two approaches. However, there are empirical problems, such as those here presented in this chapter, that allow for a supplementary clearing up.

The aim of this chapter is to replicate some of the results from Rips (1990, 1994) with three premise problems which included as first premise a conjunction or disjunction, followed by two conditionals. We controlled the type of task (either evaluation or construction) and also manipulated the order in which each premise was presented. Finally, our two most recent studies are presented that sought to get at the types of strategy used by the participants when trying to puzzle out these problems.

RIPS'S CONJUNCTION–DISJUNCTION AND CONDITIONALS PROBLEMS

In Rips (1990, 1994, pp. 365–369) participants were asked to evaluate the necessity of the given conclusion for a series of arguments like the following ones:

(1)	p AND q	(2)	p OR q
	IF p, r		IF p, r
	IF q, r		IF q, r
	----------		----------
	r		r

The two arguments were probably chosen by Rips because according to the mental model theory their representation, and hence the predictions that can be drawn from them, are quite different in each. The problems differ only in the first premise, but the mental model predicts that Problem 1 will probably be easier than Problem 2.

Argument 1 in particular would be specially easy in the light of the mental model theory. Reasoners are called on to build up their model for the first premise (the conjunction) and then the initial representation of either of the conditionals, in order to achieve a multiple representation allowing to infer that "*r*" is necessarily true. The process would be carried out as follows: The initial representation of the first premise "*p AND q*" would be the model

P   Q

The second premise, "*IF p, r*," is a conditional whose initial representation is:

[P]   R
...

The initial representation of the conditionals consists of two models, a first and explicit one representing the antecedent and consequent of the conditional statement and a second, implicit model expressed by the three dots. The brackets that enclose the first component of the explicit model indicate that the antecedent of the conditional has been fully expressed, that is, it cannot be otherwise represented in any other model. This initial representation of the conditional could be fleshed out either as a conditional in the strict sense (material implication) or as a biconditional (equivalence), thus offering a full range of models for conditionals:

Conditional		Biconditional	
P	Q	P	Q
¬P	Q	¬P	¬Q
¬P	¬Q		

However, the final explicit representation of the conditionals is not really called for, given that from the initial representation of the second premise, reasoners could easily put together a composite representation of both premises within a single model (see the psychological algorithm in Johnson-Laird et al., 1992) such as this one:

P   Q   R

The fact that "*r*" is necessarily valid can then be immediately inferred.

The mental model theory would claim that the reasoning process for the second type of Argument 2 would be very alike although the result would be very different. The key here is to be found in how the first and disjunctive premise "*p OR q*" is to be represented, this requiring the building up of two initial models:

P

　　Q

Given the "economy principle" in representation, it seems that reasoners would not make a complete fleshing out of the models but rather work upon initial models, be this for disjunctions or conditionals. This being so, the second premise "*IF p, r,*" would be represented thus:

[P]   R
...

Likewise, the third premise, "*IF q, r,*" would be expressed like this:

[Q]   R
...

Hence the combining process of the models would lead to a compound representation like:

P　　　　R
　　Q　　R

From this representation of two models, it would be possible to draw the necessarily true conclusion "*r.*" A fully explicit representation of the models for disjunction, be it inclusive or exclusive, would lead to the building up of final models like the following:

Inclusive Representation			Exclusive Representation		
P	Q	R	P	~Q	R
P	~Q	R	~P	Q	R
~P	Q	R			

Table 3.1.
PSYCOP's rules to solve Rip's conjunction–disjunction and conditionals problems.

	Arguments		*Rules*
One model problems	(1) P AND q IF p, r IF q, r ---------- r	(3) NOT p AND NOT q IF p, r P IF q, r ------------------------ r	Forward And Elimination P AND Q Forward IF Elimination IF P THEN R P ------------------------------- R
Mutiple model problems	(2) p OR q IF p, r IF q, r -----------	(4) NOT p OR NOT q IF NOT p, r IF NOT q, r ----------------------	Forward Dilemma P OR Q IF P THEN R IF Q THEN R ---------------------- R

Although some participants could well be up to a full fleshing out of the models, the cognitive economy principle would lead us to believe that most would draw their inferences upon the initial representation of the disjunction.

However, whereas for the theory of mental models it seems clear that the Arguments 1 and 2 present different degrees of difficulty, the predictions of the rules theories do not seem to be the same. Argument 1 would call for the applying of two rules drawn from the basic set of inference schemes (see Braine, 1990; Braine et al., 1984; Rips 1983, 1994), being the schema for conjunction and that for the conditional. For Argument 2, the rules theories would offer a single rule to be directly applied to reach a conclusion.

To solve Problem 1, Rips's most recent PSYSCOP theory of logical reasoning postulates an applying of forward AND and elimination IF rules, whereas for Problem 2, its Forward Dilemma rule (Rips, 1994, p. 368) would be brought into play. The rules can be seen in Table 3.1, where a further two Arguments 3 and 4 are included, their only significant variation being that they present negated propositions that would, however, call for no changes in the basic predictions proper to either theory. The mental model representation of negated conditionals is problematic. Although Johnson-Laird and Byrne (1991) proposed that the initial representation of negative conditionals would include the affirmative propositions, more recently Evans, Clibbens, and Rood (1995) and Schaeken, García Madruga, and Johnson-Laird (1995) have proposed that there would be no difference between the representation of conditionals without a negative and with a negative. Only the antecedent (positive or negative) and the consequent (positive or negative) are represented in the initial models. Likewise, to explain other effects of negation on conditionals, the authors have proposed that some differences of difficulty can appear during the fleshing out of the models when people have to negate a negated antecedent or consequent; that is, when people have to make a "double negation."

Hence, according to the theory of Rips, the problems with a single mental model call for applying two different rules and the problems with multiple models only call for one. A cursory glance would seem to indicate the two theories suggesting opposed predictions, but this is not so. According to Rips (1994), applying the Dilemma rule is *"somehow harder,"* given that it calls for coordinating three premises, while the rules to be applied in the case of the other two arguments only call for coordinating one or two. Thus, as Rips himself has put it: *"There is no reason to think that one of these methods should be much easier than the other"* (1994, pp. 368–369).

Table 3.2.
Percentage of correct responses by type of task in Experiment 1. Results found by Rips are included in parentheses.

	Argument	% Correct Eval.-Construct.		Argument	% Correct Eval.-Construct	
One model problems	p AND q IF p, r IF q, r	94.2 (89.2)	97.4	NOT p AND NOT q IF NOT p, r IF NOT q, r	88.5 (94.6)	92.3
	r			r		
Multiple model problems	p OR q IF p, r If q, r	86.5 (89.2)	76.9	NOT p OR NOT q If NOT p, r IF NOT q, r	82.7 (81.1)	66.7
	r			r		

In Rips' study there were different groups of participants for the different problems: A group of participants was given the two problems that included affirmative conjunction and disjunction, whereas a second group of participants received the problems that included the negated conjunction and the negated disjunction premise. Furthermore, reasoners were also given two filler arguments that were not valid. They had to answer as to whether the conclusions were "necessarily true" or "not necessarily true." As Table 3.2 shows, there were no differences at all between the first column problem solutions, whereas with the negated arguments, the difference was in the direction predicted by model theory, even though it was only marginally significant. The overall difference between one-model and multiple-model problems was thus unreliable (Rips, 1990, p. 297). To sum up, the results seem to run against the model theory prediction.

EVALUATION AND CONSTRUCTION TASKS

Any analysis of Rips' study will reveal two characteristics that characterize the majority of the studies made by the theorists of the rules school. First, the problems they employ are indeed simple and easy. The marked preference by the mental logicians for problems with which the participants are going to be successful (O'Brien, 1997, p. 174) surely lies in the fact they will better allow an explanation in terms of mental rules. On the other hand, problems and tasks of a greater difficulty, such as syllogistic reasoning or Wason's selection task, are usually left aside by mental rules' theorists.

The second characteristic, which ties in with the first one, is the use of an evaluation task in which the participant is faced with a conclusion and then asked if it is true or false. Evaluation tasks can indeed make problems easier to solve as the participants are saved the labor of putting the conclusions into words. However, as Johnson-Laird (1997) has underlined, one of human reason's salient characteristics is the capacity to generate conclusions of itself. On the other hand, construction tasks, when used, prove most informative: They allow a precise analysis of the linguistic characteristics of the participants' answers (be these correct or not) which, in themselves, may be quite revealing (see, e.g., the figural effect in syllogistic reasoning).

Rips' use of evaluation tasks has a signal importance in his theory given that in such tasks it is possible not only to employ his basic forwards rules but also another set of backwards ones. The first ones are nearly automatically employed "*whenever a triggering assertion appears in the database*" (Rips, 1994, p. 122). Backwards rules are set to work after the forward ones and are, furthermore, more complex as they call for specific control processes. However, as mentioned earlier, solving our examples requires only using forward rules. Hence, apart from the minimal difficulty of actually formulating a conclusion, in Rips' theory, the shift from an evaluation to a construction task should not imply a noteworthy difference. However, besides the supplementary difficulty of putting the conclusions into words, mental model theory suggests that reasoners may adopt different strategies with evaluation and construction tasks; particularly, they can work backwards from the given conclusion in the evaluation task, whereas this strategy is not possible in construction one.

The purpose of Experiment 1 was to assess reasoning performance when facing the problems presented in Table 3.1, using both evaluation and construction tasks. There were two groups of participants, each group with a different task. The participants in either group had to solve the four previous problems where there is a valid conclusion for each, as well as four other filler problems that had no valid conclusion. In both conditions (evaluation and construction tasks) participants received a booklet in which the task was explained and the importance of necessity underlined, this along with an example demonstration of a Modus Ponens inference. The second page of the booklet set out the eight problems in random order. The problems' content was close to that of those used by Rips and, like the earlier examples, made mention of people and places.

The results (see Table 3.2) showed that in the evaluation task there was no reliable difference in people's accuracy when dealing with one-model and multiple-models problems, this with both affirmative or negative arguments. However, when it came to dealing with the construction task, conjunction problems proved to be significantly less difficult than disjunctive ones, this with both affirmative or negative arguments.

These results clearly replicate those found by Rips in his evaluation task: The differences between arguments are in the direction of mental model predictions but they are not significant. In the case of the construction task, results do confirm the mental model theory. Arguments including as a first premise a disjunction are reliably harder to solve than those including a conjunction. In an evaluation task, the absence of any difference between either type of problem is probably due to a ceiling effect. Bringing in a somewhat more difficult task, such as a construction task, leads to show some differences hitherto obscured by the ease and simplicity of the problems. It should be pointed out that the differences among correct answers are always in favor of the predictions by the model theory.

In the next experiment, another modifier is used that in no way affects the logical model of the problem: the manipulation of the order in which the premises are presented which has already shown to be important in other propositional reasoning tasks.

THE ORDER OF THE PREMISES

One of the truly robust findings in deductive reasoning research is the difference in difficulty between the Modus Ponens and Modus Tollens (see Evans et al., 1993): The Modus Ponens is almost universally solved whereas the Modus Tollens presents noteworthy difficulties for most participants. Both theoretical approaches, rules and models, give a good explanation for the difference. What is important here is that the mental models explanation predicts a change in the order of the premises to affect one of the two types of argument, and the other not at all.

The Modus Ponens is an argument like the following:

If Raquel is in León, then William is in Oviedo.
Raquel is in León.
William is in Oviedo.

According to the mental model theory, the participant does not need to use the final, totally explicit representation of the problem in order to solve it but can manage to do so on the basis of the initial representation of the conditional.

[L]   O

...

In this initial representation, the minor categorical premise (L) refers directly to the explicit model, thus allowing the elimination of the implicit model and the drawing of the correct conclusion.

However, a different prediction has to be made with a Modus Tollens argument like the following:

If Raquel is in León, then William is in Oviedo.
William is not in Oviedo.
∴ Raquel is not in León

According to the mental model theorists, in order to deduce the valid conclusion, more mental effort is expected in order to flesh out the entire model:

L   O
¬L   O
¬L   ¬O

In this totally explicit representation, the minor categorical premise (¬O) does away with the first two models thus allowing for a correct conclusion from the third model. In this case, and according to Girotto, Mazzoco, and Tasso (1997; see also Legrenzi, Girotto, & Johnson-Laird, 1993), the presentation of the categorical premise (¬O) before that of the conditional statement means that the reasoners would be focusing on the negated consequent (¬O) from the very start and thus would be able to flesh out the models in an easier way. In their own words: "*When the categorical premise is presented in the traditional order, reasoners have already received the conditional premise, that is, their working memory is pre-occupied with the models of the conditional. By contrast, when reasoners have to treat the categorical premise before the conditional one, they can easily represent the negated consequent from the start. When they then begin to consider the conditional, they can eliminate the model representing the antecedent and the consequent, and thus free up the working memory capacity.*" (Girotto et al., 1997,

p. 4; for another discussion of order effects, see Dekeyser, Schroyens, Schaeken, Spittaels, & d'Ydewalle, chap. 4, this volume).

To sum up, a change in the order in which the categorical premise is presented, should make the Modus Tollens easier while not affecting the Modus Ponens where the conclusion is drawn from the initial presentation and reasoners are focused on the correct model from the outset. Girotto et al. (1997) confirmed this prediction empirically.

In Rips' problems, the conditional premise is always presented after the conjunctive or disjunctive ones, which means that the problem is thus focused on the conjunction or disjunction. With the conjunctive Arguments 1 and 3, the information in the conditional can be tied in directly and simply with the conjunction's single model. In the case of the disjunctive Arguments 2 and 4, the reasoner is called upon to build up an initial representation of two models to which the content of the conditionals can also be easily and simply aggregated. A change in the order of the premises, by setting the conjunction or the disjunction after the conditionals, should thus not necessarily imply any real change in the case of the conjunctive arguments, as they require only a single model, but could somewhat affect the disjunctive ones when the participant has to build up a two-model representation. It is worthwhile to point out that the increased difficulty is probably going to be small, because the problems are all very simple and can be solved from an initial representation; that is to say, reasoners do not need to fully flesh out the models of disjunction to reach the correct conclusion. In other words, changing the order of premises allows to set aside the ceiling effect in Rips' study.

The purpose of Experiment 2 was to test this hypothesis by using the same problems but with changes in the order of the statements, the conjunction–disjunction being presented as the final premise. As for Experiment 1, there were two groups of participants, either with a task of evaluation or construction. The materials and procedure were identical with those used in Experiment 1, except the change in the order in which the premises were presented. The results (see Table 3.3) confirm the model theory. As for the evaluation task, one-model problems were reliably easier than multiple-model ones; likewise, using the construction task, conjunction problems were significantly easier than disjunction ones.

The change in the order of the premises has produced the predicted effect: Evaluating the answer as necessarily true has become significantly more difficult for the participants in the problems that included a disjunction than in the ones that had a conjunction. As for the construction task, the same predicted results were found. However, if we leave aside the new significant differences in the evaluation task, it would appear that the change in the order of the premises does not seem to have specially affected the performance of the participants. This is what we indeed expected, given that even in the case of the disjunction, the reasoner could reach a valid conclusion from the initial representation of the problem. A more pronounced effect of the change of order might be predicted when more processing demands are being requested from the participant.

Table 3.3.
Percentage of correct responses by type of task in Experiment 2.

	Argument	% Correct Eval.-Construct.		Argument	% Correct Eval.-Construct	
One model problems	IF p, r IF q, r p AND q ---------- r	100	95.8	IF NOT p, r IF NOT q, r NOT p AND NOT Q -------------------------- r	100	93.7
Multiple model problems	IF p, r IF q, r p OR q --------- r	77.3	81.3	IF NOT p, r IF NOT q, r NOT p OR NOT q ------------------------ r	79.6	77.1

When grouping the findings from Experiment 1 and 2, it is clear that the conjunctive problems are significantly easier than the disjunctive ones (in the evaluation task, 95.3% vs. 81.8%; in the construction task, 94.8% vs. 75.9%). Likewise, the single model problems are significantly easier than the multiple models, both when using Rips's ordering of premises (conjunction–disjunction first; 93.4% vs. 79.1%) or when they were presented in inverse order (conjunction–disjunction last; 97.3% vs. 78.8%). The tendency to find affirmative arguments easier than negative ones is only marginally significant (89% vs. 87%; $p < .06$). Accordingly, the predictions of Rips' theory are not borne out. On the contrary, the results confirm the basic predictions of the mental model theory. What is more, the manipulation of variables (task and order of premises) was based directly on the theoretical assumptions of the model theory. We next attempt to obtain evidence about the strategies the participants use to solve a given problem.

EXPLICIT AND IMPLICIT STRATEGIES

The heuristic strategic nature of human cognition arises from its limited cognitive resources. It is only by coordinating and orchestrating the resources that it can carry out complex cognitive tasks (e.g., the safe driving of a vehicle or the reading of a newspaper). The concept of "strategy" refers to a set of actions all aimed at satisfying a goal in the simplest, quickest thus most economical way (see Van Dijk

& Kintsch, 1983); that is, with minimal demand on cognitive resources and lowest load on the working memory. There is, however, another basic principle of human cognition which also has a important bearing on the question of the mind's strategies. We are referring to the adaptive character of thought. The feature was incorporated as a basic principle within Piaget's theory of intelligence (Piaget, 1967), and has come to the forefront again in cognitive science (see Anderson, 1990). The adaptive component of human cognition manifests itself in various ways. For example, a minor change to a problem will lead to an alteration in the way the participant will treat it (Reder & Schunn, 1996).

Traditionally, the notion of cognitive strategy has been used in research about solving other types of problems, such as the breaking down of a complex problem into its simpler and more accessible components or the means–end analysis (Newell & Simon, 1972). This kind of problem-solving strategy tends to be explicit, accessible to consciousness and communicable through verbal protocols. Thus registering human conduct while solving a problem along with a careful use of the information from verbal protocols during the task have become a key method in information processing approaches (see Ericsson & Simon, 1980). If deductive tasks are to be considered problem-solving tasks, why has the study of these strategies through verbal protocols never been made in the field of logical inferences?

The answer is to be found in the fact that a larger part of the strategies are more language processing strategies than problem solving ones. Logical problems are linguistically formulated, and the solution basically depends on a language comprehension process that is mainly automated and thus inaccessible to the conscious mind (Van Dijk & Kintsch, 1983).

Let us now look at the role strategies play in our two theories: rules and mental models. For mental rules, the two basic formulations show a close parallelism when it comes to distinguishing between the two levels of application of the theories (Evans & Over, 1997). On the one hand, we have the schemes or rules of simple inference (Braine, 1990; Braine et al., 1984) which would be directly, automatically, and unconsciously brought into play and that correspond directly to Rips' forward rules (Rips, 1994). On the other hand, we have the "strategic component" that only comes into operation when the direct reasoning routine fails to determine a response (O'Brien et al., 1994, p. 715); This is similar to Rips' backwards rules. In other words, strategies, supposing them to be conscious and explicit, will be used when participants are confronted with more complex problems, which cannot be solved by means of a simple routine.

To data, the mental model theory cannot be said to have given much thought to strategies (see, however, Bucciarelli & Johnson-Laird, in press; see also Johnson-Laird, Savary, & Bucciarelli, chap. 11, this volume). The theory postulates, as a core claim, the existence of a validation stage at which reasoners have to falsify their conclusions while searching for counterexamples. Thus, this stage is a strategic search stage for alternative conclusions. Putting this activity aside for a moment, the theory's basic principle rests upon   constructing and combining models from which the participant can then "read off" the conclusions. As this process is not deterministic, it admits a wide range of strategies about which many questions remain. When are the models for any premise constructed? Do the participants construct the models for each premise while reading them off? When are the meanings of the premises brought together? Are the meanings of the premises brought together while they are being read off or only after the final question has been encountered? What does the choice of one and not another strategy depend on? There is still little to offer in attempting to answer those questions. However, what we do know is that when facing multiple conditional problems, participants probably maintain the information from the early premises as a kind of buffer. They wait thus to build models in order to integrate them at the end of the problem when presented the final premise or when they are asked to give the conclusions (García Madruga & Johnson-Laird, 1994).

Not every reasoning strategy is implicit, nor accessible to conscious examination, and the issue here is not one of all or nothing (d'Ydewalle, 1996). We go along with Evans and Over (1997; see also Evans, chap. 1, this volume; Johnson-Laird et al., chap. 11, this volume) in considering that counterexample search could and should be investigated through verbal protocols. In this sense and in keeping with rules theory, Moshman (1990) holds that the search for counterexamples as the *reductio ad absurdum* is a kind of conscious metalogical strategy. According to the author, this type of metalogical strategy is developed relatively late as it calls for developing a metalogical understanding of prior concepts such as logical necessity. Velasco and García Madruga (1997), in studying the development of metalogical processes and logical learning with categorical syllogisms, have confirmed this hypothesis by discovering that the counterexamples search strategy first appears during adolescence, at about age 15 and is preceded by the acquisition of the concept of logical necessity. Likewise, and again in keeping with the mental models theory, the authors showed that the search for counterexamples is closely tied in with the reasoners' performance when solving syllogisms of greater difficulty.

Yet again, the need for using high-level strategies such as the search for counterexamples is determined by the nature of the problems. If only simple problems, such as those here under analysis, are presented, it is more likely that the participant will solve them by a coordinated application of linguistic and implicit metacognitive strategies which will escape the conscious mind. It is in this sense that Reder and Schunn (1997) have emphasized that metacognition does not imply awareness and that important aspects of metacognition are implicit.

"It is important to distinguish between the strategy-selection processes and the strategies themselves. Although we argue that people are unaware of what causes them to select one strategy rather than another, we make no claims about their awareness of the results of the strategy selection. For example, people might not be aware of what led them to decide to use a calculator, but usually they are aware that they decided to use the calculator. On the other hand, when the processes or strategies are executed rapidly, it is quite possible that people are even unaware of the strategy that was selected." (p. 47)

All this implies that participants would not be able to inform us about their strategy selection processes as well as the strategies they used. Besides verbally externalizing the participant's strategies, other methods of analysis could be considered, as, for example, a computer tracing of the cognitive behavior or inviting the participants to use diagrams (see Bauer & Johnson-Laird, 1993; Bucciarelli & Johnson-Laird, in press). First, we analyze the results from a study in which the problems were presented on a computer's visual display that recorded online time measures and allowed participants to go through each argument both forward and backward. Second, we present another study in which the student's task was to rate the difficulty of each problem on a five-point scale and to write down reasons for doing so.

Experiment 3 was aimed at gathering evidence about implicit strategies in solving intuitively simple reasoning problems. Although one of the most striking characteristics of the literature on strategies is the large within- and between-subjects variability (Siegler, Adolph, & Lemaire, 1996), we still expected to find some general pattern. A group of participants was given Rips' four basic problems, along with the nonvalid four fillers; they were presented at random, in an evaluation task. As we have already mentioned, the principal innovation here was the use of a computer that allowed people to run forward and backward through each problem. The three premises and the question as to the conclusion for each of the arguments were presented, one at a time, on the visual display of the computer.

Table 3.4.
Means of reading times of first premise and response times, for each kind of argument in Experiment 3. Percentage of correct responses given in parentheses.

	Argument	Reading and response times	Argument	Reading and response times
One model problems	p AND q IF p, r IF q, r	12.9 s	NOT p AND NOT q IF NOT p, r IF NOT q, r	14.4 s
	---------- r	2.2 s (90%)	----------------------- r	2.0 s (90%)
Multiple model problems	p OR q · IF p, r IF q, r	14.9 s	NOT p OR NOT q IF NOT p, r IF NOT q, r	16.2 s
	--------- r	2.3 s (76%)	----------------------- r	2.6 s (67%)

The main results are given in Tables 3.4 and 3.5. Table 3.4 includes the mean reading times for the first premise, the mean response times, and the percentage of correct conclusions. The reading times of the first premise seem to be in the predicted trend, being faster for conjunction than for disjunction.

However, none of the differences was significant. As to the response times, the trend was also in the predicted direction, but now the negated conjunctive argument was reliably faster than the negated disjunctive one. Likewise, the percentage of correct responses was always significantly higher for conjunction problems than for disjunction ones, but was significant only in the case of the conjunctive negative arguments. As can be observed, the results are quite similar to those in Experiment 1.

Table 3.5 includes the means for the backward steps. Unexpectedly, although there are no reliable differences, it appears that people tend to go backward more often in conjunction arguments than in disjunction ones. We computed the times that people reason back to a first conjunction–disjunction premise as well as the mean time that people spent re-reading it. There was again a tendency to go back more often to the first premise when it was a conjunction (1.85 times), than when it was a disjunction (1.60 times), although the difference was not reliable. However, although people went back to disjunction premises less often than to conjunction ones, the time they spent when doing so was reliably the larger for disjunction than conjunction (5.8 vs. 5.2 s).

Table 3.5.
Means of backward steps for the three premises in Experiment 3 for each kind of argument.

	Argument	Backward	Argument	Backward	Overall
One model problems	p AND q IF p, r IF q, r		NOT p AND NOT q IF NOT p, r IF NOT q, r		
	----------		------------------------		
	r	3.51	r	3.81	3.66
Multiple model problems	p OR q IF p, r IF q, r		NOT p OR NOT q IF NOT p, r IF NOT q, r		
	---------		----------------------		
	r	3.19	r	3.44	3.32
Overall		3.35		3.63	

Although the results are not reliable, the fact that the participants tended to go backward more often in the conjunctive problems and, yet, to spend more time over the disjunctive ones, suggested that they were using partially different strategies for each. When dealing with the conjunctive problems, the simplicity of the problems perhaps led the participants to draw a direct conclusion without having to think deeply; they only went back to establish the conjunctive nature of the problems. On the other hand, when dealing with the disjunctive problems and as the mental model theory would have predicted, the reasoner (having to think things out more) spent a little more time in so doing and thus felt less need to go back. Does this then mean that there is a strategic pattern that is different for conjunction and disjunction? The findings we have considered are not solid enough to establish this, although they do suggest that the strategy for dealing with conjunction could be more speedy and automatic than that for disjunction.

The objective of Experiment 4 was to check out people's metaknowledge of the problems' difficulty along with the ability to explain verbally why problems are more or less difficult. Participants received a booklet in which, following some instructions, they were faced with Rips' four basic problems, with an evaluation task, and with a conjunction–disjunction premise presented before two conditional ones. Half of participants received the four problems at random, the other half in inverse order. The participants' task was to rate the difficulty of the deduction on a five-point scale and to write down the reasons for that evaluation. Results are given in Tables 3.6 and 3.7.

Table 3.6.
Means of difficulty's rates in Experiment 4 for each kind of argument.

	Argument	Rate of difficulty	Argument	Rate of difficulty	Overall
One model problems	p AND q IF p, r IF q, r		NOT p AND NOT q IF NOT p, r IF NOT q, r		
	r	3.05	r	3.40	2.25
Multiple model problems	p OR q IF p, r IF q, r		NOT p OR NOT q IF NOT p, r IF NOT q, r		
	r	2.70	r	3.05	2.90
Overall		2.40		2.73	

Table 3.6 shows how participants rated the difficulty involved in the activity. They were aware that multiple-model problems are harder than one-model ones, (likewise with affirmative and negative arguments). They also considered the negative arguments harder than the affirmative ones. Therefore, it would appear that people enjoy a metacognitive awareness of the difficulty of the problems. The awareness does not however seem to be very precise: The difference between problems with affirmative and negative arguments was not reliable in the previous experiments and yet, here, the negative arguments were indeed considered to be more difficult.

As to the explanations of the evaluations, participants' responses were sorted by two judges who classified the responses into seven different categories as shown in Table 3.7. In the first category, here labeled "Content," we have grouped the participants' answers that restated a problem, paraphrased it, or referred to its content. In the second category, Negation–Affirmation, the participants' explanations refer to the greater or lesser difficulty of the arguments in terms of being negated or affirmed. The third and fourth groupings refer to disjunction: In the third category, the replies refer to how the problem is to be understood; in the fourth one, to the simple fact of its being more difficult. The fifth and sixth categories are the same as the preceding two categories but applied to conjunction. In the seventh category are the answers we considered irrelevant or which could not be accommodated in any of the previous categories.

Table 3.7.
Categories used when classifying the explanations offered by participants in Experiment 4.

Categories	Examples
C = Content	"Because it follows that if Carlos is in Rome or Ruth is in London then Grace will be in Rome."
NA = Negation/Affirmation	"The negative conditional gives rise to doubts."
ID = Interpretation of Disjunction	"You have to bear in mind that Carlos and Ruth are not in London or Paris and that takes some doing."
DD = Difficulty with Disjunction	"Because 'or' throws you out."
IC = Interpretation of Conjunction	"You need two conditions for conjunction. Grace to be in Rome."
DC = Difficulty with Conjunction	"It's more difficult with 'and' the conjunction joining the premises."
IR = Irrelevant	"Easy really for the time it takes."; "It's obvious, isn't it?".

Table 3.8.

Percentages of responses' categories given by participants in Experiment 4.

Argument	Percentages of categories						
	C	NA	ID	DD	IC	DC	IR
p and q	38.5	20.5	2.5		2.5	5.1	28.2
not p and not q	28.2	28.2			5.1	2.6	35.8
overall conjunction	33.4	24.4	1.3		3.8	3.9	32.0
p or q	8.3	12.5	25.0	25.0			18.8
not p or not q	11.1	14.8	24.1	18.5		1.8	18.5
overall disjunction	9.7	13.7	24.6	21.8		1.4	18.7

Table 3.8 presents the percentage of answers in each category. It is worth pointing out that, when conjunctive arguments are being considered, the participants showed a tendency to give more answers in the "Content," "Negation–Affirmation," and "Irrelevant" categories, whereas the greater part of the answers given as to disjunctive arguments refers to the overall difficulty or the understanding of the problem. As to the high proportion of answers in the category "Content" in the case of conjunctions, they could be understood along the same lines as the results in the preceding experiment: It seems as if the participants found themselves unable to recall any explanation other than the simple repetition of the conclusion. This might be interpreted in line with the more automatic and implicit nature of solving conjunction arguments. At any rate, the explanations confirm the idea of a different strategic pattern for either type of argument. Likewise, they seem to hint that people are not up to offering much in the way of explanations, showing the likely implicit nature of the strategies (particularly in the case of conjunctions).

CONCLUSIONS

We commented earlier, following Evans and Over (1997), that on an empirical basis, it is difficult to decide between the theoretical approaches of the rules and models. We also agree with them that it is all but impossible to set up a crucial experiment that would allow us to reject either standpoint: At most, certain empirical results could perhaps no more than question a version of a specific theory (Johnson-Laird, Byrne, & Schaeken, 1994). Notwithstanding, the results of the studies that were presented here seem to be quite conclusive in some respect.

The problems here analyzed touch on a key aspect of the theory of rules, the difference between conjunction and disjunction in human reasoning. There is a good body of mainly developmental data that makes it clear that disjunction tends to be more difficult and that its application comes later on. We have shown that the difference in difficulty is also encountered by adults when they are faced with three-premise arguments, which also include two conditionals. The two major rules theories postulate a single basic rule in the case of disjunctive arguments, and two rules in the case of conjunctive ones. The theory of mental models offers the opposite prediction: one model to meet the conjunctive arguments and two models for the disjunctive ones. The addendum by Rips (1994), that the rule for disjunctive arguments is more complex given that three premises are in need of coordination, seems to be somewhat ad hoc. The number of premises is exactly the same for either type of problem: What does distinguish them, is the number of models or rules they postulate. We thus have some reasoning problems that are sufficiently decisive, as the two theories of rules postulate an immediate and direct employing of basic rules. What is more, the predictions of both the theory of rules and models are here not only different but in opposition to each other. The results seem to be both clear and robust: Reasoners have more difficulty with disjunctive arguments than with conjunctive ones, and this confirms the theory of mental models.

The lack of any reliable difference in the findings of Rips could be due to ceiling effects as Experiments 1 and 2 suggest. Of the four conditions in the two experiments, only in one does the tendency toward a greater difficulty with disjunctive arguments not reach the significant level.

As to the strategies by our reasoners, the time measures agree well with the findings on accuracy. It was also found that disjunctive problems are more difficult; reasoners seem to be aware of this and able to give some verbal information on the matter. Last, as to back-tracking while solving a problem, the results suggest a different strategic pattern for conjunctive and disjunctive arguments. People use speedy and automatic strategies to cope with conjunctive problems, whereas with disjunctive arguments reasoners use some deeper and more time-consuming strategies. The divergent basic strategic patterns are confirmed by the written explanations from the participants to explain the difficulties they had met when solving the problems.

ACKNOWLEDGMENTS

Phil Johnson-Laird suggested the original idea for this chapter as part of his contribution to the "Comprehension and inference in conditional reasoning" research project funded by the Spanish Ministry of Education and Science (PB94-0394).

REFERENCES

Anderson, J. R. (1990). *The adaptive character of thought.* Hillsdale, NJ: Lawrence Erlbaum Associates.

Bauer, M. I., & Johnson-Laird, P. N. (1993). How diagrams can improve reasoning. *Psychologycal Science, 4,* 372–378.

Braine, M. D. S. (1990). The "Natural Logic" approach to reasoning. In W. F. Overton (Ed.), *Reasoning, necessity and logic: Developmental perspectives* (pp. 135–157) Hillsdale, NJ: Lawrence Erlbaum Associates.

Braine, M. D. S., Reiser, B. J., & Rumain, B. (1984). Some empirical justification for a theory of natural propositional reasoning. In G. H. Bower (Ed.), *The psychology of learning and motivation. Vol. 1* (pp. 313–371). New York: Academic Press.

Bucciarelli, M., & Johnson-Laird, P. N. (in press). Strategies in syllogistic reasoning. *Cognitive Science.*

d'Ydewalle, G. (1996). Implicit memory and learning. In E. De Corte & F. Weinert (Eds.), *Encyclopedia of developmental and instructional psychology* (pp. 399–402). Oxford, UK: Pergamon Press.

Ericsson, K. A., & Simon, H. A. (1980). Verbal reports as data. *Psychological Review, 87,* 215–251.

Evans, J. St. B. T., Clibbens, J., & Rood, B. (1995). Bias in conditional inference: Implications for mental models and mental logic. *Quarterly Journal of Experimental Psychology, 48A,* 644–670.

Evans, St. B. T., Newstead S. E., & Byrne, R. M. J. (1993). *Human reasoning.* Hove, UK: Lawrence Erlbaum Associates.

Evans, J. St. B. T., & Over, D. (1997). Rationality in reasoning: The problem of deductive competence. *Cahiers de Psychologie Cognitive/Current Psychology of Cognition, 16,* 3–38.

García Madruga, J.A., & Johnson-Laird, P. N. (1994, September). *Multiple conditionals: Rules or Models?* Paper presented at the Seventh Meeting of European Society for Cognitive Psychology. Lisbon, Portugal.

Girotto, V., Mazzoco, A., & Tasso, A. (1997). The effect of premise order in conditional reasoning: A test of the mental model theory. *Cognition, 63,* 1–28.

Johnson-Laird, P. N. (1993). *Human and machine thinking.* Hillsdale, NJ: Lawrence Erlbaum Associates.

Johnson-Laird, P. N. (1997). Rules and illusion: A critical study of Rips' The psychology of proof. *Minds and Machines, 7,* 387–407.

Johnson-Laird, P. N., & Byrne, R. M. J. (1991). *Deduction.* Hillsdale, NJ: Lawrence Erlbaum Associates.

Johnson-Laird, P. N., Byrne, R., & Schaeken, W. (1992). Propositional reasoning by model. *Psychological Review, 99,* 418–439.

Johnson-Laird, P. N., Byrne, R., & Schaeken, W. (1994). Why models rather than rules give a better account of propositional reasoning: A reply to Bonatti and to O'Brien, Braine & Yang. *Psychological Review, 101*, 734–739.

Legrenzi, P., Girotto, V., & Johnson-Laird, P. N. (1993). Focussing in reasoning and decision-making. *Cognition, 49*, 37–66.

Moshman, D. (1990). The development of metalogical understanding. In W. F. Overton (Ed.), *Reasoning, necessity and logic: Developmental perspectives* (pp. 205–225). Hillsdale, NJ: Lawrence Erlbaum Associates.

Newell, A., & Simon, H. A (1972). *Human problem solving.* Englewood Cliffs, NJ: Prentice-Hall.

O'Brien, D. P. (1997). The criticisms of mental-logic theory miss their target. *Cahiers de Psychologie Cognitive/Current Psychology of Cognition, 16*, 173–180.

O'Brien, D. P., Braine, M. D. S., & Yang, Y. (1994). Propositional reasoning by mental models: Simple to refute in principle and practice. *Psychological Review, 101*, 711–724.

Piaget, J. (1967). *Biologie et connaissance.* Paris: Gallimard.

Reder, L., & Schunn, C. D. (1996). Metacognition does not imply awareness: Strategy choice is governed by implicit learning and memory. In L. Reder (Ed.), *Implicit memory and metacognition* (pp. 45–77). Mahwah, NJ: Lawrence Erlbaum Associates.

Rips, L. J. (1983). Cognitive processes in propositional reasoning. *Psychological Review, 90*, 38–71.

Rips, L. J. (1990). Paralogical reasoning: Evans, Johnson-Laird, and Byrne on liar and truth-teller puzzles. *Cognition, 36*, 291–314.

Rips, L. J. (1994). *The psychology of proof: Deductive reasoning in human reasoning.* Cambridge, MA: MIT Press.

Schaeken, W., Garcia Madruga, J., & Johnson-Laird, P. N. (1995). *Conditional reasoning and the effects of negation.* Unpublished manuscript, University of Leuven.

Siegler, R. S., Adolph, K. E., & Lemaire, P. (1996). Strategy choices across the life-span. In L. M. Reder (Ed.), *Implicit memory and metacognition* (pp. 79–121). Mahwah, NJ: Lawrence Erlbaum Associates.

Van Dijk, T. H., & Kintsch, W. (1983). *Strategies of discourse comprehension.* New York: Academic Press.

Velasco, J., & García Madruga, J. A. (1997). El desarrollo de los procesos meta-lógicos y el razonamiento lógico durante la adolescencia [The development of the meta-logical processes and logical reasoning during adolescence]. *Cognitiva, 9*, 139–152.

Wason. P. C., & Johnson-Laird, P. N. (1972). *Psychology of reasoning.* London: Batsford.

4

Preferred Premise Order in Propositional Reasoning: Semantic Informativeness and Co-Reference

Mathias Dekeyser
Walter Schroyens
Walter Schaeken
Olaf Spittaels
Géry d'Ydewalle

The mental model theory of propositional reasoning has received many critiques pertaining to its inability to account for intermediate conclusions in multiple-premise problems. In response Johnson-Laird, Byrne, and Schaeken (1994) postulated that reasoners tend to start with the maximally semantically informative premise and tend to work in an order that maintains co-reference. In Experiment 1 our participants were facing the problems used by Braine et al. (1995), such that they could not see the content of the problems fully. Participants were requested to choose the order in which they preferred to see the premises. Experiments 2 and 3 presented reasoners with all two-premise problems conceivable, combining a categorical premise, a conjunction, a conditional, a biconditional, an inclusive disjunction, or an exclusive disjunction. Results confirm the importance of co-reference but indicate that the mental model theory is in need for a more refined and psychologically valid notion of semantic informativeness.

Johnson-Laird (1983) specified the general processing assumptions of the mental model theory of reasoning. The mental model theory holds that the basic processes of human reasoning competence are based on the construction and manipulation of mental models: representations of a possible state of affairs as described by structural relationships expressed in the premises. Reasoning by model is broken down into three processing stages (Johnson-Laird, 1983; Johnson-Laird & Byrne, 1991). The processing stages embody the principle of eliminating states of affairs when reasoners try to construct an integrated model of the premises. First, on the basis of the meaning of the premises and other general knowledge triggered during the process of interpretation, reasoners build a mental model representing a state of affairs. Second, while eliminating inconsistent models, reasoners conjoin the various models of the premises to form an integrated model. The integrated mental model forms the basis to formulate a putative conclusion. Third, in order to validate the putative conclusion, reasoners search for alternative models (possibilities) which might falsify it. If there is such a counterexample, reasoners need to return to the second stage to determine whether there is any conclusion that holds over all the models constructed thus far. When no alternative models can be constructed, the putative conclusion could not be falsified and is valid. The central expectation is that the more models that need to be constructed in order to derive a valid conclusion, the harder the inferential task will be. This prediction gained support from studies of syllogistic reasoning (Johnson-Laird & Bara, 1984), reasoning with multiple qualifiers (Johnson-Laird, Byrne, & Tabossi, 1991), spatial and temporal reasoning (Byrne & Johnson-Laird, 1989; Schaeken, Johnson-Laird, & d'Ydewalle, 1996; Rauh, chap. 9, this volume; Vandierendonck & De Vooght, 1996; Vandierendonck, De Vooght, Desimpelaere, & Dierckx, chap 10, this volume) and propositional reasoning (Johnson-Laird, Byrne, & Schaeken, 1992).

The mental model theory of propositonal reasoning (Johnson-Laird et al., 1992), that is reasoning about sentences containing connectives such as "if, then," "or," "and," or operators such as "not," has received much critique from the main alternative and historically dominant approach to deductive reasoning competence (Bonatti, 1994; Braine & O'Brien, 1991; Rips, 1994). These rule-based theories hold that the basic processes of human reasoning competence are those of applying mental rules of inferences or inference schemata to propositional representations. The more rules that need to be applied to reach a particular conclusion, the more likely people will err.

One of the aspects of propositional reasoning by model that has been criticized by mental logicians is the mental model theory's account of the strategies people use in a chain of inferences. Indeed, research efforts of mental modelers have focused primarily on reasoning about two-premise problems. Whereas the combination of subsets of premises is mostly determined by the particular mental rules of inference, mental logicians have argued that the algorithms proposed as a specification of reasoning by model do not provide an unequivocal way of determining which premises reasoners would combine in constructing a chain of inference. As such, Braine et al. (1995) have shown that the rule-based approach has a theoretical advantage over the mental models based approach in predicting and explaining the intermediate conclusions drawn in constructing a line of inference.

In response to these and other critiques to propositional reasoning by model, Johnson-Laird, Byrne, and Schaeken (1994) made several suggestions as to amend the criticized thesis. We focus our attention on the amendment that is supposed to capture the way in which reasoners combine premises in constructing a line of inference. That is, Johnson-Laird et al. (1994) postulated that:

If possible, reasoners will tend to start with a premise that is maximally semantically informative (e.g., a categorical assertion) and they will tend to work in an order that maintains co-reference, drawing, when possible, informative intermediate conclusions. (p. 736)

Co-reference and semantic informativeness are thus believed to be two key concepts in the explanation of human inferential behavior. We present three studies testing these assumptions (for other relevant studies, see Garcia-Madruga, et al., chap. 3, this volume; Girotto & Gonzalez, chap.13, this volume). Experiment 1 focuses on the assumption that people tend to work in an order that maintains co-reference. Experiments 2 and 3 were set up to investigate reasoners' tendency to start reasoning with the semantically most informative premise. Before reporting these studies one should note that our theorizing depends extensively on the procedures of constructing and manipulating mental model sets, as described by Johnson-Laird et al. (1992). It is these procedures that we consider expanded with the aforementioned principles of semantic informativeness and co-reference. With respect to propositional reasoning people are supposed to represent multiple models simultaneously, hence we say that people construct model sets rather than models.

PROPOSITIONAL REASONING BY CONSTRUCTING AND MANIPULATING MENTAL MODEL SETS

Johnson-Laird et al. (1992) proposed three algorithms: an artificial intelligence algorithm, a general algorithm, and a psychological algorithm. They differ on two main features. First, they differ in what reasoners are to reason about, that is, the type of mental model sets constructed from the premises. A mental model set contains the different mental models people construct to represent the different states of affairs that are possible given the meaning of a premise. Second, the algorithms differ in how the mental model sets are combined. The method of integrating mental model sets is dependent on the type of model sets. For the present discussion mainly the first feature is of interest, thus we concentrate here on different types of model sets. Model set combination is not discussed but one important feature of this procedure for all proposed algorithms is treated briefly: symmetry.

The AI Algorithm: Fully Explicit Model Sets.   The mental model sets on which the AI algorithm operates correspond to the truth conditions of propositions. In propositional logic, truth tables provide a semantic definition of compound propositions. The truth-value of a proposition is defined as a function of the truth-values of the component propositions (its atoms). For instance, the logical product $p \wedge q$, which would have "and" as its counterpart in natural language, is true only when both atoms are true. Hence the model set would consist of one model. The material implication $p \rightarrow q$, which would have "if, then" as its natural language analogue, is false only when the antecedent p is true and the consequent q is false. Hence, the model sets of the conditional "*If there's an A, then there's a 2*" would incorporate three models: one representing both atoms as true, one representing the false antecedent in combination with the false consequent, and one representing the false antecedent in combination with the true consequent:

$$A \qquad 2$$
$$\neg A \qquad \neg 2$$
$$\neg A \qquad \neg 2$$

The General and the Psychological Algorithm: Partially Explicit Models. Johnson-Laird et al. (1992) argued on the basis of working memory constraints that reasoners represent as little information explicitly as possible. Reasoners initially do not represent the complete set of possible states of affairs consistent with a proposition. In Table 4.1, we give the initial model sets that were proposed by Johnson-Laird et al. (1992) and Johnson-Laird and Byrne (1993). Let us take the example of the earlier conditional *"If there's an A, then there's a 2"*:

$$[A] \qquad 2$$
$$....$$

Table 4.1.
Model sets of compound propositions, according to Johnson-Laird et al. (1992).

	Initial Model Sets		*Initial Model Sets With Exhaustiveness Marks*		*Explicit Model Sets*	
p	p		p		p	
p and q	p	q	p	q	p	q
p or q, or both		p		p	p	$\neg p$
		q		q	$\neg q$	q
					P	q
either p or q	p		p		p	$\neg q$
		q		q	$\neg p$	q
if p, then q	p	q	$[p]$	q		pq
	...		...		$\neg\text{-}p$	q
					$\neg p$	$\neg q$
iff p, then q	p	q	$[p]$	$[q]$	p	q
	...		...		$\neg p$	$\neg q$

This model set denotes that reasoners would initially represent only the situation explicitly expressed in the proposition, namely the contingency in which there is an *A* and a *2*. However, reasoners note that there are alternative states of affairs. They do this by representing a completely implicit mental model, denoted by the ellipsis. In addition, people would make a mental footnote that none of these alternative models would represent a situation in which there is an *A*. The square brackets in the explicit model denote that the *A* is exhaustively represented: There are no other situations in which there is an *A* than those in which there is also a *2*.

Finally, the specification of the mental model sets used in the psychological algorithm is rather straightforward. The psychological algorithm employs the same models as the general algorithm but does not keep count of exhaustiveness. "*If there's an A, then there's a 2*" is thus represented as:

A   2
....

Symmetry of Model Set Combination.   For purposes that will become clear in specifying our expectations about people's tendency to work in an order to maintain co-reference, it is important to note that the procedure for combining model sets is symmetrical. This holds for all proposed algorithms, but we illustrate this property for only one: the general algorithm. Consider for instance the conditional "*If there's an A, then there's a 2*":

[A]   2
....

This model set can be conjoined with the information "*There's an A*":

[A]

The combination results in the following model set:

[A]   2

If the conditional were to be interpreted last and combined with the categorical premise already represented, the result would be the same:

[A]   2

Nothing in the procedure hints as to why the integrated model of, for instance, a conditional and a categorical premise would be different from the integrated model of a categorical premise and a conditional (but see Girotto, Mazzocco, & Tasso, 1997). An asymmetrical procedure would result in different integrated models as a function of whether, for instance, a conditional or a categorical premise would have been taken as the starting point.

EXPERIMENT 1: MAINTAINING CO-REFERENCE

In order to test the thesis that reasoners tend to combine premises in an order that maintains co-reference we devised a procedure in which participants had to select the order in which they want to see the premises, without them actually being able to draw conclusions at this point. The problems we used in the present study were taken from Braine et al. (1995). To obtain a measure of reasoners' preferred sequence of processing the premises we first presented the participants (48 psychology students at the University of Leuven) with an incomplete formulation of the premises on a computer screen. Take for instance the following problem:

[1]	*Ms. P and Mr. B are not both a suspect.*
[2]	*If Mr. O was in the dining room, then Ms. P is a suspect.*
[3]	*Mr. O and Ms. V were both in the dining room.*
[4] Conclusion:	*Mr. B is not a suspect.*

Initially, reasoners would be confronted with the incomplete premises presented next. These incomplete premises do not present the predicate assigned to the subject and exclude the negation if any is present in the complete premises:

[1]	*Ms. P and Mr. B are ....*
[2]	*If Mr. O was ...., then Ms. P is ....*
[3]	*Mr. O and Ms. V were ....*
[4] Conclusion:	*Mr. B is ....*

The participants could specify the preferred order of seeing the premises in full by typing it on a command line as, for instance, 2314. Once they typed in their preferred sequence, the premises would be presented one at a time in a self-paced manner by pressing the space bar if they wanted to see the next premise in the preferred sequence.

What would one expect if reasoners do tend to maintain co-reference while drawing intermediate conclusions, if possible? Given that the participants' task was to evaluate the given conclusion as correct or incorrect, we would be able to trace their line of inference backward from the given conclusion. In the foregoing problem this means that, first, since the conclusion [4] makes reference to a Mr. B and Mr. B is only referred to in [1], one would expect that people prefer to see [1] last before they evaluate the conclusion. In addition, [1] makes reference to Mr. P, who is also being referred to in [2]. Hence, one might expect that people would opt to see [2] before [1], such that the preferred sequence would be:

[3]	<u>Mr. O</u> *and Ms. V were both in dining room.*
[2]	*If <u>Mr. O</u> was in the dining room, then* **Ms. P** *is a suspect.*
[1]	**Ms. P** *and Mr. B are not both a suspect.*
[4] Conclusion:	*Mr. B is not a suspect.*

However, expecting a preference of [3] before [2], does not keep count of the thesis that, if possible, people will draw intermediate conclusions. When people produce intermediate conclusions, the idea of maintaining co-reference provides no basis as to prefer [3] before or after [2]. In both cases people would draw the same intermediate conclusion about Ms. P such that co-reference with [1] is maintained. Given that people develop a strategy of drawing intermediate conclusions, there need not be a preferred order in the first two of the premises when maintaining co-reference for three premise problems. However, remember from our introduction that there are other reasons why people might prefer to see one premise before another.

Let us take another example of a three-premise problem:

[1]	*Mr. O and Ms. V are ....*
[2]	*Mr. O is ....*
[3]	*Mr. P is ....*
[4] Conclusion:	*Ms. V and Mr. P are ....*

For this problem both [1] and [3] are co-referential to the conclusion [4], such that one would expect that reasoners tend to prefer either one of these premises as the last premise. On the basis of co-reference with the conclusion, neither one of these premises would be preferred above the other. But, because premise [3] is linked only to the conclusion, whereas [1] has a co-referential clause to both the conclusion [4] and [2], one might expect a somewhat larger preference for premise [3] as the last premise.

The structure of the previous two problems corresponds to two of the problems used by Braine et al. (1995), who looked primarily at the intermediate conclusions that people draw when a problem comprises more than two premises. Braine et al. (1995) also presented two-premise problems. We already suggested that maintaining co-reference does not result in preferring one or the other of two premises before the other in the case of two-premise problems. Conclusions drawn on the basis of the two premises would not change as a function of one of the two premises being presented first. In both cases they would evaluate their conclusion against the given conclusion they would receive in full after the premises have been presented in their preferred sequence. Obviously, other factors might contribute to preferring one premise before the other. Indeed, semantic informativeness is one of them. Because Experiments 2 and 3 were set up to test the assumption that reasoners tend to start with the semantically most informative premise, we do not elaborate this factor at this point.

The content of the premises was about particular persons (five persons) being in a particular room of a house (five places) or about being a suspect or not. Other premises were about certain objects (five of them) being found in a certain room, or being a murder weapon or not (for a detailed description, see Dekeyser, Schroyens, Schaeken, Spittaels, & d'Ydewalle, 1998). The participants first received the instructions, which they could scroll through at a self-paced manner. These instructions explained that they were to solve a murder plot. They would be given 22 small subproblems to solve by indicating whether the given conclusion for these problems was correct or incorrect. Their conclusion for 10 of these 22 problems would be used to provide the premises for the final murder-plot problem (who committed the murder, in what room and which was the murder weapon). Hence, they were told, it would be very hard to solve the final murder plot if they solved any of these problems incorrectly. To provide the participants with an extra motivation, we gave an award to the fastest three participants who would solve the murder plot correctly (500, 300, and 150 BF).

In specifying the expected frequencies for the χ^2 goodness-of-fit tests (Siegel & Castellan, 1988) on the observed frequencies of preferred sequences, the total number of observations was reduced by the number of times the conclusion was not selected to be seen last. In the case of two-premise problems, this means that each of the two possible sequences has a 50% chance of being selected under the null hypothesis. In the case of three-premise problems, there are six possible premise sequences, each of which would be selected 1 out of 6 times under the general null hypothesis. For instance, when the expectations were that either premise [1] or [3] would be the last premise in the preferred sequence, and that there would be no preference in the presentation of the first two premises, the expected frequency would be 4/6 of the total number of observations.

Table 4.2 presents the percentages of preferred sequences according to the thesis that the third premise in a sequence of three premises will have a co-referential clause with the conclusion. As can be seen in Table 4.2, only when problems have one premise with a co-referential clause to the conclusion, the proportion of participants selecting a sequence with the co-referential premise last is reliably larger than chance level (33.3%). For the problems in which two premises could be preferred as the last premises on the basis of their co-reference with the conclusion, only two showed a reliable effect in the expected direction (chance level being 66%). Given that either one of the two co-referential premises was selected last, there was at least a reliable tendency to prefer the categorical premise first in these two problems (31% vs. 42%; 25% vs. 39% respectively). Interestingly, the three problems that failed to support the predictions all have a similar structure: two conditionals and one disjunction. We will return to this issue further on.

Table 4.2.
Percentages of selected orderings of three-premise problems in which co-reference is maintained. The representation of the problems corresponds to the initial representation. Premises with a co-referent to the conclusion are typed bold and the co-referential clause is underscored.

Premise 1	Premise 2	Premise 3	Conclusion	%	χ^2
	One co-referential premise				
p	**q and r**	p or s → q	r	53.2	8.27**
p → q	p and r	**q and s**	s	63.8	19.56***
p → q	**q and r**	p	r	59.6	14.47**
p → q	**q or r**	p	r	59.6	14.47**
	Two co-referential premises				
p or q	p	**r**	q and r	87.5	9.38**
p and q	p	r	q or r	84.8	6.75*
p or q	**p → r**	**q → r**	r	63.8	0.16
(p and q) or (p and r)	**q → s**	**r → t**	s or t	51.1	5.09
(p and q) or (p and r)	**p and q → s**	**p and r → t**	s or t	62.5	0.54

* p < .01, ** p < .005, *** p < .001.

Table 4.3.
Percentages of selected orderings in which the co-referential premise in two premise problems is preferred as the second premise. The representation of the problems corresponds to the initial representation.

Premise 1	Premise 2	Conclusion	%	χ^2
p	p or q → r	r	50.0	0.00
p	p → p and r	q or r	61.7	3.13
p and r	p and q	q	76.1	12.52**
(p and q) or (p and r)	p or s → t	t	59.5	1.72
p	p and q	q	51.1	0.02
p	p or q	q	36.2	3.59
p	p → q	q	53.2	0.83

* p < .005.

Table 4.3 presents the percentages of preferred sequences in the case of two-premise problems. Given the 50% chance level of selecting either one of the two premises as the last premise before the conclusion, the results seem to indicate that co-reference has only a marginal impact on preferring one premise before or after the other premise in the case of two-premise problems.

The present experiment illustrated that the tendency to maintain co-reference in drawing inferences is preserved in the case of three-premise problems, but is not observed in the case of two-premise problems. Indeed, the procedure of combining two model sets is not conceptualized as an asymmetrical procedure. In the case of three (or more) premise problems, co-reference does not constrain the preferred order of the first two premises. In the case of a conclusion that is to be evaluated, the premise preferred last would maintain co-reference with both the conclusion to be evaluated and the intermediate conclusion drawn on the basis of the first two premises. However, the present experiment does not provide a strong test of the influence that semantic informativeness might exert on selecting a premise to start reasoning with. First, reasoners were given a conclusion to evaluate such that the processing sequence would be restrained by this goal. Second, in the two-premise problems there was no control for the semantic informativeness of the two premises. Third, a preference to start reasoning with the semantically most informative premise might interact with the tendency to construct a chain of reasoning that maintains co-reference up to the conclusion to be evaluated.

The thesis that, when possible, people would draw intermediate conclusions can be taken to account for the larger preference for one of two premises, both of which are linked to the conclusion. If one of these premises, say [1], is linked to only the conclusion, whereas the other premise, say [2], is also linked to another premise (such that these premises form the basis for drawing an intermediate conclusion), then [1] is preferred above [2]. The problem set presented to the participants included some problems in which co-reference between the premises and the conclusion is intertwined even more. For these problems the two premises linked to the conclusion were not selected more frequently than by chance. In presenting the results we already alluded to the fact that all these problems had a particular structure. Take for instance the following problem:

[1]   *Mr. O or Ms. V is ....*
[2]   *If Mr. O is ...., then Mr. P is ....*
[3]   *If Ms. V is ...., then Mr. P is ....*
[4] Conclusion: *Mr. P is ....*

Both [2] and [3] are linked with the conclusion [4], such that either [2] or [3] would be preferred last. However, both [2] and [3] are also linked to premise [1], such that [2] or [3] would not be preferred one before the other. That is, neither combination of a subset of two of the premises would suffice to draw an intermediate conclusion. Do these problems indicate that the possibility to draw intermediate conclusions would determine which premises people combine, without a role for co-reference to a conclusion figuring in reasoners' preferred order of working? Participants' behavior with three-premise problems with two premises linked to the conclusion and one of these two linked to the third premise suggests this is not the case. They tended to prefer as the last premise that premise which was linked only to the conclusion.

In sum, the assumption that reasoners *"will tend to work in an order that maintains co-reference, drawing, when possible, informative intermediate conclusions"* (Johnson-Laird et al., 1994, p. 736), is supported by the present set of results. However, the results indicated that co-reference and the possibility to draw intermediate conclusions are dependent on one another; neither one is sufficient by itself to account for reasoners preferred order of working.

EXPERIMENT 2: THE MOST INFORMATIVE PREMISE FIRST?

After investigating reasoners tendency to maintain co-reference, we address the problem of semantic informativeness. If reasoners prefer to process the most informative premise first, how can we test this? Johnson-Laird (1983) proposed a quantified notion of semantic informativeness for propositional logic. He proposed a procedure to calculate the informativeness (I) of a proposition as the complement of its truth-table probability. Every atomic proposition has a probability of .5. The truth table probability of a sentence can be calculated recursively. For example the probability of a conjunction is the product of the probabilities of its constituents:

$$P(p) = .5 \qquad\qquad I(p) = 1 - P(p) = .5$$
$$P(p \wedge q) = P(p) \bullet P(q) = .25 \qquad\qquad I(p \wedge q) = 1 - P(p \wedge q) = .75$$

The probability of p equals .5, so its informativeness is the complement of that probability, again .5. For two atomic propositions connected as a conjunction (AND), an exclusive disjunction (ORE), an inclusive disjunction (ORI), a conditional (IF) or a biconditional (IFF) respectively, the probabilities are .25, .5, .75, .75, and .5. Thus the informativeness for propositions consisting of atomic propositions connected by these operators is .75, .5, .25, .25, and .5. With these values, one can make a prediction concerning the order in which reasoners prefer to see two premises:

1. AND
2. CP, ORE, IFF
3. ORI, IF

A premise with a conjunction (AND) is preferably seen before any of the other premises. The categorical premise (CP) and premises with an exclusive disjunction (ORE) or biconditional (IFF) are preferably viewed before premises with an inclusive disjunction (ORI) or a conditional (IF). With these preference orderings one has a precise prediction concerning reasoners ordering behavior. If they are free to order two premises, they will do so as described before. Again, other factors might come to play in people's premise ordering. One has no predictions for premises with equal semantic informativeness.

To test these predictions, we set up an experiment with 43 logically untrained participants, all first year students of educational sciences. It was important to avoid tendencies to order premises according to the position of co-referential atomic propositions in the premises. Therefore we presented participants premises lacking crucial referential information. Based on those incomplete premises, they were able to choose the presentation order of the completed premises. As an example we present a sequence of a conjunction (AND) and a conditional (IF) below, both in incomplete and completed form:

There is ... chalk and ... chalk in the box.
If there is ... chalk then there is also ... chalk in the box.

There is <u>white</u> chalk and <u>red</u> chalk in the box.
If there is <u>green</u> chalk then there is also <u>red</u> chalk in the box.

We used compound premises with atomic propositions as arguments for one of the main connectives. Thus six types of sentences were formed: categorical premises, conjunctions, exclusive disjunctions, inclusive disjunctions, conditionals, and biconditionals. The sentences were combined to form pairs of premises. Each of the 15 premise pairs shared one atom at the same location in the sentence: at the left or the right. Thus co-reference effects were avoided during inference. Participants were unable to predict the location of the shared atom or the colors involved, as these were counterbalanced across trials. Each type of premise combination was presented twice, albeit in a different order. As in the previous experiment, the completed premises were presented one at a time at a self-paced manner. Once both premises were seen, participants could formulate their conclusion.

We considered a premise sequence to be a participant's consistently preferred sequence only if the participant chose this sequence twice over its opposite. Table 4.4 presents the count of those preferences per premise pair. From the significant differences, the following premise order seems to be preferred consistently: CP, AND, and ORE preferably precede IF and IFF. ORE preferably precedes ORI. However, we suspected participants to behave quite different from one another. Therefore a hierarchical cluster analysis was performed on the participants' preferences using HICLAS (De Boeck & Rosenberg, 1988). The program searches for groups of participants with similar preference patterns. First, a preference matrix or pattern was made for every participant, in which participants got a one-value if they chose a sequence at least once, and a zero otherwise. The overall matrix consisted for 65% in ones. The cluster solution in Rank 2 had an overall goodness of fit of 0.738. Table 4.4 presents the preferences for two resulting groups of participants: Group 1 and Group 2. A third group generally selected most sequences once. Some of these participants always accepted the suggested premise order but it is hard to tell why. Either they had no preference or their preference shifted over trials.

As shown in Table 4.4, almost half of the participants typically select sequences according to the general pattern: CP before all other premises, AND before all but CP, ORE before ORI, IF, and IFF, ORI before IF and IFF, IF before IFF. Of all other participants showing any preference consistency—Group 2—this is not true. On the contrary, they seem to select sequences according to the opposite pattern, at least for sequences containing atomic propositions and the conjunctive connective (Table 4.4). For premise pairs containing neither premise, these participants typically prefer every sequence once.

We had a prediction according to the semantic informativeness principle: The most informative premise is preferably seen first. Thus conjunctions (AND) would be seen preferably before any other premise; inclusive disjunctions (ORI) and conditionals (IF) preferably last. The overall results of our experiment confirm this prediction, although participants showed additional preferences for premise pairs of equal semantic informativeness. It is the cluster analysis that confronts us with more crucial problems. From the semantic informativeness principle, we would predict that CP is preferably processed after AND, and IF and ORI after IFF, but we obtained the opposite effect for the majority of participants showing a consistent sequence preference. The rest of the participants with a consistent preference—Group 2—flout the semantic informativeness principle just as well: They generally like to see AND—the most informative premise—after any other premise. In an attempt to save the principle, one could argue that these participants have reversed the informativeness principle and adopted a strategy of processing the most informative premise last. In that case, how to explain these participants preferring to see AND before CP? Whatever the reason for their behavior, all participants with a consistent preference force us to refute both the informativeness principle and its reverse. We must conclude that the predictions were false and we must acknowledge that participants don't all order premises according to the same strategy. However, this does not mean that the concept of semantic informativeness should be abandoned. We believe that there is need for the concept in explaining participants' behavior.

Let us reconsider the way this concept was quantified. Johnson-Laird (1983) calculated the notion of a premise's semantic informativeness as the complement of its probability. At the same time he admitted that calculating a probability and its complement are not the psychologically most plausible way of judging the information conveyed by a premise. There are, however, other ways of deciding on two premises relative informativeness.

Table 4.4.
Results of χ^2 and Group analyses on sequence preferences for Experiment 2.

	n	χ^2	G1	G2	G3
Sequences according to both concepts of informativeness					
cp, ori	17 vs. 13	0.53	+	-	0
cp, if	25 vs. 11	5.44*	+	-	0
and, ore	18 vs. 14	0.50	+	-	0
and, ori	18 vs. 14	0.50	+	-	0
and, if	25 vs. 8	8.76**	+	-	0
and, iff	22 vs. 9	5.45*	+	-	0
ore, if	24 vs. 5	12.45***	+	0	0
Sequences according to the logical concept of informativeness					
and, cp	9 vs. 16	1.96	-	+	0
ore, ori	21 vs. 7	7.00**	+	0	0
iff, if	10 vs. 16	1.39	-	0	0
iff, ori	13 vs. 16	0.31	-	0	0
Sequences according to the psychological concept of informativeness					
cp, ore	15 vs. 19	0.47	+	-	0
cp, iff	22 vs. 8	6.53*	+	-	0
ore, iff	21 vs. 7	7.00**	+	0	0
ori, if	18 vs. 9	3.00	+	0	0
ori, iff	16 vs. 13	0.31	+	0	0

* $p < .05$, ** $p < .01$, *** $p < .001$. Column n contains the number of participants selecting a sequence twice vs. the number of participants selecting the opposite sequence twice. A + symbol indicates preference for a sequence, an 0 symbol indicates preference for both the sequence and its opposite, a - symbol indicates preference for the opposite sequence.

A simple rule of thumb does the job: The premise with the smallest model set is the most informative one. This rule leads to the same comparisons as Johnson-Laird's quantificational approach, as long as both premises are constructed of the same number of atomic propositions. For in that case, the smaller a premise's model set, the lower the probability that this premise is true and the higher its semantic informativeness. It is impossible to compare premises with a different number of atomic propositions with just this rule. One can not tell whether a categorical premise is more informative than a conjunction.

What if participants apply the rule of thumb, but ignore its prerequisite for equal number of atomic propositions? Then we would predict that both categorical premises and conjunctions are considered more informative than any other premise, because they convey only one model. Disjunctions are considered more informative than conditionals because the exact size of their model set is known, both in an initial and a completed representation. The size of (bi)conditionals' complete model sets is intrinsically unknown from their initial representation. The purpose of the implicit model or "ellipse" in their model set is precisely to reduce the size of the set, notifying that the real size is in fact larger. This notification might be enough to make participants consider these premises' model sets "probably larger" than any other premise's model set. They expect the number of models involved during inference to be higher than the number of models contained in the initial representation. Based on the rule of thumb mentioned earlier, we propose a notion of psychological informativeness as opposed to logical informativeness: A premise is psychologically more informative than a second premise if its observed or expected complete representation contains less models.

Hence the semantic informativeness principle would explain the behavior of most participants with a consistent preference: Categorical premises and conjunctions are preferred on the first position, and conditionals on the last. The reversed principle could explain the behavior of the participants of Group 2, preferring to see the premises with the smallest model set last. Even when both groups of participants select sequences according to opposite patterns, the number of models conveyed by the premises always seems to guide their decisions.

From examining response latency and accuracy we hoped to gain some insight in the performance of participant groups. The latency was calculated per person over selecting the premises' order, reading the completed premises and starting to type the answer. Response latencies were different for participant groups, because participants of Group 1 responded faster than those of Group 2 (26.8 s vs. 34.3 s). The average latency of Group 3 was in between both (28.6 s) The accuracy is the percentage of correct responses per person. The responses were first transformed subjectively, independent from the problem or participant that originated them. This means that all eight possible box contents were checked for every response, to see whether the response allowed for that content as a possible state of affairs, whether tacitly or explicitly. Thus a set of possibly intended box contents was obtained for every response. Every transformed response was then compared with the correct set of possible box contents. If a transformed response did not allow at least for the correct set of possible contents, it was considered false. Responses thus had to be valid to be correct, but not precise. They had to convey at least the information conveyed by the premises. A Mann-Whitney U test showed the averaged accuracies not to differ significantly for participant groups (66%, 62%, and 70% respectively). Participants from Group 2 were thus generally performing worse. They were not less accurate but took more time to find a conclusion. One might argue that they weren't as acquainted with abstract propositional reasoning as their colleagues. They only had preferences for problems containing categorical premises or conjunctions. It seems as if they didn't discern for the specific properties of disjunctions and conditionals. The higher latencies of this group of participants seem to confirm their lack of experience, although it is just as well possible that the sequences they selected are harder to solve.

EXPERIMENT 3: LOGICAL VERSUS PSYCHOLOGICAL INFORMATIVENESS

It may be that no reasoner is really consistent in processing premise pairs. In the previous experiment we did force participants to make a choice that they may not make in daily life. Almost half of all participants hardly showed any preference at all. We possibly elicited spurious ad hoc rules for those reasoners that made consistent decisions. At the same time, our considerations of psychological informativeness were considerations post hoc. Therefore we decided to repeat the experiment with a new set of participants. They could indicate their preference or indicate that they didn't have any preference. We expected them nevertheless to order premises according to the size of their model set. The prediction we made is that premises are ordered as follows:

1.   *CP, AND*
2.   *ORE, ORI*
3.   *IF, IFF*

A categorical premise and a conjunction are preferably seen first. When a conditional or biconditional are involved, they are preferably seen last. As in the previous experiment, we expected those reasoners that behave contrary to these predictions to do precisely the opposite. If our prediction were to prove right, then we have gained evidence that the size of a premise's model set determines its position in the line of processing, depending on the reasoners' preferences.

However, we also wanted to compare the predictive power of our psychological alternative to its logical counterpart. The best way to do this is to look at contradictory predictions, but there is only one. Processing ORI before IFF is preferable from a psychological informativeness point of view, whereas the opposite order is preferable from a logical informativeness point of view. Other predictions can be made exclusively from applying the informativeness principle with one of the informativeness concepts (compare Table 4.4 and 4.5). Thus from a logical concept preferred sequences are: AND before CP, ORE before ORI, IFF before IF. From a psychological concept preferred sequences are: CP before IFF, CP before ORE, ORE before IFF, ORI before IF, ORI before IFF. We ran this experiment on 34 first-year medical students from the University of Leuven. We hoped that participants would consistently select sequences applying the informativeness principle according to the psychological concept of informativeness.

Table 4.5.
Results of χ² and Group analyses on sequence preferences for Experiment 3.

	n	χ^2	G1	G2	G3
Sequences according to both concepts of informativeness					
cp, ori	16 vs. 4	7.20**	+	0	0
cp, if	19 vs. 7	5.54*	+	-	0
and, ore	15 vs. 6	3.86*	+	-	0
and, ori	17 vs. 7	4.17*	+	-	0
and, if	16 vs. 5	5.76*	+	-	0
and, iff	17 vs. 3	9.80**	+	0	#
ore, if	14 vs. 5	4.27*	+	0	0
Sequences according to the logical concept of informativeness					
and, cp	6 vs. 8	0.29	0	+	0
ore, ori	15 vs. 3	8.00**	0	+	0
iff, if	9 vs. 13	0.73	0	+	0
iff, ori	10 vs. 10	0.00	0	+	0
Sequences according to the psychological concept of informativeness					
cp, ore	6 vs. 7	3.52	+	0	0
cp, iff	20 vs. 4	10.67**	+	-	0
ore, iff	14 vs. 4	2.33	+	0	0
ori, if	11 vs. 7	0.89	0	-	0
ori, iff	10 vs. 10	0.00	0	-	0

* $p < .05$, ** $p < .01$, *** $p < .001$. Column n contains the number of participants selecting a sequence twice vs. the number of participants selecting the opposite sequence twice. A + symbol indicates preference for a sequence, an 0 symbol indicates preference for both the sequence and its opposite, a - symbol indicates preference for the opposite sequence. Explicit lack of preference is indicated with a #.

It turned out that participants hardly used the opportunity to indicate lack of preference, which means that the results of the previous experiment are not artificial. Table 4.5 presents the count of consistent preferences per premise pair. From the significant differences, the following premise order seemed to be preferred: CP was preferably put before ORI, IF, and IFF; AND before ORI and IF; ORE before ORI, IF and IFF. Again, a hierarchic cluster analysis was performed on the participants' responses using HICLAS. The global matrix consisted for 65% in positives. The solution in Rank 2 had an overall goodness of fit of 0.725. Table 4.5 presents the data for two resulting groups of participants (Group 1 and Group 2 conveying 18 and 3 participants respectively). A third group consists of persons generally selecting most of the sequences once. One person always indicated lack of preference. In this experiment, participants were not obliged to select a premise order. Still, one third of participants chose almost all sequences at least once. It is hard to think of their responses as showing a mere lack of preference. We believe that some of them preferred seeing the completed premises in the same order as the incomplete premises, as they consistently abided by the suggested sequence. Others appear to change their preference during the experiment, which might indicate some learning from experience.

Table 4.5 shows that more than half of all participants typically selected sequences according to the pattern found in the overall preference matrix, although they didn't have any typical consistent preference with respect to ORI in relation to IF or IFF. They typically didn't indicate any consistent preference with respect to CP in relation to AND, with ORE in relation to ORI or with IF in relation to IFF. Of all other participants showing any preference consistency (Group 2), the opposite is true. They didn't have many consistent preferences, but when they did, they preferred to see CP and AND last. For premise pairs consisting of AND and IFF they typically had an explicit lack of preference.

As far as participants had consistent preferences, they behaved as we predicted. More than half of all participants typically selected CP and AND—both one model premises—before any other premise, and they preferred to see IF and IFF—conveying indefinitely many models—last. Thus when confronted with two premises, most reasoners prefer to process the premise with the smallest model set first. Three participants did the opposite; they preferred to see premises with smaller model sets last. The relative notion of semantic informativeness defined as smaller model set size does make sense in understanding reasoners premise ordering behavior.

If we reconsider participants' preferences with a logical concept of informativeness, we see a different picture. If we consider the participants of Group 2 to behave according to the informativeness principle with a logical concept, then several preferred sequences are the opposite of our expectations (compare Table 4.5): IF preferably precedes CP, and ORE, ORI and IF precede AND, ORI precedes IF, and CP and ORI precede IFF. If we consider them to behave according to the reversed principle, then other sequences oppose our expectations: AND before CP, ORE before ORI, IFF before IF, and IFF before ORI. With a logical concept of informativeness, we can not address participants' behavior without making predictions contrary to the facts. We therefore believe our psychological concept of informativeness to have more predictive power than its logical counterpart.

Response latencies were not significantly different for participant groups (32.4, 38.2, and 32.6 s respectively). Averaged accuracies were calculated over percentages of correct responses per person but were not significantly different for participant groups (53%, 52%, and 53% respectively).

A DISCUSSION OF SEMANTIC INFORMATIVENESS

In our experiments, we have studied preferences of untrained reasoners for sequences of premises with main connectives. Three groups of reasoners emerged from our analyses. One group of reasoners has no consistent preferences. They either change preferences during the experiment or abide by suggested sequences. A second group rarely prefers sequences in which the complete model set is observed or expected to be larger for the first premise. A third group rarely prefers sequences in which the complete model set is observed or expected to be smaller for the first premise. To behave according to this pattern, reasoners with consistent preferences must have information about premises that is equivalent to a premise's initial model set.

We argue that reasoners build initial model sets when confronted with these premises, hence comparing the observed or expected number of models involved or the load on working memory. The number of models involved in a proposition's initial model set indicates its psychological informativeness: The less models involved, the more informative the proposition. Therefore one-model propositions like a categorical premise or a conjunction are highly informative. The size of conditionals' or biconditionals' complete model sets is unknown from their initial representation. All one can tell from inspecting the initial representation is that they might convey "many" possibilities. Therefore these propositions are hardly informative.

To explain the opposite behavior of two groups of participants, the semantic informativeness principle has proved useful. Either reasoners apply it and prefer to see the most informative premise first, or they apply its reverse and prefer to see the most informative premise last. Unfortunately, this principle cannot explain all results. Often reasoners have consistent preferences for sequences of premises considered equally informative. In Experiment 2 a large number of participants consistently preferred to see categorical premises before conjunctions, exclusive disjunctions before inclusive disjunctions, and conditionals before biconditionals. As Girotto et al. (1997) argued, different individuals may build different representations of a given statement. Thus, some participants might represent an inclusive disjunction initially with three models and therefore consider an exclusive disjunction more informative. It is possible for participants to use exhaustiveness marks and therefore to consider a conditional with less exhaustiveness marks as less informative than a biconditional with more exhaustiveness marks.

Another relevant factor may be the number of atoms involved, which would explain the consistent preference for a conjunction after a categorical premise. The majority of participants with a preference does not consistently prefer other predicted sequences, which might be explained on the same grounds. For example, a large number of participants of Experiment 3 showed no consistent preference for sequences involving inclusive disjunctions and conditionals. With three models or even an ellipse in the initial representation, the psychological informativeness of an inclusive disjunction might be equal to that of (bi)conditionals. However, these unexpected findings do not refute the semantic informativeness principle or its reverse. Categorical premises and conjunctions are highly informative, and (bi)conditionals have very low informativeness. Therefore participants typically select the categorical premises and conjunctions first and (bi)conditionals last.

It is obvious that we can not tell from our experiments whether participants really process premises in the self-paced order. A reasoner can remember one premise and introduce it after processing another premise. Most people are very bad at analyzing their reasoning behavior from retrospection (see Evans, chap. 1, this volume). It might prove fruitful to offer participants the completed premises before having them make inferences, rather than presenting them incomplete premises. We are indeed a long way from proving that reasoners process premises according to the semantic informativeness principle or its opposite. We have nevertheless shown that untrained reasoners have some knowledge or expectation considering the complete model set size of premises. Whatever may be the actual behavior of reasoners, their opinion on the order of premise processing is guided by psychological informativeness.

GENERAL DISCUSSION

The present studies attempted to investigate the strategies that people employ in constructing a chain of inferences. These strategies would reflect conscious control processes in a line of reasoning (see Evans, chap. 1, this volume). To investigate these control processes we questioned which premise people tend to start reasoning with and which order of presenting the premises they prefer. A rule-based approach dictates the processing sequence of the premises by the rules applicable to them. No control procedures are required to determine a chain of inference. The sequence of inference steps in a line of reasoning is demarcated by the mental rules of inference themselves. The procedures of constructing and manipulating mental models do not constrain which model sets of premises to combine with one another. To overcome this critique to reasoning by model Johnson-Laird et al. (1994) provided a principle that would guide people in constructing a chain of inference. Hence we investigated the assumption that people tend to start reasoning with the semantically most informative premise and tend to work in an order that maintains co-reference, drawing intermediate conclusions when possible.

Experiment 1 shows that the idea that people tend to maintain co-reference is a viable one. However, maintaining co-reference does not seem to form a stringent constraint on people's ordering of premises. Co-reference is dependent on the possibility of drawing intermediate conclusions. In the case of two premise problems the participants in Experiment 1 did not share a consistent preference for one or the other premise to be presented first. Indeed combining two model sets is conceptualized as a symmetrical procedure (see the Introduction; but see Girotto et al., 1997). Irrespective of whether premise X is integrated with premise Y, or the other way around, the resulting model set and its co-reference with the conclusion is the same. For those three-premise problems in which combining the premises' model sets does not result in a single model, reasoners have no intermediate conclusion and no consistent preference. They cannot maintain co-reference between an intermediate conclusion and the conclusion to be evaluated. As it seems that maintaining co-reference is constraint by the possibility to draw intermediate inferences it is most interesting to note that the combination of a compound premise and a categorical premise almost always results in the possibility to draw an intermediate conclusion. Hence, the assumption that people "*tend to start with a premise that is maximally semantically informative (e.g., a categorical assertion)*" (Johnson-Laird et al., 1994, p. 736) is compatible with the idea that people tend to draw intermediate conclusions.

Our last experiments show that semantic informativeness as specified by Johnson-Laird (1983; Johnson-Laird & Byrne, 1991) is not a factor that adequately reflects people's preference in the premise they tend to start reasoning with. However, there is no need of evidence that this formal notion of semantic informativeness is psychologically inadequate. Its calculation requires exact knowledge of both the included and the excluded number of states of affairs from the premises' model set. Johnson-Laird et al. (1992) proposed that working memory constraints would induce reasoners to represent as little information as possible explicitly. Reasoners construct an initial model set which does not include all the possible state of affairs. Calculation of formal semantic informativeness, which presupposes fully fleshed out model sets, would therefore be implausible as a modulating factor in human reasoning. Hence we proposed a notion of psychological informativeness based on the number of models in the initial model sets. The more models involved, the less informative a proposition is.

The results of Experiments 2 and 3 bear out that psychological informativeness might indeed be a modulating factor in people's premise ordering behavior. Although there is a general tendency to start reasoning with the semantically most informative premise, there are also large individual differences. Cluster analyses showed that a large subset of participants selects the first premise in function of its larger informativeness, where others select it in function of its smaller informativeness. This means that people almost invariably use the informativeness of premises to decide which premise to start reasoning with. The detection of consistent interindividual differences would have been impossible without our cluster analysis, as would have been our general conclusion. As such, this investigation can be considered to be an example of successful application of this method in reasoning research. However, as shown by Rauh (chap. 9, this volume), the structure of experimental results doesn't always favor this approach.

Numerous questions remain unanswered on the basis of our study. One problem is that of the relation between individual differences and working memory constraints. Drawing intermediate conclusions is functional in freeing working memory resources. Once an intermediate conclusion is drawn, one does not need to retain in memory the representation of the respective premises on the basis of which the intermediate conclusion was drawn. Indeed, the self-paced presentation of premises in Experiment 1 might have placed a heavy load on working memory because the respective premises could only be seen once, and one at a time. Another problem is that of the relation between ordering premises according to semantic informativeness and drawing intermediate conclusions. As noted earlier, the possibility to draw a determinate, intermediate conclusion is related to the semantic informativeness of the respective premises. Integrating the initial model set of a compound proposition with the model of a conjunction or a categorical premise more frequently yields a single model, which can serve as an intermediate conclusion. More research needs to be conducted in order to discover the function of checking semantic informativeness and maintaining co-reference.

ACKNOWLEDGMENTS

Mathias Dekeyser and Géry d'Ydewalle are funded by the IUAP/PAI convention P4/19. Walter Schroyens and Walter Schaeken are supported by the FWO-Flanders.

REFERENCES

Bonatti, L. (1994). Propositional reasoning by model. *Psychological Review, 101,* 725–733.

Braine, M. D. S., & O'Brien, D. P. (1991). A theory of If: A lexical entry, reasoning program, and pragmatic principles. *Psychological Review, 98,* 182–203.

Braine, M. D. S., O'Brien, D. P., Noveck, I. A., Samuels, M. C., Lea, R. B., & Yang, Y. (1995). Predicting intermediate and multiple conclusions in propositional logic inference problems: Further evidence for a mental logic. *Journal of Experimental Psychology: General, 124,* 263–292.

Byrne, R. M. J., & Johnson-Laird, P. N. (1989). Spatial reasoning. *Journal of Memory and Language, 28,* 564–575.

De Boeck, P., & Rosenberg, S. (1988). Hierarchical classes: Model and data analysis. *Psychometrica, 53,* 361–381.

Dekeyser, M., Schroyens, W., Schaeken, W., Spittaels, O., & d'Ydewalle, G. (1998). *Preferred premise order in propositional reasoning: Semantic informativeness and co-reference.* Internal Report nr. 237, University of Leuven.

Girotto, V., Mazzocco, A., & Tasso, A. (1997). The effect of premise order in conditional reasoning: A test of the mental model theory. *Cognition, 63,* 1–28.

Johnson-Laird, P. N. (1983). *Mental models.* Cambridge, UK: Cambridge University Press.

Johnson-Laird, P. N., & Bara, B. G. (1984). Syllogistic inference. *Cognition, 16,* 1–62.

Johnson-Laird, P. N., & Byrne, R. M. J. (1991). *Deduction.* Hillsdale, NJ: Lawrence Erlbaum Associates.

Johnson-Laird, P. N., & Byrne, R. M. J. (1993). Precis of deduction. *Behavioral and Brain Sciences, 16,* 69–84.

Johnson-Laird, P. N., Byrne, R. M. J., & Schaeken, W. (1992). Propositional reasoning by model. *Psychological Review, 99,* 418–439.

Johnson-Laird, P. N., Byrne, R. M. J., & Schaeken, W. (1994). Why models rather than rules give a better account of propositional reasoning: A reply to Bonatti and to O'Brien, Braine, and Yang. *Psychological Review, 101,* 734–739.

Johnson-Laird, P. N., Byrne, R. M. J., & Tabossi, P. (1991). Reasoning by rule or model: The case of multiple quantification. *Psychological Review, 96,* 658–673.

Rips, L. J. (1994). *The psychology of proof: Deductive reasoning in human thinking.* Cambridge, MA: MIT Press.

Schaeken, W., Johnson-Laird, P. N., & d'Ydewalle, G. (1996). Mental models and temporal reasoning. *Cognition, 60,* 205–234.

Siegel, S., & Castellan, J. N. (1988). *Nonparametric statistics for the behavioral sciences.* New York: McGraw-Hill.

Vandierendonck, A., & De Vooght, G. (1996). Evidence for Mental-model-based reasoning: A comparison of reasoning with time and space concepts. *Thinking and Reasoning, 2,* 249–272.

5

Counterexample Availability

Ruth M. J. Byrne
Orlando Espino
Carlos Santamaria

Little is known about the process by which reasoners search for counterexamples. Is the search for counterexamples an unconscious automatic component of the reasoning mechanism or is it a deliberate conscious strategy? As a first attempt towards answering such questions, we consider four possible interpretations of 'if' and we outline the impact that these different interpretations have on the nature of the models that reasoners construct and the counterexamples that are available to them in those models. We suggest that the process of fleshing out models, that is, carrying out revisions to the initial set of models constructed to understand a conditional, is central to the discovery of counterexamples. We discuss empirical evidence on how people deal with ready-made counterexamples that have been made explicitly available to them.

One of the central proposals of the mental model theory of deduction is that people make deductions according to a semantic principle of validity: An argument is valid if there are no counterexamples to it, that is, if there are no situations in which the premises are true but the conclusion is false (Johnson-Laird, 1983; Johnson-Laird & Byrne, 1991). How is the search for counterexamples carried out? Not much is known about the process and our aim in this chapter is to examine some of the issues surrounding counterexample discovery (see also Byrne, Espino, & Santamaria, 1998). Is the search for counterexamples an unconscious automatic component of the reasoning mechanism? Failures to search for counterexamples may reflect constraints on reasoning in general, such as working memory limitations on the number of models that can be kept in mind. Alternatively, is the search for counterexamples a deliberate conscious strategy (as suggested by Evans, chap. 1, this volume; see also Handley, Dennis, Evans, & Capon, chap. 12, this volume)? Failures to search for counterexamples may reflect a deliberate decision made by reasoners who consider that a plausible, possible rather than necessary, conclusion is sufficient for their current purposes. As a first attempt toward answering such questions, we consider in this chapter how people deal with counterexamples that have been made explicitly available to them.

The role of counterexamples in making deductions can be illustrated by considering one of the common fallacies—the Denial of the Antecedent inference. Given a conditional, such as:

If Paul went fishing, then he had a fish supper.

and the denial of its antecedent:

Paul did not go fishing.

consider whether the following conclusion is valid:

He did not have a fish supper.

A counterexample to the inference is the situation where Paul did not go fishing but he did have a fish supper. Reasoners may engage in different processes to make the inference, and only some of these processes will lead to the correct answer. Some reasoners may construct only the initial models of the conditional:

fishing   fish supper
. . .

where "fishing" represents the idea that Paul went fishing, "fish supper" represents the idea that he had a fish supper, and separate models are represented on separate lines. The second model is wholly implicit, and the three dots indicate that there may be alternatives to the explicit model (In fact, models may contain "mental footnotes" to indicate how they can be fleshed out, but for these more technical details, see Johnson-Laird & Byrne, 1991.) Reasoners who fail to flesh out their models to be more explicit will not be able to combine the information from the second premise with the models for the conditional. They may consider that nothing follows.

Some reasoners may flesh out the initial models to a biconditional interpretation:

fishing   fish supper
not fishing   not fish supper

where "not" is a propositional-like tag to indicate negation. The information from the second premise can be combined readily with the second model, and so reasoners who flesh out their models to this interpretation will make the Denial of the Antecedent: They will conclude that Paul did not have a fish supper.

Finally some reasoners may flesh out the initial models to a conditional interpretation:

fishing   *fish supper*
not fishing   *not fish supper*
not fishing   *fish supper*

They can integrate the information from the second premise, that Paul did not go fishing, with the explicit models of the conditional. It is consistent with two of the models, the second and third model. The conclusion that Paul did not have a fish supper is consistent with the second model but it is countermanded by the third model. The third model provides an explicit counterexample to the putative conclusion for the Denial of the Antecedent inference. Reasoners will conclude that Paul may or may not have had a fish supper. As is illustrated by this example of the processes that reasoners may engage in when they consider the Denial of the Antecedent inference, fleshing out the models of a conditional is central to the discovery of counterexamples. People construct an initial set of models and the revision of the initial set of models to be more explicit is crucial for the discovery of counterexamples. Fleshing out models is costly in terms of working memory constraints and it is well known that inferences are easier if they can be based on the initial set of models rather than a more fully fleshed out set (Johnson-Laird, Byrne, & Schaeken, 1992).

Table 5.1.
Different interpretations of 'if' illustrated for the assertion, "*If Paul went fishing, then he had a fish supper.*"

Interpretation	*Models*		*Inferences*	*Sufficiency/ Necessity*
Biconditional	fishing	fish supper	MP, MT,	Sufficient
	not fishing	not fish supper	DA, AC	Necessary
Conditional	fishing	fish supper	MP, MT	Sufficient
	not fishing	not fish supper	not DA, AC	Not necessary
	not fishing	fish supper		
Reversed	fishing	fish supper	not MP, MT	Not sufficient
Conditional	not fishing	not fish supper	DA, AC	Necessary
	fishing	not fish supper		
Nonconditional	fishing	fish supper	not MP, MT	Not sufficient
	not fishing	not fish supper	not DA, AC	Not necessary
	not fishing	fish supper		
	fishing	not fish supper		

The interpretation that people reach of a conditional has a profound impact on the nature of the models they construct, the counterexamples that are available to them in those models, and the inferences that they consider are supported by the conditional (see Byrne et al., 1998). As Table 5.1 shows, there are at least four alternative interpretations that people may reach for a conditional (e.g., Staudenmayer, 1975).

The biconditional interpretation is consistent with just two models:

> *fishing*   *fish supper*
> *not fishing*   *not fish supper*

and it supports all four of the standard inferences, including the two inferences that are considered valid on a "material implication" reading of "if", that is the Modus Ponens inference:

> *If Paul went fishing then, he had a fish supper.*
> *Paul went fishing.*
> *Therefore he had a fish supper.*

and the Modus Tollens inference:

> *If Paul went fishing, then he had a fish supper.*
> *Paul did not have a fish supper.*
> *Therefore he did not go fishing.*

It also supports the two inferences that are invalid on a material implication interpretation of "if" but are valid on a material equivalence interpretation, that is, the Denial of the Antecedent inference:

> *If Paul went fishing, then he had a fish supper.*
> *Paul did not go fishing.*
> *Therefore he did not have a fish supper.*

and the Affirmation of the Consequent inference:

> *If Paul went fishing, then he had a fish supper.*
> *Paul had a fish supper.*
> *Therefore he went fishing.*

There are no counterexamples to these four inferences available in the models for the biconditional, as Table 5.1 shows. The antecedent of the conditional "*Paul went fishing*" is interpreted as both sufficient and necessary for the consequent "*he had a fish supper.*"

The conditional interpretation is consistent with three models:

fishing	*fish supper*
not fishing	*not fish supper*
not fishing	*fish supper*

and it supports two of the inferences, the Modus Ponens and Modus Tollens inferences. The other two inferences, the Denial of the Antecedent and Affirmation of the Consequent inferences can be rejected: The third model contains a counterexample to them. The antecedent is interpreted as sufficient but not necessary for the consequent.

The biconditional and conditional interpretations of "if" correspond to the material "equivalence" and "implication" relations long studied by philosophers. Staudenmayer (1975) conjectured, using persuasive examples from everyday discourse, that a third meaning of "if" is possible, which he termed a "reversed conditional" interpretation. The reversed conditional interpretation is again consistent with three models:

fishing	*fish supper*
not fishing	*not fish supper*
fishing	*not fish supper*

but it differs from the conditional interpretation in the nature of the third model. It supports two of the inferences, the Denial of the Antecedent and Affirmation of the Consequent inferences. The other two inferences, the Modus Ponens and Modus Tollens inferences can be rejected: The third model contains a counterexample to them. The antecedent is interpreted as necessary but not sufficient for the consequent.

Staudenmayer also speculated that a further interpretation of "if" is possible, which we will call a "non-conditional" interpretation. The nonconditional interpretation is consistent with four models:

fishing	*fish supper*
not fishing	*not fish supper*
not fishing	*fish supper*
fishing	*not fish supper*

and it does not support any of the inferences. The Denial of the Antecedent and Affirmation of the Consequent inferences can be rejected (the third model contains a counterexample to them), and the Modus Ponens and Modus Tollens inferences can also be rejected (the fourth model contains a counterexample to them). The antecedent is interpreted as neither sufficient nor necessary for the consequent.

In this chapter we suggest that the reversed conditional and the nonconditional interpretations of "if", although neglected by psychologists and philosophers interested in the meaning of "if" may in fact be common in everyday interpretations of conditionals. To illustrate this point we consider the role of the availability of counterexamples in the suppression of fallacies and the suppression of valid inferences.

THE AVAILABILITY OF COUNTEREXAMPLES AND THE SUPPRESSION OF INFERENCES

Consider the pair of conditionals:

If there is a dog in the box then, there is an orange in the box.
If there is a lion in the box then, there is an orange in the box.

Given the premise:

There is a dog in the box.

the Modus Ponens conclusion follows validly:

There is an orange in the box.

The counterexample to the inference, that is, the situation in which there is a dog in the box and there is not an orange in the box is not available and so the inference is readily endorsed. But given the premise:

There is not a dog in the box.

the Denial of the Antecedent conclusion:

There is not an orange in the box.

does not follow. The counterexample to the inference, that is, the situation in which there is not a dog in the box and there is an orange in the box is readily available from the premises: There is not a dog in the box but there is a lion in the box and so there is an orange in the box. As a result, the modus ponens inference is made (and so is the Modus Tollens inference) from a pair of conditionals that contain alternative antecedents, but the Denial of the Antecedent inference is resisted (and so is the Affirmation of the Consequent inference) from such premises (Rumain, Connell, & Braine, 1983).

Consider now the pair of conditionals:

If Paul goes fishing, then he has a fish supper.
If Paul catches fish, then he has a fish supper.

Given the premise:

Paul goes fishing.

the Modus Ponens conclusion does not seem to follow:

Paul has a fish supper.

The counterexample to the inference, that is, the situation in which Paul goes fishing and does not have a fish supper is readily available from the representation of the premises: Paul goes fishing and does not catch any fish and so he does not have a fish supper. Given the premise:

Paul does not go fishing.

the Denial of the Antecedent conclusion seems to follow:

He does not have a fish supper.

The counterexample to the inference, that is, the situation in which Paul does not go fishing but he has a fish supper is not available and so the inference is readily endorsed. As a result, the Modus Ponens inference is resisted (and so too is the Modus Tollens inference) from a pair of conditionals that contain additional antecedents, and the Denial of the Antecedent inference is made (and so too is the Affirmation of the Consequent inference) from such premises (Byrne, 1989).

The proper interpretation of the suppression of valid inferences is a matter of debate (Byrne, 1991; Byrne & Johnson-Laird, 1992; George, 1995; O'Brien, 1993; Politzer & Braine, 1991). Our interpretation of the suppression of the fallacies and the suppression of the valid inferences is that it hinges on the interpretation that reasoners come to of "if" (see also Fillenbaum, 1993). The provision of an alternative antecedent (e.g., *a lion* instead of *a dog*) in a pair of conditionals leads reasoners to have readily available a counterexample to the fallacies. Their representation of "if" resembles the conditional interpretation. The provision of an additional enabling antecedent (e.g., *catching fish* as well as *going fishing*) in a pair of conditionals leads reasoners to have readily available a counterexample to the valid inferences. Their representation of "if" resembles the reversed conditional interpretation.

Our interpretation of the suppression of inferences in terms of the availability of counterexamples leads to the following straightforward prediction: Just as reasoners can be led to a conditional or a reversed conditional interpretation by the provision of either an alternative or additional antecedent respectively, so too, they should be led to a nonconditional interpretation of "if" by the provision of both an alternative and an additional antecedent. They will have readily available a counterexample to the valid inferences and a counterexample to the fallacies.

Consider for example, the following set of conditionals:

If Paul goes fishing, then he has a fish supper.
If Paul goes to the fishmarket then, he has a fish supper.
If Paul catches fish then, he has a fish supper.

Given the premise:

Paul goes fishing.

the Modus Ponens conclusion:

He has a fish supper.

will be suppressed because there is a counterexample available from the provision of the third premise: Paul goes fishing but he does not catch any fish and so he does not have a fish supper.
Likewise, given the premise:

Paul does not go fishing.

the Denial of the Antecedent conclusion:

He does not have a fish supper.

will be suppressed because there is a counterexample available from the provision of the second premise: Paul does not go fishing but he goes to the fishmarket and so he has a fish supper. We expect suppression of all four inferences from this set of premises. The nonconditional interpretation, in which the antecedent is neither necessary nor sufficient, does not support any of the four standard inferences. The first conditional is embedded in a set of conditionals that are coherent and consistent, yet it does not support any inferences.

We tested this prediction in an experiment in which 88 undergraduate students from the University of La Laguna, Tenerife, were assigned to one of four groups. One group received a pair of conditionals that contained alternative antecedents, the second group received a pair of conditionals that contained additional antecedents, the third group received a set of three conditionals that contained both alternative and additional antecedents, and the fourth group received single conditional arguments (for details, see Byrne et al., 1998). Each participant received 12 inferences, three each of the Modus Ponens, Modus Tollens, Denial of the Antecedent, and Affirmation of the Consequent inferences, instantiated in different contents, and their task was to select a conclusion from a set of three conclusions, indicating, for example, that p occurred, p did not occur, or p may or may not have occurred.

The results corroborated our counterexample explanation of the suppression of inferences. The results show that it is possible to suppress all four inferences from a conditional embedded in a set of conditionals that contain alternative and additional antecedents. The valid inferences, such as Modus Ponens, were suppressed from the pair of conditionals that contained both alternatives and additional antecedents (58%), as they were from the set of conditionals that contained additional antecedents (47%), compared to the pair of conditionals that contained alternative antecedents (96%). Likewise, the fallacies, such as the Denial of the Antecedent, were suppressed from the pair of conditionals that contained both alternatives and additional antecedents (21%), as they were from the set of conditionals that contained alternative antecedents (18%), compared to the pair of conditionals that contained additional antecedents (44%).

The results support our suggestion that the suppression of inferences arises because the provision of extra conditionals with additional or alternative antecedents changes the interpretation that reasoners reach of conditionals. Alternative antecedents encourage a conditional interpretation and the availability of a counterexample (not going fishing but eating a fish supper anyway) ensures the suppression of the fallacies. Additional enabling antecedents encourage a reversed conditional interpretation and the availability of a counterexample (going fishing but not eating a fish supper) ensures the suppression of the valid inferences. Alternative and additional antecedents encourage a nonconditional interpretation and the availability of counterexamples of both sorts (not going fishing but eating a fish supper anyway, and going fishing but not eating a fish supper) ensures the suppression of all four of the inferences.

THE RELATIVE IMPORTANCE OF COUNTEREXAMPLES

The inferences reasoners make can be influenced by counterexamples that they generate themselves rather than just by counterexamples that they are explicitly given. Consider the following problem:

When David has homework to do, he gets into a bad mood.
I saw David after school today and he was in a bad mood.
Can you imagine what could have put David into a bad mood?

When people were given problems of this sort, the more alternatives they generated, the fewer fallacies they made (Markovits, 1984). Thinking of other antecedents that could lead to the consequent ensures the availability of a counterexample (David not having homework to do but being in a bad mood anyway, because he had a fight with a friend, or failed a test, and so on), which suppresses the fallacies.

Consider the following problem:

Rule: If Joyce eats candy, then she will have cavities.
Fact: Joyce eats candy often, but she does not have cavities.
Write down as many circumstances as you can that could make this situation possible.

When people were given problems of this sort, the more additional antecedents they generated, the fewer valid inferences they made (Cummins, Lubart, Alksnis, & Rist, 1991; Elio, 1997). Thinking of other antecedents that could block the consequent ensures the availability of a counterexample (Joyce eating candy often but not getting cavities, because she brushes her teeth often, or has a genetic predisposition for strong teeth, and so on) which suppresses the valid inferences.

However, it does not seem to be the case that people gain any general insight into the need to search for counterexamples. When reasoners are given alternative conditions and both of the conditions are denied, for example:

If Paul went fishing, then he had a fish supper.
If he went to the market, then he had a fish supper.
He did not go fishing or to the market.

they make the Denial of the Antecedent inference:

Therefore, he did not have a fish supper.

When people are given additional conditions and both of the conditions are affirmed, for example:

If Paul went fishing, then he had a fish supper.
If he caught some fish, then he had a fish supper.
He went fishing and he caught some fish.

they make the Modus Ponens inference (Byrne, 1989):

Therefore, he had a fish supper.

Perhaps people do not spontaneously engage in a counterexample search, at least in these experimental situations, unless they are prompted to do so, say, by the content, context, or task, or by their beliefs and emotions.

When both of the additional conditions are affirmed implicitly, for example:

If Paul goes fishing, then he will have a fish supper.
If Paul catches a fish, then he will have a fish supper.
Paul is always lucky when he goes fishing.
Paul goes fishing.

they readily make the Modus Ponens inference (Stevenson & Over, 1995):

Therefore, he will have a fish supper.

The premise that Paul is always lucky when he goes fishing indirectly informs reasoners that he always catches fish. The affirmation of the antecedent can be modified by including *"almost always," "sometimes,"* and so on, and suppression is increased (Stevenson & Over, 1995).

Another way in which suppression of inferences is increased or decreased is by manipulating how important reasoners perceive the counterexamples to be. For example, consider the following pair of conditionals:

> *If Steven is invited, then he will attend the dance party.*
> *If Steven knows the host well, then he will attend the dance party.*

People rate the additional condition as less important than the first antecedent. The valid inferences are only weakly suppressed, for example, reasoners make the Modus Ponens inferences on 69% of occasions. But consider instead the following pair of conditionals:

> *If Steven is invited, then he will attend the dance party.*
> *If Steven completes the report tonight, then he will attend the party.*

People rate the additional condition as more important than the first antecedent. The valid inferences are more strongly suppressed, for example, reasoners make the Modus Ponens inferences on 46% of occasions (Chan & Chua, 1994).

Perhaps the results indicate that suppression depends on general knowledge in memory schemas, as Chan and Chua suggest? Alternatively, perhaps the strength of additional conditions can differ in importance without differing in content? We carried out an experiment to test these possibilities (see Byrne et al., 1998, for details). We gave participants pairs of conditionals that contained additional antecedents, but we phrased some additional conditions as biconditionals, for example:

> *If Paul went fishing, then he had a fish supper.*
> *If and only if he caught some fish, then he had a fish supper.*

and we phrased some additional conditions as conditionals, for example:

> *If Paul went fishing, then he had a fish supper.*
> *If he caught some fish, then he had a fish supper.*

The biconditional emphasizes the importance of the additional enabling condition. Given the premise for the Modus Ponens inference:

> *Paul went fishing.*

We expect that from both pairs of premises people will resist the conclusion:

> *He had a fish supper.*

because the counterexample is readily available: He went fishing but he did not catch any fish and so he did not have a fish supper. But we expect that there will be more suppression from the biconditional additional condition than from the conditional additional condition. In fact, reasoners may even flesh out the biconditional premise to represent the counterexample explicitly:

fishing	*caught*	*fish supper*
fishing	*not-caught*	*not-fish supper*
. . .		

We assigned 135 undergraduate students from the University of La Laguna, Tenerife, to five groups. One group received arguments based on a pair of conditionals, a second received arguments based on a pair of biconditionals, the third received arguments based on a conditional first premise and a biconditional second premise, and the fourth group received arguments based on a biconditional first premise and a conditional second premise. The final group were given single conditional arguments. Participants in each group were given three Modus Ponens and three Modus Tollens inferences, instantiated by different contents, and their task was to select a conclusion from a set of three options (see Byrne et al., 1998).

The results corroborated our prediction showing that an additional enabling condition phrased as a biconditional led to more suppression than an additional enabling condition phrased as a conditional. Participants who were given a pair of premises with the enabling condition phrased as a biconditional made reliably fewer inferences (regardless of whether the first premise was a conditional, 26%, or a biconditional, 32%) than participants who were given a pair of premises with the enabling condition phrased as a conditional (regardless of whether the first premise was a conditional, 41%, or a biconditional, 43%). And of course, participants in the four groups who were given a pair of premises that contained additional conditions made fewer inferences than participants in the group who were given a single conditional (91%).

The results indicate that the strength of a counterexample, as manipulated by the phrasing "if" and "if and only if," influences how strongly the inference is suppressed. The perceived strength of a counterexample need not depend on background knowledge in memory, instead it can be determined by the phrasing of the assertion as a conditional or a biconditional.

CONCLUSIONS

Little is known about how people search for counterexamples and our aim in this chapter has been to shed some light on the process. We have concentrated on situations where counterexamples are made explicitly available to people. The results of our experiments and others show clearly that people can avail of counterexamples when they are given them, and the influence of counterexamples on the frequency of inferences that people make is profound. We have illustrated the role of counterexamples by focusing on the suppression effect. Our suggestion is that the suppression of inferences occurs because alternative conditions provide a ready-made counterexample to the fallacies (i.e., an instance where the antecedent condition does not occur but the consequent occurs anyway). Alternatives encourage reasoners to construct a conditional interpretation of "if", in which the antecedent is considered sufficient but not necessary. Additional conditions provide a counterexample to the valid inferences (that is, an instance where the antecedent condition occurs but the consequent does not). Additional antecedents encourage a "reversed conditional" interpretation of "if," in which the antecedent is considered necessary but not sufficient.

Our counterexample account leads us to expect that all four inferences could be suppressed from a conditional embedded in a set of conditionals that contained alternative and additional conditions. The results of our experiment supported this prediction: The provision of both an alternative and an additional antecedent provides counterexamples to all four inferences and encourages a "nonconditional" interpretation of "if." Counterexamples can have a greater or lesser influence on inferences depending on how important the counterexample is perceived to be. When the additional condition is phrased using a biconditional there is even greater suppression than when the additional condition is phrased using a conditional.

Counterexample search may be an automatic process carried out unconsciously, that frequently fails because it depends on multiple models to be borne in mind when the initial set of models is fleshed out to be more explicit. Alternatively, it may be an optional process carried out consciously, that frequently remains uncalled because reasoners are content to settle for plausible rather than valid conclusions. Whichever it turns out to be, it seems clear that the deductions people make are influenced by the semantic principle of deduction: An argument is valid if there are no counterexamples to it. The influence that counterexamples have on the inferences people make shows that reasoners can represent counterexamples explicitly and they can use them. It may even be the case that adult reasoners spontaneously develop strategies to help them discover counterexamples. Adult reasoners spontaneously develop control strategies to help them chart their path through complex and novel deductive problems (e.g., Byrne & Handley, 1997; Byrne, Handley, & Johnson-Laird, 1995). They may construct their new strategies by re-assembling component parts of existing strategies in novel ways guided by a growing familiarity with particular types of deductive problems (Byrne & Handley, 1997). Counterexample search strategies could span a wide range of tactics, whether conscious or unconscious, from using ready-made explicitly presented counterexamples, to incorporating readily-retrieved relevant information into the set of models, to constructing the negation of the premise and conclusion (e.g., p and not-q) and assessing the plausibility of the two alternatives (p and not-q vs. p and q). It remains for future research to determine the nature of counterexample search strategies, their development, and the situations in which they are deployed.

REFERENCES

Byrne, R. M. J. (1989). Suppressing valid inferences with conditionals. *Cognition, 31,* 61–83.

Byrne, R. M. J. (1991). Can valid inferences be suppressed? *Cognition, 39,* 71–78.

Byrne, R. M. J., Espino, O., & Santamaria, C. (1998). *Counterexamples and the suppression of inferences.* Manuscript submitted for review.

Byrne, R. M. J., & Handley, S. J. (1997). Reasoning strategies for suppositional deductions. *Cognition, 62,* 1–49.

Byrne, R. M. J., Handley, S. J., & Johnson-Laird, P. N. (1995). Reasoning with suppositions. *Quarterly Journal of Experimental Psychology. 48A,* 915–944.

Byrne, R. M. J., & Johnson-Laird, P. N. (1992). The spontaneous use of propositional connectives. *Quarterly Journal of Experimental Psychology, 45A,* 89–110.

Chan, D., & Chua, F. (1994). Suppression of valid inferences: Syntactic views, mental models, and relative salience. *Cognition, 53,* 217–238.

Cummins, D. D., Lubart, T., Alksnis, O., & Rist, R. (1991). Conditional reasoning and causation. *Memory and Cognition, 19,* 274–282.

Elio, R. (1997). What to believe when inferences are contradicted: The impact of knowledge type and inference rule. In M. Shafto & P. Langley (Eds.), *Proceedings of the Nineteenth Annual Conference of the Cognitive Science Society* (pp. 211–216). Hillsdale, NJ: Lawrence Erlbaum Associates.

Fillenbaum, S. (1993). Deductive reasoning: What are taken to be the premises and how are they interpreted? *Behavioural and Brain Sciences, 16,* 348–349.

George, C. (1995). The endorsement of premises: Assumption-based or belief-based reasoning. *British Journal of Psychology. 86,* 93–111.

Johnson-Laird, P. N. (1983). *Mental models.* Cambridge, UK: Cambridge University Press.

Johnson-Laird, P. N., & Byrne, R. M. J. (1991). *Deduction.* Hillsdale, NJ: Lawrence Erlbaum Associates.

Johnson-Laird, P. N., Byrne, R. M. J., & Schaeken, W. (1992). Propositional reasoning by model. *Psychological Review, 99,* 418–439.

Markovits, H. (1984). Awareness of the "possible" as a mediator of formal thinking in conditional reasoning problems. *British Journal of Psychology, 75,* 367–376.

O'Brien, D. P. (1993). Mental logic and human irrationality: We can put a man on the moon so why can't we solve those logical-reasoning problems? In K. I. Manktelow & D. E. Over (Eds.), *Rationality* (pp. 110–135). London: Routledge.

Politzer, G., & Braine, M. D. S. (1991). Responses to inconsistent premises cannot count as suppression of valid inferences. *Cognition, 38,* 103–108.

Rumain, B., Connell, J., & Braine, M. D. S. (1983). Conversational comprehension processes are responsible for reasoning fallacies in children as well as adults. *Developmental Psychology, 19,* 471–481.

Stevenson, R. J., & Over, D. E. (1995). Deduction from uncertain premises. *Quarterly Journal of Experimental Psychology, 48A,* 613–643.

Staudenmayer, H. (1975). Understanding conditional reasoning with meaningful propositions. In R. J. Falmagne (Ed.), *Reasoning: Representation and process* (pp. 55–79). New York: John Wiley.

6

Pragmatics and Strategies for Practical Reasoning

Ken I. Manktelow
Neil Fairley
Steve G. Kilpatrick
David E. Over

This chapter is concerned with the strategic role of pragmatics in practical reasoning. Three studies are reported. In Study 1, scale of violation of deontic rules was explored, along with aggravating and mitigating circumstances for the specified offenses (road traffic violations). It was found that these factors all had significant, systematic effects on inference. In Study 2, problem components were presented serially: Inferences from deontic rules varied qualitatively and quantitatively as relevant information was encountered. In Study 3, a well-known effect in deontic reasoning, the perspective effect, was shown to extend to causal reasoning. Both effects are attributed to uncertainty about the condition relations of necessity and sufficiency. A modified account based on the theory of mental models is proposed. These studies show that pragmatic factors help to define initial representations, determine the sorts of inferences made, and motivate the search through problems which is at the heart of the connection between these elements of thought.

Philosophers have for many years made a broad distinction between two forms of reasoning: pure or theoretical reasoning on the one hand, and practical reasoning on the other. Pure reasoning is largely about matters of fact: It is the kind of thinking we are doing when we try to figure out what is the case, as when we consider whether a certain statement is true or not. For instance, suppose we assume that the following statement about students is true:

If one works hard, then one does well on tests.

We learn that a certain student, Jasper, works hard. We conclude, validly, that he does well on tests. Practical reasoning, by contrast, is largely concerned with inferences about which actions may be performed or not. Suppose now that one accepts the following statement:

If one works hard, then one should rest on Sundays.

Note that now we are talking about *accepting* a statement, rather than assuming truth, and that the consequent contains a modal auxiliary verb, *should*, instead of the plain indicative construction in the first example. Such features mark out this second statement as one calling for practical reasoning. Now again we learn that Jasper works hard, and so we conclude that Jasper should rest on Sundays. This particular example illustrates a form of deontic reasoning involving a conditional obligation; other varieties have to do with permission, promise, and so forth.

Deontic (practical) reasoning can be sharply distinguished from indicative (pure) reasoning by considering what follows from discovering that the antecedent (Jasper works hard) is true while the consequent is not. In the first case, the fact that Jasper works hard but does not do well on tests implies that the claim made in the statement is false. However, in the second case, the fact that Jasper works hard but does not rest on Sundays does not falsify the sentence. Rather, what we say is that Jasper has broken, transgressed, violated, or some such, the rule expressed by the conditional statement. The rule itself stands.

Psychological research has shown this kind of thinking is richly pragmatic: That is, we need to take account of a wide variety of types of information that dictate not only what is represented when people are given tasks to solve which involve practical reasoning, but also influence the progress of inference-making. We focus initially on deontic reasoning, and briefly review some recent work which informs our approach to practical reasoning. We report some work on particular pragmatic aspects of deontic inference: Those concerned with the circumstances against which such inferences are performed. Next, we reconsider a well-known and well-researched aspect of deontic thought—the perspective effect—and offer a reinterpretation of it in terms of the theory of mental models. Finally, we draw some general conclusions about pragmatics and strategies in practical reasoning. We shall see that pragmatic aspects of practical thinking play a dual strategic role in this form of thought: They act as a framing system to delineate the type of inference in question (as in the opening example), and they direct inferences via the resulting representations.

DEONTIC REASONING

The contemporary study of deontic reasoning owes much of its existence to the efforts of several groups of researchers in the 1970s, who set themselves the goal of explaining the effects of content on reasoning, and in particular, on performance on the Wason selection task. When first introduced, the Wason task contained abstract contents (Wason, 1968). For instance, a conditional claim in "*If p then q*" form such as the following would be made about four cards:

If a card has a vowel on one side, then it has an even number on the other side.

Experimental participants were presented with four cards, which they were told had a single letter on one side, and a single number on the other side. The cards showed an instance of p (in this example, a vowel), *not-p* (a consonant), q (an even number), or *not-q* (an odd number). The task was to select which cards would test the truth value of the conditional claim. Only the p and *not-q* combination can do this, by showing the claim to be false, so participants should select the p card (which might have a *not-q* value on its reverse) and the *not-q* card (which might have a p value on its reverse). Under 10% usually do so (see Evans, Newstead, & Byrne, 1993, and Manktelow, 1999, for reviews).

It had been discovered very early in the history of the selection task (by Wason & Shapiro, 1971) that using a more realistic, that is, semantically enriched, problem format gave rise to improved performance (by standard logical norms). Following some fairly sterile debate about the locus of this facilitation effect, as it came to be known, it began to emerge that the most effective way of improving selection task performance was to make it into a deontic problem.

The earliest indication of this was in the experiments reported by Johnson-Laird, Legrenzi, and Legrenzi (1972). They gave participants a selection task in which they took the role of a postal worker sorting the mail. The rule was:

If an envelope is sealed, then it has a 5d stamp on it.

The "cards" this time were envelopes, one sealed (p), one unsealed (*not-p*), one with a 5d stamp on it (q) and one with a 4d stamp on it (*not-q*). The task was to choose those letters which might be breaking this rule. Over 80% chose the p and *not-q* cards this time.

In retrospect, it can be seen that this was the first deontic selection task. This became clear in the pivotal paper by Cheng and Holyoak (1985), in which the postal content was used (among others) in an explicitly deontic context. That is, their version of the postal rule used a modal auxiliary verb:

If the letter is sealed, then it <u>must carry</u> a 20c stamp.

and they also provided (in one condition) a rationale for the rule, setting out the benefits obtained by having a letter sealed.

Cheng and Holyoak proposed that the high levels of accurate reasoning observed in their versions of this task were explicable in terms of pragmatic reasoning schemas—content-dependent routines abstracted from experience. Cosmides (1989), on the other hand, attributed the effect to the operation of innate algorithms, which she held to be necessary for adaptive social inference. She maintained that all facilitating contents contained conditionals which could be reduced to a single canonical form:

If you take a benefit, then you pay a cost.

People were said to have a natural tendency to search for cheaters, those who take a benefit (p) without paying a cost or, in some cases, meeting a requirement (*not-*

q). This account has been disputed (see Cheng & Holyoak, 1989; Manktelow & Over, 1995).

Our own approach to deontic reasoning owes something to both these theories, but is not allied to either. Manktelow and Over (1991) appealed to decision-making constructs to explain a novel finding: the perspective effect. This effect occurs when participants take alternative roles when solving the deontic selection task. For instance, Manktelow and Over (1991) presented the following conditional permission rule:

If you tidy your room, then you may go out to play.

This was said to have been uttered by a mother to her son. Four cards, said to record on one side whether the room had been tidied or not, and on the other side whether the boy had gone out to play (or been let out to play) or not, showed the following values: room tidied (p), room not tidied (*not p*), went out to play (q), did not go out to play (*not q*).

Participants can be asked to detect possible violations of this rule from either the son's or the mother's perspective. From the son's perspective, they should be sensitive to cases where he tidies his room (p) but is not let out (*not q*); but from the mother's perspective, they should be sensitive to cases where he does not tidy his room (*not p*) but still goes out (q)—the mirror image of the "correct" solution endorsed by standard logic, the one usually said to have have been "facilitated" by deontic contents. Strong support for these predictions was found in a set of experiments (see also Gigerenzer & Hug, 1992; Light, Girotto, & Legrenzi, 1990; Politzer & Nguyen-Xuan, 1992 for consistent findings).

Deontic facilitation and perspective effects have been the subject of much theoretical attention. Mental logic theorists account for the apparently better performance in deontic selection tasks first by proposing that the abstract selection task is beyond the scope of ordinary mental logic, where the deontic task is not. The abstract task is, on this account, a meta-logical task requiring the knowledge and application of the truth-table for material implication, something beyond ordinary untutored logical expertise, whereas the rule in a deontic task can be used for direct reasoning (O'Brien, 1993, 1995; O'Brien calls deontic selection tasks quasi-selection tasks). Holyoak and Cheng (1995) extend their pragmatic reasoning schema theory to concern the complementarity of rights (asserted by permission statements) and duties (asserted by obligation statements) in order to explain perspective effects. Oaksford and Chater (1994) allow that deontic tasks constitute an exception to their general probabilistic account of selection task performance, and include the construct of subjective utility in explaining performance on the deontic task.

Manktelow and Over (1991, 1995) adapted the theory of mental models, introduced by Johnson-Laird (1983; Johnson-Laird & Byrne, 1991), in explaining deontic facilitation and perspectives. As with some of the other approaches just mentioned, they invoked decision-making constructs in doing so, especially that of subjective utility, and have argued that deontic reasoning may usefully be considered in decision-making terms (Evans, Over, & Manktelow, 1993; Manktelow & Over, 1991, 1995; Over & Manktelow, 1993). One advantage of this approach over others is that it provides deontic reasoning with a semantic base, which in turn enables an explanation of why deontic statements should be made in the first place.

Consider again the mother–son rule given earlier. Two crucial assumptions must be fulfilled for this to be a felicitous utterance in ordinary circumstances. The assumptions concern the preferences, and hence the utilities, of the two parties in the exchange: the *agent*, who utters the rule, and the *actor*, whose behavior is its target. The first assumption is that the agent prefers p to *not-p* (e.g., tidy to untidy rooms). Without this assumption, the rule would never be uttered. The second assumption is made by the agent: That the actor prefers q to *not-q* (e.g., going out to staying in). If the agent did not make this assumption, again, the rule would not be uttered; if the assumption is not justified, and the actor does not prefer q to *not-q*, then the inducement expressed by the rule will not work. It is also likely, though not crucial, that the agent will either be indifferent between q and *not-q*, or prefer q to *not-q*. Mental model sets expressing these preferences can be used to predict a range of potential transgressions (see Manktelow & Over, 1991, 1995), most of which have been empirically confirmed.

Of course, the normative theory of decision making is expressed in terms of subjective *expected* utility. Thus, it should be possible to detect the influence of subjective probability as well as subjective utility on deontic reasoning, following the argument that deontic reasoning can be construed in decision-making terms. This was explored by Manktelow, Sutherland, and Over (1995). They adapted a scenario introduced by Cheng and Holyoak (1985), concerning immigration. The following rule was used in a selection task:

If a person has ENTERING on one side of their immigration form, then they must have CHOLERA on the reverse side.

The task was to take the role of an immigration officer trying to detect possible violators of this rule. A rationale for the rule was given, together with the additional, probabilistic information that cholera was particularly common in tropical countries. A large array of cards was used, with multiple instances of the logical items p, *not p*, etc. This enabled the probabilistic variable to be included on the cards in the form of countries of origin: Some of them gave tropical countries such as Thailand; others gave European countries such as Holland. It was predicted that the European cards would be less frequently selected than the Tropical cards, and this was observed, both when the country information was added to the antecedent and to the consequent cards. Participants seemed to view passengers coming from European countries as less of a risk, and hence less worthy of attention, than passengers coming from tropical countries, as was predicted on decision-making grounds. Logically, of course, a person violating this rule is just as much a violator wherever they come from.

We thus have evidence for the influence of semantic and pragmatic factors, centering on perspective and the decision-making constructs of utility and probability, on deontic reasoning. In the next section, we report some further work on the pragmatics of violation of deontic rules. We return to perspective effects and the mental model approach to practical reasoning later in this chapter.

CONTEXTS OF TRANSGRESSION: MITIGATING AND AGGRAVATING CIRCUMSTANCES

Treating deontic reasoning as allied to decision making allows a range of possible influences to be explored. In general, anything that affects the representation of utility or probability will be expected to affect deontic reasoning. In recent work, we have begun to study the effects of variables which are likely to modify people's judgments of the degree of violation of a deontic conditional, a utility variable.

Pragmatic variables are already known to affect the ways in which people reason with conditionals, even in the theoretical context. For instance, Byrne (1989; see also Byrne, Espino, & Santamaria, chap. 5, this volume) found that the logically sanctioned Modus Ponens and Modus Tollens inferences could be suppressed by the introduction of additional premises, an effect attributed by Stevenson and Over (1995) to induced uncertainty about the major premise—a probabilistic variable. Similarly, Cummins and her associates have demonstrated that causal conditional inferences can be suppressed by information, (either explicit or implicit) about alternative causes or disabling conditions (Cummins, 1995; Cummins, Lubart, Alksnis, & Rist, 1991) associated with the cause–effect relationships expressed in conditional statements.

In the deontic domain, rule violation is often assessed in the context of mitigating and aggravating circumstances. Courts of Law recognize these factors in determining penalties. Mitigating circumstances are those that bring about a less severe judgment of violation; they may sometimes be used to excuse rule violation altogether. Aggravating circumstances have the opposite property: They lead to a more severe assessment of violation.

In Study 1 (reported by Manktelow, Over, & Kilpatrick 1996), we used the example of road traffic offenses. There was an initial evaluation stage to the experiment, followed by an inference stage. In the evaluation stage, 20 participants were given the case of either driving above the speed limit or driving while under the influence of alcohol, together with 36 additional statements describing attributes of the driver, the road and weather conditions, time of day, purpose of journey, and so on. For each case, participants indicated on a 10-point scale the degree of seriousness of the offense as they viewed it.

Table 6.1.
The eight items for aggravating and mitigating circumstances used in Study 1,
with their ratings under either offense.

Aggravating	Drink	Speed	Mitigating	Drink	Speed
Poor visibility	9.1	9.3	Good visibility	9.4	6.4
Rain and fog	9.8	9.3	Empty road	9.0	4.1
5pm	9.7	8.1	2am	9.7	6.0
In an accident	9.9	9.0	Wife in labor	6.5	3.0
Teacher on trip	9.9	9.4	Doctor on call	8.8	3.2
Late for a party	9.6	7.9	Late for a plane	8.6	5.8
15 y.o. joyrider	9.9	9.5	Experienced	9.3	6.3
Disqualified	9.9	9.1	driver		
driver			No previous	9.4	7.5
			convictions		
Mean	9.72	8.95	Mean	8.84	5.29

One unexpected outcome of this part of the study was that although for both offenses aggravating circumstances were evaluated significantly more severely than were mitigating circumstances, ratings were much more variable in the case of speeding than in the case of drink-driving: Only in one circumstance was a drink-driving offense given an average rating of below 8.5 (on a scale with a maximum of 10). This was for a driver taking his expectant wife to hospital. In contrast, average ratings for speeding varied between 3.0 (wife in labor, again) and 9.8 (wet and icy road).

For the inference experiment, we extracted eight pairs of contrasting items, where possible, representing mitigating and aggravating circumstances as rated in the evaluation study. The pairs of items and their ratings are given in Table 6.1.

Participants were given inferences in the following form (e.g., for speeding):

If a car driver travels above 30 mph in a built-up area and is stopped by the police, then she or he is liable to a fine.
A car driver travels above 30 mph in a built-up area and is stopped by the police.
[Circumstance]
What follows?

Nine response options were available, designed to be scored for strength of inference; these are shown in Table 6.2.

Table 6.2.
Scoring system and mean scores for the inference stage of Study 1.

Scoring system			
"What follows?"			
The driver	must	be fined	2
	should		3
	ought to		4
	may		5
	may not		6
	ought not		7
	should not		8
	must not		9
None of these	(penalty < fine)		10
	(penalty > fine)		1

Table of means			
	Aggravating circumstances		
	Control	*Minor*	*Major*
Drink	Over limit	2.5 pints	5 pints
	2.5	2.6	1.8
Speed	Over limit	35 mph	60 mph
	3.0	4.1	2.8
	Mitigating circumstances		
	Control	*Minor*	*Major*
Drink	3.8	3.5	2.4
Speed	5.1	6.0	4.9
	Baseline scores (no circumstances)		
	Control	*Minor*	*Major*
Drink	3.2	2.9	2.8
Speed	2.9	5.4	3.6

A further variable was also addressed in this experiment: scale of violation. There were three levels of this factor, as follows:

Drink-	Control:	Exceeded the limit
driving	Minor:	Has drunk 2.5 pints of beer
	Major:	Has drunk 5 pints of beer
Speeding	Control:	Exceeded the limit
	Minor:	Traveling at 35 mph
	Major:	Traveling at 60 mph

In addition, there was also a "baseline" case in which the circumstance was omitted. A different group from the same population as those in the evaluation stage took part in the inference stage.

Under the scoring system, each inference could be given a score between 1 (*strongly follows*) and 10 (*strongly doesn't follow*), as shown in Table 6.2. A split occurs between scores of 5 (*may be fined*) and 6 (*may not be fined*) where participants decide whether or not to levy a penalty at all. Mean scores in each of the six groups, omitting the baseline scores, are also given in Table 6.2, with the baseline scores listed separately for comparison. Scores were pooled across participants, and means under each circumstance were analyzed.

For drink-driving, there was a main effect of circumstance (aggravating– mitigating), a main effect of scale (control/ minor/ major), and an interaction between these two factors. The major offense produced stronger inferences than the minor and control offenses, whereas aggravating circumstances produced stronger inferences than mitigating circumstances across all conditions; the interaction reflects the lack of differences between minor and control offenses with aggravating circumstances. All the average scores were below 5, indicating that participants tended to infer that some kind of penalty should always be levied for this offense.

For speeding, there was a main effect of scale and a main effect of circumstance. There was no significant interaction. Again, the major offense produced stronger inferences than the minor offense, and aggravating circumstances produced stronger inferences than mitigating circumstances. Unlike the drink condition, although, average scores with mitigating circumstances were all around 5, indicating that participants may have been uncertain under such circumstances about whether to impose a sanction for speeding.

The inference results both confirm and add to the evaluation results. Drink-driving was always seen as a punishable offense, whereas speeding could be readily condoned given additional information. However, it appears that participants were prepared to vary their inferences according to circumstance to a far greater degree than for their evaluations: Both speeding and drink-driving could be mitigated as far as inferences were concerned, whereas evaluations of drink-driving were rigidly punitive.

In Study 2, we presented similar materials in serial mode, one item of information after another, instead of all at once on the same page. This was to assess the degree to which initial judgments would be changed as succeeding pieces of information were encountered. We expected that this kind of practical reasoning would resemble judgment and decision making in showing a degree of defeasibility, a matter that has provoked some comment in the area of deductive reasoning (e.g., Oaksford & Chater, 1993, 1995). As before, the task contained three forms of information: category of offense, scale of offense, and circumstance. These were presented, in this order, on successive pages; at the bottom of each page, participants were asked to indicate how much of a penalty they would levy, before proceeding. A scale of fines from 0–£100 was used for this purpose. Two examples of each circumstance were used: disqualified/joy-rider for aggravating, and doctor/wife for mitigating. The same values for scale of offense were used as before.

Presenting the information serially in this way allowed for some qualitative as well as quantitative predictions among the various task conditions, on the basis of the findings of Study 1. We would predict, first, that initial penalties for drink-driving should be higher than those for speeding, as they were before. Second, that there should be less difference between major and minor offenses for drink-driving than for speeding, because all drink-driving tends to be judged as a major offense. Thus, third, aggravating circumstances should have less of an effect on drink-driving penalties than on speeding penalties, because the former are already highly rated, whereas, fourth, mitigating circumstances should have similar effects in each, and should lead to reduced penalties.

Table 6.3.
Average penalties levied at each stage of Study 2.

Stage 1: Category	Stage 2: Scale	Stage 3: Circumstance
Speeding 41.67	Minor 22.50	Aggravating 73.33
Speeding 50.83	Minor 26.67	Mitigating 18.33
Speeding 42.50	Major 56.67	Aggravating 90.00
Speeding 46.67	Major 55.83	Mitigating 20.83
Drink-driving 81.67	Minor 59.17	Aggravating 88.33
Drink-driving 81.67	Minor 73.33	Mitigating 43.33
Drink-driving 70.83	Major 83.33	Aggravating 80.00
Drink-driving 90.83	Major 79.17	Mitigating 48.33

The results of this study are shown in Table 6.3. In the first column, the penalties are those levied when the information is simply that of the category of offense, speeding or drink-driving. In the second column, the penalties are those levied once the scale of offense is known, major or minor. In the third column, the penalties are those after the circumstance is known, aggravating or mitigating (i.e., after receiving all three types of information). For drink-driving, there was a main effect of circumstance but not of scale; there was a significant interaction between circumstance and scale, however. As predicted, therefore, scale made no difference to penalties for drink-driving, as all such episodes were treated as major offenses (overall initial mean for drink-driving was 81.25, near the maximum of 100: Compare this with the overall initial mean for speeding of 45.42; we can see from these figures that drink-driving was, as predicted, considered a more serious offense than speeding). The interaction shows that aggravating circumstances made little difference, whereas mitigating circumstances reduced penalties, again as predicted (see Table 6.3).

For speeding, there were main effects of scale and circumstance, and a significant interaction between these two factors. For this offense, we can see that, as in Study 1, penalties did depend on scale, and that, as predicted, not only did mitigating circumstances lead to a lowering of penalties, but aggravating circumstances led to a heightening.

These studies have shown that evaluations and inferences about transgressions of deontic rules are subject to a wide range of pragmatic influences. People first consider the kind of transgression, and this determines how later inferences about its scale are made, and whether and to what extent circumstances will affect their conclusions. The circumstances themselves are variable in their effects. It is hard to capture this kind of thinking using any kind of rule-based system; a decision-based approach seems much more fruitful. We have argued before that this kind of approach can be brought into contact with reasoning theory via the theory of mental models, as long as we allow that models can express aspects of thinking such as probability (to which it has been applied; see Johnson-Laird, 1994) and utility.

In the next section, we return to the perspective effect, and again consider how a mental models account of this effect may be developed.

PERSPECTIVES IN DEONTIC AND NON-DEONTIC REASONING

Many theorists, as we have seen, consider that there is a real, categorical distinction between theoretical reasoning (assessed using indicative rules such as those in the original Wason selection task) and practical reasoning (assessed using deontic versions). One of the strongest lines of evidence for this distinction comes from the perspective effect: It has only been observed up to now in experiments on deontic reasoning. As we saw, it is possible to obtain the mirror image of the "facilitated" selection task response by switching participants' role, or point of view, in a deontic task: From the actor's point of view, the normal p, not-q response is forthcoming, whereas from the agent's point of view, the not-p, q response is produced. In fact, the situation is more complex than this, as we shall see.

In previous papers, we have emphasized the social aspect of deontic reasoning; the terminology of agents and actors implicitly includes this. Moreover, Holyoak and Cheng (1995) derive a rationale for the perspective effect from legal theory, in particular, the constructs of rights and duties. They argue that the normal "correct" pattern or its reverse will be observed when people focus on their own rights, and others' duties. Rights equate with permission (if p then *may* q) whereas duties equate with obligation (if p then *must* q). Thus, the mother–son rule would be read, by the mother, as a permission, like this:

If he tidies his room, then he may go out to play.

She will be sensitive to the case of the abuse of this right, and hence will look for cases of q without p. However, the son will read the rule as, for instance:

If I tidy my room then, she must let me out to play.

—a duty, and an obligation. He will therefore look for cases where this duty was not fulfilled, that is, where he did p but did not receive q (p, not q).

In recent work (reported by Fairley, Manktelow, & Over, in press), we have used a different analysis in terms of condition relations, and shown that the perspective effect can be generalized from the deontic to the causal domain, hence that it may not depend on considerations such as those set out by Holyoak and Cheng, or on any specifically social or even deontic factors at all.

The analysis was based on Cummins' (1995) observation that the constructs of necessity and sufficiency operate differently in the causal and indicative (or truth-functional) domains. The standard logic of material implication entails that the antecedent is sufficient for the consequent, while the consequent is necessary for the antecedent. However, in causal conditionals, which may express causality typically in this way:

If cause (C), then effect (E),

the cause C can be sufficient or necessary (or both) for the effect E; and knowing that E has occurred can be sufficient to infer C (when C is necessary for E) or necessary to infer it (when C is sufficient for E). Cummins found that causal conditional inferences can be suppressed when doubt is cast on either the causal sufficiency or necessity of C for E. We applied this argument to predict a perspective effect with causal conditionals.

The factors identified by Cummins as undermining belief in causal sufficiency or necessity are known as disabling conditions and alternative causes. A disabling condition prevents the effect given the cause, hence C is no longer sufficient for E; an alternative cause allows E to occur without C, hence C is not necessary for E. In one study, we used the following conditional:

If you study hard, then you do well on tests.

A scenario was used in which doubt was cast on this rule by saying that it might not be true either because students may *cheat* (an alternative cause for doing well, hence questioning the necessity of C for E), or because students may *feel terribly nervous* (a disabling condition, hence questioning the sufficiency of C for E).

A large-array selection task (LAST) format was used (following Manktelow et al., 1995; see earlier) in which each logical type (p, *not-p*, q, *not-q*) was presented along with explicit information as to the presence or absence of the alternative cause (in the necessity condition) or the disabling condition (in the sufficiency condition), making 16 cards in all, four for each type. It was predicted that in the necessity condition, participants would choose the *not-p* and q cards, but *only those which showed the alternative cause* (this is the advantage of using the LAST). Similarly, participants in the sufficiency condition should select the p and *not-q* cards, but *only those showing the disabling condition.*

These predictions were confirmed: In each condition, there was a statistically significant tendency for the predicted card of each type to be selected most often. There was also an unpredicted tendency to select the 'studied hard and cheated' p card in the necessity condition.) A differential test was conducted by allotting each participant's selection to a contingency table using a strict criterion: If a participant made at least one predicted or unpredicted selection, and none of the other, their score was entered in the appropriate cell, otherwise it was regarded as a tie and omitted. The resulting scores are shown in Table 4; there was a highly significant effect in the predicted direction.

Table 6.4.
Contingency table for predicted and unpredicted selections in the perspective experiment.

	p+DC or not-q+DC	not-p+AC or q+AC
Necessity condition	0	9
Sufficiency condition	12	2

DC: disabling condition, AC: alternative cause
or = inclusive or

We thus have strong evidence for what would be called a perspective effect, if it occurred in a deontic experiment. Clearly, however, in the present study this effect has nothing to do with social roles, or rights and duties. What has happened is that uncertainty has been introduced with respect to one or other of the *condition relations* inherent in a causal conditional: sufficiency or necessity. Perhaps, then, explanations such as Holyoak and Cheng's (and our own, in previous papers) are high-level explanations which can be restated in terms of condition relations.

Can this analysis be applied in the deontic context? Consider again the mother–son rule. The mother could be said, in uttering the rule in the first place, to be specifying that tidying the room is a *necessary* precondition before the child will be let out. She will therefore be interested in cases where necessity has been violated: The child has gone out for some other reason, or none. This is the *not p, q* case. On the other hand, the child's construal of the rule may be that his tidying the room is a *sufficient* condition for his being let out. He will therefore be interested in cases where this relation did not seem to hold: where he tidied his room but was not let out (the *p, not q* case).

It seems therefore that highlighting condition relations in this way could be seen as leading to a focussing effect among mental models, along the lines suggested by Legrenzi, Girotto, and Johnson-Laird (1993). However, the argument is not as easily applicable as it might seem. Mental model theorists propose that reasoners represent deontic sentences as biconditionals:

[t]   *[o]*
. . .

where *t* indicates tidying the room and *o* indicates going out to play. The square brackets denote exhaustive representation (i.e., neither *t* nor *o* can appear in another model), and the three dots indicate possible implicit models with no present explicit content. This initial representation is fleshed out to include the "invited inference" (following Geis & Zwicky, 1971) that if you don't tidy your room then you may not go out to play:

[t]   *[o]*
[¬t]   *[¬o]*

Perspective effects are accounted for by the proposal that only one of these models is explicitly represented, depending on the point of view. From the mother's point of view, this will be

¬t   ¬o
. . .

and, because the task concerns violations, the critical case, by logical negation, will be

¬t   o

From the boy's perspective, the initial representation will be

t   o
. . .

and the possible violation will be represented as follows (Johnson-Laird & Byrne, 1995):

t   ¬o

There are problems with this account, however. In Manktelow and Over (1991), it was shown that complementary forms of "violation" could also be elicited readily from reasoners: From the mother's perspective, a boy who tidies up but does not go out (is there something wrong with him?) and from the son's perspective, a mother who lets him out even though he hasn't tidied up (she's weak). We also argued, although without testing it, that reasoners would be sensitive to the case where neither action is performed, as when the child as an act of defiance neither tidies his room nor goes out to play (Manktelow & Over, 1995): The *not p, not q* case is not a violation of a conditional or a biconditional.

Now we turn to the causal domain. We have seen that causal conditionals do not fit neatly into a characterization as either conditional or biconditional, because causal necessity and sufficiency do not map directly on to their truth-functional equivalents: A cause can be sufficient for an effect, necessary for an effect, or both necessary and sufficient. In the first case the conditional is consistent with a single-conditional reading, and in the third it is consistent with a biconditional reading, but in the second case it fits neither. And yet, this analysis predicts "perspective" effects not only in causal selection tasks but also, we argue, in deontic contexts as well.

The current model theory interpretation of perspective effects in terms of a default biconditional, selective initial explicit models, focusing, and negation (Johnson-Laird & Byrne, 1995) therefore seems to require some modification. This needs to include the possibility of *three* initial model representations, to reflect the present evidence concerning the importance of condition relations in bringing about perspective effects.

Here are the three possible construals of the condition relations in causal statements (Fairley & Manktelow, 1997):

1.   C is sufficient (but not necessary) for E
2.   C is necessary (but not sufficient) for E
3.   C is necessary and sufficient for E.

Generalizing to the *If p, then q* conditional, these can be expressed as:

1'   *p suff q*
2'   *p nec q*
3'   *p necsuff q.*

Cases 1' and 3' correspond to the truth conditions of the indicative conditional and biconditional, respectively, as noted earlier. We can now state initial and fully explicit models for these three construals:

	Initial models		*Explicit models*	
1. p suff q	[p]	q	p	q
	. . .		¬p	q
			¬p	¬q
			•p	¬q
2. p nec q	p	[q]	p	q
	. . .		p	¬q
			¬p	¬q
			•¬p	q
3. p necsuff q	[p]	[q]	p	q
	. . .		¬p	¬q
			•p	¬q
			•¬p	q

The bullet-point marks indicate within each set of possible models the cases that are ruled out under each of the three possible construals of a causal conditional, as follows. 1: Sufficiency entails that there can be no cases of p without q; 2: Necessity entails that there can be no cases of q without p; 3: Necessity + Sufficiency entails that there can be no cases of p without q or of q without p. It is an open question whether these prohibited cases are or are not explicitly represented; the • device is used here only for exposition.

Now to return to the argument that the interpretation of causal perspectives in terms of condition relations can also be applied to deontic perspective effects. We should note at this point that it is often overlooked that there are more than two such effects to be explained, as we have mentioned. The four cases are:

(i) The agent sees that p is true but does not allow q	p, not q
(ii) The agent sees that p is not true but allows q	not p, q
(iii) The actor makes p true but does not make q true	p, not q
(iv) The actor does not make p true but makes q true	not p, q

Predictions for the selection task are given after each sentence. The mental models account of focusing and negation presented by Johnson-Laird and Byrne (1995), outlined earlier, can account only for cases (i) and (iv), since it assumes an initial model based on a biconditional reading, focusing due to point of view, and logical negation. It is not clear how this explanation could account for causal perspective effects, since causal conditionals are not (usually) biconditionals in the first place. To illustrate this point, consider a causal conditional where *p* is sufficient for *q*: *If you have your head cut off then you will die*. The "invited inference" here would have to be *If you do not have your head cut off then you will not die*; not a very useful inference to have in mind as you step into the traffic.

We propose therefore that the task scenario leads to a focus on an initial model defined in terms of condition relations, namely 1 and 2 above. The four cases of violation can therefore be recast as follows:

(i)   *Violates sufficiency*
(ii)   *Violates necessity*
(iii) *Violates sufficiency*
(iv)   *Violates necessity.*

Thus the perspective effect, in both causal and deontic contexts, depends on whether the task induces a construal of the problem in terms of necessity or sufficiency.

CONCLUSIONS

The research reported here leads to some proposals about two general strategic aspects of practical reasoning. First, we can see from the work on the perspective effect that the terms in which a problem is framed can define for the reasoner which initial representations, in mental model terms, are made. These initial representations in turn determine the sorts of inference that are available. If the task is framed in terms of necessity, then the reasoner will be sensitive to, and search for, cases that bear on perceived necessity. If the task concerns sufficiency, then the cases in point will be those that bear on sufficiency; they are different cases.

In the causal domain, this "framing" is in terms of known or specified disabling conditions or alternative causes, respectively. Clearly, these are probabilistic variables, and have to do with the availability of those cases represented by the ● models shown earlier. The utility aspects of this area of inference seem to be concerned with the usefulness of being able to derive accurate causal beliefs (cf. the construct of epistemic utility: Evans & Over, 1996). In the deontic domain, the framing factors are the goals and intentions of the two parties, the agent and the actor, which, as we have seen, can be specified in terms of both preferences (utility) and probabilities.

The work on circumstances and scale of violation of deontic rules shows how the search through representations of such cases may be motivated, and directed. It is clearly in reasoners' material interests, as Cosmides and others have argued, for them to perform accurate inferences about what is allowed, forbidden, promised, and obligated. Without such general abilities, individuals would be open to exploitation, to the detriment of individual welfare and social cohesion. The pragmatic factors we have begun to explore thus reveal aspects of the "engine" of practical reasoning: the need to make justified inferences about the material world. Johnson-Laird and Byrne (1993; see also Byrne, Espino, & Santamaria, chap. 5, this volume) have similarly argued for a motivating aspect to the more general area of inferential reasoning—inferences which are noncausal and nondeontic: the need to believe and infer what is true. As yet, we have little direct evidence for the role of the kinds of pragmatic factors in this domain which have been demonstrated in the "practical" areas we have considered here. A general criticism along these lines has been made of the theory of mental models, and of the theory of mental logic: that such "core" theories have, paradoxically, a peripheral role in areas of thought rich in pragmatic influences (Evans & Over, 1996; Manktelow, 1997). In this chapter, we have seen that it is possible to begin to specify the role of pragmatics in practical reasoning, and hence to enlarge on aspects of thought which have perhaps been underspecified so far: practical reasoning, its pragmatic influences, and the strategic relation between them.

ACKNOWLEDGMENTS

We express our thanks to Walter Schaeken, for organizational and editorial assistance, and to Phil Johnson-Laird, for helpful suggestions on the analysis of the results of the third study reported here.

REFERENCES

Byrne, R. M. J. (1989). Suppressing valid inferences with conditionals. *Cognition, 31,* 61–83.

Cheng, P. W., & Holyoak, K. J. (1985). Pragmatic reasoning schemas. *Cognitive Psychology, 17,* 391–416.

Cheng, P. W., & Holyoak, K. J. (1989). On the natural selection of reasoning theories. *Cognition, 33,* 285–313.

Cosmides, L. (1989). The logic of social exchange: Has natural selection shaped how humans reason? Studies with the Wason selection task. *Cognition, 31,* 187–316.

Cummins, D. D. (1995). Naive theories and causal deduction. *Memory and Cognition, 23,* 646–658.

Cummins, D. D., Lubart, T., Alksnis, O., & Rist, R. (1991). Conditional reasoning and causation. *Memory and Cognition, 19,* 274–282.

Evans, J. St. B. T., Newstead, S. E., & Byrne, R. M. J. (1993). *Human reasoning: The psychology of deduction.* Hove, UK: Lawrence Erlbaum Associates.

Evans, J. St. B. T., & Over, D. E. (1996). *Rationality and reasoning.* Hove, UK:

Psychology Press.

Evans, J. St. B. T., Over, D. E., & Manktelow, K. I. (1993). Reasoning, decision making, and rationality. *Cognition, 49*, 165–187.

Fairley, N., & Manktelow, K. I. (1997). Causal and conditional reasoning: A comment on Cummins (1995). *Memory and Cognition, 25*, 413–414.

Fairley, N., Manktelow, K. I., & Over, D. E. (in press). Necessity, sufficiency, and perspective effects in causal and conditional reasoning. *Quarterly Journal of Experimental Psychology.*

Geis, M. C., & Zwicky, A. M. (1971). On invited inferences. *Linguistic Inquiry, 2*, 561–566.

Gigerenzer, G., & Hug, K. (1992). Domain-specific reasoning: Social contracts, cheating and perspective change. *Cognition, 43*, 127–171.

Holyoak, K. J., & Cheng, P. W. (1995). Pragmatic reasoning with a point of view. *Thinking and Reasoning, 1*, 289–313.

Johnson-Laird, P. N. (1983). *Mental models.* Cambridge, MA: Cambridge University Press.

Johnson-Laird, P. N. (1994). Mental models and probabilistic thinking. *Cognition, 50*, 189–209.

Johnson-Laird, P. N., & Byrne, R. M. J. (1991). *Deduction.* Hove, UK: Lawrence Erlbaum Associates.

Johnson-Laird, P. N., & Byrne, R. M. J. (1993). Models and deductive rationality. In K. I. Manktelow & D. E. Over (Eds.), *Rationality: Psychological and philosophical perspectives* (pp. 170–210). London: Routledge.

Johnson-Laird, P. N., & Byrne, R. M. J. (1995). A model point of view. *Thinking and Reasoning, 1*, 339–350.

Johnson-Laird, P. N., Legrenzi, P., & Legrenzi, M. S. (1972). Reasoning and a sense of reality. *British Journal of Psychology, 63*, 395–400.

Legrenzi, P., Girotto, V., & Johnson-Laird, P. N. (1993). Focussing in reasoning and decision making. *Cognition, 49*, 37–66.

Light, P., Girotto, V., & Legrenzi, P. (1990). Children's reasoning on conditional promises and permissions. *Cognitive Development, 5*, 369–383.

Manktelow, K. I. (1997). Rationality and reasoning theory: The ever-elusive deductive component. *Current Psychology of Cognition, 16*, 147–155.

Manktelow, K. I. (1999). *Reasoning and thinking.* Hove, UK: Psychology Press.

Manktelow, K. I., & Over, D. E. (1991). Social roles and utilities in reasoning with deontic conditionals. *Cognition, 39*, 85–105.

Manktelow, K. I., & Over, D. E. (1995). Deontic reasoning. In S. E. Newstead & J. St. B. T. Evans (Eds.), *Perspectives on thinking and reasoning. Essays in honour of Peter Wason* (pp. 91–114). Hove, UK: Lawrence Erlbaum Associates.

Manktelow, K. I., Over, D. E., & Kilpatrick, S. G. (1996). *Pragmatic constraints on deontic inference.* Paper presented at the XXVI International Congress of Psychology, Montreal, Canada.

Manktelow, K. I., Sutherland, E. J., & Over, D. E. (1995). Probabilistic factors in deontic reasoning. *Thinking and Reasoning, 1*, 201–220.

Oaksford, M. R., & Chater, N. (1993). Reasoning theories and bounded rationality. In K. I. Manktelow & D. E. Over (Eds.), *Rationality: Psychological and philosophical perspectives* (pp. 31–60). London: Routledge.

Oaksford, M. R., & Chater, N. (1994). A rational analysis of the selection task as optimal data selection. *Psychological Review, 101,* 608–631.

Oaksford, M. R., & Chater, N. (1995). Theories of reasoning and the computational explanation of everyday inference. *Thinking and Reasoning, 1,* 121–152.

O'Brien, D. P. (1993). Mental logic and irrationality: We can put a man on the moon, so why can't we solve those logical reasoning problems? In K. I. Manktelow & D. E. Over (Eds.), *Rationality: Psychological and philosophical perspectives* (pp. 110–135). London: Routledge.

O'Brien, D. P. (1995). Finding logic in human reasoning requires looking in the right places. In S. E. Newstead & J. St. B. T. Evans (Eds.), *Perspectives on thinking and reasoning. Essays in honour of Peter Wason* (pp. 189–216). Hove, UK: Lawrence Erlbaum Associates.

Over, D. E., & Manktelow, K. I. (1993). Rationality, utility, and deontic reasoning. In K. I. Manktelow & D. E. Over (Eds.), *Rationality: Psychological and philosophical perspectives* (pp. 231–259). London: Routledge.

Politzer, G., & Nguyen-Xuan, A. (1992). Reasoning about conditional promises and warnings: Darwinian algorithms, mental models, relevance judgements or pragamtic schemas? *Quarterly Journal of Experimental Psychology, 44A,* 401–412.

Stevenson, R. J., & Over, D. E. (1995). Deduction from uncertain premises. *Quarterly Journal of Experimental Psychology, 48A,* 613–643.

Wason, P. C. (1968). Reasoning about a rule. *Quarterly Journal of Experimental Psychology, 20,* 273–281.

Wason, P. C., & Shapiro, D. A. (1971). Natural and contrived experience in a reasoning problem. *Quarterly Journal of Experimental Psychology, 23,* 63–71.

7

Mechanisms and Strategies for Rephrasing

Thomas C. Ormerod

This chapter reviews research into rephrasing, and describes a model-theoretic mechanism for rephrasing between sentential forms. The results of a recent investigation into effects of task format are outlined, which allow a test between competing proposals for a general reasoning mechanism. The different kinds of strategy that can be invoked by people in rephrasing are also reviewed. The role of thematic content is then discussed, and the integration of thematic information at two different points in the construction of a mental representation of sentences is considered. In accounting for contextual and task demand effects, it is suggested that reasoning in general, and model theory in particular, might be reconceptualized as problem solving. Model construction offers a fundamental mechanism for developing the reasoning space, and is a continuous process rather than simply a response to the presentation of premise information. Minimal completion operates as general constraint, limiting model construction and strategy choice to the minimum required to satisfy the task demands (or goal state). Strategies (e.g., searching for alternatives) are applied to constrain or expand the reasoning space. They enable the application of operators (e.g., 'reading off' model sets, applying inference rules, or invoking heuristics) that generate solution components.

Consider the sentence *"Either the chemical is not iodide or its viscosity is 14."* What of the case when the chemical *is* iodide? To communicate this situation to someone, you might complete the rephrasing *"If the chemical is iodide, then,"* with the consequent *"its viscosity is 14."* Although these sentences use different connectives, they are logically equivalent. Despite this, the task of rephrasing between them is nontrivial. Indeed, the author witnessed an experienced chemical engineer rephrase a similar example as *"If the chemical is iodide, then its viscosity is not 14."* It was only some minutes later that the engineer realized that this rephrasing was incorrect, noticing that it did not coincide with his knowledge of the properties of iodide. He did so by rephrasing the rephrasing itself, stating *"Hang on, so in that case, either the chemical is iodide or its viscosity is 14 which is clearly wrong."* Why he was unable to rephrase between disjunctive and conditional forms, and why he chose this approach to testing the validity of his rephrasing, exemplify the research questions that are explored in this chapter.

Although researchers have occasionally used rephrasing to explore human reasoning (e.g., Cheng & Holyoak, 1985; Fillenbaum, 1975), it remains in the shadow of tasks that involve the generation or evaluation of inferences. This is perhaps not surprising, because the task of rephrasing does not derive novel information, which means it is necessarily incomplete for studying deductive reasoning. However, there are three reasons why the study of rephrasing is of value.

First, despite the apparent simplicity of rephrasing, it can be accomplished in a number of ways depending on the "strategy" adopted. The use of the word strategy in this chapter derives from the problem-solving literature (e.g., Newell & Simon, 1972). Strategies such as means–ends analysis are mechanisms for exploring and constraining the problem space, typically by decomposing problems into smaller subgoals that can then be solved through the application of "operators." A distinction between strategies for exploration and constraint, and operators for producing solution components, has proved to be valuable in problem-solving research, and it may be equally valuable in studying reasoning. The representation and manipulation of premises (the "reasoning space") is at least analogous to, if not the same as, the exploration and constraint of the problem space. This contrasts with the application of heuristics (e.g., matching), inference rules, "reading off" model sets or even simply guessing, which are operators from which solutions to components of reasoning tasks are derived. This notion of strategy can be applied at more than one level. For example, we propose that reasoners adopt a "meta-strategy" to minimize the exploration of the reasoning space: In essence, as soon as one can apply an operator that produces a satisfactory task solution one ceases exploration. This contrasts with the exhaustive search that underlies Johnson-Laird and Byrne's (1991) mental models theory. However, we also describe "microstrategies," the mechanisms used by participants to construct the reasoning space as far as task demands necessitate. For example, where we describe meaning-based and heuristic-based strategies later in this chapter, these are strategies that construct the reasoning space to a point where meaning-extraction or heuristic operators can be applied. Although the *meta* and *micro* tags are not used explicitly, both levels influence the construction of a reasoning space.

In addition, unlike the majority of paradigms used in reasoning research, such as Wason's selection task as well as most syllogistic and spatial reasoning tasks, rephrasing plays an important role in a wide range of practical applications. Two examples are in the domains of computer programming and in the specification of requirements for industrial, engineering, and architectural design. These are discussed later in relation to our own work in these areas. For now, the practical application of rephrasing is nicely illustrated by an example taken from the teaching and assessment of English as a second language (ESL). For example, Swan and Walter (1997) provide the following exercise for training students in the correct use of the word "unless" (p. 264):

Which of these sentences can be rewritten with "unless" ?
1. I'll be surprised if he doesn't have an accident soon.
2. It will be better if we don't tell her anything.
3. You can have the car tonight if Harriet doesn't need it.

Rephrasings between logically equivalent forms are also used as part of linguistic skill assessment such as the Cambridge proficiency certificate in ESL (e.g., Naylor & Hagger, 1993). What is interesting about the use of a rephrasing task here is the implicit assumption that what is being assessed is a linguistic rather than a reasoning skill. It turns out, for the model-theoretic account of rephrasing proposed in this chapter, that this distinction is irrelevant.

Next, the very fact that rephrasing does not involve the derivation of novel information makes it a valuable paradigm for exploring the comprehension of sentences independent of the processes that are employed in drawing conclusions. It allows the study of the psychological processes that underlie interpretation and representation of information contained in a premise without invoking other factors (e.g., response biases) that affect later stages in reasoning. As such, it might be described as an immediate inference task.

Consider another example. A child told by her mother *"Either you tidy your room or I'll be angry"* might spontaneously rephrase this command, in conversation or perhaps subvocally, as *"I must tidy my room or else my mother will be angry."* This replaces "either" with an "else" construction but retains the disjunctive form of the original, although a conditional rephrasing such as *"If I don't tidy my room, then my mother will be angry"* sounds just as natural. Depending on the context, other rephrasings, such as *"If I tidy my room, then my mother won't get angry,"* are possible. Curiously, a slightly less natural-sounding rephrasing is *"Either I tidy my room or my mother will be angry."* In this example, the sentence seems to carry a threat that goes beyond the logical imperative of the disjunctive form, and which makes a precise reflection of the original sentence inappropriate.

Although interesting in themselves, nuances such as this are not the focus of this chapter. What is of concern here is that some rephrasings seem so much easier to accept or to generate than others. For example, it is unlikely that a child would rephrase the earlier sentence as *"If I don't tidy my room then, my mother won't be angry,"* unless they were confident on the basis of prior experience that the threat was a hollow one (cf. Manktelow & Over, 1991) and consequently wanted to express their rejection of the original command. Clearly, the presence or absence of familiar thematic content is important in mediating rephrasing performance. However, other factors such as negation and syntactic form also play a part, and it is to these that we first turn.

REPHRASING IN THE ABSENCE OF CONTEXTUAL INFORMATION

Our initial interest in rephrasing originated in the domain of computer programming (Ormerod, 1990). Program coding can be described as the statement of data, actions, and plans in terms of conditional expressions. We began our investigations with the language Prolog, to address claims that had been made about the equivalence of the predicate calculus underlying Prolog and the nature of human thought (e.g., Kowalski, 1979). The Prolog syntax for expressing rules is "Q if P," which necessitates that any other sentential expression is rephrased into this form. It struck us that this might be problematic, especially for programmers experienced with languages like Pascal and C where conditional expressions are of the form "if P, then Q." Thus we investigated reasoning with these conditional forms, and also included "P only if" Q for comparison (Ormerod, Manktelow, & Jones, 1993).

It turned out that participants were able to rephrase between "if P, then Q" and "Q if P" forms with approximately 75% accuracy (Ormerod et al., 1993, Experiment 2). Curiously, although rephrasings between "if P, then Q" and "P only if Q" rules were at chance level (i.e., approximately 50% correct), those between "Q if P" and "P only if Q" rules were at floor (i.e., almost always wrong). The "if P, then Q" and "Q if P forms also showed similar temporal order and matching biases in a truth-table evaluation task, both forms favoring an order in which the antecedent P temporally precedes the consequent Q, in contrast with the opposite temporal order bias found with "P only if Q" rules (Experiment 1).

In addition to establishing performance patterns for the previously unexplored "Q if P" form, these data are important for three main reasons. First, they establish rephrasing as a useful paradigm for studying human reasoning: Despite the absence of a requirement to generate a conclusion, task performance is neither at ceiling nor (usually) at floor. Second, the results demonstrate how the processing of sentences containing logical connectives depends more on the interpretation of the connective than on the order of the sentence, though crucially not on the *logical* interpretation of the connective. In particular, the processing of temporal context (in this case abstract event orders) is linked to the mental representation determined by the connective rather than the sentential order. Third, they show how the strategies adopted by participants in a rephrasing task can vary across sentential forms.

Ormerod et al. (1993) provides a model-theoretic account of the main body of their findings. Following Johnson-Laird and Byrne (1991), we argue that both "if P, then Q" and "Q if P" sentences are initially represented with a single model, whereas a "P only if Q" sentence is initially represented with two models, as illustrated in the first two models of the abstract models shown in Table 7.1. Although differences in initial model set may account for most of their data, they argue that the floor effect in rephrasings between "Q if P" and "P only if Q" sentences arises because participants do not engage in the construction of a mental representation to uncover the sentence meaning, but simply adopt the flawed strategy of adding or removing the word "only."

Table 7.1.
Initial mental model sets for If P, then Q, P only Q and disjunctives depending upon the availability of contextual information (note that whilst other terms may in principle be exhaustively represented, there is no requirement in the initial model sets that this be made explicit).

Context	If P then Q	P only if Q	Either not P or Q
Abstract	P Q ...	$[P]$ Q $\neg P$	$\neg P$ Q
Causal unfamiliar	P Q $\neg P$ $\neg Q$	$[P]$ Q $\neg P$ $\neg Q$	$\neg P$ P Q
Familiar noncausal	P Q ...	$[P]$ Q $\neg P$ $\neg Q$	$\neg P$ Q P Q

In a similar vein to our research on rephrasing between conditionals, our interest in disjunctives began as part of an applied research program to develop a design methodology. An important task in writing a design requirements document is to convert an informal statement of needs into a rigorous and unambiguous formal notation, a task that necessarily entails rephrasing from a multitude of syntactic forms into a subset specified by the methodology in use. A common problem in design specification is the failure to state important assumptions that are implicitly obvious to the operator but not to the designer. Thus, a disjunctive notation was initially chosen for the methodology that formed the basis for our research (the SGT method of Shepherd, 1993). Using a disjunctive to express operating conditions and action choices had the advantage of highlighting both expected and the alternative courses of action, as in the following example, where a failure to specify the alternative scenario might have disastrous consequences:

> *Either the tank reaches pressure (in which case open valve A)*
> *or the tank fails to reach pressure (in which case alert supervisor).*

It rapidly became apparent that neither designers nor operators were able to use the disjunctive notation effectively (Shepherd & Ormerod, 1992). We therefore redesigned the notation, using a conditional form with an additional negative antecedent, of the form "*if P, then Q; if not P, then*" (Ormerod, Richardson, & Shepherd, 1998), which resolved the problem satisfactorily.

The problem of rephrasing between disjunctives and conditionals is of theoretical interest for examining the relationship between logical and psychological interpretations of sentential forms, and has a long history. Stoic logicians viewed conditionals with negative antecedents as being psychologically equivalent to their logically equivalent disjunctive counterparts. In the second century Galen stated that conditionals with a negated antecedent "are called conditionals by those who pay attention only to the sounds, but a disjunction by those who pay attention to what is meant" (cited in Wason & Johnson-Laird, 1972). In other words, a conditional "*If not P, then Q*" will always be interpreted as the disjunctive "*Either P or Q.*"

This assumption plays an important role in Johnson-Laird and Byrne's (1991) mental models theory. They argue that, for a conditional with a negative antecedent, the affirmative counterpart is represented in the initial model set as well as the negative antecedent. As a consequence, the mental representations of conditionals with negative antecedents and their logically equivalent disjunctives are approximately the same. This enables Johnson-Laird and Byrne to account for the phenomenon of matching bias in the selection task (e.g., Evans & Lynch, 1973). According to them, given the rule "*If there is not an A on one side of the card, then there is a 7 on the other side*" participants select the *A* and *7* cards because the antecedent is represented positively in their initial model set along with the consequent.

Richardson and Ormerod (1997) conducted an empirical study into the generation of rephrasings between conditionals and disjunctives. Participants were required to produce a rephrasing in the alternative syntax of a rule given in either disjunctive or conditional form. As well as manipulating syntactic form, we also varied the polarity, familiarity and causality of the given rule. In Experiment 1, participants rephrased between "*if P, then Q*" conditionals and their disjunctive equivalents, and in Experiment 2 participants rephrased between "*P only if Q*" conditionals and their disjunctive equivalents. There are two key findings from the experiments that relate to the rephrasing abstract sentences, which are discussed next (effects of thematic content are discussed later).

First, an advantage for rephrasing from conditionals with negated antecedents did not emerge. This finding challenges the Stoician assumption that conditionals with negated antecedents are psychologically equivalent to their disjunctive counterparts, and casts doubt upon the account of matching bias offered by Johnson-Laird and Byrne (1991). Indeed, the incorporation of this assumption into model theory does not seem to follow in any principled way from the procedural semantics of the theory, a view shared by Evans, Clibbens, and Rood (1995) who offered an alternative account of matching bias that does not invoke this assumption. Second, conditional→ disjunctive rephrasings were more accurate than disjunctive → conditional rephrasings in Experiment 1. This asymmetry was not found in Experiment 2, where the conditional *P only if Q* was used.

To account for these results, Richardson and Ormerod proposed that rephrasing is achieved through a process that they call *minimal completion*, in which participants construct the minimal set of mental models necessary to generate a putative rephrasing. They argued that this entails four steps:

1. *Create an initial model set through accessing a predetermined sentential representation: In the case of an "if P, then Q" conditional of any polarity this will consist of a single model, and in the case of a disjunctive or a "P only if Q" conditional the set will contain two models (cf. Johnson-Laird & Byrne, 1991);*
2. *Use this initial model set to generate a first component of the rephrasing;*
3. *Complete the initial model set only so far as is necessary to represent a second possible component for the rephrasing;*
4. *Read off the complete rephrasing from the model set.*

In essence, a rephrasing is generated by constructing a partial mental representation of the original rule only, and "reading off" the rephrasing from this representation. The syntactic form asymmetry results from the greater load created by representing the two models of a disjunctive or "*P only if Q*" conditional than the single model of an "*if P, then Q*" conditional. The asymmetry indicates that rephrasing is not simply a process of syntactic translation, but must involve the construction of an intermediate mental representation. It also suggests that the mental representation is minimal: A representation based on fully fleshed-out model sets would not lead to the asymmetry.

EXPERIMENTS WITH RESPONSE FORMATS

Effects of syntactic form offer a useful asymmetry for determining the processes involved in creating a mental representation of premise information. Another asymmetry concerns the effects of different response format such as generation and evaluation. We have recently undertaken a program of work to investigate the effects of response format in a rephrasing paradigm, which provides a test of competing theories that propose a general reasoning mechanism (Richardson & Ormerod, 1998). Rephrasing is an ideal task for exploring response format effects because it does not involve the derivation of novel information. Thus, effects of response format cannot be ascribed simply to differential information provision.

Hardman and Payne (1995) found a response format asymmetry with syllogistic reasoning, where participants performed better in evaluating than generating conclusions to syllogisms. They account for the asymmetry in model-theoretic terms: The generation of conclusions can require the construction of more than one model set, whereas the evaluation of a conclusion can always be achieved through the construction of a single model set. Thus, evaluation of given conclusions is always at least as easy as, and often easier than, generation.

Hardman and Payne offer only a model theoretic interpretation of the response format asymmetry in syllogistic reasoning, and it is difficult to see how most other theories of reasoning could explain it. Pragmatic reasoning schemas (Cheng & Holyoak, 1985) cannot, because schemas are elicited by contextual information that remains static across response formats. Similarly, the heuristic or rationality$_1$ mechanisms proposed by Evans and Over (1996; see also Evans, chap. 1, this volume) should apply equally to both generation and evaluation formats. Rule-theoretic approaches (e.g., Braine & O'Brien, 1991, Rips, 1994) assume that reasoners apply a set of formal rules to the logical forms of the premises in order to construct a conclusion, and then translate this conclusion back into the original content of the premises. Evaluation necessarily entails the application of the same steps as generation, so there should be no response format asymmetry. In our view, the only other theory that clearly predicts this response format asymmetry is that of Chater and Oaksford (1999). They provide a set of heuristics that operate under a general principle of information gain to generate candidate conclusions which are then evaluated for, and chosen on the basis of, their informativeness. Because this is inherently a generate and test procedure, evaluation would be easier than generation as it involves only the test component.

There are two problems in using evidence from syllogistic reasoning to differentiate between reasoning theories. First, the observed asymmetry is consistent with both model-theoretic and information gain accounts. Second, other theorists might reasonably argue that, although their theory does not specifically predict the asymmetry, an advantage for evaluation over generation would be expected on intuitive grounds. Participants may judge a presented conclusion as being more relevant than a self-generated conclusion, or an evaluation format might make available conclusions that participants would be unlikely to generate for themselves. Evaluation may also have lower demands on memory retrieval, it may allow reasoners to work through a reasoning procedure in both directions, either in parallel or alternating depending on which generates the lowest task demand (cf. Rips, 1994), or it may in some other unspecified way make it easier to apply relevant schemas or heuristics. Thus, an advantage for evaluation over generation does not provide a convincing case for accepting one theory in preference to any other. We suggest that examining response format effects in the rephrasing paradigm may provide a more compelling test of alternative theories than can be gained from syllogistic reasoning, simply because the opposite prediction can be made.

The model-theoretic account of minimal completion makes two key predictions concerning response format effects in rephrasing. First, an evaluation task creates a demand that the participant compare model sets representing the given rule and its rephrasing. To do this, the evaluation format necessitates the construction of two model sets whereas the generation format requires only one model set. Therefore, evaluation performance should be poorer than generation performance, which is precisely the opposite response format asymmetry to that expected on intuitive grounds alone. Second, whereas a generation task should favor rephrasings from conditional to disjunctive, this asymmetry should disappear in an evaluation task, in as much as model sets must be constructed for both the given rule and the putative rephrasing.

There is no reason for any of the theoretical alternatives to mental models to predict response format effects in rephrasing that differ from those found in syllogistic reasoning, nor would they predict a removal of the syntax asymmetry (assuming they could account for it in the first place). A rule-theoretic account would indicate that the same number of steps should apply to evaluating and generating rephrasings, with a possible facilitation for evaluation performance, because the final step is arguably provided by the rephrasing to be evaluated. Information gain should predict that evaluating rephrasings is easier than generating them, since evaluation only involves one stage whereas generation involves both. Finally, under the general intuitive prediction argued earlier, evaluation performance should be the same as, or easier than, generation performance, and so this should also be the prediction of pragmatic reasoning schemas and heuristic accounts.

We conducted three experiments to test our predictions regarding the existence of a task format asymmetry in rephrasing. The first two experiments investigated rephrasing performance in two evaluation formats using the same sentences that Richardson and Ormerod (1997) gave participants in their rephrasing generation study. In Experiment 1, participants were given a rule to read, and then this was removed and a rephrasing was presented for evaluation. Experiment 2 consisted of a multiple-choice evaluation task, in which participants selected from a set of eight possible rephrasings, all those that were semantically equivalent to an original rule. In both experiments, evaluation performance was approximately 25% poorer than generation. Thus the first prediction of minimal completion is confirmed by these results.

The second prediction was also confirmed by the results of Experiment 1, in which no effect of given rule syntax was found. The evaluation format requires the construction of model sets for both rules, so no asymmetry was present. Performance in Experiment 2 was poorest overall, and interestingly, the syntactic form asymmetry found with generation was actually reversed, the evaluation of conditional rephrasings of a disjunctive original being easier than the opposite. Presumably the requirement to construct eight conditional model sets is easier than the construction of eight disjunctive model sets. This again supports the contention that the demands of evaluation are qualitatively different from those of generation, in necessitating the construction of model sets for both original and rephrasing.

Experiment 3 was conducted as a within-subjects comparison of generation against evaluation, using abstract sentences only. It replicated the basic finding of Experiments 1 and 2, while at the same time remedying a number of potential methodological inadequacies of the other experiments. For example, it employed new sentences, to address a potential "language as fixed-effect fallacy" critique discussed by Richardson and Ormerod (1997). Again, the rule format asymmetry was found with generation but not evaluation. Also, the within-subjects design allowed a more sensitive comparison of response format effects, again showing approximately a 25% advantage for generation. In particular, the recording of response time data for both task formats allowed us to dismiss the possibility that the response format effect was simply the result of a speed-accuracy tradeoff: Generation times (22.2 s) were slightly but nonsignificantly longer than evaluation times (19.4 s). Third, during evaluation trials, the given rule remained on the screen whilst the rephrasing was evaluated, thereby removing the memory load that the task format of Experiment 1 generates. Surprisingly, evaluation performance was slightly though nonsignificantly better in the separate presentation format of Experiment 1 than in Experiment 3.

Another difference across the experiments of Richardson and Ormerod (1998) was that a post hoc debriefing took place after Experiment 3, in which participants were encouraged to give an account of which they found to be the easier task format, and how they believed they went about the generation and evaluation of rephrasings. Evidence for strategies in rephrasing is discussed in the next section.

STRATEGIES FOR REPHRASING

We have described evidence favoring the minimal completion account of rephrasing on the assumption that everyone uses the same strategy (for generation, of constructing a minimal representation of the given rule and reading a rephrasing off the representation, and for evaluation, of constructing and then comparing minimal representations of both rules). The generation strategy entails a smaller expansion of the reasoning space than the evaluation strategy. However, there are obviously other ways of tackling these tasks. For example, participants might simply guess, on the assumption they will be correct half the time. Indeed, performance in some tasks is roughly 50% correct. A guessing strategy maximally constrains the reasoning space—it simply is not searched systematically. However, the time taken by participants to generate and evaluate rephrasings, and the accounts they give of their rephrasing performance, lead us to believe that most of the time participants use a more sophisticated, if not particularly more successful, strategy than guessing.

The finding by Ormerod et al. (1993) of a floor effect in rephrasing between "Q if P" and "P only if Q" suggests that participants are capable of coming up with a strategy that is far worse than guessing. In this case, we suggest that participants adopt a strategy that constrains the reasoning space to the given linguistic representations, to which the only operator that can be applied is that of syntactic comparison, in which differences between given and required sentential forms are resolved linguistically. Superficially, the linguistic forms of "Q if P" and "P only if Q" are so similar that participants are prepared to add or drop the word "only" as if it served no function. For example, they would rephrase sentences such as "*It is a mammal only if it is an animal*" as "*It is a mammal if it is an animal.*" As Ormerod et al. (1993) found, the presence of familiar thematic content (participants were rephrasing self-generated rules) was no help in overcoming their difficulties with this rephrasing.

As described earlier, Richardson and Ormerod (1998) conducted a post hoc elicitation of participants' accounts of their own rephrasing performance. The fact that these accounts are post hoc means that they must be treated with caution. Indeed, that participants have imperfect insight into their own performance is well illustrated by the fact that of the 32 participants, 28 claimed the evaluation format was easier for them than the generation format, yet for 20 of these 28 people, their performance was better in the generation format. Notwithstanding these data, it is interesting to review the kinds of strategy that participants described, because it suggests that the construction and testing of mental representations of sentence meaning is only one (albeit a dominant one, in our view) of the strategies that are employed in rephrasing, and by implication, in any other reasoning task that requires the manipulation of sentential forms.

On the basis of post hoc verbal descriptions of the generation of rephrasings, we can divide participants into three broad groups:

Meaning-Based.   This group includes 16 participants whose account outlined a strategy that involved accessing the meaning of the presented sentences. Some of these reported using an imaging strategy. For example, in rephrasing the sentence "*If it is a triangle then it is blue,*" participant four stated "*I tried to imagine blue triangles and triangles that were not blue.*" Others reported using a strategy of considering the possible combinations of antecedent and consequent that the given rule allowed by name rather than by image, and then generating a rephrasing that described these possibilities. Both of these fit in a straightforward way with the minimal completion account. However, some participants appear to have used additional strategic elements to assist in the process of constructing a mental representation of the sentence meaning. For example, one participant stated that "because the first one was about Mary, the manager of a hotel . . . and I found that really easy . . . so for all the others . . . I put Mary as the first bit and the manager job as the second bit . . . and then I imagined whether the rule was making her the manager or someone else. . . ."

Heuristic-Based.   This group includes 10 participants who described a strategy of manipulating sentence components using a heuristic that operates independently of sentence meaning (though eight of these participants also stated that they used a meaning-based approach for some of the trials). This group was less successful in generating rephrasings than the meaning-based group (66% vs. 78%), though they were slightly more successful in evaluating rephrasings (54% vs. 47%). One participant reported using what one might argue is the ideal strategy of counting the negatives in the given rule, and simply making sure that the rephrasing had one fewer or one more (each participant was asked specifically whether they had used such a strategy). Curiously, this participant was not particularly successful in applying this "foolproof" strategy, since he generated only five out of eight rephrasings correctly. The most common strategy, reported by eight participants, was one of trying to reduce the presence of negatives, typically by treating the first component of the sentence as an affirmative case, and then considering the need for a negative in the second component. Only one participant reported using a strategy that bears any relation to the application of logical rules, stating "*I tried accessing the logical structure of the parts of the sentence . . . you know, what implies what else . . . and then seeing if I could get a rule out of it that implied the same things . . . .*" As well as being perhaps somewhat ambiguous in its description, this strategy did the participant no favors, in that he only generated two out of eight rephrasings correctly.

Ambiguous. This group includes eight participants whose verbalizations could not be classified reliably as reflecting either a meaning-based or heuristic-based strategy. No participants reported the extensive use of a guessing strategy.

Participants were also asked what kinds of strategy they used for evaluating rephrasings. Typically, verbalizations were less satisfactory from the point of view of trying to classify them according to strategy (e.g., "*I don't know, I just compared them and sort of saw if they were saying the same or not.*") Participants were asked directly whether they used a strategy of generating their own rephrasing and comparing this against the given rephrasing. Ten participants reported using a strategy similar to this. If participants are employing the mechanism of minimal completion, then this strategy should reduce the task format effect, because it allows them to evaluate by constructing a single model set. It is interesting to note that evaluation performance with these 10 participants was better (though nonsignificantly so) than the other participants. However, this strategy still entails an extra demand of comparing the generated and given rephrasings.

In general, it appears that a majority of participants report using a strategy that is consistent with a model-theoretic approach, though a number do not fit comfortably into this category. What is perhaps most interesting is that, even within each strategy group, there appear to be wide variations in performance. It is as if one can optimize a mechanism such as minimal completion to the current task by adopting extra strategic elements. Conversely, one can also adopt strategies that impair rather than complement the underlying mechanism used for rephrasing.

REPHRASING CONTEXTUAL INFORMATION

So far, we have considered the task of rephrasing between sentences containing arbitrary or unfamiliar content and in pragmatically impoverished contexts. Yet, as a comparison of the two examples given in the Introduction reveals, rephrasing is much easier when sentences describe familiar or meaningful relationships. This is consistent with the large quantities of evidence showing facilitatory effects of familiar thematic content in many reasoning tasks. Facilitation effects are often so great, that some theories dispense with general reasoning mechanisms in favor of contextuallybound heuristics, schemas, or judgment systems (e.g., Cheng & Holyoak, 1985; Gigerenzer & Hug, 1992; Oaksford & Chater, 1994).

The importance of contextual information in rephrasing is nicely illustrated by the work of Cheng and Holyoak (1985, Experiment 3) who used a task of rephrasing between "*if P, then Q*" and "*P only if Q*" conditional forms to test predictions deriving from their pragmatic reasoning schemas theory. They found that rephrasings from "*if P, then Q*" into "*P only if Q*" were facilitated by the presence of content relating to permission statements of the form "*If the action is to be taken, then the precondition must be satisfied.*" This sentence could be rephrased either as "*The action is to be taken only if the precondition is satisfied*" or as "*The precondition must be satisfied only if the action is to be taken.*" The latter rephrasing is, they argue, equivalent to saying "*If the action is not to be taken, then the precondition need not be satisfied.*" This rule, one of four that make up a permission schema in their theory, is not a natural way of rephrasing the original statement, so participants avoid that particular rephrasing.

Although this account may appear adequate at first sight, there are two reasons why it is less than satisfactory. First, their predictions should only apply to the specific rephrasing that they test, since they argue that the effect arises out of the fact that the "*P only if Q*" form emphasises necessity of the consequent for the antecedent. However, we have found the same effect with rephrasings between disjunctives and "*if P, then Q*" conditionals (Ormerod, 1998), a point we discuss in more detail shortly. Second, pragmatic reasoning schemas theory cannot deal with rephrasing in the absence of contextual information, and therefore could not in principle account for either the rule syntax or task format asymmetries discussed in previous sections. Thus the challenge is to develop a theory that can deal with both context-free and context-dependent rephrasing. Manktelow and Over (1991; see also Mantkelow, Fairley, Kilpatrick, & Over, chap. 6, this volume) have argued that model theory is able to deal with deontic contexts such as permission at least as well as pragmatic reasoning schemas theory. Thus, our task is to extend minimal completion to deal with effects of contextual information.

As their critics are keen to point out, neither model theories (e.g., Johnson-Laird & Byrne, 1991) nor rule theories (e.g., Braine & O'Brien, 1991; Rips, 1994) currently offer particularly compelling accounts of how thematic content affects reasoning. Thematic content effects are deeply problematic for rule theorists, who must posit extralogical mechanisms of premise interpretation as their source. Why should it be easier to rephrase "*either it is not raining or we will get wet*" into "*if it is raining, then we will get wet*" than it is to rephrase "*either not P or Q*" into "*if P, then Q*"? Any theory that requires the extraction of an abstract intermediate representation from a thematic sentence as a precursor to applying a reasoning mechanism will struggle to accommodate such a phenomenon. On the face of it, the problem is smaller for model theories, as they allow a role for thematic content in aiding the construction of a meaningful intermediate representation. However, Johnson-Laird and Byrne's (1991) account, as we found to our cost in trying to generate predictions about the effects of thematic content on rephrasing, tends to state *that* thematic content facilitates the construction of mental models, without offering a precise account of *how* it might do so and at what stage in model construction.

In dealing with causality, Johnson-Laird and Byrne (1991) suggested that people rely on their general knowledge that in causal events a consequent does not usually occur in the absence of its antecedent, which directs them to form a biconditional interpretation of causal conditional relationships. They propose that an initial model set is formed which contains two models, one for the actual situations and one for the counterfactual situation (as illustrated by the first causal unfamiliar model shown in Table 7.1). Their account of the effects of familiar content is less explicit, although we can generalize from their account of effects of causality. If causal content completes initial model sets through the representation of general knowledge about causal relationships, then the effect of familiar content is presumably to complete initial model sets through the representation of specific knowledge about familiar instances. In both cases, the completion of model sets happens through two processes: First, the addition of new models that are not already present in the initial model set as a result of representing the sentence syntax, and second, the completion of models that are only partially complete after representing the sentence syntax. It turned out that this account was adequate for the effects of causality but not for those of familiarity on rephrasing performance.

In our experiments on the generation and evaluation of rephrasings, we manipulated both the familiarity and causality of sentence content. Examples of each condition are as follows:

causal familiar:	*If it is raining, then the ground will become wet.*
causal unfamiliar:	*If the isopropanol rises, then the valve will open.*
noncausal familiar:	*If it is a flamingo, then it is pink.*
noncausal unfamiliar:	*If it is iodide, then its schmidt number is 36.*

The results of Richardson and Ormerod (1997, Experiment 1) are summarized in Table 7.2, and the effects of familiarity and causality were replicated in Experiments 1 and 2 of Richardson and Ormerod (1998). As Table 7.2 indicates, although the causality was found to facilitate both rephrasing orders, familiar thematic content facilitated only disjunctive → conditional rephrasings. This interaction between familiarity and rule syntax is problematic for the account of thematic content just offered: If the effect of familiar content were both to add new models to the initial model set and to complete existing partial models, then there should be no reason why familiar content should not also facilitate conditional → disjunctive rephrasings.

Table 7.2.
Data from Richardson and Ormerod (1997, Experiment 1), showing the percentage of rephrasings correctly generated for each rule syntax and content.

		Causal	*Noncausal*
Conditional → disjunctive	Familiar	86	64
	Unfamiliar	85	73
Disjunctive → conditional	Familiar	94	83
	Unfamiliar	67	44

Richardson and Ormerod (1997) proposed a revised model-theoretic account of familiarity effects in rephrasing. In this, the role of familiar content is restricted to completing models that are already partially represented in the initial model set as a result of representing the syntactic structure of the original rule. Familiar thematic content does not add new models to the initial model set. To borrow their example to illustrate the point, being told *"If it is a flamingo, then it is pink"* does not immediately make one think of things that are not flamingos and things that are not pink. Thus, in the absence of any requirement to draw or test a novel conclusion, participants do not retrieve additional models in rephrasing familiar indicative rules such as this. However, given the sentence *"Either it is not a flamingo or it is pink,"* participants are already primed, by the representation of two incomplete models in the initial model set, to retrieve from memory information about things that are not flamingos and things that are pink. Thus, familiarity acts in this case to complete the partial models entailed in representing a disjunctive's syntax.

Altough this appears to be a plausible account of familiarity effects in rephrasing it cannot be complete, because it seems to suggest that familiar content plays only a secondary and relatively minor role in human reasoning. This is clearly not the case, a point illustrated by Manktelow and Over's (1991; see also Manktelow et al., chap. 6, this volume) demonstration of a "perspective effect" on deontic versions of the selection task. They found (Experiments 1 and 2) that they were able to alter radically the card selections made in testing the rule *"If you tidy your room, then you may go out to play"* by giving participants different perspectives. Participants who were given a scenario of the child monitoring whether the mother keeps to her side of the bargain tended to choose the P card ("*I tidied my room*") and the *not Q* card ("*Mother did not let me go out to play*"), whereas participants who were given the scenario of a mother monitoring whether a child follows the rule tended to select the *not P* card ("*I did not tidy my room*") and the Q card ("*Mother let me go out to play*"). One version of a familiar deontic context allows participants to make the logically correct card selections for testing an "*if P, then Q*" rule, whereas another version of the same context leads participants to completely different selections. Clearly, the role of context is fundamental here, and is not accounted for by the completion of partial models in an initial model set.

We are currently conducting a study of the generation of rephrasings between "*if P, then Q*," "*P only if Q*," and their disjunctive equivalents containing thematic content (Ormerod, 1998). Our findings so far show similar effects with deontics to those of Manktelow and Over. In the first experiment, participants generated rephrasings of a given rule using one of the alternative syntaxes. The given rules contained either unfamiliar relationships, or familiar relationships that were deontic (e.g., "*If you are over 18, then you can drink alcohol*") or indicative (e.g., "*If it is a flamingo, then it is pink*"). There are two important findings from this experiment. First, the strongest facilitation was found with rephrasings of deontic sentences from "*if P, then Q*" into "*P only if Q*" (90% correct, compared with 67% in the reverse direction), a finding consistent with the results of Cheng and Holyoak (1985). However, familiar indicative content also facilitated this rephrasing, though more strongly in one direction than the other (from "*if P, then Q*" into "*P only if Q*" = 66%, from "*P only if Q*" into "*if P, then Q*" = 79%, compared with performance on unfamiliar sentences, from "*if P, then Q*" into "*P only if Q*" = 36%, from "*P only if Q*" into "*if P, then Q*" = 48%). Second, rephrasings of deontic sentences between both conditional forms and their disjunctive equivalents were facilitated in both directions by deontic content (ranging between 73% and 78% correct).Although rephrasings between "*Q only if P*" conditionals and their disjunctive equivalents were facilitated by familiar indicative content (from "*Q only if P*" into disjunctive = 72%, from disjunctive into "*Q only if P*" = 69%), this content facilitated only from disjunctive into "*if P, then Q*" rephrasings (80%) and not from "*if P, then Q*" into disjunctive rephrasings (58%).

The results complement those of Manktelow and Over (1991), and extend the study of deontic contexts to the rephrasing paradigm. They also show how a deontic context facilitates performance across all sentence forms, and as such challenge the generality of Cheng and Holyoak's (1985) pragmatic reasoning schemas account of rephrasing. We are currently conducting a second experiment in which we are investigating whether rephrasing generation is affected by perspective, in an extension of Manktelow and Over's method. The results so far indicate that the order in which a rephrasing is generated can be altered by the perspective given to participants. Given a deontic such as "*If you are over 18, then you can drink alcohol,*" participants who are given a law enforcement perspective tend to generate the correct rephrasing "*Either you are over 18 or you cannot drink alcohol,*" whereas participants who are given a rule obeying/violation perspective are much more prone to error, and when they do generate the correct rephrasing, tend to generate it in the form "*Either you are drinking alcohol or you are not over 18.*" One perspective emphasizes conditions for remaining within the law, whereas the other emphasizes possible violating conditions.

How can the account of familiarity offered by Richardson and Ormerod (1997) be reconciled with effects of deontic contexts? The answer seems to be that familiar content plays two very different roles in the construction of a mental model set. In the contextually impoverished task of rephrasing between rules that have indicative contents, familiarity acts merely to complete models that are already represented in the initial model set. There is no additional information, such as a perspective or general knowledge about the reciprocity of actor–agent roles, that makes additional models available. Nor is there any apparent task demand for the participant to consider cases that are not already represented in the initial model set determined by the syntax of the rule to be rephrased. In the case of deontic rules and perspective effects, on the other hand, what is represented in the initial model set goes beyond the syntax of the given rule. The initial model set also includes models that represent important outcomes of deontic relationships. In representing deontic rules where a specific perspective is not established, then the outcomes that are represented depend on general knowledge. For example, with a rule "*if you are over 18, then you can drink alcohol,*" the force of the deontic is to raise awareness of the possibility of not being 18, and the consequences thereof. Where a perspective is established prior to rule presentation, it is the perspective itself that is represented.

This second role of thematic content suggests that additions can be made to an initial model independently of the rule that forms the major premise of a reasoning task. This raises the possibility that participants begin the construction of an initial model set, not at the point where premises are presented, but as soon as there is any information at all which they can usefully represent. In the case of the rephrasing generation task used by Richardson and Ormerod (1997), the syntax of the initial rule provides the first usable piece of information. Thus, the role of familiar indicative content is restricted to completing established models rather than adding new ones. In the case of the perspectives used by Manktelow and Over (1991) and the deontics used in our recent experiments, it is the perspectives themselves that are first represented in an initial model set, the representation of the rule syntax being a secondary (and possibly minor) addition to the model set. Thus, familiar deontic content *can* add new models to the reasoner's representation.

IMPLICATIONS FOR A MODEL THEORY OF REASONING

This chapter has presented an overview of research into the task of rephrasing. In particular, it has examined four main phenomena:

1. *asymmetries in rephrasing from one syntactic form into another*
2. *asymmetries across task response format*
3. *a restricted role for familiar indicative content in rephrasing*
4. *a broader role for causal and deontic contents and perspectives in rephrasing*

The results of the experiments have important implications for choosing between theories of human reasoning. Only a theory that posits the use of intermediate representations and processing stages in reasoning can account for the effects of rule syntax and response format. Of these, a mental models framework offers the most compelling explanation, particularly of task format asymmetries.

We have proposed a model-theoretic account of rephrasing which we term "minimal completion." Although broadly in line with Johnson-Laird and Byrne's (1991) account, it makes specific predictions regarding, first the order in which syntactic and semantic components are added to model sets in the construction of an initial mental representation of a reasoning task, and second, the extent to which initial model set construction is dependent on the reasoner's current goal(s). A general principle of minimal completion is that model construction is pursued only as far as the task demands require it. For example, differences in Modus Tollens acceptance in a conditional truth-table evaluation task and selection of the *not-q* card in the abstract selection task can be accounted for by different demands of the two tasks creating qualitatively different goals for the reasoner in the treatment of Modus Tollens-related cases (Ormerod, 1997).

In the Introduction, an analogy between reasoning and problem solving was proposed, in part as a way of pinning down the elusive term "strategy." In accounting for contextual and task demand effects, it is suggested that reasoning in general, and model theory in particular, might profit from being reconceptualized as problem solving. The representation of premise and contextual information in reasoning parallels the exploration of a problem space. One could take the analogy further, describing premises as dictating the state space of reasoning and contextual information as providing the task environment. Of more interest is the underlying mechanism for developing the reasoning space, because it is here that problem solving may actively learn from reasoning research. We suggest that the process of model construction may be a fundamental representational mechanism for constructing the reasoning space, and it may be that model construction is general to both reasoning and problem solving.

Minimal completion operates to restrict the expansion of the reasoning space to the minimum necessary to satisfy the current goal of the reasoner. As such, minimal completion is satisficing (e.g., Simon, 1981). However, it alone cannot account for how the reasoning space is explored. Again, taking our lead from the problem-solving literature, we suggest that reasoners use strategies to expand or further constrain the reasoning space to a point where operators can be applied. At this point, the account begins to diverge from traditional model theory, because a search for alternative models is fundamental to Johnson-Laird and Byrne's (1991) theory, but here is simply one of a number of possible strategies that the reasoner might apply. Indeed, because it violates the dictates of minimal completion, we suggest it is only under extreme task demands (e.g., where the context of task performance requires absolute certainty about the uniqueness of a conclusion) that the strategy of searching for alternatives will be invoked (see also Evans, chap. 1, this volume; Handley, Dennis, Evans, & Capon, chap. 12, this volume).

In the description of rephrasing offered in this chapter, the main "operator" used to derive rephrasings is to read off a sentence from a model set, though other operators (e.g., linguistic comparison) are feasible. We would go further, to suggest that reading off unique values from model sets is the default operator. However, a consequence of the distinction between the reasoning space, strategies, and operators is that it enables an account to be developed of how reasoners switch between model-theoretic and other forms of reasoning. For example, when I do the Wason selection task, I apply operators to identify and select the P and $not\text{-}Q$ cases regardless of the rule content (perspective effects just don't happen with me!), which incidentally also minimize the expansion of the reasoning space. I know in advance that these operators give me a normatively correct solution, thereby saving embarrassment in front of other reasoning researchers. Similarly, it is feasible if uncommon to learn to apply logical inference rules accurately. These are not accounts of model-theoretic reasoning, but they do not undermine model construction as a representational mechanism, as they are merely describing the choice of operator that is applied. Model-theoretic reasoning in Johnson-Laird and Byrne's (1991) account necessitates developing a reasoning space through model construction, deriving conclusions through applying the "read off" operator, and expanding the reasoning space through strategic search for alternatives. In minimal completion, the process of model construction is mandatory, the "read off" operator is the default though others are available, and the strategy of searching for alternatives is rare.

The application of strategies and the subsequent appropriateness of different operators are in response to the task demands as perceived by the reasoner. Task demands are conceived of as determining the current goal(s) of the reasoner and are a function of both the requested solution type (cf. the goal state of a problem) and the context under which a task is performed (e.g., requirements for accuracy vs. speed of response). An interesting question for further research is how the current goal of the reasoner is itself represented. One possibility is that it acts as a kind of frame for model construction, perhaps even itself being represented as a putative model set whose values are instantiated during task performance. In this sense, the reasoning space contains a representation both of initial (premise information) and goal states (required solution type).

The re-analysis of the minimal completion account of thematic content effects leads to a subtle but potentially important shift of emphasis in model-theoretic accounts of reasoning. All reasoning theories, model theory included, appear to deem the beginning of the construction of a mental representation to be at the point where major or minor premises are provided. However, as the case of perspective effects illustrates, the process of mental representation in general, and of model construction in particular, may be continuous rather than being initiated by the provision of premises. When participants are given a rule to test in the selection task, or a sentence to evaluate or generate in a rephrasing task, after having received a preamble that establishes a perspective, they may already have the model set that determines their task performance. The extent to which premises or further thematic information lead them to extend that model set depends on whether it adds or completes models that are necessary in achieving the current goal of the reasoner. More generally, when participants represent premises, they may be adding these to a partial model set that already represents contextual and goal state information.

REFERENCES

Braine, M. D. S., & O'Brien, D. P. (1991). A theory of If: A lexical entry, reasoning program and pragmatic principles. *Psychological Review, 98,* 182–203.

Chater, N., & Oaksford, M. (1999). The probability heuristics model of syllogistic reasoning. *Cognitive Psychology, 2,* 191–258.

Cheng, P. W., & Holyoak, K. J. (1985). Pragmatic reasoning schemas. *Cognitive Psychology, 17,* 391–416.

Evans, J. S. B., & Over, D. E. (1996). *Rationality and reasoning.* Hove, UK: Psychology Press.

Evans, J. St. B. T, Clibbens, J., & Rood, B. (1995). Bias in conditional inference: Implications for mental models and mental logic. *Quarterly Journal of Experimental Psychology, 48A,* 644–670.

Evans, J. St. B. T., & Lynch, J. S. (1973). Matching bias in the selection task. *British Journal of Psychology, 64,* 391–397.

Fillenbaum, S. (1975). If: Some uses. *Psychological Research, 37,* 245–260.

Gigerenzer, G., & Hug, K. (1992). Domain-specific reasoning: Social contracts, cheating and perspective change. *Cognition, 43,* 127–171.

Hardman, D. K., & Payne, S. J. (1995). Problem difficulty and response format in syllogistic reasoning. *Quarterly Journal of Experimental Psychology, 48A,* 945–975.

Johnson-Laird, P. N., & Byrne, R. M. J. (1991). *Deduction.* Hillsdale, NJ: Lawrence Erlbaum Associates.

Kowalski, R. (1979). *Logic for problem solving.* Amsterdam: North-Holland.

Manktelow, K. I., & Over, D. E. (1991). Social roles in reasoning with deontic conditionals. *Cognition, 35,* 85–105.

Naylor, H., & Hagger, S. (1993). *Paths to proficiency.* Harlow, UK: Longman.

Newell, A., & Simon, H. A. (1972). *Human problem solving.* Englewood Cliffs, NJ: Prentice-Hall.

Oaksford, M., & Chater, N. (1994). A rational analysis of the selection task as optimal data selection. *Psychological Review, 101,* 608–631.

Ormerod, T. C. (1990). Human cognition and programming. In T. R. G. Green., J. M. Hoc, R. Samurçay, & D. J. Gilmore (Eds.), *Psychology of programming* (pp. 63–98). London: Academic Press.

Ormerod, T. C. (1997). Rationalities 1 and 2: Dual processes or different task demands. *Cahiers de Psychologie Cognitive, 16,* 181–189.

Ormerod, T. C. (1998). *Contextual effects in rephrasing.* Manuscript in preparation, University of Lancaster.

Ormerod, T. C., Manktelow, K. I., & Jones, G. V. (1993). Reasoning with three types of conditional: Biases and mental models. *Quarterly Journal of Experimental Psychology, 46A,* 653–677.

Ormerod, T. C., Richardson, J., & Shepherd, A. (1998). Enhancing the usability of a task analysis method: A notation and environment for requirements specification. *Ergonomics, 41,* 1642–1663.

Richardson, J., & Ormerod, T. C. (1997). Rephrasing between disjunctives and conditionals: Mental models and the effects of thematic content. *Quarterly Journal of experimental Psychology, 50A,* 358–385.

Richardson, J., & Ormerod, T. C. (1998). *Response format and reasoning.* Manuscript submitted for publication.

Rips, L. J. (1994). *The psychology of proof.* Cambridge MA: MIT Press.

Shepherd, A. (1993). An approach to information requirements specification for process control tasks. *Ergonomics, 36,* 805–817.

Shepherd, A., & Ormerod, T. C. (1992). *Development of a formal method of user requirements specification for process plant displays.* Report for British Gas plc.

Simon, H. A. (1981). *The sciences of the artificial* (2nd ed.). Cambridge MA: MIT Press.

Swan, M., & Walter, C. (1997). *How English works.* Oxford: Open University Press.

Wason, P. C., & Johnson-Laird, P. N. (1972). *Pychology of reasoning: Structure and content.* Cambridge, MA: Harvard University Press.

8

Spatial Strategies in Reasoning

Merideth Gattis
Caroline Dupeyrat

This chapter describes how spatial strategies may be used in deductive and inductive reasoning. It reports three experiments investigating when and how people construct spatially organized representations for reasoning. People solved either a spatial, temporal, social, or logical problem, and then received either an indirect or a direct probe, aimed at uncovering the underlying representation. The results indicated that during reasoning people use spatial organization to preserve order between elements, to identify relations between dimensions, and to identify polarity within a dimension. Two limitations of spatial strategies were also noted: people did not appear to use spatial strategies to solve conditional reasoning problems, and for all problems, the number of spatial dimensions used for problem organization was extremely limited.

A friend of mine who is an artist recently produced a series of drawings called 24 Hours a Day (Langenhuizen, 1998). In each drawing, green root-like figures stretch horizontally across the page, at times bulbous, and sprouting knobs, at other times narrow and sometimes constricted by black fetters. She explained that the drawings represented the movement of her spirit during the 24 hours in a day. Scanning a drawing from left to right, it was easy to identify the times of growth, times of boredom, and times of pain. I saw that at night, when she is sleeping and dreaming, her spirit has space for roaming, as the roots grew thick and knobby. Daytime also offers opportunities for movement and growth, but at times is constricted, perhaps by duties and obligations. The spatial organization of the drawing, with the 24 hours marked in horizontal intervals, allowed me to quickly infer which times of the day most often lead to growth and which lead to stagnation.

This ability to infer new knowledge from spatial representations of nonspatial information not only helps us interpret drawings and gestures made by others as they communicate, it often leads us to create or adopt spatial representations during difficult reasoning tasks. In this chapter, I will refer to the creation or adoption of a spatial representation during reasoning as a spatial strategy in reasoning. A strategy in reasoning, as defined by Johnson-Laird, Savary, and

Bucciarelli (chap. 11, this volume), is simply a series of steps taken to solve an inferential problem. A spatial strategy is the use of spatial organization during at least one of those steps.

Spatial strategies are often adopted for solving both spatial and nonspatial deductive problems. When Byrne and Johnson-Laird (1989) gave people spatial layout problems such as "*A is on the right of B and C is on the left of B*," and then asked them about the relative location of two of the objects (i.e., *A* and *C*), the results indicated that people were imagining the spatial layout described in the premises, and drawing a conclusion from that model. Similarly, De Soto, London, and Handel (1965) reported that adults given logical reasoning tasks about relations between indefinite entities (e.g., *Tom is taller than Sam* and *John is shorter than Sam*) created mental arrays of items and relations given in the premises (e.g., Tom–Sam–John) to make transitive inferences about the unstated relations (e.g., *Tom is taller than John*). Since that time several empirical studies have suggested that spatial strategies account at least in part for adults' and children's performance on linear syllogisms (Huttenlocher, 1968; Sternberg, 1980; Trabasso, 1975). More recently, other researchers have also suggested that people may solve categorical syllogisms (e.g., inferring that the statements "*all x are y*," and "*all y are z*" yield the conclusion, "*all x are z*," among others) by using a variant of Euler circles, based on an analogy between spatial inclusion and set membership (Ford, 1995, Stenning & Oberlander, 1994; Stenning & Yule, 1997).

A growing body of research on diagrammatic and visual reasoning indicates that spatial strategies play an important role in inductive reasoning as well. Larkin and Simon (1987) demonstrated that reasoning with diagrams in physics and a variety of other domains can lead to faster search and recognition compared to reasoning with sentential representations because diagrams allow reasoners to chunk several steps into one. People also use diagrams and imagined models of physical systems as a form of quasi-empirical evidence to induce rules that are not otherwise available (Schwartz & Black, 1996), relying on correspondences between the imagined model and the real physical system to generate new knowledge. Correspondences also underlie the use of more abstract spatial representations depicting nonspatial concepts. Gattis and Holyoak (1996) found that people made more accurate inferences with spatial representations that preserve structural correspondences between spatial and conceptual relations. Adults comparing rates of change represented by two function lines were more accurate when those rates were represented by the slope of the lines (so that *steeper* equals *faster*) than when they were represented the inverse of the slope (so that *steeper* equals *slower*). Further research shows that young children and adults rely on structural correspondences between spatial and conceptual relations to interpret novel diagrams (Gattis, 1998a, 1998b).

SPATIAL STRATEGIES IN EVERYDAY REASONING

Many studies of spatial strategies in reasoning have involved formal types of reasoning (e.g., conditional or categorical syllogisms) or expert representations (e.g., graphs and other specialized diagrams), but few have examined the role of spatial strategies in informal reasoning. We wondered when and how people use spatial strategies in everyday reasoning tasks, and whether those strategies are similar to those used in logical and scientific reasoning tasks. Because we were interested in the conditions in which people spontaneously construct internal, spatially organized representations for reasoning and problem solving, we looked for tasks in which cultural artifacts and anthropological research collectively indicate that the majority of individuals in a culture, and even multiple cultures, commonly use space for abstract reasoning and problem solving. We chose two domains in which spatial organization is well-documented: time (Boroditsky, 1998) and social values (Needham, 1973). We asked people to solve a spatial, temporal, social, or logical problem either in the context of a narrative (Experiments 1 and 2), or in reference to themselves (Experiment 3), with the spatial and logical problems serving as cases against which the social and temporal problems could be compared. In all three experiments, problem solving was followed by either an indirect or a direct probe aimed at uncovering the underlying problem representation (Gattis & Dupeyrat, 1997, 1998).

Reasoning in a Narrative Context

Experiments 1 and 2 used a fictional narrative to provide a context for problem solving. The narrative introduced spatial, temporal, and social facts relevant to the main character and which were relevant to solving the subsequent problems. The narrative began, "*Anne walks in the front door of her house. In her left hand is a letter. The letter is from her lover. She reads*" and followed the character through several rooms in her house, and through thoughts of a personal dilemma between her marriage and a lover as well as many time constraints on her schedule. The narrative ended, "*At that moment, the phone rings. She walks to the bedroom to answer the phone. Hello?*" Immediately following the narrative, all participants were given either a spatial, temporal, social, or logical problem to solve.

The spatial problem was to identify the location of a letter mentioned several times in the narrative in different physical locations: "*On the other end, she hears the voice of her lover. 'We need to talk. Do you have the letter?'*" She looks down and realizes she doesn't. Where could the letter be?" Because prior research demonstrates that identifying a lost object involves coordinating and updating information about spatial relations (de Vega, 1994; Franklin & Tversky, 1990), we reasoned that using such a problem provided a standard against which representations for more abstract, nonspatial problems could be compared.

The temporal problem was to identify an open time slot in the main character's very busy schedule for an appointment: "*On the other end, she hears the voice of her lover. 'We need to talk. When do you have a couple of hours free?' She knows she is busy now. When does she have time to see him?"* This problem involves the coordination of ordered relations which may be organized linearly (a continuous, linear stream of events for any given time period) or two-dimensionally (events organized hierarchically, e.g., day and time of day). A case study of one brain-damaged patient (Clarke, Assal, & de Tribolet, 1993) suggests that temporal planning problems may involve the construction and scanning of an internal, two-dimensional spatial representation, and that when unable to construct such a two-dimensional representation, humans resort to a less efficient linear construction. We wondered whether most people create spatial representations for temporal planning, and whether those people doing so would organize temporal information linearly or two-dimensionally.

The social problem involved choosing between two relationships, both of which had a variety of positive and negative qualities described in the narrative: *"On the other end, she hears the voice of her lover. 'We need to talk. Will you leave your husband?' She realizes she needs to make a decision. What should she do?"* This problem involves organizing and evaluating multiple pieces of information, much like the spatial and temporal problems, but the essential relations may be best characterized as oppositional rather than ordered. We wanted to compare problems containing oppositional and ordered relations because anthropological studies (Hertz, 1909/1973; Needham, 1973) indicate that in many cultures, space plays an important role in the organization of social reasoning, particularly reasoning about oppositions.

The logical problem was a conditional syllogism concerning the identity of the caller: *"At the other end, she hears the voice of John. If John asks about the letter, then John is Anne's lover. John doesn't ask about the letter. What can you conclude?"* Because conditional syllogisms, like the previous problems, require the coordination of several pieces of information, and because nothing can be validly concluded from this information, we considered this problem about equal in difficulty to the other three problems. We used this comparison to examine whether space plays a role in reasoning about conditional relations, which are neither clearly ordered nor clearly oppositional. Although conditional problems can be diagrammed spatially, and some have suggested spatial strategies for solving such problems, we reasoned that people would be less likely to use spatial strategies in a problem domain which is neither ordered nor oppositional, nor contains inherently spatial relations.

After solving one of the four problems, each person received either an indirect or a direct probe aimed at uncovering the underlying representation. The indirect probe (Experiment 1) was a card-sorting task. Participants were given 55 cards containing each statement from the narrative and from the target problem and were instructed, *"Sort the cards in a way that helps you solve the problem."* Participants who selected a subset of the cards and retained that subset in their hands were scored as having used a nonspatial solution strategy, as were those who selected a subset of the cards and placed that subset in a single stack on the table. Participants who further divided the subset and created any spatial arrangement (i.e., two opposing stacks, or a linear order of five cards) on the table were scored as having used a spatial solution strategy. The results were as follows:

Spatial problem:	*60% created a spatial organization.*
Temporal problem:	*43% created a spatial organization.*
Social problem:	*57% created a spatial organization.*
Logical problem:	*0% created a spatial organization.*

The spatial organization constructed by participants solving the spatial problem was usually one-dimensional (see Figure 8.1). Linear spatial organization often reflected a sequence of locations to be searched, and sometimes deviated from the linear organization of the text. For example, if the kitchen, laundry room, and bedroom were mentioned in that order in the text, some participants organized them in some other order, for instance, bedroom, kitchen, and laundry room, and identified that order as the ideal search order.

Participants solving the temporal and social problems, in contrast, usually created a two-dimensional spatial organization. The solutions given for these two problem types were very similar, indicating that participants often conflated temporal and social information, perhaps due to the compelling nature of the social problem in the narrative. Two-dimensional organizations of cards were usually divided into several categories or dimensions relevant to the problem (such as "time," "work," or "dreams") and then divided into oppositions or polarities, which were often explicitly marked as positive and negative (see Figure 8.2). In stark contrast to the other three problem conditions, none of the participants given the logical problem created a spatial organization with the cards.

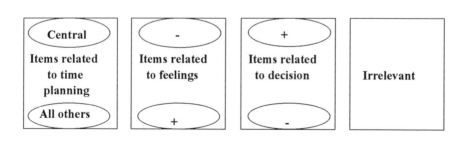

FIG. 8.1. A typical one-dimensional arrangement of cards produced by a participant who solved the spatial problem, "*Where could the letter be?*," in Experiment 1.

As she reads, she walks upstairs to the bedroom.	She closes the laundry door and walks upstairs to the kitchen.	She opens the patio door to let some fresh air into the house.	She walks to the bedroom to answer the phone.	Where could the letter be?

FIG. 8.2. A typical two-dimensional arrangement of cards produced by a participant who solved the temporal problem, "When does she have time to see him?," in Experiment 1. The descriptive labels were provided by the participant.

The card-sorting task thus allowed us to measure the frequency and type of spatial organizations used in different reasoning problems. The most striking results were the selective use of one-dimensional or two-dimensional space according to problem type (ordered, oppositional, or neither), and the explicit oppositional labeling of the ends of dimensions as positive and negative.

In order to gather more detailed information about spatial strategies in reasoning, we collected self-reports from new participants in the same reasoning contexts as Experiment 1. Collecting self-reports from participants has the advantage of both broadening (by revealing general patterns) and narrowing (by supplying counterexamples) initial hypotheses. In fact, the earliest studies of spatial strategies for reasoning were reports of participants' introspections about their reasoning strategies in logical reasoning tasks (De Soto et al., 1965), and these later facilitated more traditional experimental investigations of spatial strategies in reasoning (e.g., Huttenlocher, 1968).

The direct probe used in Experiment 2 was a series of retrospective questions about the reasoning process, which followed the narrative in written form. After solving either the spatial, temporal, social, or logical problem, participants were asked, "Was the problem you just solved a mostly verbal task or a mostly visual task?" Those who answered "mostly visual" were then asked to draw and label the image they used to solve the problem, and finally to select which of four common diagrams most resembled their problem representation, a two-dimensional table, a network/path, a hierarchy, or a Venn diagram. The results, largely consistent with the indirect probe, were as follows:

Spatial problem:	86% said the problem was visual.
Temporal problem:	35% said the problem was visual.
Social problem:	48% said the problem was visual.
Logical problem:	21% said the problem was visual.

Significantly, of those who reported that the logical problem was visual, only one person produced a visual representation of the logical problem; the remaining people represented some other aspect of the narrative rather than the syllogism itself. Because those drawings did not depict the syllogism, we did not analyze their content further.

Participants solving the spatial problem nearly always drew an image of objects in a physical environment. This image frequently depicted the spatial framework within which the main character moved, and highlighted locations that might be searched for the lost letter, as seen in the diagram of a house layout produced by one participant (Figure 8.3). Fitting with the idea of a sequence of possible locations where the letter might be found, most participants solving the spatial problem reported that their image of the problem resembled a network/path diagram.

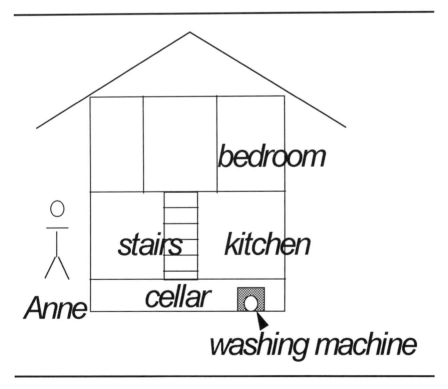

FIG. 8.3. Reproduction of a drawing made by a participant who solved the spatial problem, "*Where could the letter be?*," in Experiment 2. The person who drew this diagram identified the mental image as similar to a network/path.

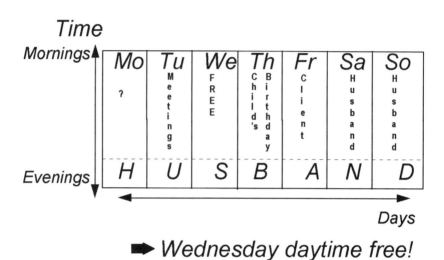

FIG. 8.4. Reproduction of a drawing made by a participant who solved the temporal problem, "*When does she have time to see him?*," in Experiment 2. The participant identified this image as a matrix.

In contrast to the concrete images produced by participants solving the spatial problem, participants solving the temporal problem drew abstract representations, using space to depict non-spatial relations (for one example, see Figure 8.4). As in Experiment 1, however, the drawings of many participants solving the temporal problem indicated that they had conflated the temporal and social problems, rather than separating the two

Participants solving the social problem also drew abstract representations which frequently used space to depict nonspatial relations. The most common type of drawing divided space into two regions representing two options: the protagonist's husband, work, and family responsibilities versus her potential life in a new place with her lover (see Figure 8.5). People in both the temporal and social conditions, as in the other two conditions, also reported that their image of the problem resembled a network/path. The narrative context appears to have played some role in this choice, perhaps because mental models constructed from narratives often depict movements of a character through a sequence of locations (de Vega, 1994; Franklin & Tversky, 1990).

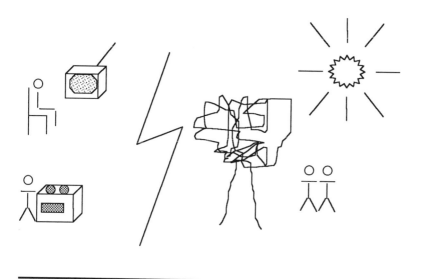

FIG. 8.5. Reproduction of a drawing made by a participant who solved the social problem, "What should she do (about her relationships)?," in Experiment 2. This image utilizes oppositional space, as is clearly demonstrated by the jagged dividing line in the center, but was identified as a network/path.

In general the results of the direct probe were consistent with the results of the indirect probe, both in terms of frequency and type of spatial organization. Spatial organization was most common with the spatial problem, least common with the logical problem, and moderately common for temporal and social problems. People again used one-dimensional or two-dimensional space selectively according to problem type, although two-dimensional organizations were more frequent in the spatial condition in Experiment 2 than in Experiment 1. People also used oppositional space to denote positive and negative values, as illustrated in Figure 8.5, similar to the valence labeling found in Experiment 1.

One difficulty with the results of Experiments 1 and 2 is that some people in the temporal, logical, and spatial conditions produced drawings that seemed to represent the social dilemma as well as the assigned problem. Because we wanted to create a situation in which people in all four conditions started with approximately the same set of complex information, and to ask how, once given a problem, they organized that information, all participants were given the same initial narrative. As a result, many participants appeared to have focused on the most memorable aspect of the story: the dilemma of choosing between husband and lover. Despite the obvious differences between the results of the four conditions, people tended to produce solutions and drawings that combined information relevant to the different problems, and thus diluted our efforts to find out how spatial representations and strategies vary according to problem type. Because we wanted to be certain about the differences in spatial strategies for different problem types, we designed a third experiment asking people to solve similar problems with reference to their own lives, rather than a fictional character's.

Reasoning in a Self-Referential Context

In Experiment 3 participants were asked to imagine a problem as their own. The spatial problem was, "*Imagine that you lost an object in your house. How would you search for it?*" The temporal problem was, "*Imagine that I would like to make a 3-hour appointment with you next week. How would you decide when you have time?*" The social problem was, "*Imagine that you are in a relationship, and meet someone new. How would you decide with whom you should stay?*" Because the results of Experiments 1 and 2 indicated that spatial strategies do not play a large role in solving conditional reasoning problems, we did not include a logical syllogism in Experiment 3. Instead, we created a new problem concerning a dilemma between two jobs, which we thought would serve as an interesting comparison against the social problem. The work problem was, "*Imagine that you have received two job offers, both of them interesting. How would you decide which job you should take?*" The work problem thus shared a similar structure to the social problem, but had less personal emotional content.

Following one of these four problems, participants were given the same direct probe used in Experiment 2, containing a series of questions about whether the problem was mostly verbal or mostly visual, drawing and labeling the image, and selecting which one of four diagrams most resembled their problem representation. The results were as follows:

Spatial problem:	87% said the problem was visual.
Temporal problem:	58% said the problem was visual.
Social problem:	43% said the problem was visual.
Work problem:	56% said the problem was visual.

The self-reference problems had the desired effect of producing more clearly differentiated results in the different experimental conditions. Whereas in Experiments 1 and 2 participants had tended to include extraneous information in their reasoning representations, in Experiment 3 the basis of spatial organization for the spatial problem was the search path (Fig. 8.6), for the temporal problem was temporal information (Fig. 8.7), and for the social and work problems was comparative information about two possibilities (Figs. 8.8 and 8.9, respectively). As in the previous two experiments, spatial organization for the spatial problem was often one-dimensional, and two-dimensionally organized representations often highlighted the linear sequence of a search path. Spatial organization for the other three problems was usually two-dimensional, mostly strikingly so for the temporal problem, since the comparative use of oppositional space often found in the social and work problems could be said to contrast two locations in only one dimension of space, while the spatial organization of temporal information was clearly two-dimensional.

The diagrams reported to resemble the mental image of participants in each of the four conditions was similarly well-differentiated. Those solving the spatial problem said their image resembled a network/path, those solving the temporal problem said their image resembled a matrix, those solving the social problem said their image resembled a Venn diagram, and those solving the work problem said their image resembled a network/path.

Overall the results were quite consistent across all three experiments: A majority of participants used spatial representations for reasoning about spatial problems, about half for temporal and social/comparative problems, and very few for logical problems. From these and other results, several characteristics and limitations of spatial strategies emerge. These will be described further in the next two sections.

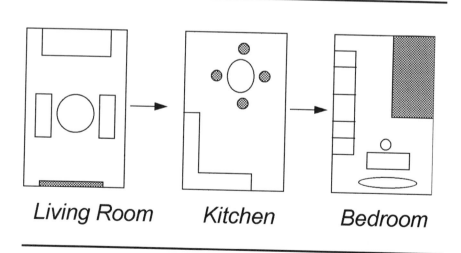

Living Room   Kitchen   Bedroom

FIG. 8. 6. Reproduction of a drawing made by a participant who solved the spatial problem, "How would you search for it (a lost object)?," in Experiment 3. This image was identified as a network/path.

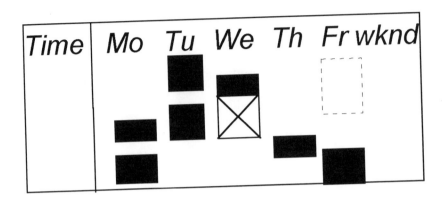

FIG. 8.7. Reproduction of a drawing made by a participant who solved the temporal problem, "*How would you decide when you have time?*," in Experiment 3. This image was identified as a matrix.

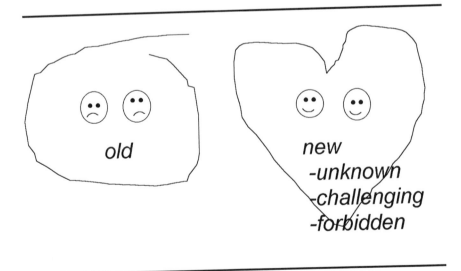

FIG. 8.8. Reproduction of a drawing made by a participant who solved the social problem, "*How would you decide with whom you should stay?*," in Experiment 3. This image was identified as a Venn diagram.

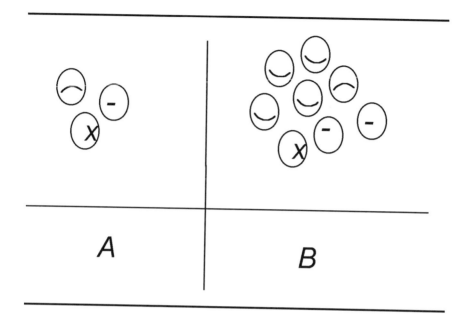

FIG. 8.9. Reproduction of a drawing made by a participant who solved the work problem, *"How would you decide which job you should take?,"* in Experiment 3. This image was identified as a network/path.

WHY DO PEOPLE USE SPATIAL STRATEGIES IN REASONING?

People use spatial strategies in reasoning because spatial representations are very effective for integrating information, and reasoning is often a matter of integrating multiple pieces of information. Once we have identified the relevant information, and integrated it, we can simply check the resulting problem representation for appropriate inferences. Finding the appropriate spatial representation for a problem is not straightforward, however, as illustrated by the confusing figures found in many textbooks and scientific papers! The experiments described earlier, combined with other research, indicate that during reasoning people use spatial organization to perform three basic functions: to preserve order between elements, to identify relations between dimensions, and to identify polarity within a dimension.

To Preserve Order

To reason accurately, we often need to maintain or infer ordered relations between several elements. Unfortunately, maintaining multiple ordered relations places a high demand on working memory, and thus limits inference. Because spatial relations are explicit, using ordered space to represent ordered elements facilitates reasoning by making explicit those relations which would otherwise need to be inferred. For example, a spatial model containing a linear order in which A is to the left of B and B is to the left of C also explicitly represents that A is to the left of C. In the earlier experiments, people most often used spatial representations to preserve order when reasoning about space and when reasoning about time. A sequence of spatial locations to be searched was often represented in a one-dimensional spatial organization (see also Figs. 8.1 and 8.6), whereas temporal sequences were organized hierarchically and two-dimensionally, often with horizontal space ordered by days of the week and vertical space ordered by time of day (see also Figs. 8.4 and 8.7). Ordered space was also used to convey importance, as can be seen for example in Fig. 8.2, in which one participant ordered several dimensions horizontally according to relevance to the problem being solved.

Ordered space is particularly useful for reasoning about transitive relations, and not surprisingly, many studies have investigated the role of spatial strategies in transitive reasoning. A relation is transitive when the relation between stimuli a and b, aRb, and between stimuli b and c, bRc, is also true for stimuli a and c, aRc. Combining the first two premises to infer the relationship between a and c, aRc, is called transitive inference. Because the relation between a and c has not been stated or observed, arriving at the correct answer requires a deductive process of some sort. De Soto et al. (1965) proposed that this deduction is based on the internal construction of ordered spatial representations, such as linear arrays, to represent stated conceptual relations. When a reasoner constructs a linear spatial array, ABC, to represent ordered conceptual relations of elements, abc, inferencing about implicit conceptual relations can be based on explicit spatial relations.

Despite its appealing simplicity, the idea that transitive inference and other forms of reasoning about orders are based on the use of a mental spatial array has had a controversial history, largely due to arguments that linguistic phenomena including markedness can explain performance patterns more accurately and more parsimoniously (Clark, 1969). However, many studies of transitive inference in non-human animals concern nonverbal relations (e.g., Boysen, Berntson, Shreyer, & Quigley, 1993; Davis, 1992; Gillan, 1981; McGonigle & Chalmers, 1977; Roberts & Phelps, 1994). In these studies, animals are trained to discriminate between object pairs in which one object is rewarded and the other not. When tested on non-trained pairs, animals' choice patterns indicate that the premise pairs are integrated in some way that allows transitive inferences about non-presented pairs. Comparative psychologists have observed that linguistic explanations of human transitive performance seem less suited to nonhuman transitive performance, and this breach again raises the question of whether spatial coding may in fact play a role in transitive performance in both humans and other animals (Davis, 1992; Roberts & Phelps, 1994). Recent research with children indicates that linearly ordered space may indeed play an important role in transitive reasoning. Schnall and Gattis (1998) presented young children with reward–nonreward relations between four overlapping pairs of elements (A through E) which were either organized in a linear spatial order, or in a random spatial order. On a subsequent test of a non-presented pair (B and D), children in the linear order condition chose transitively, whereas children in the random order condition did not. Schnall and Gattis concluded that when ordered space corresponds to ordered relations, children readily use available spatial relations to make subsequent inferences.

To Identify Relations Between Dimensions

We often need to reason about relations that are more complex than a single set of ordered relations, such as the relationship between two different orders of the same set of elements, or orders of different elements across different dimensions. Spatial representations are particularly useful in such situations because space has more than one dimension, and the integrated nature of multiple spatial dimensions can be exploited to coordinate multiple conceptual dimensions. Spatial representations of temporal information are a familiar example of how naturally multiple spatial dimensions can be used to coordinate conceptual dimensions and identify the relations between them. The drawings seen in Figs. 8.4 and 8.7, for instance, use vertical and horizontal space to organize two temporal dimensions (day of the week and time of day), and to identify the hierarchical relation between them. The frequent use of two-dimensional space to convey hierarchical temporal relations does not appear to be accidental: In addition to the neuropsychological study mentioned earlier (Clarke et al., 1993), other psychological studies of the organization of temporal memory indicate that temporal information is hierarchically rather than sequentially organized. Huttenlocher, Hedges, and Prohaska (1992) asked people about the time of occurrence of a past event and compared participants responses to a categorization model that predicted boundary and prototype effects if temporal organization is indeed hierarchical. The resulting errors indicated that memory for past events utilizes a multiple-entry, hierarchically organized representation rather than a sequential, timeline representation.

Spatial dimensions convey other types of conceptual relations as well, by relying on structural correspondences between spatial and conceptual relations. Gattis (1998a) asked young children with no experience with graphs or related representations to reason about quantity or rate using graph-like diagrams. Children were asked to map time and quantity to horizontal and vertical lines, and then taught to integrate those values to form "a story line" (a function line in conventional Cartesian graphs) representing a quantity changing across time. When asked to judge the quantity represented by one story line relative to another, children's judgments corresponded to the height of the line: Children judged the higher of two lines as representing greater quantity, and the lower of two lines as representing lesser quantity. In contrast, when asked to judge the rate represented by one story line relative to another, children's judgments corresponded to the slope of the line. Regardless of the relative heights of the lines, children reported that the steeper line represented a faster rate, and the shallower line represented a slower rate. Young children thus inferred quantity from height and rate from slope, indicating that they can exploit structural correspondences between spatial and conceptual relations to distinguish between relations between elements and relations between relations. The ability to use spatial relations judiciously to reason about conceptual relations thus appears to support the use of spatial strategies by adults and children alike.

To Identify Polarity Within a Dimension

Perhaps the most surprising result in these experiments was the frequency with which people marked card arrangements or diagrams with positive and negative valences. This was most common in the social problem and the work problem, both of which involved comparison of two possibilities. The drawings shown in Figs. 8.5, 8.8, and 8.9 were typical of such oppositions: Right and left divisions of space were used to characterize the contrast between two options, and those options were then assigned positive and negative values.

In what may be one of the earliest discussions of spatial metaphor, Hertz (1909/1973) proposed that the organic asymmetry of the human body that leads to right-handedness in a majority of humans also provides a metaphor for social constructs, such as the oppositions between good and evil, superior and inferior, light and darkness, sacred and profane. Since then, numerous anthropological studies of the dual classification of social values attest to the prevalence of a right–left organizational scheme for social communication and reasoning in many cultures (Needham, 1973). The pervasiveness of this mapping is also witnessed by the double meanings of right and left in many languages to refer to political and social orientation, and by the evaluative phrases "on the one hand . . . on the other hand" and their accompanying spatial gestures. More recent cross-cultural studies of spatial representation systems, however, indicate that the right–left scheme is not a privileged spatial scheme. Instead, it is the concept of opposition, including not only egocentrically defined points, such as right and left, but also allocentrically defined points, such as north and south, which often organizes spatial conception (Levinson & Brown, 1994).

In addition to its influence on language via directional metaphors, the concept of opposition also plays a role in the organizational structure of conceptual dimensions. The linguistic organization of dimensions into oppositions is referred to as polar grading or polarity (Sapir, 1944). Many oppositions are asymmetric in character, such as *"good"* and *"bad,"* or *"long"* and *"short,"* and this asymmetry in polarity is known as marking (Clark, 1969; Greenberg, 1966). For each of these adjective pairs, the first term, called the positive or unmarked term, is more general, and can refer neutrally to the dimension itself, as well as to the positive end of that dimension. The second term in each pair is marked, in that it derives its meaning from its relation to the first term, and refers only to the negative end of the dimension.

The idea that linguistic marking of direction influences reasoning was first proposed as a counterargument to discussions of spatial coding in transitive inference. Clark (1969) argued that because unmarked adjectives like *good* can be interpreted in the neutral nominal sense, comprehending them does not always require reference to the opposite and negative end of the dimension. As a result, they are less complex and more easily retrieved from memory. Clark argued that this difference in ease of comprehension and retrieval better accounted for performance on linear syllogisms than contemporaneous theories of spatial arrays.

Interestingly, however, the polarity of dimensions clearly precedes linguistic organization of thought. Smith and Sera (1992) demonstrated that young children are sensitive to the polarity of dimensions before they acquire the linguistic polarity implicit in marking structure, and that perceptual polarity and linguistic polarity interact in a complex pattern across development. In a nonlinguistic cross-dimensional matching task, 2-year-olds not only paired *"big"* with *"more"* (both positive and unmarked terms) and *"small"* with *"less"* (both negative and marked terms), but also paired *"dark"* with *"big"* and *"light"* with *"small,"* even though *dark* and *light* are not an unmarked-marked pair. Older children and adults, in contrast, did not pair *dark–light* with *big–small* in a reliable pattern, indicating that the acquisition of linguistic polarity influences perceptual polarity.

Perceptual and linguistic polarity may interact in many reasoning tasks involving visuospatial representations, though the question is as yet relatively unexplored. Gattis (1998a) noted that children asked to judge the rate or quantity represented by function lines judged the steeper of two lines as *"faster,"* and the shallower of two lines as *"slower,"* and correspondingly the higher of two lines as *"more,"* and the lower of two lines as less. Children's verbal responses thus matched the perceptual polarity of the stimulus, even though the words *"steeper,"* *"shallower,"* *"higher,"* and *"lower"* were never used in the experiment. Furthermore, when children were asked to explain their answer, although they identified many different perceptual differences such as height, slope, length, width (which were often in fact erroneous), the adjective chosen (i.e., *longer*) always corresponded in markedness to their answer on the judgment task (i.e., *faster*). This suggests that polarity may influence the interpretation and creation of spatial representations during reasoning in subtle, even implicit ways of which we are as yet unaware.

CONSTRAINTS ON SPATIAL STRATEGIES

An important alternative approach to understanding spatial strategies is not only to understand how they benefit cognition, but also understanding how they do not help, or how they are limited. In the experiments reported here, two limitations of spatial strategies were noted: People did not appear to use spatial strategies to solve conditional reasoning problems, and for all problems, the number of spatial dimensions used for problem organization was extremely limited.

Limited Forms of Reasoning

An interesting prospect raised by the principle of ordered space is that for reasoning problems in which maintaining ordered relations is not essential, the use of ordered space may be less useful, and therefore might be less frequently observed. This conjecture is supported by the results of the experiments described before. In Experiments 1 and 2, people frequently used spatial strategies to solve spatial, temporal, and social problems, but not for solving conditional syllogisms.

These results are consistent with results of other studies using a very different method, a dual-task paradigm, to investigate the role of visuospatial working memory in reasoning. In this paradigm, in addition to a primary reasoning task, adults perform one of several secondary tasks assumed to utilize various components of working memory. Vandierendonck and De Vooght (1997) asked adults to solve linear syllogisms about spatial or temporal relations and at the same time to tap in a spatial pattern, repeat a string of digits, or shadow a random pattern. All three tasks decreased reasoning performance on linear syllogisms compared to a control condition in which no secondary task was performed. Vandierendonck and De Vooght concluded that reasoning about linear orders, regardless of whether those orders are spatial or temporal, involves visuospatial working memory during premise uptake, and suggested that this may reflect the construction of an internal spatial array.

In contrast, Toms, Morris, and Ward (1993) reported that neither of two tapping tasks interfered with accuracy or speed of syllogistic reasoning about conditional relations, but a memory-load task (repeating a random string of digits) did interfere. Toms, Morris, and Ward concluded that reasoning about conditional relations does not involve visuospatial working memory. Similarly, Gilhooly, Logie, Wetherick, and Wynn (1993) reported that a spatial tapping task did not interfere with syllogistic reasoning about categorical relations, but random number generation did interfere. Gilhooly et al. concluded that people use heuristic strategies, such as matching qualifiers (i.e., *all* or *some*), rather than visuospatial memory to solve categorical syllogisms. Together the results of these studies suggest that spatial representation may play an important role in reasoning about ordered relations, such as spatial or temporal linear orders, but a lesser role in reasoning about nonordered relations, such as conditional or categorical relations.

Limited Dimensions of Space

Although many examples of efficient and accurate reasoning with spatial representations have been discussed here, it is important to note that all of the research discussed here appears to have involved one and two-dimensional spatial representations. The spatial representations created for reasoning about spatial, temporal, and social problems were always one or two-dimensional organizations. In both the indirect and direct probe tasks, people solving the spatial problem (locating a lost object) usually created a one-dimensional organization, a sequence of locations to be searched (see Figs. 8.1 and 8.6). People solving the social and work problems (choosing between two relationships) also frequently produced one-dimensional organizations (Figs. 8.5, 8.8, and 8.9) which were divided into two opposing spaces (i.e., right and left). The remaining representations were always two-dimensional. Significantly, participants never created three-dimensional organizations; when problem solvers produced three-dimensional images, these were drawings of single scenes rather than novel organizations of conceptual information.

There are many reasons to doubt that spatial strategies are as fruitful with three-dimensional representations. Imagery research demonstrates that people have difficulty maintaining and manipulating internal spatial representations of more than two dimensions (Kerr, 1993; Kosslyn, 1980). When asked to image either a two-dimensional matrix or a three-dimensional matrix, and imagine a route through that matrix as specified by a sequence of directional terms, people prefer slower presentation rates of directional terms for three-dimensional matrices, and faster presentation rates impair performance more dramatically for people imagining three-dimensional matrices than those imagining two-dimensional matrices (Kerr, 1993). These and other similar results have been taken as evidence that spatial mental imagery is not inherently three-dimensional, and have led to the formulation of *array theories* of imagery, which propose that mental imagery is constructed from the activation of two-dimensional arrays (Kosslyn, 1980; Tye, 1991). According to array theories, information about three-dimensional spatial relations can be extracted from two-dimensional arrays, but doing so requires additional time and computation, and is likely to lead to characteristic error patterns. Array theories and related experimental work on the internal construction and manipulation of spatial representations thus propose an important constraint on imagery which may in turn constrain spatial strategies in reasoning: The actual internal representation is likely limited to two dimensions, and representing information about additional dimensions is difficult and costly.

Research on reasoning with internal and external spatial representations also indicates that spatial strategies in reasoning are more effective with extremely limited spatial dimensions. Wright (1977) asked adults to solve transportation problems involving multiple variables with either a one-dimensionally organized table or a two-dimensionally organized table. Use of the two-dimensional table led to more judgment errors than the one-dimensional table. Wright concluded that the increased number of dimensions led to increased errors because a two-dimensional table required the integration of decisions from two dimensions, whereas the one-dimensional table allowed reasoners to make decisions about each dimension sequentially. Surprisingly, these sequential judgments from one-dimensional tables were not due to any kind of speed–accuracy tradeoff: Reasoning speed was not affected by the number of spatial dimensions. These results indicate that spatial representations may benefit reasoning most when limited to one-dimensional spatial organization.

Strict bounds on imagery capacity thus appear to lead to limited use of the dimensionality of space in reasoning. In some sense, the ideal spatial representation for reasoning seems to be one-dimensional, because every additional dimension adds processing demands and errors. The studies reported here, in concert with other work, indicate that when constructing internal spatial representations for reasoning, reasoners usually create spatial organizations limited to one or two dimensions. These bounds may in turn lead us to create external spatial representations for reasoning, which can overcome computational and memory limitations.

UNDERSTANDING STRATEGIES THROUGH GENERAL PRINCIPLES

This chapter identifies three principles influencing the use of spatial strategies in reasoning, and two constraints which may limit the use of spatial strategies. People use spatial representations during reasoning to preserve order between elements, to identify relations between dimensions, and to identify polarity within a dimension. People appear to be less likely to use spatial strategies for reasoning about relations that are neither ordered nor oppositional, and more generally, people use only limited spatial dimensions during reasoning.

The idea that understanding strategy use in reasoning involves general principles may at first seem puzzling, as it contradicts the notion that strategies exist only where general processing mechanisms do not. According to the latter notion, cognition may be explained either by fundamental processing mechanisms which are thought to be uniformly true across individuals and time, or by strategies that are seen as complementary but external to fundamental mechanisms (see, e.g., Roberts, chap. 2, this volume). The division of cognition into uniform and fundamental processes versus varying and acquired processes implies that the acquisition and implementation of strategies is less fundamental to cognition.

However, the notion that strategies are not fundamental to cognition contradicts an important fact about cognition, namely that cognition is remarkably flexible: Many tasks can be performed by multiple processes, and when all existing processes fail, new processes can be acquired. The flexible and manifold nature of cognition suggests that to understand how the mind works, we must understand the many paths it takes. This suggests that uniformity will be found not in a single path or mechanism but in the principles and constraints influencing all paths. For this reason, we have focused on general principles and constraints influencing the use of spatial strategies in reasoning. Rather than identifying when people use spatial (as opposed to verbal) strategies and representations, these three principles, preserving order between elements, identifying relations between dimensions, and identifying polarity within a dimension, broadly describe how space is used in reasoning. As such, these principles characterize the spatial strategies used by humans with a wide variety of age and experience, across many reasoning tasks.

REFERENCES

Boroditsky, L. (1998). Evidence for metaphoric representation: Understanding time. In B. Kokinov (Ed.), *Advances in analogy research: Integration of theory and data from the cognitive, computational, and neural sciences* (pp. 308–319). Sofia, Bulgaria: New Bulgarian University.

Boysen, S. T., Berntson, G. G., Shreyer, T. A., & Quigley, K. S. (1993). Processing of ordinality and transitivity by chimpanzees *(Pan troglodytes)*. *Journal of Comparative Psychology, 107*, 208–215.

Byrne, R. M. J., & Johnson-Laird, P. N. (1989). Spatial reasoning. *Journal of Memory and Language, 28*, 564–575.

Clark, H. (1969). Linguistic processes in deductive reasoning. *Psychological Review, 76*, 387–404.

Clarke, S., Assal, G., & de Tribolet, N. (1993). Left hemisphere strategies in visual recognition, topographical orientation and time planning. *Neuropsychologia, 31*, 99–113.

Davis, H. (1992). Transitive inference in rats *(Rattus norvegicus)*. *Journal of Comparative Psychology, 106*, 342–349.

de Vega, M. (1994). Characters and their perspectives in narratives describing spatial environments. *Psychological Research, 56*, 116–126.

De Soto, C. B., London, M., & Handel, S. (1965). Social reasoning and spatial paralogic. *Journal of Personality and Social Psychology, 2*, 513–521.

Ford, M. (1995). Two modes of mental representation and problem solution in syllogistic reasoning. *Cognition, 54*, 1–71.

Franklin, N., & Tversky, B. (1990). Searching imagined environments. *Journal of Experimental Psychology: General, 119*, 63–76.

Gattis, M. (1998a). *Structure-driven mapping in visual reasoning*. Manuscript submitted for review.

Gattis, M. (1998b). Mapping conceptual and spatial schemas. In B. Kokinov (Ed.), *Advances in analogy research: Integration of theory and data from the cognitive, computational and neural sciences* (pp. 210–220). Sofia, Bulgaria: New Bulgarian University.

Gattis, M., & Dupeyrat, C. (1997). *Using space to organize reasoning and problem solving*. (Paper No. 1997/4). Munich, Germany: Max Planck Institute for Psychological

Research.

Gattis, M., & Dupeyrat, C. (1998) *Using space to organize reasoning.* Manuscript in preparation.

Gattis, M., & Holyoak, K. J. (1996). Mapping conceptual to spatial relations in visual reasoning. *Journal of Experimental Psychology: Learning, Memory, and Cognition, 22,* 231–239.

Gilhooly, K. J., Logie, R. H., Wetherick, N. E., & Wynn, V. (1993). Working memory and strategies in syllogistic reasoning tasks. *Memory & Cognition, 21,* 115–124.

Gillan, D. J. (1981). Reasoning in the chimpanzee II: Transitive inference. *Journal of Experimental Psychology: Animal Behavior Processes, 7,* 150–164.

Greenberg, J. H. (1966). *Language universals.* The Hague, Netherlands: Mouton.

Hertz, R. (1973). The pre-eminence of the right hand: A study in religious polarity. In R. Needham (Ed. and Trans.), *Right & left* (pp. 3–31). Chicago: University of Chicago Press. (Original work published 1909)

Huttenlocher, J. (1968). Constructing spatial images: A strategy in reasoning. *Psychological Review, 75,* 550–560.

Huttenlocher, J., Hedges, L. V., & Prohaska, V. (1992). Memory for day of the week: A 5 + 2 day cycle. *Journal of Experimental Psychology: General, 121,* 313–325.

Kerr, N. H. (1993). Rate of imagery processing in two versus three dimensions. *Memory & Cognition, 21,* 467–476.

Kosslyn, S. M. (1980). *Image and mind.* Cambridge, MA: Harvard University Press.

Langenhuizen, E. (Artist). (1998). 24 Stunden pro Tag (Drawings). (Available from Ellie Langenhuizen, Kunstpark Ost, Grafingerstrasse 6, 81671 Munich, Germany)

Larkin, J. H., & Simon, H. A. (1987). Why a diagram is (sometimes) worth ten thousand words. *Cognitive Science, 11,* 65–99.

Levinson, S. C., & Brown, P. (1994). Immanuel Kant among the Tenejapans: Anthropology as empirical philosophy. *Ethos, 22,* 3–41.

McGonigle, B., & Chalmers, M (1977). Are monkeys logical? *Nature, 267,* 694–696.

Needham, R. (Ed.). (1973). *Right & left.* Chicago: University of Chicago Press.

Roberts, W. A., & Phelps, M. T. (1994). Transitive inference in rats: A test of the spatial coding hypothesis. *Psychological Science, 5,* 368–374.

Sapir, E. (1944). Grading, A study in semantics. *Philosophy of Science, 11,* 93–116.

Schnall, S., & Gattis, M. (1998). Transitive inference by visual reasoning. In M. A. Gernsbacher (Ed.), *Proceedings of the 20th Annual Conference of the Cognitive Science Society.* Hillsdale, NJ: Lawrence Erlbaum Associates.

Schwartz, D. L., & Black, J. B. (1996). Shuttling between depictive models and abstract rules: Induction and fallback. *Cognitive Science, 20,* 457–498.

Smith, L. B., & Sera, M. D. (1992). A developmental analysis of the polar structure of dimensions. *Cognitive Psychology, 24,* 99–142.

Stenning, K., & Oberlander, J. (1994). Spatial inclusion and set membership: A case study of analogy at work. In K. J. Holyoak & J. A. Barnden (Eds.), *Analogical connections: Advances in connectionist and neural computation theory, Vol. 2* (pp. 446–486). Norwood, NJ: Ablex.

Stenning, K., & Yule, P. (1997). Image and language in human reasoning: A syllogistic illustration. *Cognitive Psychology, 34,* 109–159.

Sternberg, R. J. (1980). The development of linear syllogistic reasoning. *Journal of Experimental Child Psychology, 29,* 340–356.

Toms, M., Morris, N., & Ward, D. (1993). Working memory and conditional reasoning. *Quarterly Journal of Experimental Psychology, 46A*, 679–699.

Trabasso, T. (1975). Representation, memory, and reasoning: How do we make transitive inferences? In A. D. Pick (Ed.), *Minnesota symposium on child psychology, Vol. 9* (pp. 135–172). Minneapolis: University of Minnesota Press.

Tye, M. (1991). *The imagery debate*. Cambridge, MA: MIT Press.

Vandierendonck, A., & De Vooght, G. (1997). Working memory constraints on linear reasoning with spatial and temporal contents. *Quarterly Journal of Experimental Psychology, 50A*, 803–820.

Wright, P. (1977). Decision making as a factor in the ease of using numerical tables. *Ergonomics, 20*, 91–96.

9

Strategies of Constructing Preferred Mental Models in Spatial Relational Inference

Reinhold Rauh

A reanalysis of the preferred mental models to indeterminate three-term series problems with Allen's (1983) interval relations as determined by Knauff, Rauh, and Schlieder (1995) revealed two kinds of general strategies people apply in constructing these preferred mental models. Furthermore, in asking (i) whether there are domain-specific strategies in the construction of initial solutions to indeterminate inference problems, and (ii) whether the abstract model construction strategies were replaced or just overlaid by domain-specific strategies, the results of a further experiment with the same problems contextually embedded and solved under two social perspectives showed that solution times for tasks where the perspective-relevant solution conformed to the abstract preferred mental model were significantly shorter than for the other tasks. This suggests that the two observed abstract model construction strategies were effective and that they were not replaced by domain-specific strategies.

In investigating representations and processes underlying relational inference, there is much evidence best explained in the framework of mental model theory (see, e.g., Evans, Newstead, & Byrne, 1993, chap. 6). This is also true in the special case of spatial relational inference (e.g., Byrne & Johnson-Laird, 1989). In a series of experiments conducted within our research project MeMoSpace (an acroynym for *Mental Models in Spatial Reasoning*), we were able to confirm many older findings (like premise order effects, term order effects) and gain some new evidence on various aspects of spatial relational inference with the help of a special set of qualitative spatial relations that is described in more detail shortly (Knauff, Rauh, & Schlieder, 1995; Knauff, Rauh, Schlieder, & Strube, 1998a, 1998b; Rauh, Schlieder, & Knauff, 1997; Rauh & Schlieder, 1997).

With the mental model theory (Johnson-Laird, 1983) as a general framework, we refer to the three phases of deduction distinguished by Johnson-Laird and Byrne (1991), that is, comprehension, description, and validation, as the phases of model construction, model inspection, and model variation. In the phase of model construction the reasoner builds an integrated representation of the situation the premises describe, that is, the mental model. This mental model can then be inspected for relationships that are not explicitly given in the premises. The third phase, the phase of model variation, comes into play if the inference task demands checking other models of the premises; this is the case in deductive inference where the reasoner has to determine whether there are other models of the premises that contradict a putative conclusion, or in verification tasks to check for the possibility of relationships between entities.

One could hypothesize that, in general, people do not only reason using mental models but that they also come up with the same initial model(s), or as we prefer to say, with the same preferred mental model of the premises. And indeed, empirical evidence for the existence of preferred mental models was gained (Knauff et al., 1995; see also Handley, Dennis, Evans, & Capon, chap. 12, this volume). These preferred mental models play an important role in the further course of reasoning because they are inspected first and are the basis of the inspection for putative conclusions. Thus, they are one important factor for facilitating or suppressing certain inferences and are one possible source of reasoning errors and cognitive biases (e.g., Byrne & Johnson-Laird, 1990). Therefore, it seems desirable to investigate the process of model construction in as much detail as possible and check for interindividual differences and/or different strategies (e.g., Roberts, 1993; see also Roberts, chap. 2, this volume).

Although the concept of a strategy is widely used, different authors seem to have different meanings in mind. Therefore, I briefly characterize the notion of *strategy* that will be used in the following. In the literature, strategy is sometimes used in a more objective sense, stating "*different ways to do things*," like solving a problem by using algorithm A, or by algorithm B, or maybe by applying heuristic C. Therefore, the mere existence of systematic qualitative individual differences justifies the use of the word strategy (e.g., Roberts, 1993). In contrast to this usage, I would like to use the concept strategy only for those cases where an information processing system has more than one method at its disposal to solve a certain task. Used this way, individual differences do not necessarily imply the existence of different mental strategies: Each individual may have only one method to solve a task, albeit different to that of another individual.

In principle, one can ask whether all processes within the three phases of reasoning are the same for all participants for all the tasks that can be constructed from a set of primitives. If this were the case, then there would be no systematic interindividual differences and no strategies in reasoning for this set of tasks, and a parsimonious theory of reasoning could be established. Evidence about the existence of systematic interindividual differences in reasoning is beyond doubt. Ford (1994), for example, found evidence for the two groups of *verbal* and *spatial* reasoners in syllogistic inference tasks. However, whether there are different strategies employed by the same participant across a set of inference tasks is still an open question.

Given these terminological distinctions that entail possible sources of variability, many combinations and interactions are conceivable. For example, there could be different strategies employed by all participants in the same way during the construction of a preferred mental model for a whole set of inference tasks. Model inspection could be the same for all participants and the whole set of tasks. And, in the phase of model variation, there could be interindividual differences with respect to the whole set of inference tasks, that is, one group using elaborated annotations to their preferred mental model thus enabling them to come up with many more models of the premises than another group of participants. More complicated combinations and interactions of strategies and interindividual differences across the three phases of inference can be easily conceived.

In the following, I concentrate on the process of model construction and report on the reanalysis of results from a former experiment conducted by Knauff et al. (1995) on whether there is evidence for the existence of strategies during the phase of model construction.

Another important issue to be addressed is the question of whether domain-specific knowledge is always a determining factor in the process of model construction. Many theories of reasoning claim that reasoning is always domain-specific (Cheng & Holyoak, 1985), and some even argue that this cannot be otherwise due to evolutionary reasons (e.g., Cosmides & Tooby, 1992).

Prior to presenting some evidence on whether or not we found systematic interindividual differences or different strategies that govern the construction of preferred mental models in spatial reasoning, I give a short overview on the material that is the basis for the set of inference tasks in our experiments. Afterward, I present an experiment that should answer the question whether or not putative model construction strategies found in the abstract version of the inference tasks are replaced by domain-specific strategies.

MATERIAL FROM RESEARCH ON QUALITATIVE SPATIAL REASONING

In our investigations on spatial relational inference, we used and still are using a set of qualitative relations from the Artificial Intelligence subfield of Qualitative Spatial Reasoning, namely the interval relations of Allen (1983). These relations have clear geometric semantics and the calculus is well understood from the algorithmic point of view. Additionally, the clear geometric semantics of these relations can be taught to people very easily. Thus, we can avoid what Evans (1972) called the interpretation problem in studies of reasoning, namely that the results of human reasoning deviates from the researcher's expectation because of a different understanding of the premises on the part of the participant compared to the semantics underlaid by the experimenter.

Allen's calculus is based on intervals, qualitative relations between these intervals, and an algebra for reasoning about relations between these intervals. First, Allen (1983) distinguished thirteen qualitative jointly exhaustive and pairwise disjoint relations describing the relative position of two intervals on a line: *"before"* (<) and its inverse *"after"* (>), *"meets"* (m) and *"met by"* (mi), *"overlaps"* (o) and *"overlapped by"* (oi), *"finishes"* (f) and *"finished by"* (fi), *"during"* (d) and *"contains"* (di), *"starts"* (s) and *"started by"* (si), and *"equal"* (=) that has no inverse. Table 9.1 gives pictorial examples of these relations and the English translations of the German natural language expressions we used in all our experiments. Additionally, the point ordering of startpoints and endpoints that define the geometrical semantics of the interval relations are listed. The first column also specifies the relation symbols that were originally introduced by Allen (1983) as a kind of shorthand notation for qualitative relationships between intervals in time.

Table 9.1.
The 13 qualitative interval relations, associated natural language expressions, graphical realization, and ordering of startpoints and endpoints (adapted and augmented according to Allen, 1983).

Relation symbol	Natural language description	Graphical realization	Point ordering (s = startpoint; e = endpoint)
X < Y	X lies to the left of Y		$s_x < e_x < s_y < e_y$
X m Y	X touches Y to the left		$s_x < e_x = s_y < e_y$
X o Y	X overlaps Y from the left		$s_x < s_y < e_x < e_y$
X s Y	X lies left-justified in Y		$s_y = s_x < e_x < e_y$
X d Y	X is completely in Y		$s_y < s_x < e_x < e_y$
X f Y	X lies right-justified in Y		$s_y < s_x < e_x = e_y$
X = Y	X equals Y		$s_x = s_y < e_y = e_x$
X fi Y	X contains Y right-justified		$s_x < s_y < e_y = e_x$
X di Y	X surrounds Y		$s_x < s_y < e_y < e_x$
X si Y	X contains Y left-justified		$s_x = s_y < e_y < e_x$
X oi Y	X overlaps Y from the right		$s_y < s_x < e_y < e_x$
X mi Y	X touches Y at the right		$s_y < e_y = s_x < e_x$
X > Y	X lies to the right of Y		$s_y < e_y < s_x < e_x$

Using these relations, one can construct n-term series problems like the following three-term series problem:

X is completely in Y.
Y is completely in Z.

When omitting the somewhat trivial relation "*equal*," one can construct 12 x 12 = 144 three-term series problems, half of them are determinate. The remaining 72 indeterminate problems fall into four classes: 42 problems with three possible solutions (models) between X and Z, 24 with five possible solutions (models), three problems with nine solutions (models), and three problems with 13 solutions (models). The complete composition table, specifying all the possible relationships between X and Z, given the relationship between X and Y, and that of Y and Z, can be found in Allen (1983).

On the basis of this rich set of three-term series problems, one can observe whole reasoning performance "profiles" of participants across these 144 tasks. Using these profiles, the commonalities and differences as described in the previous section can be uncovered.

ABSTRACT MODEL CONSTRUCTION STRATEGIES

In a previous experiment, we investigated whether or not all or at least a significant majority of participants generate the same initial solution to the 72 indeterminate three-term series problems and whether or not there are systematic interindividual differences in constructing a preferred mental model (Knauff et al., 1995; Rauh et al., 1997). Because the experimental procedure is nearly identical to the one in the following section, it is described in more detail.

The experiment was divided into three phases: In the definition phase the participants read definitions of the interval relations. For each interval relation, they were also shown a graphical example as in Table 9.1. In the learning phase participants read a one-sentence description of the relationship between a red and blue interval (e.g., *the red interval lies to the left of the blue interval*) and then had to graphically localize the blue interval with respect to the red interval. The learning phase lasted as long as it took the participant to give three consecutive correct answers to each interval relation. Thus, the learning phase should guarantee that participants acquired the geometric semantics of the interval relations, providing an answer to the above mentioned interpretation problem. In the inference phase participants first read two premises stating the relation between a red and a green interval as the first premise, and the relation of the green interval to a blue one as the second. Then, the participant had to specify one possible relationship between the red and the blue intervals.

One of the main results was that most participants generated the same initial solution to indeterminate three-term series problems (for a complete table of these preferred solutions and error rates, see Knauff et al., 1995). Figure 9.1 shows a table where the rows denote the interval relation of the first premise, and columns denote the relation symbol of the second premise. In corresponding table cells, there is the relation symbol of the solution the majority of participants drew.

	<	m	o	fi	di	si	s	d	f	oi	mi	>
<	<	<	<	<	<	<	<	<	o,< o,<	o	o	=
m	<	<	<	<	<	m	m	o	o	o	=,fi	oi,> >,oi
o	<	<	<	<,< <,o	m,o o,o	o	o	o	o^b	=	oi	>
fi	<	m	o	fi	di	di	o	d,o d,d	=^{c},fi	oi	oi	>
di	<	o	o	di	di	di	o	=^{d}	oi	oi	oi	>
si	<	o	o	di	di	si	=,s	d,oi d,d	oi	oi	mi	>
s	<	<	o	o	fi,di o,di	si	s	d	d	oi	mi	>
d	<	<	o	o	=	oi	d	d	d	oi	>	>
f	<	m	o	fi	oi^e	oi	d	d	f	oi,> oi,oi	>	>
oi	<,o <,<	o	=	oi	mi,oi oi,oi	mi,< oi,oi	d,oi oi,oi	oi	oi	>	>	>
mi	<,o <,o	si	oi	mi	>	>	oi	oi	mi	>	>	>
>	=	oi	oi	>	>	>	oi,> oi,>	>	>	>	>	>

FIG. 9.1. Comparison of empirical preferred solutions from Knauff et al. (1995; upper left cell corner), and Kuß (1998; upper right), and the predictions of the cognitive modeling of Schlieder (in press; lower left) and the cognitive modeling of Berendt (1996; lower right). Shaded cells correspond to indeterminate three-term series problems. Only where differences exist, the table cell entry was subdivided.
a. In Knauff et al. (1995), the interval relation d was equally frequently drawn.
b. In Knauff et al. (1995), the interval relation d was equally frequently drawn.
c. In Knauff et al. (1995), the interval relation f was equally frequently drawn.
d. In Kuß (1998), the interval relation di was equally frequently drawn.
e. In Knauff et al. (1995), the interval relation di was equally frequently drawn.

Because concordance of generated solutions to the 72 indeterminate three-term series problems was not perfect, we were looking for homogeneous subgroups of participants, producing similar patterns of inferences over these 72 indeterminate three-term series problems. Computing various cluster analyses over these responses did not reveal any homogeneous subgroups of people coming up with similar response profiles; instead all participants deviated from the mean response pattern to some degree.

Regarding strategies during the phase of model construction, there was evidence that participants apparently solved appropriate three-term series problems by (a) avoidance of point singularities, that means that startpoints or endpoints of intervals did not coincide, unless they are forced to be equal by a premise relation, and by (b) linearization of the intervals which means that in the case of the startpoint of interval X being left of the startpoint of interval Z, then the endpoint of X is also located left of endpoint of Z (and vice versa). Two different cognitive modelings of preferred mental models exist in which these two principles are described: Berendt (1996) calls (a) the "regularization principle," Schlieder (in press) refers to (b) as the "linearization principle." Both principles are also the basis for a suggested combination of both computational theories within one cognitive architecture (Schlieder & Berendt, 1998).

Take for example the following indeterminate three-term series problem where both principles happen to be realizable:

X overlaps Y from the left.
Y overlaps Z from the left.

Participants avoided drawing the relationship where X touches Z at the left as the initial solution (regularization principle), and most of the participants localized the interval Z to the right of X and not overlapping from the left (linearization principle).

The regularization principle was motivated by Berendt's (1996) mental imagery account to produce stable interpretations of mental images, whereas in Schlieder's (in press) cognitive modeling the linearization principle is incorporated in order to come up with a representation that allows for chunking startpoints and endpoints, which further permits a hierarchical search in which the model can be inspected at the interval level, descending to the point level only where necessary.

But interestingly, there were solutions to certain tasks that did not conform to these two principles in general, and violated the regularization principle in particular: Three-term series problems with one interval relation in the first premise and its inverse relation in the second premise were mostly solved by drawing a configuration in which "X *equals* Z" was valid—thus violating the regularization principle to the greatest extent.

As one can easily verify in Fig. 9.1 (three-term series problem with the inverse relation of the relation in the first premise are in the secondary diagonal of the table, emphasized by double lined table cells), in 9 out of 12 cases, the majority of participants drew a configuration in which X equals Z as the initial solution; in the other three cases the "equal" relation was the second preferred one, and even the most frequently drawn relation had at least one pair of points coinciding (X si Z or X fi Z), although there were other solutions that would have had no points coinciding. This pattern of results was replicated by Kuß (1998) with a slightly different drawing procedure (deviating preferences are listed in the upper right corner of table cell in Fig. 9.1). The results of the studies from Knauff et al. (1995) and Kuß (1998) are given in Fig. 9.1 together with the predictions of the two cognitive modelings of Schlieder (in press; lower left corner of table cell) and Berendt (1996; lower right corner of table cell).

To sum up, we found nearly the same pattern of inferences for all participants, but we found some variation within each participant, in that they answered inference problems differently when in the second premise the inverse relation of the relation in the first premise was used.

One obvious interpretation for this finding is that "equalizing" two objects (intervals) in a spatial configuration can reduce the complexity of the representation of the mental model and the complexity of processes when augmenting the mental model by further incoming information and inferences upon them. This can be seen as another instance of chunking and maybe accomplished by some sort of annotation or "mental footnote" in the mental model indicating that one mental entity can be handled exactly like another one (see Habel, 1998, for a discussion on how annotation can be accomplished in pictorial representations).

This indicates that there are at least two kinds of general strategies that govern the construction of initial solutions–preferred mental models in spatial relational inference tasks: (a) the equalizing of intervals when a relation and its inverse are used; (b) otherwise a strategy that conforms to the principles of regularization and linearization.

MODEL CONSTRUCTION STRATEGIES: DOMAIN-UNRELATED OR DOMAIN-SPECIFIC?

Having found that most participants generate the same initial solution to indeterminate three-term series problems that can be explained by a model construction process that incorporates at least two abstract model construction strategies, we were interested in first, whether there are domain-specific strategies in the construction of initial solutions to indeterminate inference problems, and second, whether the abstract model construction strategies were replaced or just overlaid by domain-specific strategies. Therefore, we conducted another experiment where the inference tasks were contextually embedded (details are given in Rauh & Kuβ, 1998). Because there is evidence that not only the content but also the social perspective is important (Gigerenzer & Hug, 1992), we induced also two different social perspectives to our participants (see the following).

As with the experiment of Knauff et al. (1995), the experiment of Rauh and Kuβ (1998) was also divided into three phases: The definition phase and the learning phase were identical to the ones described earlier. In the inference phase, there were three blocks. The first block consisted of the three-term series problems in abstract form. In the other two blocks, we embedded our three-term series problems in a cover story where participants had to specify one possible relationship between chemically contaminated regions of a river, either from the perspective of an owner of a chemical firm who only had to fulfill certain legal restrictions or from the perspective of an ecologist trying to detect environmental risks.

The cover story from the perspective of the ecologist was as follows (modifications of the cover story from the perspective of the owner of the chemical firm are given in brackets):

Imagine yourself as an ecologist [owner of a chemical firm]. At a straight section of a river there is a [your] chemical plant that lets out three different chemicals into the river at different places.

There are several measuring stations and filter devices situated at weirs along this section of the river. Each filter device is specialized for absorbing exactly one of the chemicals and is able to establish a constant concentration of the substance in a confined section of the river.

The three chemicals are colorless and odorless. Because some indicator tests turn the first chemical into a red color, the second one into green, and the third one into blue, we will refer to these chemicals as the "red substance," the "green substance," and the "blue substance," respectively. Contaminated sections of the river will be referred to as "red sector," "green sector," or "blue sector."

As an ecologist [owner of the chemical firm] you receive information from the measuring stations about the relative location of contaminated sectors. Due to technical reasons, you will only receive information about the relationship of the "red sector" to the "green sector," and of the "green sector" to the "blue sector."

From an ecologist's point of view there is an environmental risk if the "red sector" and the "blue sector" overlap. For this reason, there is a law stopping further effluents and even the production of the [your] chemical plant, if, according to the information from the measuring stations, there is undoubtedly a contamination of the river with the red and the blue substance.

Your task is to determine a possible relationship between the red sector and the blue sector given the information you receive from the measuring stations. Please indicate one possible relationship between the red and the blue sectors.

Indeterminate three-term series problems were selected so that the solution would or would not conform to the preferred mental model in the study of Knauff et al. (1995) depending on the social perspective of the participant. Take for example the two premises of the following indeterminate three-term series problem:

The red sector overlaps the green sector from the left.
The green sector overlaps the blue sector from the left.
How could the red and the blue sector lie to each other?

In this case, the ecologist should come up with a mental model where the red sector overlaps the blue sector from the left, whereas the chemical firm owner should come up with a solution where the red sector does not overlap the blue sector, thus obeying the (rather liberal) law and letting the production in his chemical plant continue. As one can verify easily from Fig. 9.1, the preferred mental model for the abstract condition is "*X lies to the left of Z*," which is also the relevant relationship from the "economy perspective" (see Fig. 9.2 for diagrams of supposed mental models in the abstract condition from Knauff et al., 1995, and the two induced perspectives).

Out of the 72 indeterminate three-term series problems there are 35 tasks that have relationships with overlapping and non-overlapping regions as solutions, that means they have critical solutions from both social perspectives. Fifteen of these 35 tasks have preferred solutions that are relevant for the "economy" perspective, the other 20 being relevant for the "ecology" perspective.

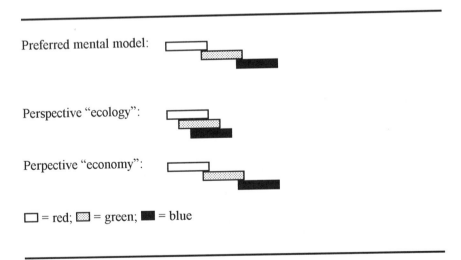

Preferred mental model:

Perspective "ecology":

Perpective "economy":

□ = red; ▨ = green; ■ = blue

FIG. 9.2. The relevant relationships of the first (red sector) and the third (blue sector) from the perspective of the ecologist and from the perspective of the economist. For this indeterminate three-term series problem the preferred mental model from the abstract condition is a relevant solution from the "economy" perspective.

That the induction of either of the two perspectives is possible has been demonstrated in a former between-subjects experiment conducted by Kuβ (1998). In all but one of the 35 cases the participants in the ecology perspective produced an initial solution where a relationship between the red and the blue sector included an environmental risk (overlapping regions) whereas the participants in the "economy" condition produced initial solutions in all 35 cases that did not violate the legal restriction (non-overlapping regions).

In the experiment of Rauh and Kuβ (1998), 20 participants first solved these 35 three-term series tasks (with 10 other practice and distractor trials) in the abstract condition, and afterwards in the two social perspective conditions (the order of social perspective conditions were counterbalanced across participants).

Comparing the solution times (drawing latencies) of three-term series tasks that conformed either to the preferred mental model (PMM+) or not (PMM-) for both social perspectives revealed the following results: There was no interaction in the 2 x 2 ANOVA with repeated measurements, and there was also no main effect of social perspective. But, as one can see in Figure 9.3, there was a main effect for the factor "concordance with the abstract preferred mental model."

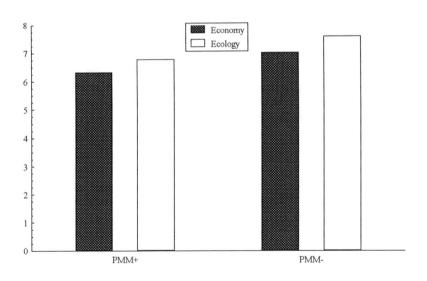

FIG. 9.3. Drawing lattencies for solutions of three-term series problems that were either compatible with domain-specific solutions or not.

Solution times for tasks where the perspective-relevant solution conformed to the abstract preferred mental model were reliably shorter (6.55 s) than for those tasks where the perspective-relevant solution did not conform to it (7.29 s). This suggests that the afore-mentioned abstract model construction strategies were effective and that they were not replaced by domain-specific strategies.

CONCLUSIONS

We have been able to show that within the set of inference tasks that are obtainable from the interval relations as its primitives most (maybe all) people treat a certain subset of tasks differently than others: Three-term series problems that incorporate in the second premise the inverse qualitative spatial relation of the relation of the first premise were answered in a way that the end terms were identical. This results in a reduction of the complexity of the mental representation of the mental model and thus freeing working memory resources for augmenting the mental model if new information has to be incorporated or in a facilitation of all the inferences where these two objects are involved.

It is an open question whether this result is only obtainable with this special set of spatial relations or whether it suggests a property of all relational reasoning with a set of relations that also contain their inverses.

We were able to show for one context (contaminated regions of a river) and two different social perspectives (economist v. ecologist) within this context that the observed preferences in the abstract condition of model construction were not replaced but just overlaid. This does not mean that heavy experience and expertise in one domain (and with one social perspective) could never result in domain-specific strategies for model construction. But what our results seem to indicate is that context-independent strategies exist which are causally effective in facilitating or suppressing valid inferences. This point must be taken into account by a general theory of reasoning and thinking, and presents a challenge to all approaches that favor content-dependent/domain-specific reasoning procedures (Cosmides, 1989; Gigerenzer & Hug, 1992).

ACKNOWLEDGMENTS

This research was supported by the German National Research Foundation (Deutsche Forschungsgemeinschaft; DFG project MeMoSpace under contract no. Str 301/5-1 to Gerhard Strube, Christoph Schlieder, and Reinhold Rauh). I would like to thank Thomas Kuβ for his extensive help in implementing the computer-aided experiment and for running the experiment, and Christoph Schlieder for fruitful discussions concerning strategies in reasoning. Thanks also to Nick Ketley for his helpful comments on an earlier draft of this chapter and to four reviewers for their suggestions.

REFERENCES

Allen, J. F. (1983). Maintaining knowledge about temporal intervals. *Communications of the ACM, 26*, 832–843.

Berendt, B. (1996). Explaining preferred mental models in Allen inferences with a metrical model of imagery. In G. W. Cottrell (Ed.), *Proceedings of the 18th Annual Conference of the Cognitive Science Society* (pp. 489–494). Mahwah, NJ: Lawrence Erlbaum Associates.

Byrne, R. M. J., & Johnson-Laird, P. N. (1989). Spatial reasoning. *Journal of Memory and Language, 28*, 564–575.

Byrne, R. M. J., & Johnson-Laird, P. N. (1990). Remembering conclusions we have inferred: what biases reveal. In J. -P. Caverni, J. -M. Fabre, & M. Gonzales (Eds.), *Cognitive biases* (pp. 109–120). Amsterdam: Elsevier Science Publishers.

Cheng, P. W., & Holyoak, K. J. (1985). Pragmatic reasoning schemas. *Cognitive Psychology, 17*, 391–416.

Cosmides, L. (1989). The logic of social exchange: Has natural selection shaped how humans reason? Studies with the Wason selection task. *Cognition, 31*, 187–276.

Cosmides, L., & Tooby, J. (1992). Cognitive adaptations for social exchange. In J. H. Barkow, L. Cosmides, & J. Tooby (Eds.), *The adapted mind: Evolutionary psychology and the generation of culture* (pp. 163–228). Oxford: Oxford University Press.

Evans, J. St. B. T. (1972). On the problem of interpreting reasoning data: Logical and psychological approaches. *Cognition, 1*, 373–384.

Evans, J. St. B. T., Newstead, S. E., & Byrne, R. M. J. (1993). *Human reasoning. The psychology of deduction*. Hove, UK: Lawrence Erlbaum Associates.

Ford, M. (1994). Two models of mental representation and problem solution in syllogistic reasoning. *Cognition, 54*, 1-71.

Gigerenzer, G., & Hug, K. (1992). Domain-specific reasoning: Social contracts, cheating, and perspective change. *Cognition, 43*, 127–171.

Habel, C. (1998). Piktorielle Repräsentationen als unterbestimmte räumliche Modelle [Pictorial representations as underdetermined spatial models]. *Kognitionswissenschaft, 7*, 58–67.

Johnson-Laird, P. N. (1983). *Mental models. Towards a cognitive science of language, inference, and consciousness*. Cambridge, UK: Cambridge University Press.

Johnson-Laird, P. N., & Byrne, R. M. J. (1991). *Deduction*. Hove, UK: Lawrence Erlbaum Associates.

Knauff, M., Rauh, R., & Schlieder, C. (1995). Preferred mental models in qualitative spatial reasoning: A cognitive assessment of Allen's calculus. In J. D. Moore & J. F. Lehman (Eds.), *Proceedings of the 17h Annual Conference of the Cognitive Science Society* (pp. 200–205). Mahwah, NJ: Lawrence Erlbaum Associates.

Knauff, M., Rauh, R., Schlieder, C., & Strube, G. (1998a). Continuity effect and figural bias in spatial relational inference. *Proceedings of the 20th Annual Conference of the Cognitive Science Society* (pp. 573–578). Mahwah, NJ: Lawrence Erlbaum Associates.

Knauff, M., Rauh, R., Schlieder, C., & Strube, G. (1998b). Mental models in spatial reasoning. In C. Freksa, C. Habel, & K. F. Wender (Eds.), *Spatial cognition—An interdisciplinary approach to representing and processing spatial knowledge* (Vol. LNCS 1404 Subseries LNAI, pp. 267-291). Berlin, Heidelberg, New York: Springer.

Kuβ, T. (1998). *Der Einfluβ der domänenspezifischen Interessenlage auf die Konstruktion präferierter mentaler Modelle beim räumlich-relationalen Schlieβen* [The influence of social perspective on the construction of preferred mental models in spatial relational inference] (Unpublished doctoral thesis). Freiburg: Albert-Ludwigs-Universität Freiburg, Psychologisches Institut.

Rauh, R., & Kuß, T. (1998). *Domain-unrelated and domain-specific spatial reasoning: On the influence of social perspective on the construction of spatial mental models.* Manuscript in preparation, Albert-Ludwigs-Universität Freiburg.

Rauh, R., & Schlieder, C. (1997). Symmetries of model construction in spatial relational inference. *Proceedings of the 19th Annual Conference of the Cognitive Science Society* (pp. 638–643). Mahwah, NJ: Lawrence Erlbaum Associates.

Rauh, R., Schlieder, C., & Knauff, M. (1997). Präferierte mentale Modelle beim räumlich-relationalen Schließ en: Empirie und kognitive Modellierung [Preferred mental models in spatial relational inference: Empirical evidence and cognitive modeling]. *Kognitionswissenschaft, 6,* 21–34.

Roberts, M. J. (1993). Human reasoning: Deduction rules or mental models, or both? *Quarterly Journal of Experimental Psychology, 46A,* 569–589.

Schlieder, C. (in press). The construction of preferred mental models in reasoning with the interval relations. In C. Habel & G. Rickheit (Eds.), *Mental models in discourse processing and reasoning.* Oxford, UK: Elsevier Science.

Schlieder, C., & Berendt, B. (1998). Mental model construction in spatial reasoning: A comparison of two computational theories. In U. Schmid, J. Krems, & F. Wysotzki (Eds.), *Mind modelling: A cognitive science approach to reasoning, learning, and discovery* (pp. 133–162). Berlin: Pabst Science Publishers.

10

Model Construction and Elaboration in Spatial Linear Syllogisms

André Vandierendonck
Gino De Vooght
Chris Desimpelaere
Vicky Dierckx

When faced with linear syllogisms, reasoners usually construct an integrated spatial representation of the premise content. As a consequence multi-model problems are more difficult than one-model problems, because the representation is more complex in multi-model problems. In the present chapter, the question is raised whether three-model problems are indeed more difficult than two-model problems. Data show that there is a reliable difference between two-model and three-model problems. However, the difference is so small that it cannot be explained by assuming that the reasoner builds an explicit representation of all three models. Overall, the last premise, the one that discloses the multi-model nature of the problem, requires more reading and processing time than other premises, and this difference is larger in multi-model than in one-model problems. The data suggest that the representation constructed leaves the additional models implicit by entering a marker that can be easily fleshed out when needed.

Given that a Rolls Royce is more expensive than a Mercedes and that the latter is more expensive than a Volvo, people easily infer that a Volvo is cheaper than a Rolls. This result is typically obtained by constructing a linear array with the elements or terms (Rolls, Mercedes, Volvo) ordered from top to bottom or from left to right, as proposed by the spatial array view (see De Soto, London, & Handel, 1965; Huttenlocher, 1968; Potts, 1974). According to a review by Evans, Newstead, and Byrne (1993), the spatial array view is the best summary of the findings reported in the literature. Basically, it may be concluded that linear reasoning problems are solved by constructing an integrated spatial representation of the premise information (see also Barclay, 1973; Foos, Smith, Sabol, & Mynatt, 1976; Gattis, chap. 8, this volume; Mynatt & Smith, 1977; Potts, 1976; Sternberg, 1980, 1981).

Nowadays this view is subsumed under the more general mental model theory (e.g., Johnson-Laird, 1983; Johnson-Laird & Byrne, 1991). This theory contends that deductive reasoning in general is based on the construction and manipulation of mental models representing the premise information. One of the major tenets of this viewpoint is that the more difficult the reasoning problem, the more models have to be considered before one can confidently arrive at a conclusion. Several studies (e.g., Byrne & Johnson-Laird, 1989; Schaeken, Girotto, & Johnson-Laird, 1998; Schaeken, Johnson-Laird, & d'Ydewalle, 1996; Vandierendonck & De Vooght, 1996) have presented evidence that corroborates this hypothesis, and dual-task experiments have testified to the spatial nature of the representation (Vandierendonck & De Vooght, 1997).

Applied to the domain of the linear syllogisms referred to earlier, the theory, nevertheless, faces a number of problems. Consider for example a problem such as the one depicted in the central panel of Fig. 10.1. Inferences concerning the relationship between A and C and between E and C are straightforward, whereas inferences about the relationship between E and A are indeterminate: Both "*A left of E*" and "*E left of A*" are possible and are consistent with the premise information. As indicated in the lower part of the central panel of Fig. 10.1, two different models are consistent with the premises.

It is interesting to note, however, that for a judgment of the correctness of the conclusion "*E left of C*" (a correct transitive inference), it does not matter whether one or two models have been constructed. As long as the relevant information is represented in memory, a correct answer is possible. Nevertheless, data show (e.g., Vandierendonck & De Vooght, 1994) that this inference elicits significantly more errors than a comparable inference in a determinate or one-model problem, as the one presented in the left panel of Fig. 10.1. A question about the relationship between A and C or between B and D in this one-model problem (left panel) appears to be easier than a similar transitive inference in a two-model problem (central panel).

A left of B	A left of B	A left of B
B left of C	B left of C	B left of C
C left of D	C left of D	C left of D
D left of E	E left of B	E left of C

A — B — C — D — E	A — B — C — D E ⌐	A — B — C — D E ⌐

ABCDE	AEBCD EABCD	ABECD AEBCD EABCD

FIG. 10.1. Examples of one-model, two-model, and three-model linear syllogisms.

Why does this happen? What causes a valid transitive inference in a two-model problem to be more difficult than a similar inference in a one-model problem? For an answer to this question, the mental model theory refers to the number of models. Indeed, the only important difference between the two situations is in the number of models that are consistent with the problem description. According to this theory, the premise information is integrated into one or more models. Under the assumption that the premise information is represented completely, the two-models problem requires the construction of two models. This increases the load on the processing system. Consequently, with a fixed quantity of resources, more resources are used for model representation and less are available for the inference engine, so that the probability of an error increases as does the time required to make the inference.

This explanation is an interesting one, and, if correct, it should be possible to extend it to three-model problems. To that end, consider the problem description in the right hand panel of Fig. 10.1. A complete representation of the premise information now requires three models. Following the argument given for the comparison between one-model and two-model valid inferences, it may be expected that the load in this three-model problem is larger than in a two-model problem. As a consequence, the resources available for making an inference should even be smaller, so that we can predict that the probability of a correct inference decreases with the number of models consistent with the premises. Indirect evidence challenges this prediction, however. In order to increase the memory load, Vandierendonck and De Vooght (1997) used three-model instead of two-model problems. Yet, the results were similar to those obtained with two-model problems.

This unexpected finding raises the following questions with respect to the mental model theory:

(a)   Is there a reliable difference in difficulty between three-model and two-model problems?

(b)   If there is indeed no reliable difference, how can this be explained by the mental model theory? Could this lack of difference be due to a strategical choice made by the reasoner (see Evans, chap. 1, this volume; Johnson-Laird, Savary, & Bucciarelli, this volume; Roberts, 1993, chap. 2, this volume).

These are straightforward questions, but a dependable answer requires a lot of control of extraneous variables. For example, compare the two-model and the three-model situation described in the examples (central and right panels of Fig. 10.1). In the three-model example, the information about the E-term describes a relation with the C-term which has been introduced more recently than in the two-model example where the E-term links to the B-term. This is clearly illustrated in the central row of Fig. 10.1: After receiving the C–D relation, the three-model problem requires we go one step back (C), whereas the two-model problem necessitates the reasoner to catch up with a term which was last presented, moving two steps back (B). Suppose that three-model problems are more difficult than two-model problems, but imagine that the recency of the premise information also affects the problem difficulty in such a way that more recent information is more easily accessed. It may happen that the two factors counteract each other, and this may lead to a no-difference result, which is then incorrectly taken to mean that three-model problems are not more difficult than two-model problems. Evidently, the chaining sequence of the premises is important (see De Vooght & Vandierendonck, 1998; Oakhill & Johnson-Laird, 1984) and has to be controlled.

NUMBER OF MODELS AND REASONING PERFORMANCE

Data were collected to find out whether solution accuracy and solution time of linear syllogisms depend on the number of models described by the premises. To that end a number of problem situations were developed in which the number of models was varied while at the same time the chaining sequence was controlled. This resulted in the five-problem situations that are described in Fig. 10.2. The first three premises in all of these problems are the same (A–B, B–C, C–D). The fourth premise determines the problem type, as follows:

addition of D-E results in a one-model problem;

addition of E-B leads to a two-model problem with a fork to the left and attaching the premise to a term two steps back;

a three-model problem with a fork to the left and an attachment of the premise one step back is obtained by the addition of E-C;

addition of C-E results in a two-model problem with a fork to the right and an attachment of the premise to a term only one step back;

similarly, an attachment of B-E, two steps back results in a three-model problem with a fork to the right.

Note that problem types 2 and 4 are both two-model problems that differ from each other in the chaining history and the orientation of the fork, and that a similar balancing is achieved in problem types 3 and 5.

The premises were presented self-paced one by one in the center of a computer screen. Each premise consisted of the two terms positioned in a spatial relationship to each other, which participants were instructed to interpret as a direct representation of the relative spatial positions of the two terms. The A–B premise, for example, consisted of the terms *A* and *B* placed at both sides of the center of the screen, such that both are on the same physical line, with *A* left and *B* right of the center. This presentation method was preferred to stress the spatial relationship of the terms and to avoid confusions sometimes evoked by the verbally formulated relations.

	Set 1	Set 2	Models
[1]	A — B — C — D — E	A — B — C — D — E	ABCDE
[2]	A — B — C — D E	A — B — C — D E	AEBCD EABCD
[3]	A — B — C — D E	A — B — C — D E	ABECD AEBCD EABCD
[4]	A — B — C — D E	A — B — C — D E	ABCED ABCDE
[5]	A — B — C — D E	A — B — C — D E	ABECD ABCED ABCDE

FIG. 10.2. Problem types and questions. The five problem types differ with respect to number of models and the place in the chain where the last premise is attached. The solid connections represent premises presented. The dashed connections indicate the terms about which an inference has to be made.

After the four premises has been read, two questions were asked. These questions queried the relative position of the two terms connected by a dashed line in Fig. 10.2. For example, in task set 1 of the one-model problem, the questions concerned the relationships between B and C and between C and E. For each question three answering alternatives were indicated; for example, B–C, C–B, or *"there is no valid answer to this question."* Over the two sets, three types of questions were asked:

1.   *repetition of a premise or recall of a presented premise (e.g., B–C?);*
2.   *a valid transitive inference (e.g., A–C);*
3.   *an inference for which no valid conclusion is possible (e.g., A–E in Problem 3).*

Twenty problems with concrete terms (5 problem types x 2 sets x 2 problem cases) with two questions per problem were presented to 47 first-year students enrolled at the Faculty of Psychology and Educational Sciences at the University of Ghent. Time needed for reading and processing of each premise, solution time, and answer were registered.

Accuracy

Table 10.1 displays the proportions of correct solutions for one-, two-, and three-model problems as a function of the three inference types in the questions. The table clearly shows that the answer to a question repeating a premise (always a nonanchored premise, namely B–C) was more often correct in one-model than in multimodel problems; the same was true for questions requiring a transitive inference. Statistical analysis on the combination of both types of questions showed that one-model problems were easier than multimodel problems, and that the difference between two-model and three-model problems was not statistically reliable. The inferences in the two- and three-model problems which do not allow a valid conclusion, were very rarely correct, but there was no difference in accuracy between the two-model and the three-model problems.

Table 10.1.
Proportion of correct verifications as a function of number of models and of inference type.

Problem type	Recall	Inference	Nonvalid
One-Model	.88	.87	-
Two-Model	.81	.75	.22
Three-Model	.81	.79	.23

Taken together, the accuracy data show that problem descriptions consistent with two or more models more often result in incorrect verification decisions both in the recall of a premise and in transitive inferences. However, no hint of such a difference was found in the comparison of three-model and two-model situations.

Premise Reading Time

The time required to read and to process each premise in turn gives information about the process of model construction. With the self-paced premise presentation procedure, the time taken to look at the premise includes reading and processing time. The variability due to reading time is expected to be small in this study because each premise consisted of two words. Spatial array and mental model theory assume, however, that the premise information is integrated into a cognitive representation. The mental model theory, more specifically, proposes that one or more (integrated) models are constructed. It may be assumed then that operations on this mental representation are more time consuming than other ones. Addition of a new model to a representation, for example, could take more time than adding a segment to an existing model. Similarly, if the new segment to be added requires a shift of attention toward another part of the model, this may require more time than a continuation at the point where the previously added segment ended (see De Vooght & Vandierendonck, 1998).

In the same vein, if the premise contains information that suggests there are several possible ways in which the model can be elaborated, the premise processing time would also increase. For one thing, the reasoner must decide how to deal with this uncertainty, and this takes some time. The decision may also result in an operation that consumes time. For instance, the reasoner may decide to start a separate model to represent the different possibilities. Alternatively, the reasoner may decide to place a marker in the model elaborated so far. This marker would indicate that at that particular place there is some uncertainty: The newly introduced term is in a specific relationship to the term at this particular position and the precise location of the new term or object is unknown. This is comparable to the "mental footnotes" discussed by Rauh (chap. 9, this volume). Observe that this action leaves the possibilities unspecified and is equivalent to the implicit models allowed in syllogistic reasoning (Johnson-Laird & Byrne, 1991).

The average premise times of the first three premises were rather similar. They did not differ as a function of the problem types, and there is certainly no reason to expect that they would do as the first three premises were similar in all problem types used. The average premise times of the fourth premise are displayed in Fig. 10.3. This figure clearly shows that the average premise reading time for the last premise was longer in multimodel problems (7.29 s) than in one-model problems (4.51 s), and within the multimodel problems, the time needed to process the fourth premise in the two-model problems was also significantly shorter (6.92 s) than the time required in the three-model problems (7.65 s). The time on the fourth premise did not vary as a function of the position of the fork in the chain (left: 7.46 s, right: 7.11 s).

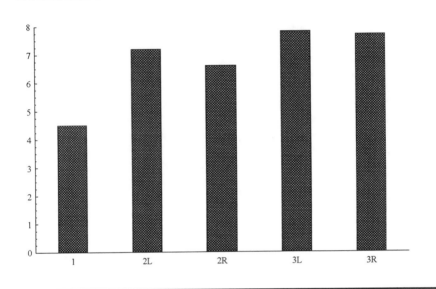

FIG. 10.3. Average premise reading time (in s) on the fourth premise as a function of problem type.

MODEL ELABORATION

In reference to one-model problems, the premise reading time of the fourth premise is slower in two-model problems. The difference is about 2.4 s, which is a big difference (about 53% of time needed for this premise in the one-model problems). This could be taken to indicate that the participants took the time to construct a second model upon encountering the premise that disclosed the two-model nature of the problem description. On the assumption that it takes about that amount of time to construct an additional model, it would be expected that an extra 2.4 s is required to construct the third model in three-model problems. However, the time difference between the two- and three-model problems was only about 0.7 s. This would imply that, if necessary a second model is constructed, but a third one is not. It is more parsimonious to explain the findings by assuming that in both two- and three-model problems, a marker is placed when the multimodel nature of the problem is detected. That this operation takes more time in the three-model problems could be due to a number of reasons: It may take more time to conclude that the information in the premise points to a three-model situation or the placement of the marker may be more complicated in the three-model situation, or a combination of both. It may also be the case that most of the participants construct an integrated representation with a marker and that a few reasoners elaborated all the models from the start. On average, the effect on the premise reading time would be the same.

The issue raised here, concerns the question whether the models are completely elaborated or fleshed out when the critical premise is read or whether they are left implicit by just placing a marker. In the study reported, an effort was made to gain some insight in this matter by asking the participants two inference questions about each problem: One question could be answered without elaborating the models (e.g., B–C? or A–C?), while for the other question (e.g., A–E? or E–C?), an elaboration of the models would enhance the proportion of correct answers.

Half of the participants always answered the questions in this order, whereas the other half received the questions in the reverse order. If participants always work with fleshed out models, then the order of the problems does not make any difference. If, on the contrary, they do not normally elaborate the models, it may be expected that when the need for elaboration comes with the first question, the consistency of the answers is larger than when the need for elaboration comes later.

Absolutely no effect of question order was apparent in the data. Even though this is consistent with the hypothesis that the models are completely fleshed out from the start, it is worthwhile to look at the consistency of the answers produced by the participants. To that end, the transitive inferences in which the last premise is involved (we call these E-inferences) were compared to the other transitive inferences (A-inferences). Such an analysis is only possible within the set of two-model problems. If both models are completely elaborated, there is no reason to expect that the E-inferences would be less often correct than the A-inferences. This expectation was contradicted: E-inferences were less often correct (68%) than A-inferences (81%). Besides, the position of the fork also had a substantial effect, such that problems with a fork on the left were less often correct (66%) than problems with a fork on the right (84%).

Moreover, both these factors (kind of inference and fork position) interacted, an effect that boiled down to the observation that E-inferences about problems with a fork to the left were less often correct (51%) than the other ones (83%). Incidentally, the poor performance is observed on a question with respect to the last premise on problems that require this premise to be connected to a term that was last encountered two steps back. Because the inference that discloses the elaboration is answered incorrectly about half of the time in the two-model problems with a fork to the left, the present findings suggest that, at least in these leftward two-model problems, a complete elaboration of the models is not performed.

Fork position interacted with question order. The difference in correctness between leftward and rightward problems was larger when the E-inference was the second question (26%), than when it was the first question (10%).

All these findings indicate that accuracy depends on the type of inference (whether the E-term is involved or not), on the structural characteristics of the problem situation (fork to the left or to the right) and question order. If the models were always fleshed out from the start, no such differences should occur. Hence, we have indications here that in two- and three-model problems, the models are left implicit, for example, by placing only a marker at the critical position in the model.

PREMISE MEMORY OR MODEL REPRESENTATION?

However, there is no way of being confident in these conclusions. The fact that accuracy is lower in two-model problems with a fork to the left, but not in three-model problems with a fork to the right, raises some questions. With respect to the issue of placing a marker when the fourth premise discloses the multimodel nature of the situation, these problems are pretty similar: Not only the representation built up so far, but also the point at which the last term is to be connected is the same. The problem here is that the orientation of the fork is confounded with the position of the marker.

In order to disambiguate the situation and to replicate the main findings, a new study was performed in which participants were presented 24 problems with three inferences per problem. Half of the participants read the premises in a "forward" order (e.g., A–B, B–C, C–D, E–B) and the other half read the premises the reverse ("backward") order (C–D, B–C, A–B, E–B). The effect of this manipulation is that the left fork position is at one step back for half of the participants and at two steps for the other half.

The study used the same 5 problem types as in the first study, but added a one-model problem in which the last premise had to be joined at the left end of the chain (A–B, B–C, C–D, E–A). Thus, these 6 problem types can be repartitioned according to a factorial combination of number of models (1, 2, or 3) and adhesion point of the last premise (left or right). The six problem types are labeled 1L, 1R, 2L, 2R, 3L, and 3R, where the digit refers to the number of models and the letter to the orientation of the fork.

At the end of the premise presentation, three inference questions were asked. To avoid the complications that may arise of having three-choice questions (left, right, or no valid answer possible), two-choice questions were used throughout. One question of each of the following groups was presented in each problem:

1. *A-inferences (transitive inferences not involving the E-term) in which the participant had to choose between two possibilities (e.g., A–C or C–A);*
2. *E-inferences (transitive inferences involving the E-term) with a similar choice (e.g., E–C or C–E);*
3. *N-inferences (inferences involving the E-term) where the question was whether or not a valid conclusion was possible.*

Note that a correct answer was always possible to the first two kinds of question, whereas the third question could receive a yes (there is a valid solution) in one-model and two-model problems or a no-answer in two- and three-model problems.

Accuracy

Table 10.2 displays the average proportions of correct responses to each of the three types of inference question in each of the 6 problem types. This table supports several conclusions. First, with respect to both the A-inferences and the E-inferences, there were no reliable differences between the problems as a function of number of models. Neither was there a reliable difference as a function of fork position.

With respect to the N-inferences, the picture is quite different. The accuracy varied as a function of the number of models, with better performance on the one-model problems (89%) than on the multimodel problems (68%). The difference between the two- and three-model problems was not statistically reliable. The table clearly shows, however, that in the multimodel problems there was an interaction of number of models with fork position. Indeed, judgment of valid conclusions was poorer in the 2L and 3R problems than in the 2R and 3L problems. Interestingly, this interaction did not depend on the order of reading the premises, and overall, the order variable did not affect performance nor did it interact with any of the other effects.

Table 10. 2.
Proportion of correct verifications as a function of number of models and of inference type in the second study.

Problem Type	A-inferences	E-inferences	N-inferences
1L	.90	.89	.86
1R	.93	.88	.92
2L	.92	.84	.60
2R	.89	.88	.72
3L	.87	.86	.76
3R	.89	.92	.63

Problem representation

It may be argued that when the problem information has been well integrated into a unified representation, the answer to all three inference questions should be correct. For one-model problems this is evident. However, multimodel problems are more complex and some of the information may get lost. As the previous analysis of the accuracy data does not allow any conclusions on this matter, a new scoring was worked out: Each problem with a correct answer on all three questions was assigned a 1; the other problems were scored 0. An analysis was performed on these derived scores.

Again, there was a clear effect of the number of models, with better performance on one-model problems (78%) than on multimodel problems (56%). The differences between two- and three-model problems did not attain significance, but within the multimodel problems, the number of models interacted with fork position.

Solution Time

The solution time of the correctly answered questions also revealed a number of effects. In addition to an effect of the number of models, with faster solution in the one-model (3.60 s) than in the multimodel problems (4.00 s), solution time was slower in problems with a leftward fork (4.02 s) than in problems with a rightward fork (3.71 s). Moreover, these two variables interacted, in such a way that the difference was smaller in the one-model problems (.04 s) than in the multimodel problems (.46 s).

Overall, solution latencies of the three kinds of inference questions were reliably different. A-inferences were faster (3.59 s) than E-inferences (3.95 s), but these inferential verifications did not differ from the the N-inferences (4.05 s). The contrast of A-inferences and E-inferences interacted with the contrast between one-model and multimodel problems: E-inference latencies were slightly shorter than A-inference latencies in one-model problems, while the relationship was reversed in the multimodel problems.

Premise Reading Time

An analysis of the premise reading times confirmed our expectations and replicated the findings of the first study. Premise order had no effects and did not interact with any of the factors of the design and is therefore not considered here. The reading times did not vary as a function of problem type in the first three ranks, as these premises were common to all problems, but the reading time of the fourth premise was longer overall. Fig. 10.4 shows the average reading time of the fourth premise as a function of number of models and position of fork.

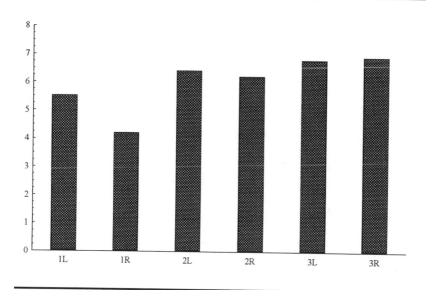

FIG. 10.4. Average premise reading time (in s) as a function of number of models and fork position in the second study.

The premise reading time of the fourth premise was shorter in one-model problems (4.87 s) than in multimodel problems (6.57 s), and within the multimodel problems reading was faster in the two-model (6.33 s) than in the three-model problems (6.81 s). The fourth premise was also read faster in the problems with a right fork (3.51 s) than in problems with a left fork (3.73 s). The latter variable interacted with the number of models. This corresponds to the observation that one-model problems with a left fork require more time to read the fourth premise than one-model problems with a right fork (see Fig. 10.4), whereas no such big differences are observed in the multimodel problems.

Strategical Issues

Given that in the studies reported here, the reasoners are confronted with a series of problems that are all rather similar, it cannot be precluded that the reasoners, once they discover the structure of the problems, decide to avoid tedious model elaborations. Within the framework proposed by Evans (chap. 1, this volume), such a decision would be a strategic one, because it qualifies as an intentional act.
    In order to find out whether such a strategic decision might have been at the basis of the present results, the premise reading times of the first and the last

problem of each type were subjected to a statistical analysis. The premise reading times of the first problems were longer (4.14 s) than those of the last problems (3.11 s). Even though this variable interacted with the premise rank, the triple interaction of first- versus-last, number of models, and premise rank failed to attain significance. Looking only at the premise reading time of the fourth premise, the difference in reading time between one-model and multimodel problems was reliable, but it did not interact with the contrast of first-to-last problem.

The findings suggest that apart from an effect of practice, resulting in faster processing of the premises as the experiment progressed, there were no changes specific to multimodel problems as compared to single-model ones. Especially the finding that the differences between the problem types did not change with practice, supports the idea that the differences observed in the present studies are not strategic ones evolved in the course of the experiment. It remains possible that reasoners have already had so much experience with spatial linear syllogisms that the strategic choices have been made prior to the participation in the experiment, probably because this type of reasoning situations occurs rather often in daily life and school contexts.

CONCLUDING REMARKS

Data of two separate studies were presented and discussed. It is clear from the accuracy data and the solution times that reasoning performance drops as the number of models increases. The difference is rather large between one-model and two-model problems and is small and not statistically reliable between two-model and three-model problems. The necessity to consider more than one model clearly adds to the difficulty of the deduction process, as measured by accuracy of verifications and verification time. Further increases in the number of models do not lead, however, to an increase in difficulty.

These findings confirm casual observations made earlier (see Vandierendonck & De Vooght, 1997) and suggest that the difference between multimodel problems and one-model problems is not due to the construction and elaboration of all possible models. It would rather seem that multimodel problems require a somewhat more complex representation than one-model problems. More specifically, in a multimodel representation information is enclosed, for example, by placing a marker, that allows later elaboration.

Such an interpretation is consistent with the findings concerning the premise reading times. The problems used in the studies discussed here consisted of four premises. The first three premises were, except for the content of the terms, the same in all problems, but the last premise depended on the problem type. It was therefore expected that premise reading times would only differ across problems in the last premise. This was confirmed. Premise reading times increased with the number of models consistent with the information, and even though all contrasts were significant, the difference between one-model and two-model problems was large, while the difference between two-model and three-model problems was small. The magnitude of these differences is consistent with the interpretation that the first three premises are used to build an integrated array representation of the situation described in the premises. In one-model problems, the fourth premise is integrated into the representation. In multimodel problems, it is obvious that the fourth premise adds ambiguous information and the information is integrated in the model constructed so far. In addition, a marker or a tag is entered to indicate that the model can be elaborated to represent two or more situations.

Comparison of the premise reading time of the fourth premise in 1R and 1L problems showed that the distance between the last term of the third premise and the repeated term of the last premise had an effect on the premise reading times. When the first term of the fourth premise was a repetition of the second term of the third premise (as in 1R problems), the last premise required less reading time than when the connection was less direct (as in 1L problems). This suggests that refocusing of the attention to another part of the (integrated) spatial representation is monotonically related to the distance of this shift.

This factor also plays a role in multimodel problems, but in addition, the reasoner must recognize that the fourth premise introduces information about the number of valid models. From the finding that the difference in premise reading time of the fourth premise between multimodel problems and the 1R problem is larger than the corresponding difference between the 1L and the 1R problems, it may be concluded that disambiguation of the new information takes some time. In combination with the finding that refocusing of attention also takes time, all these findings may be taken to suggest that during model construction, the complete representation is available in memory. In other words, model construction is an online process.

The question arises, however, how this conclusion can be reconciliated with the finding that two-model problems with a fork to the left and three-model problems with a fork to the right (both problems have the B and E-terms in their fourth premise) were more prone to errors of validity judgment than the other multimodel problems. One straightforward interpretation of this finding is that there is some loss of information from memory and the loss tends to be higher the larger the amount of time elapsed since the relevant information was presented. However, this interpretation is at variance with the finding that both, inferences involving the E-term and inferences involving the A-term, were very accurate in all six types of problems used. Moreover, variations in the order of premise presentation did not affect performance and did not interact with any of the other variables, not even with the contrast between problems with E–B and E–C as the last premise. Because of this, it might be suggested that the effect is linked to the structure of the representation: Irrespective of the time elapsed since this part of the representation was constructed, it would seem that making an inference about the validity of the conclusions that involve the marked premise is more difficult if the position of the marker is further from the right end of the left–right chain of events. Of course, this is a rather speculative interpretation which should be subjected to empirical verification.

If correct, this interpretation also implies that elaboration of the representation at the marked position is less likely when the B-position is marked than when the marker is at the C-term. In the first study, half of the problems started with a question that required some model elaboration for a correct answer. It was found, however, that this variation had no effect. This would mean either that the representation is usually elaborated or that it is rarely ever elaborated. Taking into account that there was a rather strong association between all kinds of inference questions asked in both studies, and that the solution time of the E-inferences was longer than the solution time of the A-inferences, the data indicate that the models are elaborated when needed.

By way of summary, it may be said that when faced with linear syllogisms, reasoners construct an integrated spatial representation of the premise information which is left implicit when more than one model is consistent with the information; this implicit information is fleshed out when needed. As a consequence, there is an economy in the representation constructed that explains why three-model problems are not substantially more difficult than two-model problems, even though two-model problems are more difficult than one-model problems because of the necessity to add a marker. Placement and orientation of the fork in multimodel problems seems to affect performance, but it is clearly shown that this is not caused by deterioration of older fragments in the representation. The structure of the representation rather seems to be responsible for these effects, which are not yet clearly understood. Future work could help to clarify the findings concerning fork position and orientation.

It is also not yet clear to what extent the reasoning method is based on strategical choices. A comparison of premise reading times in the first and the last problems in the experiment, shows that it is quite unlikely that a strategy was developed in the course of the experiment. Future research could help to find out whether or not reasoning in linear syllogisms is based on strategic choices.

ACKNOWLEDGMENTS

The chapter presents research results of the Belgian programme on Interuniversity Poles of Attraction initiated by the Belgian State, Prime Minister's Office, Science Policy Programming, Grants nr. P3/31 and nr. P4/19 from the Department of Science Policy to the first Author. The scientific responsibility is assumed by its authors.

REFERENCES

Barclay, J. R. (1973). The role of comprehension in remembering sentences. *Cognitive Psychology, 4*, 229–254.
Byrne, R. M. J., & Johnson-Laird, P. N. (1989). Spatial reasoning. *Journal of Memory*

and Language, 28, 564–575.

De Soto, C. B., London, M., & Handel, S. (1965). Social reasoning and spatial paralogic. *Journal of Personality and Social Psychology, 4,* 513–521.

De Vooght, G., & Vandierendonck, A. (1998). Spatial mental models in linear reasoning. *Kognitionswissenschaft, 7,* 5–10.

Evans, J. S. B. T., Newstead, S. E., & Byrne, R. M. J. (1993). *Human reasoning: The psychology of deduction.* Hillsdale, NJ: Lawrence Erlbaum Associates.

Foos, P. W., Smith, K. H., Sabol, M. A., & Mynatt, B. T. (1976). Constructive processes in simple linear-order problems. *Journal of Experimental Psychology: Human Learning and Memory, 2,* 759–766.

Huttenlocher, J. (1968). Constructing spatial images: A strategy in reasoning. *Psychological Review, 75,* 550–560.

Johnson-Laird, P. N. (1983). *Mental models.* Cambridge, MA: Cambridge University Press.

Johnson-Laird, P. N., & Byrne, R. M. J. (1991). *Deduction.* London: Lawrence Erlbaum Associates.

Mynatt, B. T., & Smith, K. H. (1977). Constructive processes in linear order problems revealed by sentence study times. *Journal of Experimental Psychology: Human Learning and Memory, 3,* 357–374.

Oakhill, J. V., & Johnson-Laird, P. N. (1984). Representation of spatial descriptions in working memory. *Current Psychological Research & Reviews, 3,* 52–62.

Potts, G. R. (1974). Storing and retrieving information about ordered relationships. *Journal of Experimental Psychology, 103,* 431–439.

Potts, G. R. (1976). Artificial logical relations and their relevance to semantic memory. *Journal of Experimental Psychology: Human Learning and Memory, 2,* 746–758.

Roberts, M. J. (1993). Human reasoning: Deduction rules or mental models, or both? *Quarterly Journal of Experimental Psychology, 46A,* 569–589.

Schaeken, W., Girotto, V., & Johnson-Laird, P. N. (1998). The effect of an irrelevant premise on temporal and spatial reasoning. *Kognitionswissenschaft, 7,* 27–32.

Schaeken, W., Johnson-Laird, P. N., & d'Ydewalle, G. (1996). Mental models and temporal reasoning. *Cognition, 60,* 205–234.

Sternberg, R. J. (1980). Representation and process in linear syllogistic reasoning. *Journal of Experimental Psychology: General, 109,* 119–159.

Sternberg, R. J. (1981). Reasoning with determinate and indeterminate linear syllogisms. *British Journal of Psychology, 72,* 407–420.

Vandierendonck, A., & De Vooght, G. (1994). The time-spatialization hypothesis and reasoning about time and space. In M. Richelle, V. De Keyser, G. d'Ydewalle, & A. Vandierendonck (Eds.), *Temporal reasoning and behavioral variability* (pp. 99–125). Liege: Interuniversity Pole of Attraction, Temporal Reasoning and Behaviorial Variability, Issue 3.

Vandierendonck, A., & De Vooght, G. (1996). Evidence for mental model based rea soning: A comparison of reasoning with time and space concepts. *Thinking and Reasoning, 2,* 249–272.

Vandierendonck, A., & De Vooght, G. (1997). Working memory constraints on linear reasoning with spatial and temporal contents. *Quarterly Journal of Experimental Psychology, 50A,* 803–820.

11

Strategies and Tactics in Reasoning

Philip N. Johnson-Laird
Fabien Savary
Monica Bucciarelli

This chapter reports three experiments that investigated the strategies that individuals developed for themselves in various sorts of reasoning. The results suggest that there are four levels of thinking: at the topmost level, there is metacognitive thinking, which can yield novel strategies for reasoning; at the second level are the strategies themselves; At the third level are the components of strategies, which are a variety of 'tactics', such as representing a premise in a diagram; and at the fourth level are the largely unconscious processes that underlie the tactics. Any feasible theory of these various levels must, at present, contain many nondeterministic components, and the best way to express such a theory is in the form of a grammar.

Not long ago, a visiting speaker, a distinguished cognitive scientist, came to Princeton. He visited our laboratory, and one of us, by way of entertaining him gave him a tricky inferential problem, one that almost everyone gets wrong. He got it wrong, too. Later, he explained:

> I said to myself, "This is one of Phil's silly inference problems, and so I've got to be careful." But I still got it wrong!

Despite his insight—a metacognitive one, our visitor failed to come up with an appropriate strategy for dealing with the inference—as indeed had we when we first attempted the inference in checking the output of a computer program.

Current theories of deductive reasoning have largely neglected the topic of inferential strategies, their variety, and the constraints that determine the particular strategy that a reasoner adopts (see Evans, Newstead, & Byrne, 1993, for a review of current theories). The aim of the present chapter is to make good this neglect. But, what exactly *is* a strategy in reasoning? The best way to answer this question is to consider an example, although not the tricky problem that we gave our distinguished visitor. Consider instead the following simple problem about marbles in a box:

There is a red marble in the box if and only if there is a brown marble in the box.
Either there is a brown marble in the box or else there is a gray marble in the box, but not both.
There is a gray marble in the box if and only if there is a black marble in the box.
Does it follow that:
If there is not a red marble in the box then there is a black marble in the box?

You, the reader, are invited to solve this problem, and then to try to characterize how you went about it.

The correct answer to the problem is "yes": If there is not a red marble in the box, then there is a black marble in the box. But, how did you solve the problem? One strategy is to use a supposition, that is, an assumption for the sake of argument. Thus, you might have said to yourself:

Suppose that there is not a red marble in the box. It follows from the first premise that there is not a brown marble in the box, either. And, in this case, it follows from the second premise, that there is a gray marble in the box. The third premise now implies that there is a black marble in the box. So, if there is not a red marble in the box, then it follows that there is a black marble. Hence, the conclusion follows.

This protocol, which in fact is typical of what some reasoners say, reveals one strategy that can be used to solve the problem: the suppositional strategy. But, as we will see, it is not the only strategy that people use to solve this problem.

A working definition of a *strategy* is that it is the sequence of steps that an individual follows in solving, or attempting to solve, a problem. Thus, the first step in the foregoing strategy is to make a supposition (corresponding to the antecedent clause of the conditional conclusion). The second step is to combine this supposition with the first premise in order to draw an intermediate conclusion. And the next step is to use this conclusion to make another inference, and so on, until one arrives at the consequent proposition in the conclusion.

Each step in a strategy is what we refer to as a *tactic*. The mental processes underlying a tactic are seldom, if ever, available to consciousness. Thus, noone knows for sure how people make an inference of the form known as Modus Ponens, the tactic that occurs in the earlier second step. People do not report how they carry out tactical steps in their "think aloud" protocols. Their nature is therefore highly controversial. Some psychologists argue that Modus Ponens depends on the use of a formal rule of inference (see Braine & O'Brien, 1991; Rips, 1994). Other psychologists, including the present authors, argue instead that the minds of logically untrained reasoners do not contain tacit rules of inference, and that an inference such as Modus Ponens depends on constructing mental models of the premises (see Johnson-Laird & Byrne, 1991). In contrast to tactics, the overall strategy that reasoners use is potentially available to introspection, and can be revealed by reasoners' verbal reports, especially if they have to think aloud as they tackle a problem (see also Evans, chap. 1, this volume). In our view, reasoning tactics probably depend on the manipulation of mental models, but reasoning strategies are, as yet, almost wholly unknown. They are a matter for empirical investigation.

The plan of the present chapter is simple. It begins with a brief account of how psychologists have thought about strategies in the past. It presents an experimental investigation of the strategies underlying reasoning with sentential connectives (such as *"if"* and *"or"*). The results call for a distinction between strategies and tactics, that is, the components of strategies, which in turn depend on unconscious processes. The chapter then formulates a new way to frame theories that are nondeterministic, and illustrates this method in an account of one particular strategy for sentential reasoning. The chapter then turns to reasoning with quantifiers (such as *"all"* and *"some"*). It reports a study in which the participants had to construct models of premises that refuted putative conclusions, and it then describes a study of syllogistic reasoning. The results of these two studies suggest that all current theories of syllogistic reasoning need to be revised. The chapter concludes with an appraisal of strategic and tactical thinking in reasoning.

STRATEGIES IN REASONING: A BRIEF REVIEW

In the past, psychologists have defended two main views about reasoning strategies. On the one hand, some have argued that reasoners rely on a single deterministic strategy. This view is explicit in Rips' (1989) account of the suppositional strategy that he claims reasoners use to solve so-called "knight-and-knave" problems, such as:

> There are only two sorts of people: knights, who always tell the truth, and knaves, who always lie.
> Arthur says 'Lancelot is a knight and Gawain is a knave'.
> Lancelot says 'Arthur is a knave'.
> Gawain says 'Arthur is a knave'.
> What are Arthur, Lancelot, and Gawain?

Likewise, Rips' (1994) more recent PSYCOP computer program for reasoning in general follows a single deterministic strategy. A similar view is defended by Martin Braine and his colleagues (see Braine & O'Brien, 1991). On the other hand, Johnson-Laird and Byrne (1990) have argued that naive reasoners use a variety of different strategies for knight-and-knave problems. Consider the previous problem, for example. Many people report that they solved it when they noticed that Lancelot and Gawain are making the same assertion and so they must both be either knights or else knaves. Hence, Arthur's assertion cannot be true, because he assigns Lancelot and Gawain to different categories. Johnson-Laird and Byrne modeled five distinct strategies for knight-and-knave problems, including both a suppositional strategy and the one sketched for the previous problem, which is outside Rips' account. Subsequently, Byrne and Handley (1997) obtained good evidence for the use of several strategies for these problems.

There are other embarrassments to the thesis that there is just a single deterministic strategy. Girotto, Mazzocco, and Tasso (1997) report robust effects of the order of the premises on simple conditional inferences. Such effects seem inexplicable in terms of a single strategy using formal rules of inference. Likewise, reasoners use suppositions relatively rarely in reasoning (see Wason & Johnson-Laird, 1972), which is surprising if the single strategy is based on them. In the light of these results, we began to suspect that the main reason for postulating a single strategy is that previous experimental studies of reasoning had tended to use pairs of premises at most, which leave little room for alternative strategies. They had also failed to gather pertinent evidence about strategies. In order to remedy these defects, we carried out a study of reasoners' strategies in coping with a set of deductions that hinged on sentential connectives.

A STUDY OF STRATEGIES AND TACTICS IN SENTENTIAL REASONING

In our first experiment, participants were given a set of different inferences about marbles in a box. The problem in the introduction is a typical example of such an inference. Here it is again in an abbreviated form:

> Red if and only if Brown.
> Either Brown or else Gray, but not both.
> Gray if and only if Black.
> Does it follow that:
> If not Red then Black?

The inferences had premises that were mainly exclusive disjunctions or biconditionals, as the example illustrates, and their conclusions were either conditionals or disjunctions. For half the problems the conclusions were valid, and for the other half they were invalid. The important feature of the problems, however, is that most of them supported only two alternative possibilities. Each mental model represents a possibility, and so each problem called for two mental models. The premises of the preceding problem, for example, yield the following two models, shown here on separate lines:

> Red   Brown
>
>   Gray   Black

It is evident that the conclusion follows from the premises.

The participants were encouraged to use paper and pencil to evaluate the inferences. They were told to "think aloud" as they tackled each inference, and we video-recorded what they had to say and what they wrote down or drew. The camera was above them and focused on the paper on which they wrote, and they rapidly adapted to the conditions of the experiment.

Problem:
Red iff brown
Brown ore gray
Gray iff black
If not red then black?

Verbal protocol:	Diagram:
Red iff brown	
If brown then red	**Br → R**
Brown ore gray	
If not brown or red then gray	**G**
	Br → R
Gray iff black	
If gray then black:	**Bl → G**
	Br → R
Yes	
Brown ore gray	
Red if brown	
If black then gray	
Not possible (brown and gray)	
If not red then necessarily gray	
Gray only if black	
Yes	

FIG. 11.1. A typical protocol of a participant solving a reasoning problem transcribed using the interface devised by the second author. The protocol begins with the problem, stated in abbreviated form in which "iff" denotes "if, and only if," and "ore" denotes an exclusive disjunction. The left-hand side of the protocol summarizes what the participant said in thinking aloud, and the right-hand side shows what the participant drew. The participant, in fact, drew a single diagram, and the bold components show what was drawn contemporaneously with the verbal assertions on the left.

We tested eight Princeton students, who had no training in logic. The problems were easy, and none of the participants made any errors in evaluating them, although they were not always right for the right reasons. We devised a computer program that allowed us to transcribe each protocol, including any diagrams drawn by the participant, into a format that was readable in the high-level programming language, LISP.

Figure 11.1 presents a typical protocol of a participant (no. 5) tackling the problem above. The participant drew a single diagram, adding components to it incrementally. The finished diagram was:

$$Bl \rightarrow G$$
$$Br \rightarrow R$$

where "*Bl*" stands for "*Black*," "*G*" for "*Gray*," "*Br*" for "*Brown*," and "*R*" for "*Red*." Each row represents a possibility, that is, a mental model.

We believe that our protocols are typical of intelligent individuals thinking aloud as they make inferences. The protocols showed most of the major steps, and they allowed us to identify the participants' strategies and their component tactics. What they did not reveal, however, are the insightful processes in developing or creating the strategies, or the processes underlying the tactical steps, which are largely unconscious.

Our participants used four principal strategies in evaluating the inferences, and we were able to categorize every single protocol, though some protocols showed that the participant had changed mid-problem from one strategy to another. We describe each of the four principal strategies and present examples of them.

The Suppositional Strategy.   In this strategy, reasoners begin by making an assumption, which corresponds either to the antecedent or to the consequent of the conditional conclusion. They use this supposition to derive a conclusion from a premise. They then use this intermediate conclusion to derive another conclusion from another premise, and so on, until they derive the other proposition (or its negation) in the conditional conclusion. Where individuals base their supposition on the antecedent clause (p) of a conditional of the form: "*if p then q*," then the strategy is closely related, if not identical, to the suppositional strategies postulated in formal rule theories (e.g., Braine & O'Brien, 1991; Rips, 1994) and to the suppositional strategy postulated by Johnson-Laird and Byrne (1991).

In some cases, however, reasoners invalidly based their supposition on the consequent clause (q) of the conditional conclusion and discharged the supposition when the derivation lead them to its antecedent clause (p). This strategy is not valid. If a conclusion of the form "*if A then C*" is interpreted as a "one-way" conditional, that is, *A* implies *C*, but *C* doesn't necessarily imply *A*, then the supposition must correspond to the antecedent, *A*, of the conditional. And if the conclusion is interpreted as a biconditional, that is, "*if A then C and if C then A*," then the suppositional strategy needs to be used twice, for example, once to show that the supposition of *A* yields the consequent, *B*, and once to show that the supposition of *C* yields the antecedent, *A*. None of our participants ever made such double suppositions.

There are two diagnostic signs of a suppositional strategy: Reasoners start by stating a supposition (or assumption), and they then derive a series of simple categorical conclusions, beginning by combining their supposition with a premise. Figure 11.2 is a typical protocol of a participant using a suppositional strategy.

Problem:
Pink iff black
Black ore gray
Gray iff blue
If not pink then blue?

Verbal Protocol:	Drawing:
Pink iff black	
Black ore gray	
Gray iff blue	
If not pink then blue	
Assuming we have no pink	
There is no pink	Crosses out pink in printed premise
So there is no black	Crosses out black in both premises
There is gray	Circles gray
There is blue.	
Yes	
Not pink and blue	
Yes	

FIG. 11.2. The suppositional strategy: a typical protocol. Figure 11.1 explains the abbreviations. As the protocol shows, the participant starts by reading the premises aloud.

The key phrase indicating the participant is making a supposition is, "*Assuming we have no pink*," which corresponds to the antecedent of the conditional conclusion. The participant then uses this assumption to draw a conclusion from the first premise. This step, in turn, leads to a further inference, and so on, in a series culminating in a conclusion corresponding to the consequent of the conclusion.

The Compound Strategy.   Reasoners draw a conclusion from a pair of premises, or from one premise and a diagram of another premise, or from two diagrams representing separate premises. The conclusion is expressed either verbally or in the form of another diagram, or both. By combining such pair-wise inferences, reasoners derive the answer to the questioned conclusion. Figure 11.3 shows a typical protocol in which the reasoner combines the first two premises to yield an intermediate conclusion, and then combines this conclusion with the third premise to draw the final conclusion. One feature of the strategy is that even though neither the premises nor the conclusion to be evaluated made use of any modal terms, such as "*possibly*," the participants often drew a modal conclusion.

Problem:
White iff blue
If blue then pink
Pink ore brown
White or brown?

Verbal Protocol:	Drawing:
...	[draws a diagram of the first premise]
	Points to: blue → white
White if blue	
If blue then pink	
If blue then pink	Writes down premise
If pink then white [an intermediate conclusion]	Draws: pink → white
Pink ore brown	
Pink and white	Points to previous diagram
If brown then not white [conclusion]	Writes: brown, ~~white~~
White ore brown	
Yes	

FIG. 11.3. The compound strategy: a typical protocol. "If" in the premises refers to a "one-way" conditional, and "or" refers to an inclusive disjunction. The participant started by drawing a diagram for the first premise; we have omitted this stage from the protocol below.

When the participant draws the conjunctive conclusion, "*Pink and white*," in Fig. 11.3, he is really referring to a possibility rather than drawing a categorical conclusion. In other cases, however, the participants were quite explicit about the modal nature of their conclusions, for example:

Red or else blue
Blue or else gray
∴ Possibly grey and red

The Chain Strategy.   This strategy is not one that we had encountered before, and we can find no mention of it in either the psychological or logical literature. The reasoner constructs a chain of conditionals leading from one constituent of a conditional conclusion to its other constituent. There is a resemblance to the suppositional strategy, but two crucial distinctions. First, reasoners do not announce that they are making an assumption. Indeed, they are not making an assumption, because they do not draw any intermediate conclusions. Second, they convert any premise that is not a conditional into a conditional, either verbally or in the form of a diagram representing a conditional. These conversions include cases where a biconditional, such as:

Gray if and only if red

yields the inference, either from the verbal premise or from a diagram representing it:

If not gray, then not red

Problem:
Gray iff red
Red or else white
White iff blue
If not gray then blue?

Verbal Protocol:	Drawing:
. . .	[Draws separate diagrams for each premise]
	Points to diagrams:
If not gray then not red	r → g
If not red then white	r X w
White comes from blue	b → w
Yes	

Problem:
Pink iff green
Green or else red
Red iff white
If not pink then white?

Verbal Protocol:	Drawing:
. . .	[Draws separate diagrams for each premise]
	Crosses out color
	terms in diagrams:
if not pink then not green	~~pink~~ = ~~green~~
if not g then r	~~green~~ or red
if red then white	red = white
yes	

FIG. 11.4. The chain strategy: two typical protocols. We have omitted the initial verbal protocol when the participants draw separate diagrams for each premise.

The aim is to make a chain in which the consequent of one conditional matches the antecedent of the next conditional. Figure 11.4 presents two typical examples of the chain strategy. The chain strategy is valid provided that reasoners construct a chain leading from the antecedent of the conditional conclusion to its consequent. However, reasoners often worked invalidly in the converse direction.

The Model Strategy.   From our standpoint, the most interesting strategy was one in which the reasoners explicitly represented the possibilities compatible with the premises. As Fig. 11.5 shows, they drew a single integrated diagram that represented the possibilities. Some participants drew a vertical line down the page and wrote down the colors in the two possibilities on either side of it. Others arranged them horizontally. One participant, as Fig. 11.5 shows, merely drew circles around the terms in the premises themselves to pick out one of the two possibilities. Figure 11.1 gives a complete protocol of this strategy. A tell-tale sign of the model strategy is that the participants using it work through the premises in the order in which they are stated, and they include in the diagrams information from premises that are irrelevant to evaluating the conclusion.

Problem: Final diagram:

Blue or else brown   blue   white   red
Brown or else white   brown
White iff red
If blue then red?

Problem: Final diagram:

Black or else pink   black | pink
Pink or else grey   white grey |
Grey iff white
If black then white?

Problem and drawing:

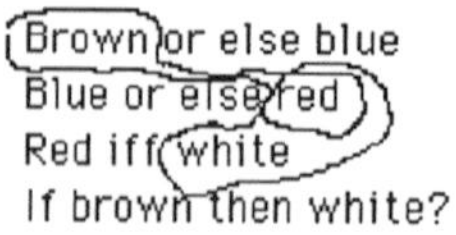

FIG. 11.5. The model strategy: three typical protocols. We have presented only the premises and the final diagram that the participants drew (see Fig. 11.1 for a complete example of this strategy).

There were lines in the protocols that we could not understand, and there were also false starts and derivations that petered out. But, every participant correctly evaluated every problem, and we were able to categorize all their protocols into cases of one or more of the four strategies outlined. On the basis of the data, we worked out the relative proportions of the four sorts of strategies, that is, we calculated the total number of times each strategy occurred in the protocols, and then expressed them as percentages of the sum of the totals. The results were as follows:

Suppositional strategy:	*21% of overall use of strategies*
Compound strategy:	*19% of overall use of strategies*
Chain strategy:	*25% of overall use of strategies*
Model strategy:	*34% of overall use of strategies*
Unknown strategies:	*0% of overall use of strategies*

The most salient feature of the protocols was that the participants mix strategies, and switch from one strategy (compound) to another (chain) in ways that seem wholly unpredictable. Sometimes a switch occurs in the middle of a problem; sometimes from one problem to the next. Reasoners sometimes revert to a strategy that they used earlier in the experiment. They are plainly not following a single deterministic strategy of the sort postulated in current formal rule theories. Likewise, although the problems are all within the scope of sentential reasoning, the participants quite often draw intermediate conclusions that go beyond the scope of current formal rule theories. Sometimes, these conclusions are about possibilities. On other occasions, however, reasoners take a step that is difficult for formal rule theories to explain, for example:

If red then not white
brown for white [where the participant points to a diagram of the form: brown → white]
∴ not (if red then brown)

The most striking strategy, the model strategy, is entirely beyond the scope of rule theories. Yet, it was used at least one or more times by half the participants.

In our view, the four strategies are all entirely compatible with the use of models at the tactical level, and so we examine each strategy from this point of view. People reason from suppositions in many circumstances, and the strategy is compatible with the use of models. In an unpublished study carried out in collaboration with Victoria Bell, we asked the participants to draw possible conclusions or necessary conclusions from such suppositions as:

Suppose everyone spoke the same language.

As the model theory predicts, they were reliably faster to draw possible conclusions than to draw necessary conclusions. A key feature of our present experiment is that the participants did not make embedded suppositions; that is, having made one supposition, they did not make another before they had discharged the first. This lack of embedded suppositions may be because our problems could be solved without them, but we wonder whether logically naive individuals spontaneously embed one supposition within the domain of another (*pace* Rips, 1994). The compound strategy is also compatible with the use of models. In fact, some compound inferences can be explained at present only by the use of models, for example, those inferences yielding modal conclusions, which are beyond the scope of current formal rule theories (Braine & O'Brien, 1998; Rips, 1994). The chain strategy, likewise, can be accommodated within the model theory: The immediate inferences that convert disjunctions into conditionals, for example, could be based on models. Indeed, Richardson and Ormerod (1997; see also Ormerod, chap. 7, this volume) have studied how such conversions occur and argued that a version of the model theory gives a good account of them. Finally, the model strategy is isomorphic to the cumulative construction of a single set of models based on all the information in the premises.

NONDETERMINISM AND THEORIES OF STRATEGIES AND TACTICS

A deterministic process is one in which each step depends solely on the current state of the process and whatever input, if any, it happens to have. Thus, a deterministic strategy unwinds in a fixed way like clockwork. The mind may be deterministic, but, as theorists, we have no option but to treat it nondeterministically, that is, our theories have to allow for different possible actions in the same theoretical state. This move is forced on us because we cannot predict precisely what will happen next in a piece of reasoning. We can put some constraints on the process from our observations of common patterns in inferential behavior, but the details are beyond the predictive power of our theories. Nondeterminism could merely reflect our ignorance: If we had a better understanding of the mind, then we would discern its deterministic nature. For example, the mind could be *chaotic* in the technical sense that its behavior is deterministic but soon becomes unpredictable like, say, the dripping of a tap. Another possibility is that the mind is genuinely nondeterministic, either because it can make arbitrary decisions or because its behavior is governed in part by quantum events. We must leave to future researchers the task of deciding amongst these competing interpretations.

One question we can answer, albeit speculatively, is why the mind appears to be nondeterministic from top to bottom. The answer is that there is a value in variation. Just as variation among individuals is a precursor to the evolution of species, so there is an advantage to variation in mental life. It yields novel and unpredictable thoughts, which are a prerequisite for learning and creativity. Lack of variation is equivalent to intellectual catatonia.

Granted the need for a nondeterministic theory, we need a precise and convenient way to express it. We offer a new way in which to couch such a theory, which depends on the following steps. First, the different theoretical possibilities are captured in a grammar. In the case of reasoning, we need a grammar of strategies in which each step calls on tactics of various sorts. Second, in implementing the theory in a computer program, these tactics must be modeled in explicit mechanisms for carrying out the appropriate inferential steps. Third, the computer program includes a parser that uses the grammar to parse the protocols. In our case, the grammar should allow each "think aloud" protocol to be parsed, and control each step in the corresponding tactics, such as drawing a diagram, or making an immediate inference. Hence, as the grammar is used to parse a protocol, the program will carry out the same inferential processes that the theory attributes to reasoners following that particular strategy. A good theory of strategies should account for all humanly possible strategies and, of course, for all the strategies observed in an experiment. A grammar is merely a parsimonious way in which to capture all the strategies and the unfolding of a particular sequence of tactical steps, from many possibilities, as a specific strategy is applied to a specific problem. Just as a grammar of a language embodies a theory of all the possible syntactic structures in the language, so a grammar of strategies should embody all the different tactical structures in all the possible strategies. Hence, a good theory of strategies will be one that parses *all* the protocols and carries out all their required tactical processes.

Two computational desiderata must be met by the resulting theory. First, the power of the grammar, its position in the Chomsky hierarchy, should be compatible with plausible assumptions about the operations of working memory. Second, the processes embodied in the theory must be comparable in tractability to those carried out by the mind. Theorists sometimes worry that a theory of mental processing postulates processes that are intractable; that is, as the input increases in size, so the process demands an increasing amount of time or memory, or both (see Oaksford & Chater, 1991). We know, however, that some apparently simple classes of inference are almost certainly intractable; for example, determining whether an inference about a possibility is valid takes a nondeterministic device an amount of time that is some polynomial of the length of the premises (it is, technically speaking, "NP" hard). And we also know that as such inferences increase in complexity, for example in the number of premises on which they are based, so the human inferential system collapses under the weight of the problem. Hence, a good theory of such inferences should also postulate mental processes that are intractable.

We illustrate the construction of a grammar for strategies by considering the way in which we have modeled the chain strategy. The major tactical steps in the strategy are as follows, with options shown in parentheses:

1.   *Read each premise and grasp its meaning.*
2.   *Draw a diagram based on the meaning of a premise.*
(3.   *Check the diagram.)*

4.   Select a constituent proposition (antecedent or consequent) of the conditional conclusion.

5.   Find a premise (or diagram) containing the constituent proposition.

(6.   If the premise or diagram is not a conditional, make an immediate inference to a conditional with an antecedent that matches the constituent proposition.)

7.   If the consequent matches the other constituent in the conclusion, or its negation, then the chain is complete. Otherwise, focus on the constituent proposition expressed by the consequent of the conditional, and continue from Step 5 above.

8.   Evaluate the chain: if it reaches the other constituent of the conclusion, respond: Yes, the conclusion follows; if it reaches the negation of the other constituent of the conclusion, respond: No, the conclusion does not follow; otherwise, abandon the strategy.

The full implementational details would overwhelm the reader, but here is a sketch of how the program works. It examines each item in a protocol to determine its tactical status, which includes the following cases, for example:

READ the next premise and grasp its meaning
Make an IMMEDIATE-INFERENCE from a premise
Draw a DIAGRAM.

This procedure yields an annotated version of the protocol, and it carries out all the required tactical steps, drawing diagrams, making inferences, and so on, as it proceeds through the protocol. Indeed, its ability to carry out these steps provides a check on the accuracy of its tactical assignments to each step in the protocol. We have assumed a so-called "regular" grammar of strategies. Such a grammar corresponds to a finite-state automaton, which is the simplest hypothesis about how strategies are generated. Finite-state automata do not require any working memory for intermediate results, and so in the Chomsky hierarchy they are the least powerful computational device capable of generating infinitely many sequences. (Of course, the program as a whole makes use of working memory as do human reasoners: Our assumption of a regular grammar concerns only the identification of tactical steps in a protocol.) In the grammar representing the chain strategy, each rule corresponds to a tactical step in the strategy. It specifies the state of the system by an arbitrary numerical label such as S0, the next tactical step, and the resulting state of the system after this step is taken, for example:

S0 → read-premise S1
S1 → read-premise S2
S2 → immediate-inference S3

Grammars are useful ways to control computer programs, but they are hard for readers to digest. Figure 11.6 shows a finite-state automaton and the equivalent grammar for drawing a diagram. As the figure shows, the system starts in state S0 and then has a choice of different routes.

Finite-state device:

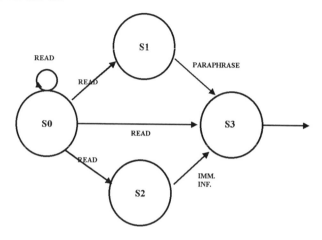

Grammar:

	READ S0
S0 →	READ S1
	READ S2
	READ S3
S1 →	PARAPHRASE S3
S2 →	IMMEDIATE-INFERENCE S3
S3 →	DRAW-DIAGRAM

FIG. 11.6. A nondeterministic finite-state device, and its corresponding grammar for reading a premise and drawing a diagram.

It reads a premise and may stay in the same state (S0)—so that it can read the premise repeatedly, or it jumps to a state (S1) where its next action is to paraphrase the premise, or to a state (S2) where its next action is to make an immediate inference from the premise, or to a state (S3) where its next action is to draw a diagram of the premise. Nothing in the automaton or grammar determines which of these routes is taken, and that is why the process is nondeterministic.

The representation of diagrams in our program is simple. One sort corresponds to individual premises, for example:

(draw a → b)   stands for drawing of one-directional arrow
(draw a ↔ b)   stands for two-directional arrow or '='

(draw a / b)   stands for some sort of separation between a and b, such as the drawing
          of separating circles round them
(draw a b)   stands for a grouping of a and b together
-a   stands for crossing out an a
+a   stands for ticking or affirming an a in some way.

Problem:
(a ore b)
(b ore c)
(c iff d))
(if a then d) Conclusion

Verbal Protocol:	Diagrams:	Tactical steps:
Drawing initial diagrams:		
(a ore b)		Read-premise
(a or b)		Immediate-inference
	(draw a / b)	Draw
(b ore c)		Read-premise
	(draw b / c)	Draw
(iff d then c)		Immediate-inference
(if d then c)		Immediate-inference
	(draw d → c)	Draw
(if d then c)		Immediate-inference
	(show d → c)	Show-diagram
Checking previous steps, showing diagrams:		
(a or b)	(show a / b)	Show-diagram
(b or c)	(show b / c)	Show-diagram
(b or c)	(show b / c)	Show-diagram
The chain strategy from d in conclusion:		
(if d then c)	(show d → c)	Show-diagram
(if c then not b)		Immediate-inference
	(draw c → - b)	Draw
(if c then not b)	(show c → - b)	Check previous two steps
(if not b then a)		Immediate-inference
	(draw - b → a)	Draw
(if not b then a)	(show - b → a)	Check previous two steps
(if a then d)		Read-evaluate-conclusion
(yes)		Assert conclusion

FIG. 11.7. An annotated protocol of the chain strategy in the format used by the computer program modeling the strategy. For simplicity, paraphrases of premises have been subsumed under the more general tactic of making an immediate inference.

Problem:
(a ore b)
(b ore c)
(c iff d))
(if a then d) Conclusion

The program's output:
Drawing initial diagrams:

(Read-premise (a ore b))
(Immediate-inference (a or b) from (a ore b))
(Diagram (draw a / b) from (a ore b))
(Read-premises (b ore c))
(Diagram (draw b/c) from (b ore c))
(Immediate-inference (iff d then c) from (c iff d))
(Immediate-inference (if d then c) from (c iff d))
(Diagram (draw d → c) from (c iff d))

. . . Checking previous steps, showing diagrams

The chain strategy from d in conclusion:
(Diagram (show d →_c) from (c iff d))
(Immediate-inference (if c then not b) from (b ore c))
(Diagram (draw c → - b) from (b ore c))
. . . checks two previous steps
(Immediate-inference (if not b then a) from (a ore b))
(Diagram (draw - b → a) from (a ore b))
. . . checks two previous steps   Chain is complete.
(Read-conclusion (if a then d))
(Asserts-conclusion (Yes))

The parse was successful.

FIG. 11.8. A computer parse of the protocol in Fig. 11.7. We have omitted the program's output for the repetitions of certain steps. Everything within parentheses is an output of the program; our comments are on separate lines without parentheses.

Another sort of diagram is built up from the premises cumulatively. For example, a diagram that uses two horizontal lines to represent two possibilities (see Fig. 11.5), such as:

a   c   d
b

is represented by showing the cumulative steps in its construction:

(draw 1 a / b)
(draw 1 a c / b)
(draw 1 a c d / b)

where "1" is a number identifying the diagram. In addition to drawing diagrams, our participants often point to an existing diagram, particularly when they are checking a previous step. The program likewise can "show" a diagram, for example (show 1 a c d / b).

Figure 11.7 shows a complete "think aloud" protocol of a chain strategy in which we have substituted "*a*," "*b*," "*c*," and "*d*" for the propositions referring to the different colours. We have also added comments that label the tactical steps, and shown the diagrams drawn by the participant using the earlier notation. Our program can parse chain strategies and carry out the corresponding inferential processes. Figure 11.8 shows its output as it parses the "think aloud" protocol in Fig. 11.7. Our general goal, yet to be achieved, is for the program to deal with all four strategies.

STRATEGIES AND TACTICS IN REFUTATIONS

We now turn to reasoning based on quantifiers, and to our attempts to identify the strategies and tactics of syllogistic reasoning. Syllogisms are logically simple inferences based on two premises, which each can be in one of four "moods":

All the A are B	*-- abbreviated as the 'A' mood*
Some of the A are B	*-- abbreviated as the 'I' mood*
None of the A is a B	*-- abbreviated as the 'E' mood*
Some of the A are not B	*-- abbreviated as the 'O' mood*

Here, are the premises of a typical syllogistic problem:

Some of the chefs are musicians.
None of the musicians is a painter.
What conclusion, if any, follows?

There are two controversies about syllogistic reasoning. The first is whether logically untrained individuals can reason at all syllogistically, or are merely selecting a conclusion that matches the mood of a premise (Chater & Oaksford, 1999; Martin Levine, personal communication, May 1994; Wetherick & Gilhooly, 1990). Granted that individuals can reason with quantifiers, the second controversy is whether they rely on formal rules of inference (Rips, 1994; Yang, Braine, & O'Brien, 1998); or on some sort of models, which may be Euler circles (Cardaci, Gangemi, Pendolino, & Di Nuovo, 1996; Fisher, 1981) or mental models (Johnson-Laird & Bara, 1984; Polk & Newell, 1995) or on both formal rules and Euler circles (Ford, 1995). The variety of theories confirms that even though syllogisms are logically simple, they are psychologically complex. What we aim to show is that none of these theories is quite right.

When we gave reasoners a paper and pencil and asked them to think aloud as they tackled syllogisms, the results were not too revealing, and so we had to devise a new procedure to help us to identify the participants' strategies (see Bucciarelli & Johnson-Laird, 1998). We gave them cut-out shapes to represent the premises, and we video-recorded them as they manipulated these shapes.

Our first study examined the competence of logically untrained individuals to search for counterexamples to putative conclusions. Part of our motivation was to check a computer program implementing the model theory (for an account of the program, see Bara, Bucciarelli, & Johnson-Laird, 1995). But, if people are unable to refute conclusions in this way, then Polk and Newell (1995) are correct in arguing that refutations play little or no role in syllogistic reasoning. The experiment was therefore designed to externalize the process of searching for counterexamples. The participants were given complete syllogisms, such as:

Some of the chefs are musicians.
None of the musicians are painters.
∴ None of the chefs are painters.

All the syllogisms referred to chefs, musicians, and painters, which were represented in cut-out shapes by chefs' hats, guitars, and palettes, respectively. The task was to add these shapes to six "stick" figures in order to construct an external model of the premises that refuted the putative conclusions. There were 20 syllogisms, four with valid conclusions, the remaining 16 with conclusions that could be correctly refuted by appropriate models of the premises.

The participants were able to construct counterexamples. The overall percentage of correct responses in cases where a conclusion could be refuted was 59%; and the overall percentage of correct responses in cases where a conclusion could not be refuted was 71%: Both results are much better than chance performance. Each participant was able to refute conclusions, and the range in performance was from 95% correct responses by the best participant to 25% correct responses by the poorest participant. This range in ability is quite characteristic of syllogistic reasoning. A major cause of error was that the participants often did not grasp what constituted a refutation of certain moods of conclusion. With conclusions in the O mood ("*Some of the A are not C*"), they often constructed a model in which some of the *A* were *C*, and they sometimes constructed a model in which none of the *A* were *C*. The correct counterexample calls for a model in which "*all the A are C.*" Likewise, the participants occasionally thought that they had refuted a conclusion in the I mood "*Some of the A are C*," when they had merely constructed a model in which some of the A were not C. Such problems should be alleviated by expressing conclusions in the O mood using the logically equivalent form:

Not all of the A are C

because the participants appeared to refute an O conclusion by constructing a model of an assertion that omitted the term "not."

The participants varied in how they interpreted the four different moods of premises. Their preferred interpretation for first premises of the form, "*All the A are B*," was the co-extensive one in which each A is a B, and each B is an A. The result is an external model of the following form:

    a   b
    a   b

which represents two individuals who are both A's and B's. This interpretation was the preferred one for most sorts of syllogisms, but when the second premise was in the O mood, the participants were more inclined to build models of the A premise in which the A's were properly included within the B's:

    a   b
    a   b
         b

Evidently, a second premise in the mood, "*Some of the B are not C*," helped reasoners to grasp that there could be B's that are not A's. Analogous patterns of influence occurred with other premises.

The most striking aspect of the results was the variety in the participants' strategies. The main strategies in a nutshell are as follows: The reasoners sometimes began by constructing a model of the first premise to which they added the information from the second premise; they sometimes proceeded in the opposite order. Sometimes, their initial model satisfied the conclusion, and so they modified the model in order to refute the conclusion; sometimes, they constructed an initial model of the premises that immediately refuted the conclusion. Here, to illustrate the variety of strategies, we summarize performance with the syllogism of the form:

Some of the A are B.
None of the B are C.
∴ None of the A are C.

Of the 20 participants, 16 correctly refuted the conclusion by constructing a model of the premises in which the conclusion was false. Five of these participants began by constructing a model of the premises that was consistent with the conclusion:

```
a
a     b
          c
```

where we have ignored the actual numbers of tokens of each type that the participants constructed. Two of the five participants then refuted the conclusion by adding a C to an A (an operation that our computer program modeling the theory also carries out):

```
a                               a             c
a    b          becomes         a     b
         c                                    c
```

Another two of the five participants added an A to a C (which the program can also do):

```
b    a                          b     a
b               becomes         b
         c                            a     c
```

The remaining participant of the five introduced a new B and an A, and added a C to the A:

```
a    b                          a     b
a                               a     b
         c      becomes               b
                                a            c
                                             c
```

In contrast, 11 of the 16 participants who were correct refuted the conclusion in their initial model of the premises. Six of them did so with the following model:

```
a         c
a    b
```

and three of them did so with the model:

```
a    b
a         c
     b
```

The other two out of the 11 built slight variants of the first of these models. Thus, the 16 participants reached a correct counterexample using at least five distinct procedures.

To what extent are these differences *strategic* as opposed to *tactical*? The distinction is harder to draw than in the case of sentential reasoning, but since we need a theory that encompasses both strategies and tactics, it may not be too important. In our view, the tactical steps are as follows:

> *Read a premise and grasp its meaning.*
> *Build a model (internal or external) based on a premise's meaning.*
> *Add information based on a premise's meaning to an existing model.*
> *Formulate a conclusion based on one or more models.*
> *Evaluate a conclusion with respect to one or more models.*
> *Construct an alternative model of the premises (in which the conclusion is false).*

Hence, some of the variation in the protocols for the previous example are different ways of carrying out a tactical step. For example, in seeking an alternative model of the premises, where a genuine alternative differs not merely in the numbers of tokens of different types, there are three main processes. Our computer program, as it happens, implements each of them. They are to add a token to one that is already in the model, to split an individual in the model into two separate tokens, and to join two separate individuals in the model into one. In principle, there is at least one other operation that reasoners could use: completely removing an individual from the model. Our participants only carried out this operation in special circumstances: They would occasionally remove an individual, only to restore the same individual immediately. The principle strategic variation in the task accordingly depends on two choices: what to model first, the first premise, the second premise, or the conclusion; and whether to model initially the conclusion or its refutation. In fact, the latter choice may only affect the external model. The internal model, we suspect, is likely to satisfy the conclusion at first, and then individuals can sometimes refute the conclusion as they an external model.

There are three major discrepancies between our program and the participants' performance. First, the program follows a deterministic strategy. Given a particular pair of premises, it always proceeds in the same way. Our participants, however, varied considerably in what they did, and they seemed likely to vary if they were to encounter the same problem twice (for evidence on this point, see Johnson-Laird & Steedman, 1978). Second, the program uses a fixed interpretation of the premises, whereas given a premise in a particular mood, our participants sometimes created one sort of model and sometimes another, a phenomenon that is much more in line with Polk and Newell's (1995) theory. Third, the program departs from human performance in its explicit representation of negation. Our participants, perhaps because they lacked any external symbols for negation, appeared to represent negatives only as "mental footnotes" on their external models.

Logically untrained individuals are able to construct external models of syllogistic premises, which are counterexamples to putative conclusions. This ability is beyond the explanatory scope of all current formal rule theories (Braine & O'Brien, 1998; Rips, 1994), which refute conclusions merely by failing to find formal derivations of them. Recursively speaking, our result is in turn a counterexample to formal rule theories. A critical issue, however, is whether individuals spontaneously use the strategy of searching for counterexamples when they have to draw syllogistic conclusions for themselves. In order to examine this issue, we carried out a further experiment.

STRATEGIES IN SYLLOGISTIC REASONING

Our final experiment was designed to observe the external models that the participants built in drawing their own conclusions from syllogistic premises. For purposes of comparison, each participant also carried out the inferential task without being allowed to construct external models. The 20 participants drew their own conclusions from a set of 48 syllogisms (all the syllogisms in three of the four "figures" of the syllogism) in two conditions one week apart. Half the participants carried out the task first using external models and then without using them; and half the participants carried out the two conditions in the opposite order.

There was no reliable effect on accuracy of whether the participants constructed external models (51% correct overall) or not (55% correct overall). Likewise, there was no reliable difference between the first session of 48 syllogisms (51% correct) and the second session of 48 syllogisms (55% correct). However, the participants drew a slightly more diverse set of conclusions (a mean of 4.3 different conclusions to each problem) when they constructed external models than when they did not (a mean of 3.6 different conclusions).

Table 11.1.
The percentages of correct responses in the experiment on syllogistic reasoning in which the participants worked both with and without external models

	No external Model	External Model
One-model with valid conclusion	93	89
Multiple model with valid conclusion	29	21
Multiple model with no valid conclusion	60	57

Table 11.1 presents the percentages of correct responses to three sorts of syllogisms: those that have only one model and hence a valid conclusion (one-model syllogisms), those that call for multiple models to reach a valid conclusion (multiple-model syllogisms with a valid conclusion); and those that have multiple models without a conclusion in common (multiple-model syllogisms with no valid conclusion). In both experimental conditions, as the model theory predicts, the participants drew a greater percentage of correct conclusions to one-model problems than to multiple-model problems with (or without) valid conclusions.

In the external model condition, the participants constructed multiple models on 39% of trials, and all 20 participants built them, ranging from two participants who built such sequences on 75% of problems, down to one participant who built them on only 8% of the problems. The results corroborated a crucial prediction of the model theory: The participants were more likely to construct two or more models for the multiple-model problems with valid conclusions (37% of such problems) and with no valid conclusions (48% of such problems) than for one-model problems (11%). All 20 participants were in accord with this prediction. These percentages probably underestimate the construction of multiple models: When the participants constructed just a single model of multiple-model problems, they often made correct responses that were not consistent with that model, which suggests that they had considered an additional model of the premises in their mind's eye.

For the one-model problems, as we have remarked, the majority of conclusions were based on a single model. It is interesting to compare the models postulated in Polk and Newell's (1995) program with those constructed by our participants. As an example, consider the one-model problem based on the premises:

Some B are A.
All B are C.

Under one interpretation of the premises, Polk and Newell's program constructs the following model:

b   c
b   a   c

and then, as a result of reencoding the first premise, it constructs the model:

b   c
     a
b   a   c

from which it generates the valid conclusion: *"Some A are C."* The most frequent response (9 participants) in our experiment was to construct just the first of these models (ignoring the number of tokens). Of the five participants who constructed multiple models, two constructed the foregoing sequence, although the first token constructed by all these participants was of the form: *b a c*.

The participants drew a less varied set of conclusions when they reasoned without the benefit of external models. The difference arises, we believe, because the reasoners constructed external models without being able to encode negative information explicitly. They then drew their conclusion based on the model without considering the presence or absence of negative tokens. Hence, they were more likely to draw a negative conclusion from affirmative premises, or an affirmative conclusion from negative premises, than when they reasoned without the benefit of external models. Yet, the participants' performance was of comparable accuracy whether or not they used external models, and the numbers of models had comparable effects in both experimental conditions (see Table 11.1).

Evidently, naive reasoners construct sequences of multiple models in drawing conclusions, especially from problems that support multiple models. This result was predicted by the model theory. Yet, the construction of multiple models is not necessarily equivalent to a search for counterexamples (see also Handley, Dennis, Evans, & Capon, chap. 12, this volume). Reasoners who construct more than one model may be just augmenting an initial model, but presumably they are not augmenting a model when, as often happened, they construct a model, modify it, revert to the original, modify it again, and so on. Likewise, participants must in general have been envisaging an alternative model when they constructed a single model from which they drew a correct response that was inconsistent with that model. But, again, we cannot be certain that refutation was the underlying motivation. Hence, a sequence of models is suggestive evidence, but no more, for the claim that reasoners are searching for counterexamples. It is bolstered, however, by the nature of the errors. Our analysis showed that there are three common causes of error. Some errors occur because reasoners overlook alternative models of the premises; some errors occur because reasoners construct the right set of models but assume that the models have nothing in common; and some errors occur because reasoners construct the right set of models but describe only one of them. To reach the right response to multiple-model syllogisms for the right reason, it is necessary to consider not just the initial models, but to search for alternatives, to grasp what, if anything, is common to all of them, and to describe it correctly.

Despite its successful predictions, the model theory and its computer implementation once again fail badly in accounting for the data. There were the same discrepancies as we observed in the previous experiment: The program uses a single deterministic strategy, it makes a single interpretation for each mood of the premises, and it represents negation explicitly. In constructing external models, our participants violated each of these principles.

REPRESENTATIONS AND TACTICS IN SYLLOGISTIC REASONING

Our results count against all current theories of syllogistic reasoning. We showed in the previous section that they are incompatible with the present theory of mental models. We turn now to other accounts. It is impossible to prove that the processes postulated by a theory play no role in reasoning, and indeed many of these processes may occur, but what we can show is that no theory by itself can explain our results. The results of our experiments demonstrate that logically untrained individuals are able to reason from syllogistic premises. They are not merely generating conclusions in accordance with the "atmosphere" of the premises (*pace* Wetherick & Gilhooly, 1990) or selecting a conclusion that matches the form of the least informative premise (*pace* Chater & Oaksford, 1999). Granted that logically untrained individuals do reason, the principal controversy is whether they rely on formal rules of inference, or some form of mental model, or both.

Could it be that some reasoners do rely on formal rules? This claim is defended by Ford (1995). She argued that some of the participants in her study relied on a verbal substitution strategy. She classified participants as using this strategy if they spoke of replacing one term in a syllogism with another, or crossed out one term and replaced it with another. But, she also classified participants as using the strategy if they rewrote a syllogism as an equation or drew arrows between its terms (see Ford, 1995, fn 2, p. 18). This evidence may be consistent with a verbal strategy, but it is hardly decisive. Consider how the strategy is supposed to work: "*the subjects . . . take one premise as having a term that needs to be substituted with another term and the other premise as providing a value for that substitution*" (Ford, 1995, p. 21). Ford proposes a set of formal rules governing these substitutions. Apart from notational differences, Braine and Rumain (1983) have proposed the same rules. But, is the substitution procedure a purely verbal one dependent on formal rules of inference? And does the model theory, as Ford implies, group "*all people together as though they basically reason in the same fashion*" (Ford, 1995, p. 3)? Johnson-Laird and Bara (1984, p. 50) wrote: "*There are undoubtedly differences from one individual to another in the way in which they make syllogistic inferences. Our alternative implementations of the theory suggest a way in which some of these differences might be explained.*" Ironically, one of these alternatives was a substitution procedure based on models rather than verbal premises, that is, one token is substituted for another in a model of the premises (see also Johnson-Laird, 1983, p. 106). In fact, no evidence shows that the substitution strategy is purely verbal as opposed to based on mental models.

Current theories based on formal rules (e.g., Braine & O'Brien, 1998; Rips, 1994) postulate such rules for syllogisms as:

All X are Y.
All Y are Z.

$\therefore$ *All X are Z.*

The drawback of these rule systems is that models play no part in them, and so they are unable to explain the ability of our participants to construct external models, or to establish models that are counterexamples to putative conclusions. However, Rips's system has the power of a Universal Turing machine, and so it can be used as a programming language in which to implement any theory, including the mental model theory. His theory in this general sense is thus almost irrefutable, that is, no empirical results could ever show it to be false unless they demonstrated that mental processes are not computable (Johnson-Laird, 1997). But, formal rules in a narrower sense cannot explain how people are able to construct external models or to refute conclusions by constructing counterexamples to them. So let us turn to a competing model-based theory.

Euler circles represent each set referred to in a premise by a circle, and they represent the relation between the two sets by a simple topological relation between the circles. Hence, a premise of the form "*All the A are B*" calls for two separate representations: In one, the circle representing A lies wholly within the circle representing B, that is, the set A is properly included with set B; and in the other, the two circles coincide, that is, the two sets are co-extensive. Analogous topological relations between the two circles represent premises in the other moods. The traditional use of Euler circles calls for the construction of all the different diagrams for each premise, and all the different combinations for the pair of premises, a demand that leads to a combinatorial explosion (see Erickson, 1974). Stenning and his colleagues have devised a novel way to use Euler circles that obviates this explosion (see Stenning & Yule, 1997). Ford (1995) postulates a similar procedure: Reasoners assume that areas enclosed by circles can be empty, and they use the verbal premises as reminders of which areas cannot be empty. This procedure, as Ford allows, is equivalent to the use of optional elements in models. Hence, the main burden of Stenning's analysis and Ford's results is that reasoners do not use the traditional method of Euler circles. These authors, however, give no account of the sequences of models that reasoners construct or of the operations that they use to generate such sequences.

There is no doubt that some people rely on Euler circles. But, do individuals who have never seen circles used to represent sets spontaneously use Euler circles? As far as we know, no logician prior to Leibniz used circles to represent sets. The idea was a major innovation, and it was later popularized by Euler's letters to a Swedish princess. If naive individuals spontaneously use the method, why wasn't it invented earlier and why did it have to be popularized? The major disadvantage of Euler circles, however, is that they do not generalize to relational inferences, such as the following example (see Russell, 1946):

All horses are animals.

∴   *All horses' heads are animals' heads.*

In contrast, mental models represent finite sets of entities by finite sets of mental tokens, and they readily accommodate relations among entities (see Johnson-Laird, 1983). Ford (1995) appears to take for granted that because some of her participants drew Euler circles, it follows that these individuals were not using mental models. She writes: *"Thus, the spatial subjects used a type of representation specifically dismissed by Johnson-Laird and his colleagues, where the class itself and not the finite members of the class is represented"* (p. 41). Readers should note the equivocation in this claim. Ford is referring to the external representations drawn by her participants; Johnson-Laird and his colleagues are referring to internal mental representations. Moreover, contrary to Ford, some of her participants whom she classified as verbal reasoners did refer to individual entities, as the following extracts from four protocols show:

i.   *. . . if there are any historians like suppose there's two historians right that means there are two weavers who are also historians so we can say some of the weavers are historians . . . (Eric)*

ii.   *. . . could have a weaver that is not a historian and is a TC member (Catherine)*

iii. *. . . all of the historians are weavers none of the historians well you actually can't conclude that because you have another some one else like a philosopher who could be a weaver who might be a tennis club member . . . (Hilary)*

iv.   *. . . if you're a playwright you're always a bookworm that means you have a chance to be a stamp collector . . . (Amy)*

Although some individuals sometimes draw Euler circles when they make syllogistic inferences, we incline to Rips' (1994) view that they rely on a vestigial memory for a procedure that they encountered in school. Euler circles, however, are a legitimate hypothesis about the nature of mental models. We do not know whether those who draw Euler circles use visual images of them either to control their drawings or to reason when they have no access to paper and pencil. But, we do know that they are not powerful enough for reasoning with relational premises, and that current psychological theories based on them cannot account for the participants' tactics in our experiments.

CONCLUSIONS

What are the main features of the reasoning strategies of logically untrained individuals? The answer is that such individuals develop strategies that are appropriate to the inferences on which they are working. For sentential reasoning, they adopt quite distinct strategies, that are compatible with the use of models at the tactical level, and which allow them to keep track, one way or another, of the relevant possibilities. The suppositional strategy pursues the consequences of one possibility, the one created by the supposition. The chain strategy likewise pursues a possibility that leads from one constituent of the conclusion to the other. The compound strategy combines pairs of premises to infer what is necessary or possible. The model strategy keeps track of all the possibilities.

In contrast, naive reasoners appear to find it impossible to envisage all the possible models of quantified premises. When reasoners are allowed to construct external models, their preferred strategies explore alternative models of the premises, though they often err by overlooking a possibility. Are they searching for counterexamples to conclusions? Certainly, they can do so when they are asked explicitly to refute conclusions. But, Polk and Newell (1995) argued that syllogistic reasoning depends on encoding and reencoding premises as mental models rather than on a search for counterexamples. They support their claim by showing that "falsification" yields little improvement in the fit of their computer program, VR, to the data. We suspect that there is little improvement because VR does some of the work of refutation in other ways. What is right about their theory, however, is its emphasis on the variety of different interpretations of the premises. What appears to be wrong is the sequences of models generated by successive reencodings of the premises. Our participants tended not to reencode the premises for one-model problems (in contrast with VR), but rather to generate sequences in the case of multiplemodel problems. In our study of syllogistic reasoning with external models, the participants generated sequences of alternative models, but whether they were searching for counterexamples is unclear (see Handley et al., chap. 12, this volume).

With hindsight, syllogisms are not an ideal test case for demonstrating a search for counterexamples. Modal reasoning is better, because the model theory predicts an obvious interaction that hinges on reasoners searching for counterexamples: It should be easier to determine that a situation is possible (one model of the premises suffices as an example) than necessary (all the models of the premises must be checked), whereas it should be easier to determine that a situation is not necessary (one model serving as a counterexample suffices) than not possible (all models must be checked). The interaction has been corroborated in reasoning both from sentential connectives (Bell & Johnson-Laird, 1998) and quantifiers (Evans, Handley, & Harper, 1998; see also Galotti, Baron, & Sabini, 1986). Hence, Polk and Newell may be right about syllogisms, but, in those tasks where counterexamples are of obvious use, reasoners appear to search for them. Indeed, as Barwise (1993) emphasized, the only way to *know* that a conclusion is invalid is by constructing a model of the premises that is a counterexample to it.

A complete theory of thinking calls for four levels. At the top level is metacognition and the sort of insightful thinking that leads to the development of a new strategy. Its manifest signs are lacking in the protocols from our experiments. Noone ever remarked, for example, *"I see now how I can solve these problems efficiently,"* and then went on to describe an insightful strategy. None of our participants was an Aristotle! Metacognitive remarks, however, might be observed in other circumstance, such as a study in which the participants are explicitly instructed to develop efficient strategies and to describe them to other people. The second level is the thinking that controls a strategy. Its signs in our protocols are a sequence of organized remarks, and diagrams in the sentential reasoning experiment, from which one can infer the strategy that the reasoner was following. At the third level are the tactics from which a strategy is composed, such as drawing a diagram of a premise, or adding information from a premise to an existing model. At the fourth, and lowest level, are the processes that underlie the tactics, that is, the largely unconscious processes that support, say, making an immediate inference, or using the meaning of a premise to control a drawing. These unconscious processes are perhaps comparable to the "instruction set" of a computer chip. Is all thinking analyzable in these terms? We conjecture that goal-driven thinking is open to metacognitive insights, governed by a strategy, and depends on tactics, which in turn rely on unconscious processes.

The strategies and tactics of reasoning call for a nondeterministic theory, which, as we have illustrated, can take the form of a grammar that is used to parse reasoners' protocols. The strategies and tactics that we have observed both in sentential and quantified reasoning are not easily reconciled with formal rules of inference, but they do seem to be compatible with the unconscious processes that construct and manipulate mental models. The study of strategies in reasoning, unlike strategies in other domains (e.g., Lemaire & Siegler, 1995), has barely begun. There are three pressing goals. Future studies should delineate the "space" of possible strategies, and their effectiveness and efficiency. They should account for the sequences of strategies that reasoners pass through as they gain experience and expertise. Logic, one could say, is the ultimate strategy that some highly gifted individuals attain. But the "Holy Grail" for future research is the discovery of how logically-untrained individuals discover new strategies of reasoning.

ACKNOWLEDGMENTS

We thank our colleague Walter Schaeken for organizing the workshop at which this chapter was presented and for his advice over the years. We are also grateful for the help of many colleagues, including Bruno Bara, Ruth Byrne, Vittorio Girotto, Paolo Legrenzi, and Yingrui Yang. The research was supported in part by ARPA (CAETI) contracts N66001-94-C-6045 and N66001-95-C-8605.

REFERENCES

Bara, B.G., Bucciarelli, M., & Johnson-Laird, P. N. (1995). The development of syllogistic reasoning. *American Journal of Psychology, 108*, 157–193.

Barwise, J. (1993). Everyday reasoning and logical inference (Commentary on Johnson-Laird and Byrne, 1991). *Behavioral and Brain Sciences, 16*, 337–338.

Bell, V., & Johnson-Laird, P. N. (1998). A model theory of modal reasoning. *Cognitive Science, 22*, 25–51.

Braine, M. D. S., & O'Brien, D. P. (1991). A theory of If: A lexical entry, reasoning program and pragmatic principles. *Psychological Review, 98*, 182–203.

Braine, M. D. S., & O'Brien, D. P. (Eds). (1998). *Mental logic.* Mahwah, NJ: Lawrence Erlbaum Associates.

Braine, M. D. S., & Rumain, B. (1983). Logical reasoning. In J. H. Flavell & E. M.

Markman (Eds.), *Carmichael's handbook of child psychology, Vol. III. Cognitive Development* (pp. 240–263). New York: Wiley.

Bucciarelli, M., & Johnson-Laird, P. N. (1998). *Strategies in syllogistic reasoning.* Unpublished manuscript, Department of Psychology, Torino University.

Byrne, R. M. J., & Handley, S. J. (1997). Reasoning strategies for suppositional deductions. *Cognition, 62,* 1–49.

Cardaci, M., Gangemi, A., Pendolino, G., & Di Nuovo, S. (1996). Mental models vs. integrated models: Explanations of syllogistic reasoning. *Perceptual and Motor Skills, 82,* 1377–1378.

Chater, N., & Oaksford, M. (1999). Rational analysis and heuristic processes for syllogistic reasoning. *Cognitive Psychology, 2,* 191–258.

Erickson, J. R. (1974). A set analysis theory of behaviour in formal syllogistic reasoning tasks. In R. Solso (Ed.), *Loyola Symposium on Cognition, Vol. 2* (pp. 305–330). Hillsdale, NJ: Lawrence Erlbaum Associates.

Evans, J. St. B. T., Handley, S. J., & Harper, C. (1998). *Deductions about what is necessary and what is possible: A test of the mental model theory.* Unpublished manuscript, Department of Psychology, University of Plymouth.

Evans, J. St. B. T., Newstead, S. E., & Byrne, R. M. J. (1993). *Human reasoning: The psychology of deduction.* Mahwah, NJ: Lawrence Erlbaum Associates.

Fisher, D. L. (1981). A three-factor model of syllogistic reasoning: The study of isolable stages. *Memory and Cognition, 9,* 496–514.

Ford, M. (1995). Two modes of mental representation and problem solution in syllogistic reasoning. *Cognition, 54,* 1–71.

Galotti, K. M., Baron, J., & Sabini, J. P. (1986). Individual differences in syllogistic reasoning: Deduction rules or mental models? *Journal of Experimental Psychology: General, 115,* 16–25.

Girotto, V., Mazzocco, A., & Tasso, A. (1997). The effect of premise order in conditional reasoning: A test of the mental model theory. *Cognition, 63,* 1–28.

Johnson-Laird, P. N. (1983). *Mental models: Towards a cognitive science of language, inference and consciousness.* Cambridge, UK: Cambridge University Press.

Johnson-Laird, P. N. (1997). Rules and Illusions: A critical study of Rips's The Psychology of Proof. *Minds and Machines, 7,* 387–407.

Johnson-Laird, P. N., & Bara, B. G. (1984). Syllogistic inference. *Cognition, 16,* 1–61.

Johnson-Laird, P. N., & Byrne, R. M. J. (1990). Meta-logical problems: Knights, knaves, and Rips. *Cognition, 36,* 69–81.

Johnson-Laird, P. N., & Byrne, R. M. J. (1991). *Deduction.* Hillsdale, NJ: Lawrence Erlbaum Associates.

Johnson-Laird, P. N., & Steedman, M. (1978). The psychology of syllogisms. *Cognitive Psychology, 10,* 64–99.

Lemaire, P., & Siegler, R. S. (1995). Four aspects of strategic change: Contributions to children's learning of multiplication. *Journal of Experimental Psychology: General, 124,* 83–97.

Oaksford, M., & Chater, N. (1991). Against logicist cognitive science. *Mind & Language, 6,* 1–38.

Polk, T. A., & Newell, A. (1995). Deduction as verbal reasoning. *Psychological Review, 102,* 533–566.

Richardson, J., & Ormerod, T. C. (1997). Rephrasing between disjunctives and conditionals: Mental models and the effects of thematic content. *Quarterly Journal of*

Experimental Psychology, 50A, 358–385.

Rips, L. J. (1989). The psychology of knights and knaves. *Cognition, 31,* 85–116.

Rips, L. J. (1994). *The psychology of proof.* Cambridge, MA: MIT Press.

Russell, B. A. W. (1946). *History of Western philosophy.* London: Allen & Unwin.

Stenning, K., & Yule, P. (1997). Image and language in human reasoning: A syllogistic illustration. *Cognitive Psychology, 34,* 109–159.

Wason, P. C., & Johnson-Laird, P. N. (1972). *Psychology of reasoning: Structure and content.* London: Batsford.

Wetherick, N. E., & Gilhooly, K. J. (1990). Syllogistic reasoning: Effects of premise order. In K. J. Gilhooly, M. T. G. Keane, R. H. Logie, & G. Erdos (Eds.), *Lines of thinking, Vol. I* (pp. 99–108). New York: Wiley.

Yang, Y., Braine, M. D. S., & O'Brien, D. P. (1998). Some empirical justifications of the mental predicate logic model. In M. D. S. Braine & D. P. O'Brien (Eds.), *Mental logic* (pp. 333–365). Mahwah, NJ: Lawrence Erlbaum Associates.

12

Individual Differences and the Search for Counterexamples in Syllogistic Reasoning

Simon J. Handley
Ian Dennis
Jonathan St. B.T. Evans
Alison Capon

In this chapter we consider whether people search for alternatives to the initial conclusions they draw from deductive arguments and the degree to which this tendency might be mediated by individual differences. We present experimental data which suggests that reasoners do not search for counter-examples when engaged in syllogistic reasoning; rather they make judgments based on a single model of the premises. This finding holds for both judgments of necessity and judgments of possibility. We go on to present a confirmatory factor analysis of the data and identify a factor which is interpreted as the degree to which people search for alternative models. This factor is a significant predictor of performance on certain problem types. Problems that can only be solved by considering alternative models to those initially constructed load positively on this factor, whereas problems that can be solved with reference to an initial model load negatively. We argue that there are clear differences in the tendency to search for alternatives but that these differences manifest themselves in different ways dependent upon the processing requirements of a particular problem type. The findings are discussed in the context of current views on the role of counter-example search in human reasoning.

Much recent debate in reasoning research has focused on the role that counterexample search plays in human reasoning (see Newstead, Handley, & Buck, in press). This chapter offers a contribution to this debate. We present a series of experimental and individual differences analyses suggesting that although searching for counterexamples may be a weak tendency overall, there are clear differences in this tendency that manifest themselves in different ways on different sorts of problems.

Our experimental work focuses on syllogistic reasoning and hence we begin by describing this reasoning paradigm. The theoretical and experimental analyses presented draw heavily on a specific theory of deduction, the model theory, and in the second section of this chapter we briefly outline this approach, together with alternative theoretical accounts of syllogistic reasoning. The model theory places a strong emphasis on the functional role that searching for counterexamples plays in human reasoning, and in the third section we review the evidence for and against this position. The remaining sections are devoted to describing the findings from our experimental program of research on syllogistic reasoning and a re-analysis of these findings from an individual differences perspective. Finally the role of individual differences in counterexample search and its impact on performance is discussed.

SYLLOGISTIC REASONING

Syllogistic reasoning is one of the most widely studied paradigms in the reasoning literature. Indeed, the earliest studies of deductive reasoning focused on the sorts of conclusions that people endorsed when they were presented with Aristotelian syllogisms (see Woodworth & Sells, 1935). A syllogism consists of two premises and a conclusion that describe set relationships between a number of terms. The premises and the conclusion of a syllogism take one of four quantified forms, *all* (A), *some* (I), *no* (E) or *some not* (O), and these forms are referred to as moods. A syllogism has two end terms and a linking or middle term, for example, in the following syllogism:

All A are B.
All B are C.

.: All A are C.

The end terms are A and C, and the linking term or middle term is B. These terms can be arranged in one of the following four ways, which are referred to as figures (Johnson-Laird & Bara, 1984):

Figure 1:	Figure 2:	Figure 3:	Figure 4:
A–B	B–A	A–B	B–A
B–C	B–C	C–B	C–B

Given that there are four quantified terms there are 16 distinct syllogistic premise sets associated with each figure, and hence 64 possible syllogistic premise combinations. Each premise combination can be presented with one of the four quantified conclusions linking the A and C terms and each conclusion can run in the direction A to C or C to A. This gives a set of 512 possible syllogisms. The conclusion to a syllogism can be necessary (determined by the premises), possible but not necessary (not determined by the premises), or impossible (falsified by the premises). So, with reference to the syllogism above, the conclusion "*All A are C*" is necessary, the conclusion "*All C are A*" is possible but not necessary, and the conclusion "*No A are C*" is impossible. We return to the distinction between possibility and impossibility later.

Research on syllogistic reasoning generally employs one of two methodologies. Participants are either presented with syllogistic premises together with a selected conclusion and asked to evaluate the conclusion in terms of its logical validity, or they are presented with syllogistic premises and asked to generate their own conclusion interrelating the end terms. Throughout the experimental work presented here we employed a conclusion evaluation paradigm, but as we see later, the type of task used may be important in influencing the strategy employed in syllogistic reasoning.

THEORIES OF SYLLOGISTIC REASONING

Theories of syllogistic reasoning can be categorized in terms of whether they explain performance by recourse to a general theory of inferential processing or whether they emphasize the role of nonlogical heuristics or response biases in predicting patterns of responding. Noninferential accounts include the atmosphere theory of syllogistic reasoning which proposes that reasoners select conclusions on the basis of the mood of the premises (Woodworth & Sells, 1935), or the matching hypothesis (Wetherick & Gilhooly, 1990), which suggests that responses are elicited which match the quantified form of one of the premises. A more recent version of these noninferential accounts is grounded in information theory, and proposes that reasoners select conclusions that match the least informative syllogistic premise (Chater & Oaksford, 1999). The specific details of these theories is not important for our purposes, but what is important is that they assign no role for explicit inferential processing in syllogistic reasoning.

Process models, on the other hand, propose that syllogistic reasoning is accomplished by engaging an explicit deductive mechanism. These accounts include rule-based theories of deduction which have been developed to account for competence in propositional reasoning and extended to reasoning with quantifiers (see Rips, 1994) and model- based theories which have been developed specifically to account for syllogistic reasoning and extended into other domains (see Johnson-Laird & Bara, 1984). According to rule theorists this deductive mechanism depends on the application of formal rules of inference to the premises of an argument in order to derive a conclusion. The systems and rules proposed have much in common with natural deduction systems and predicate logic, and the difficulty of an inference is seen as a function of the number of rules and the complexity or length of the logical proof. Errors in reasoning may arise through an inability to access appropriate rules, failure to keep track of the intermediate outputs of a complex derivation, or through mis-interpretation or mis-encoding of the premise information. Rule theorists argue that reasoning depends on the application of logical rules to the syntactic form of an argument and hence semantics plays a role only in terms of the recovery of this logical form (see Henle, 1962).

In contrast, theories of reasoning based on mental models propose that reasoning depends on the manipulation of representations that correspond to situations in the world. Mental models are constructed from discourse and their construction depends not on the syntactic structure of the discourse, but on the meaning conveyed by an assertion, together with the background knowledge elicited. According to the mental model theory reasoning proceeds in three main stages.

1.   Given a set of premises reasoners construct a set of models corresponding to the possible states of affairs in which the premises are true.
2.   These models are then inspected and an initial conclusion is drawn which is non-trivial in nature.
3.   Reasoners then search for counter-examples - that is they search for models in which the premises are true but their initial conclusion is false. If no counter-example is found then they can infer that conclusion necessarily follows from the premises.

To illustrate this process consider the following syllogism (Johnson-Laird & Byrne, 1991):

All of the bakers are athletes.
None of the bakers is a canoeist.

The computational program of the model theory elicits the following model initially

[a   [b]]
[a   [b]]
             [c]
             [c]
. . .

where the square brackets indicate that a token is exhaustively represented in the set of models and the ellipsis, ". . .", indicates that there are alternative models of the premises that are not initially represented. This initial model supports the putative conclusion:

None of the canoeists is an athlete.

and indeed this conclusion is one of the most common errors with this problem type. To appreciate that the conclusion is not necessitated by the premises reasoners must construct another model that is consistent, but in which the conclusion does not hold. The second model generated by the computer program is the following:

[a   [b]]
[a   [b]]
a   [c]
             [c]
. . .

and this refutes the initial conclusion, but supports a second conclusion:

Some of the canoeists are not athletes.

This conclusion is then refuted by a third model:

```
[a    [b]]
[a    [b]]
 a        [c]
 a        [c]
 . . .
```

All three models in conjunction with one another support the valid conclusion:

Some of the athletes are not canoeists.

Reasoners can only draw this conclusion with certainty after constructing the full set of models of the premises. The model theory proposes that these models are produced in a specific order which is determined by the way in which the models of individual quantified assertions are combined (Bucciarelli & Johnson-Laird, in press). The theory predicts that syllogisms that depend on the construction of multiple models will be more difficult than syllogisms that can be solved by constructing a single model. This prediction is made on the basis that it is difficult to keep in mind multiple alternatives and hence people are likely to lose track of the contents of their models when more than one model is required. According to Johnson-Laird and Byrne (1993) people are equipped with the psychological mechanisms that enable them to search for counterexamples to their initial conclusions, but they often fail to do so because they have no systematic search procedure. However, the search for counterexamples is a crucial stage in the reasoning process if an individual is genuinely attempting to reason deductively. After all, the judgment that a conclusion is deductively valid can only be made with certainty if there are no models of the premises in which the conclusion does not hold. Whether or not people ordinarily search for counterexamples when they reason is an issue that has attracted some debate, and in the following section we review the evidence for and against falsification strategies in deductive reasoning.

THE SEARCH FOR COUNTEREXAMPLES IN DEDUCTIVE REASONING

As we have seen many theories of syllogistic reasoning argue that performance can be explained without reference to an explicit reasoning process, but rather depends on simple heuristics that specify the type of conclusion that can be drawn. Clearly these accounts are inconsistent with the view that people actively attempt to falsify initial conclusions by considering alternative premise representations. Recently, however, theorists who favor a model-based account of reasoning have also argued that counterexample search plays a minor role in the process of reasoning.

Polk and Newell (1995) presented a model-based theory of syllogistic reasoning in which they account for performance by recourse to representational processes alone, without any assumption that falsification or counterexample search takes place. They argue that syllogistic reasoning involves the repeated re-encoding of the premises of an argument, until a legal conclusion interrelating the end terms can be generated. At this point the process is halted. Polk and Newell demonstrated that their verbal reasoning model of syllogistic reasoning provided a good fit to existing data and when they added an additional parameter to their model based on falsification they found that this explained less than 2% of the variance.

Newstead et al. (in press) provided empirical support that is consistent with this view. Their participants were instructed to produce diagrams consistent with a set of syllogistic premises, which referred to shapes and features, and then to draw a conclusion from the premises. For most syllogisms, both single and multiple model, participants constructed more than one logically distinct diagram. However, the crucial finding was that the number of logically distinct diagrams produced was not predictive of logical accuracy on the syllogistic task and further there was no difference in the number of diagrams produced for single as compared to multiple model problems. If people routinely draw putative conclusions and then attempt to falsify these conclusions by constructing alternative models, then one might expect there to be some relationship between the number of external representations constructed and logical performance. The absence of such a relationship suggests that the consideration of alternative models does not play a functional role in reasoning in that it does not lead to increased logical accuracy.

A different conclusion, however, is suggested in the research of Bucciarelli and Johnson-Laird (in press; see also Johnson-Laird, Savary, & Bucciarelli, chap. 11, this volume). They similarly asked participants to construct external models, on this occasion using cut-out shapes to represent classes of individuals. First, they found that participants were good at constructing external representations of class relations that refuted given conclusions. Second, they showed in a conclusion production task, that people constructed multiple models when asked to draw conclusions from syllogistic arguments, and contrary to Newstead et al., more models were constructed for multiple model syllogisms than single model syllogisms. However, Bucciarelli and Johnson-Laird do not report whether the number of models constructed is predictive of logical accuracy, a finding that is important in illustrating that the consideration of counterexamples plays a functional role in reasoning.

Other phenomena in syllogistic reasoning also, at first sight, seem to support a search for counterexamples. Byrne and Johnson-Laird (1990) tested their participants ability to recognize conclusions that they had earlier drawn from syllogistic premises. They found that conclusions that were recognized falsely were consistent with an initial model of the premises for syllogisms for which they had earlier responded correctly that nothing follows. Byrne and Johnson-Laird argued that this finding suggests that participants fleetingly consider the erroneous conclusion, only to reject it as a result of a counterexample. However, this finding is not as compelling as it may first seem. In the recognition phase of the study the original syllogism was re-presented and hence it was possible that reasoners were simply re-solving the syllogism, but on this occasion drawing a different conclusion. Indeed in a second study, where the recognition task was not accompanied by the original premise sets, memory for conclusions was random.

Although the data from syllogistic reasoning experiments provides equivocal evidence for counterexample search, recent research on modal reasoning has perhaps provided clearer findings. The model theory predicts an interaction in modal reasoning that rests on the assumption that reasoners do attempt to consider alternative models. Bell and Johnson-Laird (1998) argued it should be easier to judge that a conclusion is possible, as one model will suffice, than to judge that a conclusion is necessary, where all models must be checked. In contrast it should be easier to determine that a conclusion is not necessary, where only one counterexample is needed, than to judge that a conclusion is not possible, where all models must be checked. These predictions were confirmed in studies of both visual and verbal reasoning.

One point that is clear from our brief review of this literature is that the evidence for counterexample search, certainly in syllogistic reasoning, is far from convincing. In the following section we describe the findings from our experimental program of research on modal reasoning from quantified premises and discuss the implications of this research in the context of this theoretical issue.

EXPERIMENTAL PROGRAM OF RESEARCH

Experiments 1 and 2

Most research in the psychology of reasoning asks people what is necessary given some premise information. As we have seen more recently researchers have begun to investigate modal reasoning, that is the manner in which people make judgments of possibility and impossibility. The main focus of our experimental work was on judgments of necessity and possibility in syllogistic reasoning. In Experiment 1 we presented participants with an immediate inference task in which they received single quantified assertions, such as "*All A's are B's*," and were required to make a "*Yes*" or "*No*" judgment to indicate whether a second assertion, such as "*some A are C*," either necessarily followed (in the necessary group) or possibly followed (in the possible group). In Experiment 2 the same participants were presented with all 64 possible syllogistic premise pairs together with every possible conclusion, and again one group of participants were asked to judge if the conclusion necessarily followed and the second group were asked to judge if the conclusion possibly followed. The problems in both studies were classified as necessary (where the conclusion must follow), possible (where the conclusion may be, but does not have to be true), and impossible (where the conclusion cannot be true).

Our main motivation was to provide a method that could differentiate between rule-based and model-based accounts of human reasoning, without relying too greatly on the specifics of the theories. As we have seen the model theory proposes three general stages in reasoning, model construction, conclusion generation, and counterexample search. In order to judge that a conclusion is possible it is necessary only to find a single model in which the conclusion holds, and there is no need to search for alternative models that could falsify this conclusion. Hence, possible judgments depend on only the first two stages of the process. In contrast, judgments of necessity require reasoners to check that the conclusion holds in all models of the premises and hence also require the validation stage. Therefore, the model theory would predict that judgments of possibility will be made more readily than judgments of necessity.

In contrast, rule theorists do not currently have a procedure that would enable people to make modal judgments. Rule theories contain rules that allow necessary conclusions to be inferred, but do not have rules that allow modal conclusions. Within the current rule-theoretic framework a conclusion could only be shown as possible if reasoners failed to find a derivation that proved its obverse. That is, reasoners would have to assume that the conclusion was false and try to construct a derivation of this negation. If this succeeded then the conclusion could be judged as impossible; if there was no derivation then the conclusion could be judged as possible. This is an extension of current rule theories, but it is clear that such a procedure would be more resource intensive and hence, on this account, we might expect possible judgments to be more difficult than necessary judgments. Our series of experiments provide clear tests of these divergent predictions.

There were also two more specific predictions that were made, regarding the endorsement of conclusions as possible or necessary. Before examining these predictions consider the model-based checking procedures that are required for the following four possible judgments:

Yes - conclusion necessary:	The conclusion holds in all models of the premises.
No - conclusion not necessary:	The conclusion fails to hold in at least one model.
Yes - conclusion possible:	The conclusion holds in at least one model.
No - conclusion not possible:	The conclusion does not hold in any models of the premises.

In order to be certain that a conclusion follows necessarily from a set of premises all models of the premises must be checked in order to ensure that the conclusion holds in all of them. To judge that a conclusion is not necessary only a single model needs to be found that does not support the conclusion. In order to make a judgment that a conclusion is possible it is only necessary to check that the conclusion holds in a single model of the premises. In contrast, a judgment of impossibility involves checking that the conclusion does not hold in any models of the premises. The following two predictions were derived from this model-based analysis:

Prediction 1:   It will be easier to judge that a conclusion is not necessary if it is also not possible since no models of the premises support the conclusion. Specifically there will be fewer endorsements of conclusions as necessary in the necessary group when the conclusion is also not possible as compared to conclusions which are possible.

Prediction 2:   It will be easier to judge that a conclusion is possible if it is also necessary, since any model of the premises supports the conclusion. Specifically there will be more endorsements of conclusions as possible when the conclusion necessarily follows as compared to conclusions which only possibly follow.

The rationale for the first prediction is that reasoners need identify only one model of the premises that does not contain the conclusion in order to judge that it is not possible. This will be easier on impossible problems, because no models support the conclusion than on possible conclusions in which at least one model supports the conclusion. The rationale for the second prediction is that people need only identify a single model that supports the conclusion to decide that it is possible. This will be easier on necessary problems where all models support the conclusion than on possible problems where there is at least one model that does not.

The findings from both the immediate inference task and the syllogistic reasoning task were entirely consistent with our predictions. Figure 12.1 shows the percentage of conclusions endorsed, within each group and for each type of conclusion, for both experiments.

As the graphs clearly illustrate participants endorsed more conclusions under possibility instructions than under necessity instructions. Where the conclusion is necessary (the first two bars on each graph) this is the logically correct response in both cases and there is a clear and significant difference between groups on these problem types. This provides good evidence for the model-theoretic account of modal reasoning and is inconsistent with rule-based theories. Our more specific predictions were also strongly confirmed. In both the immediate inference task and the syllogistic inference task participants under necessity instructions endorsed more possible conclusions (true in one model) than impossible conclusions (false in all models). Similarly, under possibility instructions participants endorsed more necessary conclusions (true in all models) than possible conclusions (true in one model).

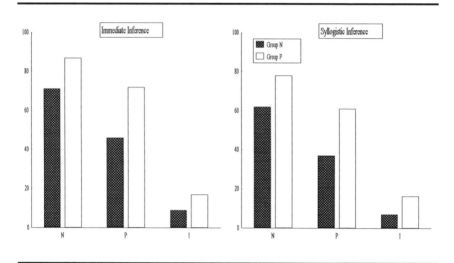

FIG. 12.1. Endorsement of the three types of syllogism in Experiments 1 and 2 as a function of instructional group. Group N is the necessary instruction group, Group P is the possible instruction group.

All the predictions that erived from the model theory were strongly confirmed, although as we have seen, the model theory also proposes that necessity judgments involve an attempt at searching for counterexamples. That is, people do not accept a conclusion as necessary if it is consistent with the first model that comes to mind, rather they attempt to refute the conclusion by searching for alternative models in which the conclusion does not hold. Although this facility may be weak, in view of the high rates of fallacies that are regularly endorsed in studies of syllogistic reasoning, our data do provide support for this view. Participants under necessity instructions clearly endorse less conclusions that are just possible than conclusions that are necessary. However, there is another possible explanation of this lower rate of endorsement of possible conclusions. Suppose syllogistic premises consistently suggest a single initial model that does or does not support the conclusion, and that reasoners base their inferences on just this single model. The result would be that possible conclusions that were present in this initial model would be as frequently endorsed as necessary conclusions. In contrast, some possible conclusions would be rarely endorsed, as infrequently as impossible problems. A re-examination of the data for both experiments provided strong support for this proposal. As an illustration consider the following syllogisms, which we label possible strong and possible weak, respectively:

Possible Strong:
All A are B.
Some C are not-B.

∴ Some A are not-C.

Endorsements: Necessary Group: 80%;   Possible Group: 87%

Possible Weak:
All A are B.
Some C are not-B.

∴ All A are C.

Endorsements: Necessary Group: 10%;   Possible Group: 17%

These examples illustrate that some fallacious conclusions which are logically possible, but not necessary, are endorsed at high rates, whereas other possible conclusions are endorsed rarely. We ran a third study to follow up this finding.

Experiment 3

Sixty-four syllogisms were selected from Experiment 2 that could be categorized into four problem types: necessary, impossible, possible strong (where there was a high rate of conclusion endorsement), and possible weak (where there was a low rate of conclusion endorsement). We presented these syllogisms to two groups of participants, a necessity instruction group and a possibility instruction group, as in Experiments 1 and 2.

The endorsement rates on these selected syllogisms are shown in Fig. 12.2, for both necessity and possibility instructions. The striking finding is that possible strong conclusions are accepted as often as necessary conclusions and possible weak as rarely as impossible conclusions. This finding only makes sense if we assume that people make validity judgments on the basis of the first model that comes to mind. This suggests that little validation or counterexample search is taking place. What it also suggests is that the higher rate of endorsement for necessary conclusions compared to possible conclusions in Experiment 2 was not because people searched for counterexamples in the case of possible conclusions, but was simply a result of averaging across the two types of possible problem.

The absence of evidence for counterexample search is a poor result for the model theory because it challenges one of the core components of the process model of deductive reasoning. However, Johnson-Laird (see Evans, Handley, Johnson-Laird, & Harper, in press) discovered that the computational implementation of the model theory produces models in a specific order that is consistent with our findings. That is, the fallacious conclusions that are highly endorsed are present in the first model constructed by the program.

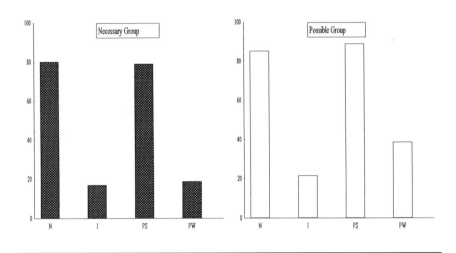

FIG. 12.2. Endorsement of the four types of syllogism in Experiment 3 as a function of instructional group. N stands for conclusion necessary, I for conclusion impossible, PS for conclusion possible strong, and PW for conclusion possible weak.

Additionally, it is clear that some instructional manipulations, or problem content, can lead to higher rate of rejection of fallacious conclusions, that is, experimental manipulations can induce people into searching for alternative models. Evans (chap. 1, this volume) argued that the validation stage of the model theory can be most usefully seen as strategic in nature; that is, it is under conscious control, explicit, and people can hence be motivated to reason deductively by a variety of task factors. Evans also argued, in line with Johnson-Laird (1983), that if alternative search is a conscious strategic process then it will be variable and people will differ in their ability to search for counterexample models. In the following section we present a re-analysis of Experiment 3 from an individual differences perspective and test these proposals.

INDIVIDUAL DIFFERENCES ANALYSIS

Our individual differences analysis of the data takes the form of confirmatory factor analysis. We made the assumption that one factor on which people will vary is their ability to search for alternatives. However, searching for alternative models will not necessarily lead to improved logical performance overall, as there are certain problems in which the logically correct solution is available from the first model constructed. In these cases searching for alternatives is not going to provide any benefit. In order to illustrate this point consider the following syllogism, together with the models that are consistent with it and the order in which the program produces them:

Syllogism:	First model:	Second model:	Third model:
All B are A	A [B] C	A [B] C	A [B] C
All B are C	A [B] C	A [B] C	A [B] C
		A	C

Consider also the following four potential conclusions to this syllogism:

Necessary:	
Some C are A.	Holds in all models of the premises.
Possible strong:	
All C are A.	Holds in the first model constructed.
Impossible:	
No C are A.	Fails to hold in any models of the premises.
Possible weak:	
Some C are not-A.	Holds in one model, but not the first model generated.

If participants are asked to make judgments of necessity for each conclusion in turn, the necessary conclusion holds in all models, and hence it is present in the first model constructed. Searching for alternative models in this case would provide no benefit and, indeed, people who consider more than one alternative may exhibit poorer performance because such a process would be more resource intensive and they may lose track of multiple models. The possible strong conclusion also holds in the first model constructed and, hence, making an inference on the basis of this first model would lead to erroneous endorsement of the conclusion and poorer logical performance. Reasoners can only correctly reject conclusions of this kind if they search for and find a model in which the conclusion does not hold. With impossible and possible weak problems the conclusion does not hold in the first model and, therefor, a judgment that the conclusion is not necessary can be made immediately without considering alternative models. So, in summary, we expect individual differences in counterexample search to manifest themselves in different ways on different problem types. In general there will be a negative relationship between performance on necessary problems and performance on possible strong problems.

For those participants who are asked to make a judgment of possibility we expect an analogous pattern to that predicted for the necessary group. For necessary and possible strong problems the conclusion is present in the first model and there is no need to consider alternative models to the one initially constructed in making a judgment that the conclusion is possible. In contrast, on impossible problems the conclusion is not present in the first model. In order to make an accurate judgment of possibility it is necessary to consider whether the conclusion holds in alternative models of the premises. If reasoners do not search for alternatives, then they will make the logically correct judgment that the conclusion is not possible on the basis of their first model. For those people who do search for alternatives there will be no benefit on these problem types and searching may lead to poorer logical performance. In contrast, on possible weak problems the conclusion is present in one model, although it is not the first one constructed. In this case searching for alternative models is necessary in order to find the model in which the conclusion holds. In summary, we expect a negative relationship between performance on impossible problems and possible weak problems in the possible instruction group, because searching for alternatives will provide differential benefits for logical performance on these problem variants.

Table 12.1 illustrates the structure of our factor analytic model for both instructional groups. A three factor model is proposed. Factor 1 is labeled "search for alternatives" (SA) and it is expected that variations in this factor will be predictive of logical performance on necessary (NE) and possible strong problems (PS) in the necessary group. Specifically, we expect necessary problems to load negatively on the factor and possible strong problems to load positively. A similar pattern is expected in the possible group for the impossible (IM) and possible weak problems (PW). A second factor, "premise integration" (PI), was proposed to capture the notion that people will vary in their ability to construct an integrated representation of the premises. Variations in this ability will manifest themselves most clearly on those problems in which a judgment can be made from the first model constructed. Hence, we expect positive loadings for the remaining problems on this second factor, IM and PW in the necessary group and NE and PS in the possible group. Finally, a third general factor (GF) was posited on the basis that one might expect variations in general ability, which would impact on logical performance across the full range of problems used.

Table 12.1.
The structure of the factor analytic model for both instructional groups in Experiment 3.

| | | Expected loadings | |
		Necessary group	Possible group
Factor 1	Search for alternatives (SA)	NE and PS	IM and PW
Factor 2	Premise integration (PI)	IM and PW	NE and PS
Factor 3	General factor (GF)	All problems	All problems

Each participant in Experiment 3 received a total of 64 problems, 16 in each problem type category. Within each problem category they received four problems drawn from each of the four syllogistic figures. Hence our analysis is based on 16 columns of data for each participant. The correlations between PS and N problems, and I and PW problems, for the necessary group are shown in Table 12.2.

The correlations between PS and N problems (those highlighted in bold in Table 12.2) are in the main negative as expected. The overall correlation between these problem types was -.29, which was marginally significant. The correlations between I and PW problems were overwhelmingly positive with an overall correlation of .71, which was highly significant. An analogous pattern of correlations was found in the possible group, as Table 12.3 shows. There were generally positive correlations between logical performance on PS and N problems (.55) and negative correlations between I and PW problems (-.45).

Table 12.2.
The pattern of correlations in the necessary instruction group.

				Necessary and Possible Strong				
	PS1	PS2	PS3	PS4	NE1	NE2	NE3	NE4
PS1	—							
PS2	.36	—						
PS3	.29	.41	—					
PS4	.31	-.54	.55	—				
NE1	**.07**	**-.08**	**.02**	**-.17**	—			
NE2	**-.14**	**-.05**	**.14**	**-.08**	.04	—		
NE3	**-.32**	**-.22**	**-.14**	**-.16**	.25	.02	—	
NE4	**-.25**	**-.49**	**-.21**	**-.36**	.27	.41	.34	—

				Impossible and Possible Weak				
	PW1	PW2	PW3	PW4	IM1	IM2	IM3	IM4
PW1	—							
PW2	.46	—						
PW3	.53	.37	—					
PW4	.40	.27	.42	—				
IM1	**.49**	**.24**	**.34**	**.57**	—			
IM2	**.60**	**.37**	**.51**	**.53**	.59	—		
IM3	**.32**	**.41**	**.35**	**.61**	.20	.35	—	
IM4	**.19**	**.23**	**.32**	**.41**	.50	.47	.38	—

Table 12.3.
The pattern of correlations in the possibility instruction group from Experiment 3.

				Impossible and Possible Weak				
	PW1	PW2	PW3	PW4	IM1	IM2	IM3	IM4
PW1	—							
PW2	.45	—						
PW3	.64	.40	—					
PW4	.50	.30	.40	—				
IM1	-.20	-.33	-.21	-.25	—			
IM2	-.25	-.06	-.26	-.46	.43	—		
IM3	-.29	-.10	-.17	-.26	.45	.42	—	
IM4	-.39	-.25	-.40	-.51	.54	.50	.60	—

				Necessary and Possible Strong				
	PS1	PS2	PS3	PS4	NE1	NE2	NE3	NE4
PS1	—							
PS2	.12	—						
PS3	.06	.03	—					
PS4	.10	.02	.36	—				
NE1	.01	.14	.28	.12	—			
NE2	.20	.22	.30	.17	.10	—		
NE3	.04	.14	-.06	.28	.19	.03	—	
NE4	.40	.20	.40	.19	.30	.24	.40	—

The correlational analysis provided some support for our proposals. In addition we ran two confirmatory factor analyses, one for each group, using the EQS structural modeling program. The maximum likelihood method was used, with robust standard error and chi-square. In addition we constrained the third general factor such that all problems loaded equally on it. Table 12.4 shows the standardized factor loadings for the necessary group.

The fit indices for the model were barely acceptable and the chi-square, although small, was also significant. However, although the fit of the model is by no means ideal, the patterns of loading are consistent with our proposals. All of the necessary loadings on SA are negative (two significantly) and all the possible strong loadings on SA were positive and significant. The patterns of loading on the premise integration factor were also consistent with those expected.

Table 12.4.
The standardized factor loadings for the necessary instruction group and the possibility instruction group in Experiment 3.

	Necessary Group			Possibility Group		
	SA	PI	GF	SA	PI	GF
NE1	-.20	—	.30*	—	.21	.30*
NE2	-.18	—	.26*	—	.11	.35*
NE3	-.39*	—	.26*	—	.28	.37*
NE4	-.69*	—	.24*	—	.93*	.35*
IM1	—	.67*	.25*	-.53*	—	.29*
IM2	—	.74*	.33*	-.55*	—	.29*
IM3	—	.51*	.25*	-.54*	—	.24*
IM4	—	.49*	.26*	-.77*	—	.27*
PS1	.43*	—	.30*	—	.37*	.32*
PS2	.75*	—	.26*	—	.05	.41*
PS3	.47*	—	.21*	—	.31*	.29*
PS4	.68*	—	.23*	—	.04	.38*
PW1	—	.66*	.26*	.70*	—	.23*
PW2	—	.45*	.32*	.48*	—	.25*
PW3	—	.59*	.23*	.66*	—	.24*
PW4	—	.69*	.27*	.65*	—	.21*

* significant loading

All the loadings of IM and PW problems were positive and significant. Also, although the loadings on the general factor are small they were also all significant. Table 12.4 also shows the results of the factor analysis on the data from the possible group.

Again the fit indices for this model were not ideal and the chi-square, although small, was also significant. However, the pattern of loadings were consistent with our proposals. NE and PS problems loaded positively on PI, although as Table 12.4 shows only four of these loadings were significant. IM problems loaded significantly and negatively on SA and PW problems loaded significantly and positively on SA. As with the necessary model the loadings on the general factor were small, but significant.

The factor analytic models for both the necessary and possibility instruction groups have provided some support for our proposals. The loadings on SA in both groups reflect differential influences of this latent variable on logical performance for different problem types. We have characterized this factor as reflecting variability in the tendency to search for alternative models. People who are good at considering alternatives show higher logical accuracy on problems in which searching is required, but this is accompanied by poorer logical performance on problems in which the accurate inference can be made from the first model, and hence searching provides no added advantage.

However, the models we have presented do not fit the data ideally. One possible reason for the less than ideal fit is that the problems presented to participants were selected on the basis of endorsement rates in Experiment 2. As a result different categories of problem were not matched in terms of premise characteristics, such as the mood of the premises. It is possible that some of the variability in performance across problem types and within subjects resulted from idiosyncratic variations in problem characteristics that could not be captured by our model. In the next section we present a test of our model on another set of data, in which the premises were kept constant for each problem type, and in which we also manipulated the believability of the conclusions.

Experiment 4

In Experiment 4, 50 participants in the necessary group and 50 participants in the possibility group were presented with a total of 32 syllogisms. Eight of the syllogisms had possible strong conclusions, eight necessary conclusions, eight possible weak conclusions, and eight impossible conclusions. We also manipulated the believability of the conclusions, such that half were believable and half were unbelievable. The overall pattern of correlations between the problem types were consistent with the findings from our first analysis. In the necessary group logical performance on NE and PS problems correlated negatively and significantly, for both problems with believable conclusions (-.35) and problems with unbelievable conclusions (-.50), and performance on PW and IM problems correlated positively and significantly for believable (.66) and positively, but nonsignificantly for unbelievable conclusions (.19). In the possible group IM and PW problems correlated negatively and significantly for both believable and unbelievable conclusions (-.57 and -.37 respectively), whereas NE and PS problems correlated positively and significantly (.33 and .64).

We made one minor change to our factor analytic model before attempting to fit it to the data. In order to take some account of variability in responding due to the believability of the presented conclusion we relaxed the constraint on our general factor (Factor 3), such that we allowed problems to load differentially on it. We will reserve discussion of this until later in this section. Table 12.5 shows the standardized factor loadings for the necessary group and the possible group.

The model of the necessary data fitted well. As predicted, N and PS problems loaded differentially on SA, with necessary problems loading negatively and possible strong problems loading positively. IM and PW problems loaded positively on PI, with three out of four of the loadings significant. The loadings on the general factor varied in magnitude and direction according to the problem type.

The model of the possible group also fitted the data well. Again the pattern of loadings were consistent with our predictions. As Table 12.5 shows IM problems loaded negatively and significantly on SA, whereas PW problems loaded positively and significantly on this factor. NE and PS problems loaded positively on the PI factor, with three out of the four loadings significant. As with the necessary group the loadings on the general factor varied in magnitude and direction according to the type of problem.

Table 12.5.
The standardized factor loadings for both instructional groups in Experiment 4.

	NEB	NEU	IMB	IMU	PSB	PSU	PWB	PWU
Necessary Group *Variables*								
SA	-.43*	-.24	—	—	.90*	.17	—	—
PI	—	—	.47*	.32	—	—	.64*	.44*
GF	.08	.91*	.69*	-.13	.43*	-.50*	.52*	-.20
Possible Group *Variables*								
SA	—	—	-.39*	-.48*	—	—	.31*	.60*
PI	.68*	.34*	—	—	.48*	.23	—	—
GF	-.03	.83*	.85*	-.18	-.30	.68*	.53*	.48*

* = significant loading

Table 12.6.
The logical response for each instructional group, for each conclusion type, together with the belief based
response and the loadings on the general factor in Experiment 4.

Problem	Logical Response Necessary Group	Logical Response Possible Group	Belief based Response Necessary Group	Loading Necessary Group	Loading Possible Group
NEB	Yes	Yes	Yes	.08	-.03
NEU	Yes	Yes	No	.91*	.83*
IMB	No	No	Yes	.69*	.85*
IMU	No	No	No	-.13	-.18
PSB	No	Yes	Yes	.43*	-.30
PSU	No	Yes	No	-.50*	.68*
PWB	No	Yes	Yes	.52*	-.53*
PWU	No	Yes	No	-.20	.48*

* = significant loading

In both factor analyzes the loadings on the general factor are variable. An interpretation of this factor in terms of general ability is not adequate to explain these variations, because we would expect performance on all problems to be predicted to a similar degree. One possibility is that people are being differentially affected by the believability of the presented conclusion, and that the general factor is capturing these individual differences. Table 12.6 shows the loadings on GF for both the necessary and possible groups, together with the logical response for each problem and the response that would be elicited on the basis of the believability of the conclusion.

As Table 12.6 shows, the significant positive loadings for both instructional groups are associated with problems in which the belief based response is at odds with the logical response (shown in bold in Table 12.6). This suggests that our general factor may be capturing individual differences in the degree to which people are able to resist the effects of empirical knowledge in making logical inferences. This pattern of loadings suggests that people who are less influenced by the believability of the conclusion in generating a response show a higher degree of logical responding on problems in which this conflict occurs than those who are influenced by the empirical status of the conclusion. If our interpretation of this factor is sound we would not expect problems in which logic-based and belief-based responses coincide (shown in italics in Table 12.6) to be predicted by variations in this factor in as much as logic and belief based responding would lead to the same response. An inspection of the data indicates that this is true in three out of the four cases, for both the necessary and possible groups in which this condition holds. The exceptions to this are the loading of possible strong unbelievable problems, in the necessary group, and possible weak believable problems in the possible group, which are significant, but negative. If our interpretation of the general factor is correct, this suggests that performance on these problems is detrimentally for those people who resist responding on the basis of their beliefs. One way of making sense of this pattern is to assume that people often respond on the basis of the first model that comes to mind. If people resist the influence of beliefs and construct an initial model of the premises they will make the logically incorrect inference, unless they consider alternative models, whereas if they respond on the basis of the believability of the conclusion they will make the correct inference. Hence resistance to empirical beliefs in these cases leads to poorer logical performance.

In summary, the factor analyses of Experiment 4, for both the necessary and possible groups, provide clear evidence that individual differences in various abilities predict performance on a syllogistic reasoning task. People who are good at searching for alternatives make the logically accurate inference on problems in which this strategy is required, whereas they perform poorly on problems in which this strategy provides no benefit. Performance on problems in which the logical inference can be made with certainty from the first model constructed is predicted by a second factor, which is interpreted as reflecting people's ability to integrate premise information into a model. Finally a third, general factor, which we interpreted as the reflecting people's resistance to respond with reference to belief, predicts variability in performance on problems in which belief and logic sanction different conclusions.

DISCUSSION

In the experimental analysis of the research presented here there was little evidence that people consider counterexample models when solving syllogistic reasoning problems. We drew a distinction between possible strong conclusions and possible weak conclusions. Possible strong conclusions are endorsed as often as conclusions that are necessary, whereas possible weak conclusions are endorsed as rarely as impossible conclusions. This finding suggests that people only construct a single model when they are engaged in syllogistic reasoning. This model contains the conclusion in the case of possible strong problems and hence these conclusions are endorsed, but it does not contain the possible weak conclusion and hence these conclusions are rarely endorsed. Interestingly the distinction between these two problem types and our interpretation of this distinction is supported by the computational program of the model theory. The program produces models in a particular order and in the vast majority of cases the first model constructed contains the possible strong conclusion, but does not contain the possible weak conclusion.

Jonathan Evans (chap. 15, this volume) argued that the search for counterexamples in reasoning or the validation stage as he termed it, may be strategic in nature. That is, people can consciously make an effort at deduction by employing such a strategy. This may be encouraged by certain experimental procedures or instructions, and it may also vary across individuals, with some people being better than others.

The individual differences analyzes presented made the assumption that people do, indeed, vary in a variety of abilities that impact on their logical performance on syllogistic reasoning tasks. Our main focus was on whether people vary in their ability to search for alternative models in validating presented conclusions. Across all four of the factor analyzes presented here, a latent variable emerged, which we interpreted as the ability to search for alternative models. Interestingly, variations in this ability do not impact on performance across all types of deductive judgment. The influence of this variable depends on the processes required for different sorts of judgments under different instructional conditions. Certain logically accurate inferences can be made with reference to the first model constructed. For example, judgments of necessity for impossible problems can be made on the basis of a single model of the premises, because the conclusion does not hold in any model of the premises. Similarly, judgments of possibility for necessary problems can be made from a single model, as the conclusion holds in all models, and to find it present in one suffices. In contrast other judgments do require people to consider alternative models. Judgments of necessity for possible strong problems require that an alternative model in which the conclusion does not hold is found, and accurate judgments of possibility for possible weak problems entail that reasoners find an alternative model in which the conclusion does hold. However, people are clearly not aware of the logical status of a conclusion before they engage in reasoning about it. Hence people may search for alternative models when it is unnecessary for generating the logically correct response. For example, judgments of necessity for necessary problems can be made accurately with reference to a single model, because the conclusion holds in all models. Judgments of possibility for impossible problems can also be made with reference to single model as the conclusion does not hold in any model. In both of these cases if people tend to search for alternatives this will not improve their logical accuracy and the analyzes suggest that searching for alternatives results in poorer performance on these problem types, together with better logical performance on problems in which it is required.

In addition, two other factors were identified that were predictive of performance on the syllogistic task. A factor that was interpreted as the ability to integrate premise information predicted performance on those problems in which the logically correct inference was available from a single model. Although one might expect a variable of this kind to predict across all problem types, we did not load those problems which we believed would be most greatly influenced by the search for alternatives variable on this factor. The reason for this was straightforward: An inability to integrate premise information may lead to chance performance (50% correct) and an ability to integrate premise information may also lead to chance performance for those problems that also require counterexample search. Hence, although the ability to integrate premise information must be important for solving syllogisms, in our model it would not have emerged as a predictive factor for problems that also require counterexample search.

The final factor we identified was a general factor that we expected to predict performance across the full range of problem types. This was the case in the analysis of the abstract problems from Experiment 3, but the introduction of thematic materials produced a range of loadings on this factor. The pattern of loadings in Experiment 4 suggested that the general factor is capturing people's ability to resist the influence of belief on the inferences that they make. This finding is consistent with recent research which suggests that there are clear differences in the degree to which people are influenced by their beliefs when solving statistical inference problems (see Klaczynski, Gordon, & Fauth, 1997).

We began this chapter by considering the evidence that people search for counterexamples when they engage in a deductive reasoning task. The search for counterexamples is a core stage in the mental model theory of reasoning, and the process ensures that at the very least people have the capability to draw deductively valid conclusions with certainty. However, the evidence that people consider counterexample models is by no means compelling and although people may construct more than one representation of a given set of premises, the number of alternatives constructed does not appear to be predictive of logical performance (Newstead et al., in press). The experimental work described earlier is clearly consistent with the view that validation plays a minor role in syllogistic reasoning. However, although it may be a weak tendency overall, the tendency to search for alternative models varies across individuals and individual differences in reasoning performance on certain types of problem may well be predicted by individual differences in counterexample search.

There still remains somewhat of an anomaly in the conclusions that can be drawn from the experimental and the factor analytic analyses presented. Why does overall performance seem to show no evidence of validation, whereas the factor analyses suggest that a significant proportion of people do search for alternative models? The answer to this question seems to lie in the nature of the influence of counterexample search on logical performance on these problem types. Consider, for example, an individual in the necessary instruction group, who is adept at searching for counterexamples. According to our account they will correctly reject possible strong conclusions, while at the same time incorrectly reject necessary conclusions. In contrast, a person who is less able to consider counterexamples will correctly accept necessary conclusions, while erroneously accepting possible strong conclusions. Averaging performance across individuals will clearly lead to similar rates of endorsement for both necessary and possible strong conclusions and mask any indication that people are searching for counterexamples on the task.

The use of an evaluation paradigm in the present research may also influence the degree to which counterexample search is evident. Recent work that has compared performance on an evaluation and production task in syllogistic reasoning (Lambell, 1998), has demonstrated that the effects of belief are restricted to the evaluation paradigm and conclusion direction effects or figural effects are restricted to a production paradigm. These findings have been interpreted as indicating that a presented conclusion guides the construction of models (see also Hardman & Payne, 1995). That is, reasoners attempt to find a model in which the conclusion holds, and hence the believability or the direction of the conclusion guides model construction. Production tasks in which reasoners are required to generate their own conclusions may well encourage less of a verification strategy and more of a motivated attempt at reasoning, which may involve the sort of counterexample search reported in recent work (Bucciarelli & Johnson-Laird, in press; see also Johnson-Laird et al., chap. 11, this volume).

The nature of the reasoning task may also influence the degree to which people are able to search for counterexamples. Syllogisms are complex deductive arguments, which involve understanding the meaning of quantifiers, and being able to integrate a representation interrelating the quantified assertions and the elements referred to within the assertions. Such a process may leave little available resource to enable people to consider alternative representations of the premises. Indeed with simpler tasks, based on visual and verbal premises, there is good experimental evidence for counterexample search (Bell & Johnson-Laird, 1998; see also Byrne, Espino, & Santamaria, chap. 5, this volume).

In conclusion, the findings reported here suggest that reasoners often make inferences on the basis of the first model that comes to mind, without considering alternative models that may verify or falsify a given conclusion. However, there are clear individual differences in the tendency to search for counterexamples that manifest themselves in different ways on different sorts of problems. If validation provides a benefit it leads to improved performance, if not, it leads to poorer performance. The identification of factors that predict individual differences in reasoning has proved a fruitful line of inquiry, and has provided some evidence of variations in strategies that may have been difficult to detect given standard experimental analyzes. The challenge remains to identify additional factors that predict individual differences in human reasoning.

ACKNOWLEDGMENTS

The authors would like to acknowledge the support of the Economic and Social Research Council who funded the research reported in this chapter (Award Number: R000221742).

REFERENCES

Bell, V., & Johnson-Laird, P. N. (1998). A model theory of modal reasoning. *Cognitive Science, 22*, 25–51.

Bucciarelli, M., & Johnson-Laird, P. N. (in press). Strategies in syllogistic reasoning. *Cognitive Science.*

Byrne, R. M. J., & Johnson-Laird, P. N. (1990). Remembering conclusions we have inferred: What biases reveal. In J. P. Caverni, J. M. Fabre, & M. Gonzalez (Eds.), *Cognitive biases* (pp. 109–120). Amsterdam: North-Holland.

Chater, N., & Oaksford, M. (1999). Rational analysis and heuristic processes for syllogistic reasoning. *Cognitive Psychology, 2*, 191–258.

Evans, J. St. B. T., Handley, S. J., Johnson-Laird, P. N., & Harper, C. (in press). Reasoning about necessity and possibility: A test of the mental model theory of deduction. *Journal of Experimental Psychology: Learning, Memory, and Cognition.*

Hardman, D. K., & Payne, S. J. (1995). Problem difficulty and response format in syllogistic reasoning. *Quarterly Journal of Experimental Psychology, 48A*, 945–975.

Henle, M. (1962). On the relation between logic and thinking. *Psychological Review, 69*, 366–378.

Johnson-Laird, P. N. (1983). *Mental models: Towards a cognitive science of language, inference and consciousness.* Cambridge, UK: Cambridge University Press.

Johnson-Laird, P. N., & Bara, B. G. (1984). Syllogistic inference. *Cognition, 16*, 1–62.

Johnson-Laird, P. N., & Byrne, R. M. J. (1991) *Deduction.* Hove, UK: Lawrence Erlbaum Associates.

Johnson-Laird, P. N., & Byrne, R. M. J. (1993). Models and deductive rationality. In K. I. Manktelow & D. E. Over (Eds.), *Rationality: Psychological and philosophical perspectives* (pp. 177–210). London: Routledge and Kegan Paul.

Klaczynski, P. A., Gordon, D. H., & Fauth, J. (1997). Goal-oriented critical reasoning and individual differences in critical reasoning. *Journal of Educational Psychology, 89*, 470–485.

Lambell, N. (1998). *Figural and belief bias in syllogistic reasoning.* Unpublished manuscript, University of Plymouth.

Newstead, S. E., Handley, S. J., & Buck, E. (in press). Falsifying mental models: Testing the predictions of theories of syllogistic reasoning. *Memory and Cognition.*

Polk, T. A., & Newell, A. (1995). Deduction as verbal reasoning. *Psychological Review, 102*, 533–566.

Rips, L. (1994). *The psychology of proof.* Cambridge, MA: MIT Press.

Wetherick, N. E., & Gilhooly, K. J. (1990). Syllogistic reasoning: Effects of premise order. In K. J. Gilhooly, M. T. G. Keane, R. H. Logie, & G. Erdos (Eds.), *Lines of thinking, Vol. 1* (pp. 99–108). New York: Wiley.

Woodworth, R. S., & Sells, S. B. (1935). An atmosphere effect in formal reasoning. *Journal of Experimental Psychology, 18*, 451–460.

13

Strategies and Models in Statistical Reasoning

Vittorio Girotto
Michel Gonzalez

The traditional literature did not directly investigate the role of strategies in statistical reasoning. According to the mental model theory, individuals may construct various representations of the same statistical problem and apply various strategies to them. However, the theory posits that the activation of these strategies does not essentially depends on the format in which information is presented (i.e., frequentist vs. probabilistic). In this chapter, we report evidence which corroborates the model theory's predictions. In particular, contrary to the assumptions of the frequentist theory, we show that Bayesian-like strategies can be activated even with probabilistic formats.

How do people draw statistical inferences? The literature on the topic has provided several answers to this question. Most of them seem to share the assumption that strategies do not play a crucial role in naive statistical reasoning. In this chapter, we show that people do solve statistical reasoning problem by using strategies, that is, they apply various sequences of operations to obtain the same solution (or different solutions).

According to one of the earliest accounts of statistical reasoning, lay people are doomed to a sort of "conservatism." In particular, in problems requiring the revision of a hypothesis in the light of new evidence, reasoners appear to underweight the impact of the latter. For example, let us consider two boxes, R and B. Box R contains 5/6 of red marbles and 1/6 of blue marbles. Box B contains 5/6 of blue marbles and 1/6 of red marbles. Suppose that a person randomly sampled a series of 32 marbles (18 red and 14 blue; i.e., the datum, or evidence E) from one box, with replacement after each marble. Suppose that you are requested to evaluate the probability that this sample has been drawn from Box R (i.e., the hypothesis H), rather than from Box B (i.e., the alternative hypothesis not-H). If you are not an expert of probability calculus, it is likely that your judgment falls around .60, that is, a value close to the proportion of red marbles in the drawn sample. In fact, the probability of getting the datum E, if the sample is drawn from Box R [i.e., the conditional probability $p(E|H)$] is 5^4, that is 625 times larger than the probability of the same datum E, if the sample is drawn from Box B [i.e., the other conditional probability $p(E|not$-$H)$]. By applying the Bayes's theorem (i.e., the normatively optimal rule for solving this problem, see below), you should obtain a probability of about 1 [i.e., 625/(625+1)] that the sample has been drawn from Box R [i.e., the posterior probability $p(H|E)$]. In other words, people appear to underweight the impact of data in their evaluation of the probability that a given hypothesis is true (see Edwards, 1968; but see Bar-Hillel, 1980).

Even the seminal studies of Kahneman and Tversky did not directly investigate the role of strategies in statistical reasoning: *"When faced with the difficult task of judging probability or frequency, people employ a limited number of heuristics which reduce these judgements to simpler ones."* For example, by the *representativeness* heuristic *"an event is judged probable to the extent that it represents the essential features of its parent population or generating process"* (Tversky & Kahneman, 1982, p. 163).

The activation of a given heuristic is a process mainly due to the content of the problem. Relatively little work has been devoted to the way in which reasoners represent and solve semantically poorer problems.

The more recently proposed *frequentist hypothesis* has stressed the role of strategies in statistical inferences. According to Gigerenzer and Hoffrage (1995), people's answers to posterior probability problems are due to the application of several different strategies. For example, consider the following problem:

According to a population screening, a person has 40% probability of having the disease H; 75% probability of showing symptom E, if she has the disease H; 33% probability of showing symptom E, if she does not have the disease H.
Mary is tested now. She shows symptom E. What is the probability that she has the disease H?
. . . %

This problem concerns single-case probabilities, and asks for the probability of H knowing E, that is $p(H|E)$. It elicits a variety of (incorrect) solution strategies.

The typical erroneous solution is 75% [i.e., the numerical value corresponding to the inverted conditional probability: $p(E|H)$]. In order to get a Bayesian answer, people should carry out a series of (relatively) complex operations. Given that the posterior probability $p(H|E) = p(H\&E)/p(E)$, people should compute the two terms of this ratio. The denominator, $p(E)$, equals the sum of the probability of getting the symptom E and the disease H [i.e., $p(H\&E)$], and the probability of getting the same symptom and not the disease H [i.e., $p(not\text{-}H\&E)$]. Now, $p(H\&E)$ equals the a priori probability of getting the disease H, times the conditional probability of getting the symptom E, if the disease H is present [i.e., $p(H) \, p(E|H)$], that is 40% x 75% = 30%. Similarly, $p(not\text{-}H\&E)$ equals the a priori probability of not getting the disease H, times the conditional probability of getting the symptom E, if the disease H is not present [i.e., $p(not\text{-}H) \, p(E|not\text{-}H)$], that is 60% x 33% = 20%. Once one gets the two terms, one can compute the required ratio: 30%/(30% + 20%) = 60%. In fact, only a minority of participants do solve this problem.

A strategy that yields a correct solution is activated by a specific way of presenting the problem information. When a problem refers to observations in form of absolute frequencies, participants solve it by applying what Gigerenzer and Hoffrage called the *Bayesian algorithm*. For example, about half of participants solve the following version of the disease problem, which is adapted from one used by Gigerenzer and Hoffrage:

According to a population screening, 4 out of 10 people have the disease H; 3 out of the 4 people with disease H show symptom E; 2 of the 6 people without disease H show symptom E.
A new sample of people is tested. They show symptom E. How many of these people do you expect to have disease H? . . . out of . . .

It should be noted that, in this version, the proportions, stated as frequencies (e.g., "4 out of 10"), are identical to the probabilities, stated as percentages, used in the previous one (e.g., "40%"). Still, performance turned out to be significantly better in the frequentist version than in the probabilistic one.

According to the frequentist hypothesis, a frequency format corresponds to the natural way in which information is acquired (Gigerenzer & Hoffrage, 1995; see also Cosmides & Tooby, 1996). For this reason, it may easily activate the Bayesian algorithm: Participants have just to consider the frequency of people presenting both the symptom E and the disease H (i.e., 3), and to compare it to the total frequency of people presenting symptom E (3 + 2 = 5). The solution ("3 out of 5") corresponds to the one you may compute by applying the Bayes' theorem (i.e., .60).

One problem with this explanation is that it implies the existence of an equivalence between the information formats and the strategies used to solve the problems. In particular, given the assumption that human mind is not tuned to probabilities, this hypothesis predicts that naive reasoners are not able to solve a posterior probability problem. In this chapter, we report evidence that Bayesian-like strategies can also be activated with probabilistic formats.

A finer analysis of strategies in naive statistical reasoning can be derived from the mental model theory, in particular from its recent application to probabilistic inferences (Johnson-Laird, 1994; Johnson-Laird, Legrenzi, Girotto, Sonino-Legrenzi, & Caverni, in press). On the basis of the representational principles of the model theory, it is possible to explain and predict many crucial phenomena of statistical reasoning. For example, it is possible to investigate the use of different strategies for solving single-case probabilistic problems, as a function of the problem representation.

In this chapter, we report evidence that problems in the same information format are solved using different strategies. Factors determining the mental representation of the problems, such as the form of the final question, appear to determine the use of a given strategy of solution. We also discuss analogous results concerning the classical paradoxes of probability (e.g., the three cards problem).

In the concluding section of the chapter, we report the results of a series of experiments that investigated the way in which the information about the datum activates different strategies for solving problems in the same information format.

THE MODEL THEORY OF STATISTICAL REASONING

The main principle of mental representation postulated by the model theory concerns *truth*. Given the limits of working memory, people tend to construct mental models that represent what is true, but not what is false. For example, given the premise:

In this box, there is at least a red marble, or else a green marble and a blue marble, but not all three marbles.

people tend to build the following representation:

Red

Green   *Blue*

in which each line denotes a separate model. The first model represents that there is a red marble (but it does not represent explicitly that it is false that there are a green and a blue marble in this situation). The second model similarly represents only that there are a green and a blue marble, but does not explicitly represent that it is false that there is a red marble in this situation. If reasoners are given the following question:

What is the probability that there is a red marble in the box?

they are likely to answer 1/2. This response is based on the assumption that the two models of the premise represent two *equiprobable* possibilities, and that the probability of an event corresponds to the *proportion* of models which represent this event, out of the entire set of models.

Similarly, given the question:

What is the probability that there is both a red and a blue marble in the box?

reasoners are likely to answer "*zero*" (see Johnson-Laird et al., in press). In fact, both answers reflect a bias. The *fully explicit* models of the premise contains three different possibilities in which there is a red marble and it is false that "there is both a green and a blue marble," as shown by the partition:

Red	*Green*	*¬Blue*
Red	*¬Green*	*Blue*
Red	*¬Green*	*¬Blue*
¬Red	*Green*	*Blue*

in which the symbol ¬ denotes negation. The application of the equiprobability and the proportionality principles to this explicit representation yield the inferences: $p(\text{Red}) = 3/4$; $p(\text{Red \& Blue}) = 1/4$.

The model theory explains these and other biased inferences about absolute and conditional probability (Johnson-Laird & Savary, 1996), as well as posterior probability judgments. For example, the frequentist version of the disease problem in the Introduction may be represented with the models:

disease $\underline{H}$	symptom $\underline{E}$	3
disease $\underline{H}$	¬symptom $\underline{E}$	1
¬disease $\underline{H}$	symptom $\underline{E}$	2
¬disease $\underline{H}$	¬symptom $\underline{E}$	4

in which each model represents a given hypothesis and the datum, and it is tagged with a numerical value which indicates its frequency.

Alternatively, individuals may build explicitly only the models containing the symptom:

disease $\underline{H}$	symptom $\underline{E}$	3/4
¬disease $\underline{H}$	symptom $\underline{E}$	2/6
. . .		

in which the ellipsis denotes the implicit models representing the absence of the symptom.

In order to answer the posterior frequency question, reasoners do not need to apply the Bayes' theorem. They may use a simpler strategy: the *subset principle*. When the models are tagged with frequencies values, one can easily compute the number of H observations among E observations, that is, the subset of E that is H. It equals the frequency of $H\&E$ observations divided by the frequency of E observations (i.e., $H\&E$ or not-$H\&E$ observations). In the models of the previous problem, there are five people who have the symptom E, and three of them have the disease H. Hence, the frequency of H observations among E observations is 3/5.

What happens when people have to solve posterior *probability* problems? One may note that, whereas in these problems the probabilities are expressed as percentages or fractions, the frequentist problems typically express information as integers. Therefore, posterior probability problems are more difficult than the frequentist problems, in part because the former involve more complex calculations than the latter (see Howson & Urbach, 1993). The point is that probabilistic information can be expressed as integers, exactly as frequentist information. Consider, for example, the following version of the disease problem, in which all information is expressed in terms of number of *chances*:

According to a population screening, a person has 4 out of 10 chances of having the disease H; 3 out of the 4 chances of having the disease H are associated with symptom E; 2 out of the 6 chances of not having the disease H are associated with symptom E.

Reasoners are likely to represent this problem with a set of fully explicit models similar to those activated by the earlier frequentist version:

disease H	*symptom E*	3
disease H	*¬symptom E*	1
¬disease H	*symptom E*	2
¬disease H	*¬symptom E*	4
. . .		

They may also construct an incomplete set of models, such as:

disease H	*symptom E*	3/4
¬disease H	*symptom E*	2/6
. . .		

In both cases, each model is tagged with values representing chances, rather than frequencies of observation. However, if asked a *conditional probability* question, such as:

Mary is tested now. She shows symptom E. How many chances are there that she has the disease H? . . . out of . . .

reasoners are unlikely to apply the subset principle to the initial models of chances.

Let us compare the latter question with the question asked earlier in the frequentist problem:

A new sample of people is tested. They show symptom E. How many of these people do you expect to have disease H? . . . out of . . .

In this case, given the expression "*How many of these people*," reasoners are explicitly lead to consider the E set (i.e., the frequency of people who show the symptom E) as the reference set, and to compare it to the $E\&H$ subset (i.e., the frequency of people who show the symptom E *and* who are infected by the disease H). In sum, reasoners are explicitly required to use the subset principle, and to apply it to the appropriate sets.

The subset principle could be used to assess $p(H|E)$ in the chance version of the disease problem. It corresponds to the subset of E that is H. In other words, the probability of getting the disease H, given the symptom E, equals the chances of getting $E\&H$, divided by the chances of getting E.

However, the *conditional probability* question seems to activate a rather different strategy of solution. On the one hand, it does not explicitly ask reasoners to compare *sets* of chances. That is to say, the conditional probability question does not ask for the probabilistic equivalent of the frequency set comparison. Such a request for a comparison of chance sets would read, for example, as follows:

Among the chances of showing the symptom E, how many chances will be associated with the disease H?

As we see shortly, an explicit request to compare the set of E chances to the subset of $E\&H$ chances does improve performance in probabilistic problems.

On the other hand, even if reasoners could grasp the need for a comparison of sets in a probabilistic problem, it could be difficult for them to make the correct comparison. Indeed, the conditional probability question requires reasoners to evaluate the occurrence of a single event (*Mary has the disease H*), given the occurrence of another one (*Mary shows symptom E*), but the initial models of the problem represent sets of chances, not single events. In particular, the *event "Mary shows symptom E"* is not represented in the set of *chances* of showing symptom E. Therefore, reasoners may fail to consider the ensemble of chances of showing that symptom.

In sum, when asked a conditional probabilistic question, reasoners are unlikely to apply the subset principle. Even those who will apply it are unlikely to make the correct comparison, which requires (a) computing the chances of showing symptom E, and (b) comparing them with the chances of showing symptom E and being infected by the disease H.

In a series of studies, we found that only 8% of participants solve the probabilistic version of the disease problem. One of the most frequent incorrect answers was "*3 out of 4*." It corresponds to what Gigerenzer and Hoffrage (1995) called the *Fisherian* strategy. We explain it in model theoretical terms. Given that the question does not ask for a comparison of the appropriate sets, reasoners tend to focus on the model of the mentioned hypothesis (*Mary has the disease*), and forget the model of the alternative one (see Legrenzi, Girotto, & Johnson-Laird, 1993). Hence, they conclude by giving the value corresponding to the chances of having the symptom, given the disease [i.e., the inverted probability: $p(E|H)$; e.g., "*3 out of 4*")]. Another frequent (incorrect) answer was "*3 out of 10*" (called *joint occurrence* by Gigerenzer & Hoffrage, 1995). This solution too is based on a strategy which seems to neglect the chances of having the symptom, without having the disease (i.e., *the false positive rate*).

One could speculate that these strategies are selectively activated by the two sets of models indicated before. That is to say, the Fisherian strategy may be more likely to be applied to the incomplete representation, whereas the joint occurrence strategy may be more likely to be applied to the fully explicit models.

In sum, in single-case problems, most reasoners tend to use strategies that lead to erroneous solutions in which the subset of *H&E* chances is not ascribed to the set of *E* chances.

STRATEGY ACTIVATION AND THE QUESTION FORM

Do single-case problems always activate incorrect strategies? In a series of experiments, we found that people can solve these problems in a correct way. In particular, when they are asked a question which de-focuses them from the model representing the hypothesis and the datum, reasoners may apply the subset principle. For example, we asked a *relative probability* question in the disease problem:

> Mary is tested now. Out of the entire 10 chances, Mary has ___ chances of showing the symptom *E*; among these chances, ___ chances will be associated with the disease *H*.

This explicit request to compute the total number of the chances of getting the datum *E* should force reasoners to consider the model representing the occurrence of the alternative hypothesis (*not-H*) and the datum (*E*). In other words, reasoners should answer this question by first computing the total number of chances of getting the symptom (5), and then, given this chance set, computing the number of chances of getting the disease (3). Indeed, when asked such a relative probability question, 53% of participants solved the problem (vs. only 8% correct in the control problem, in which participants were asked a traditional, *conditional probability* question).

One might argue that the subset principle corresponds to the Bayesian algorithm, that is the strategy which, according to the frequentist theory, is activated by frequentist formats. However, according to the frequentist theory, in order to obtain a Bayesian inference a question must ask "*for the answer as a frequency, rather than as a single-case probability*" and present "*the problem information as frequencies*" (Cosmides & Tooby, 1996, p. 22). Neither of these two criteria for successful performance were respected in our relative probability problems. Moreover, we obtained evidence that reasoners can solve probabilistic problems, even without using the subset principle.

In a study, we used questions asking for an *odds* chance estimate, such as:

> Mary is tested now. If she shows symptom *E*, there will be ___ chances that the disease *H* is associated with this symptom, and ___ chances that the absence of the disease *H* is associated with this symptom.

This is an explicit request to compute the chances that hypothesis *H* is true, *and* the chances that hypothesis *not-H* is true, given the datum *E*. In order to answer this question, reasoners do not need to compute the entire set of chances of getting the symptom *E*. They have just to consider the chances of getting the disease and the symptom (that is, the chances of the conjunction $H\&E$, i.e., "3"), and the chances of not getting the disease and getting the symptom (that is, the chances of the conjunction not-$H\&E$, i.e., "2"). Thus, they are unlikely to apply the erroneous strategies which neglect the values corresponding to the alternative hypothesis. Indeed, 66% of our participants solved single-case problems asking for an answer as an estimate of the odds chance for the two hypotheses.

A further example of the tendency to neglect the values concerning the alternative hypothesis has been found in tasks in which participants are not asked to make a posterior probability judgment, but to *select* a piece of information in order to make such a judgment. For example, suppose that: (a) you want to know whether you sister has a car X (i.e., hypothesis H) or a car Y (i.e., hypothesis not-H); (b) you know that her car does over 25 miles per gallon and has not had any mechanical problems for the first two years of ownership; (c) you know that 65% of car Xs do over 25 miles per gallon [i.e., $p(E1|H) = 65\%$]. Given this datum, you have to select only one piece of information among the following three:

1)   the percentage of car Ys that do over 25 miles per gallon [i.e., $p(E1|not$-$H)$];
2)   the percentage of car Xs that have had no mechanical problems for the first two years of ownership [i.e., $p(E2|H)$];
3)   the percentage of car Ys that have had no mechanical problems for the first two years of ownership [i.e., $p(E2|not$-$H)$].

Given that you know that 65% of car Xs do over 25 miles per gallon, you should select the percentage of car Ys that do over 25 miles per gallon. Suppose that the latter percentage is exactly 65%. In that case, the new piece of information does not help you in discovering which is your sister's car. However, suppose that that percentage is different from 65%. In that case, you have some evidence favoring either car X (when the percentage of car Y that do over 25 miles per gallon is smaller than 65%), or car Y (when the latter percentage is larger than 65%).

More formally, given that you know the datum $p(E1|H) = 65\%$, you should select the piece of information that is *potentially* diagnostic [i.e., $p(E1|not$-$H)$]. In this way, you could compute the likelihood ratio (i.e., $p(E1|H) / p(E1|not$-$H)$], which is necessary in order to obtain the posterior probability.

However, most reasoners tend to select the "pseudo-diagnostic" piece of information. For example, they select the "percentage of car Xs that have had no mechanical problems for the first two years of ownership" (see Mynatt, Doherty, & Dragan, 1993). That is to say, they prefer additional information about H over information about the alternative hypothesis not-H, selecting the second item concerning the focal hypothesis [i.e., $p(E2|H)$].

According to a model theoretical interpretation, this tendency reflects a form of focusing on the model representing the co-occurrence of the hypothesis H and the datum $E1$. Legrenzi et al. (1993) argued that reasoners represent a conjuncture relating two events, such as a hypothesis and a datum, with the models of a conditional statements. Thus, the conditional

If hypothesis H is true, then datum E1 will occur.

is represented with the models:

H   E1
. . .

in which the ellipsis denotes the implicit models of the possibilities in which the hypothesis H is false. Empirical evidence exists that reasoners tend to focus on the explicit model, in drawing both deductive (e.g., Girotto, Mazzocco, & Tasso, 1997), and probabilistic inferences (e.g., Johnson-Laird & Savary, 1996; Kleiter et al., 1997). This tendency could explain why reasoners search for information only about the focal hypothesis, thus forgetting the information about the alternative one (see also Evans & Over, 1996). The same tendency to neglect $p(E|not\text{-}H)$ has also been found in covariation judgment problems (see Arkes & Harkness, 1983; McKenzie, 1994; Wasserman, Dorner, & Kao, 1990).

Girotto, Evans, and Legrenzi (1996) provided some results that corroborate this interpretation of pseudo-diagnosticity. In one of their studies, participants were requested to select *two* items of information, rather than just one, as in the usual versions of the problem. In other words, participants were not presented with the *anchoring* item (e.g., "65% of car X do over 25 miles per gallon"), which could be the basis of the tendency to focus on a specific hypothesis (e.g., "My sister has an X car"). Indeed, Girotto and colleagues found that 71% of participants selected information in a diagnostic way (vs. 25% in the control condition). For example, they chose the potentially diagnostic couple of items: "The percentage of car X that do over 25 miles per gallon," *and* "The percentage of car Y that do over 25 miles per gallon," that is the normatively correct items $p(E1|H)$ and $p(E1|not\text{-}H)$.

In sum, on the basis of the model theory prediction, it is possible to reduce the erroneous tendency to focus on the initial model representing the focal hypothesis and the datum. In tasks requiring people to make a posterior probability judgment, or to select information in order to make such a judgment, it is possible to reduce the tendency to neglect the alternative hypothesis. The form of the question and the absence of an initial, anchoring information appear to be the main factors that determine the activation of a correct strategy of solution.

STRATEGIES, REPRESENTATION, AND THE PARADOXES OF PROBABILITY

Many classical paradoxes of probability present information in such a way that reasoners tend to represent only some of the relevant models (for a review, see Nickerson, 1996). For example, consider the classical Bertrand's (1889) paradox, also known as the three cards problem:

There are three cards in a box: One is red on both sides (RR); one is white on both sides (WW); one is red on one side and white on the other (RW). A card is drawn from the box and tossed into the air. It lands with a red face up, denoted Ru. What is the probability that the RR card was drawn?

If we were expert of the probability calculus, we could apply Bayes' theorem to this problem, and obtain the correct solution:

$$\underline{p}(RR|Ru) = \underline{p}(Ru|RR)\underline{p}(RR) / \underline{p}(Ru) = (1)(1/3) / (1/2) = 2/3,$$

where $p(RR|Ru)$ is the posterior probability that the RR card was drawn given that the evidence is Ru, $p(RR)$ is the a priori probability of drawing that card, and $p(Ru|RR)$ is the probability of obtaining the evidence Ru when the card RR is drawn.

However, participants typically answer 1/2 (see Bar-Hillel & Falk, 1982). This erroneous solution can be explained in model theoretical terms. The initial representation of the problem is likely to be:

```
R    R
R    W
W    W
```

in which each line represents the model of a single card. Given that the red face is up, people eliminate the model of the WW card. Given that just two models representing a red face are left, and they are equiprobable, people tend to apply the proportionality principle, and conclude: $p(RR|Ru) = 1/2$. In sum, this problem, as well as other paradoxes of probability (see Johnson-Laird et al., in press), are incorrectly solved because reasoners apply the equiprobability and proportionality principles to an inadequate representation of the premises.

As we have seen in the previous section, an intuitive strategy for inferring a posterior probability is the subset principle. Indeed, if we consider all the six faces (i.e., all the possible pieces of evidence), there are just three possible red faces (i.e., three occurrences of datum E), among which there are two red faces that belong to the RR card (i.e., two occurrences of the datum E, if the hypothesis H is true). Hence, there are "two out of three" chances that the hypothesis H is true, given datum E. The point is that the typical representation of this problem concerns models of *cards*, rather than models of *faces*. Therefore, it is difficult for reasoners to apply the subset principle to Bertrand's paradox.

However, it should be possible to reduce the erroneous application of the equiprobability and proportionality principles to the models of cards, by asking participants a different question.

As we have seen in the previous section, a conditional probability question tends to focus participants on the model representing the tested hypothesis and the datum. By contrast, an odds chance question makes explicit the need to estimate the chances that the hypothesis H is true *and* the chances that the alternative hypothesis *not-H* is true, given the occurrence of the datum E. This kind of question should improve performance in Bertrand's paradox. For example, participants may be required to compute the *number of chances* that the RR card is drawn, and the *number of chances* that the RW card is drawn, given that the drawn card shows a red face up. In this way, reasoners are not obliged to apply the proportionality principle to the models of cards. Therefore, they should be able to conclude that there are two chances that the drawn card is RR (each red face of the RR card provides one chance), and one chance that it is RW (the RW card has only one red face). The results of a series of experiments corroborated this prediction: Whereas only 23% of participants gave a correct answer to the probability question, 52% of them correctly solved the odds chance question (Gonzalez, unpublished studies).

In sum, as we have reported for the traditional posterior probability problems, these results show that:

1)   *Participants tend to solve Bertrand's paradox when they are asked a question that requires the chance odds for both hypotheses, because this question reduces the tendency to apply the equiprobability and proportionality principles to the typical, inadequate, representation of the problem;*

2)   *The correct solution of the problem can be reached without using the subset principle, because the chance odds question does not require a comparison of chance sets.*

Another classical puzzle of probability is the three boxes problem, or Monty Hall game (see Selvin, 1975). Many versions of this problem do not state all the critical assumptions that permit a correct computation of probabilities (see Nickerson, 1996). In the following version these assumptions are made explicit:

There are three boxes (A, B and C). A prize has been put in a random way in one of these boxes. Thus, the probability that each of the boxes contains the prize is 1/3. A person knows where the prize is, and she will open a box which does not contain it. In any case, she won't open Box A, even if it does not contain the prize. In other words, she will open, without a bias, Box B or else Box C. Now, she opens Box B. Which is more likely that the prize is in Box A or in Box C?

This problem has a Bayesian solution. If B- indicates that "Box B is open," A+ and C+ indicate "the prize is in Box A" and "the prize is in Box C," respectively, then $p(\text{B-}|\text{A+}) = 1/2$ (by assuming that, in this case, she will open Box B or C, in a random way) and $p(\text{B-}|\text{C+}) = 1$. Therefore:

$$\underline{p}(A+|B-) = \underline{p}(A+)\underline{p}(B-|A+)/\underline{p}(B-) = (1/3)(1/2)/(1/2) = 1/3.$$

Similarly,

$\underline{p}(C+|B-) = \underline{p}(C+)\underline{p}(B-|C+)/\underline{p}(B-) = (1/3)(1)/(1/2) = 2/3.$

However, virtually no participants solve it. Even expert reasoners tend to answer that there is .5 probability that the prize is in either of the two remaining boxes (for a review, see Falk, 1992). Indeed, an initial representation of this problem is likely to be:

A   +
B   +
C   +

where each line represents an alternative model of one box containing the prize (+). Because no information to the contrary is given, each model represents an equiprobable alternative (1/3). When the datum ("B is open") is provided, reasoners are likely to eliminate the model which is inconsistent with it (i.e., B+), so that they are left with only two possible models:

A   +
C   +

From this representation it is tempting to conclude, by application of the equiprobability principle, that $p(A+|B-) = p(C+|B-) = 1/2$.

However, Macchi and Girotto (1994) found that many lay people are able to solve the following problem:

There are three boxes (A, B, and C). Only one of them contains a prize. Depending on its location, either a red or a green light comes on. If the prize is in Box A, either a red or a green light comes on. If the prize is in Box B, the red light never comes on. If the prize is in Box C, the red light always comes on.
The red light comes on. Which is more likely: that the prize is in Box A or in Box C?

This problem is equivalent to the earlier three boxes problem. Opening a box corresponds to a light coming on. In particular, the events "*Box B is open*" and "*Box C is open*" correspond to the events "*the red light comes on*" and "*the green light comes on*," respectively.

Given this problem, naive reasoners can correctly grasp the different probabilities of the occurrence of a datum (*the . . . light comes on*), given each of the possible hypotheses (*the prize in box . . .*). Thus, they are likely to construct the following representation

A+   red   50%
A+   green   50%
B+   green   100%
C+   red   100%

in which each model represents the presence of the prize in each of the boxes and the light which comes on given that possibility. Each model is tagged with the appropriate probability. Thus, when the datum "the red light comes on" is considered, reasoners eliminate the models that do not contain it, but they do not consider the remaining models as equivalent:

A+	red	50%
C+	red	100%

From this representation, they can correctly conclude that the probability that the prize is in Box C is greater than the probability it is in Box A.

This finding may be explained in model theoretical terms. Versions that elicit the representation of the relevant models can be solved by the correct application of the equiprobability and proportionality principles.

THE ROLE OF INFORMATION ABOUT THE DATUM

In some cases, a piece of information concerning the datum E (i.e., the specific information) too can modify reasoners' strategies. For example, consider this simple situation:

> There is a competition among three women (Amélie, Béatrice, and Corinne, henceforth A, B, and C). Each of them will finish the competition as first, second, or third.

Given this information, it is likely that people do not construct a complete representation of all six possible ways in which the three women can be classified, rather is its likely that people tend to represent just the three events and their ranking order:

A B C 1 2 3

Now, if we give reasoners the specific information "*A is not the third*," they are likely to represent it with the following models

1	2	3
A		
	A	

in which various possible occurrences are left implicit. Therefore, when they are asked to compute the probability that A is first, they apply the equiprobability and proportionality principles to these models, and conclude:

p(A1st|A not 3rd) = 1/2.

Indeed, 78% of the participants tested by Gonzalez and Chalvidal in an unpublished study gave this answer (see Chalvidal, 1998).

However, given the same basic situation (a competition among three women) and the same question, a different piece of specific information may elicit various (erroneous) solutions. Moreover, these solutions seem to depend on the application of various strategies. For example, given the datum "*A has a better rank than C*," most people (56%) answer:

p(A1st|A better than C) = 1/2.

The participants' written protocols show that this response is frequently based on the models:

```
1      2         3
A
       A
```

This set of models was produced by half of the participants who answered, 1/2. Alternatively, this response was based on the models

```
1      2         3
A
B
```

This set was produced by the other half of the participants.

Both sets of models capture the meaning of the specific information: In the first case, they represent the fact that *A* cannot be third; in the second, they represent the fact that *C* cannot be first. However, in both cases they are incomplete. Indeed, the full set of models for this situation is:

```
1      2         3
A      B         C
A      C         B
B      A         C
```

Only 39% of participants construct this representation and correctly conclude that:

p(A1st|A better than C) = 2/3.

This and other results obtained by Gonzalez and Chalvidal using similar probabilistic problems indicate that people may represent a given probabilistic problem in different ways, and that a given inference may be drawn from different sets of models. Similar results have been recently obtained by Bucciarelli and Johnson-Laird (in press), by using categorical syllogisms.

CONCLUSIONS

The model theory of statistical reasoning does not posit an equivalence between a specific information format (e.g., frequency or single-case format) and the activation of a specific strategy. More generally, it does not claim that people always represent the same problem in the same way, nor that all individuals will apply the same strategy of solution to a given representation. The results of the studies we have discussed in this chapter appear to corroborate the main predictions deriving from the model theory.

First, naive reasoners are able to infer a posterior probability, or to search for the most relevant information in order to make such a judgment. In general, they tend to focus on the model representing one hypothesis and the datum. Thus, they tend to neglect the information concerning the alternative hypothesis. For example, they tend to answer a *conditional probability* question such as "*If datum E occur, what is the probability that hypothesis H is true?*", by giving the value of the inverted probability "*If hypothesis H is true, then the probability that datum E occur is . . .*," or by giving the value of the conjunction of the datum and the hypothesis H, that is, "*The probability that hypothesis H and datum E co-occur is . . . .*" More formally, they appear to confound $p(H|E)$ with $p(E|H)$ and $p(H\&E)$, respectively. In both cases, they fail to consider the probability that the datum E occurs when the alternative hypothesis *not-H* is true. However, we reported some evidence that people can be de-focused from the model representing the datum E and hypothesis H. For example, they correctly answered a question requiring a *chance odds* judgment, such as "If datum E occurs, there are . . . chances that the hypothesis H is associated with this datum, and . . . chances that the hypothesis *not-H* is associated with this datum." This question forced reasoners to compute the chances that the datum co-occurs with the alternative hypothesis, without asking them to compute the chances of getting the datum E. Given that their models contained the appropriate value for this occurrence, they could easily give the correct answers. Reasoners gave correct answers also when they were given a *relative probability* question, that is, an explicit request to compute the entire set of chances of getting the datum E, and to compare it with the subset of $E\&H$ chances.

These correct solutions were elicited in problems that presented probabilistic information, and asked single-event questions. In other words, they were elicited in conditions which, according to the frequentist hypothesis, should not produce correct performance, given the intrinsic limitations of human mind in dealing with single-case probabilities (see Cosmides & Tooby, 1996, p. 15; Gigerenzer & Hoffrage, 1995, p. 697). As predicted by the model theory, questions that force participants to consider the models representing the occurrence of the datum and both the focal and the alternative hypotheses, or to compute the entire set of E chances, do elicit a good rate of correct performance, regardless of the nature (frequentist or probabilistic) of the information format. High rates of correct performance have been also obtained with some classical probabilistic puzzles, such as Bertrand's paradox.

Second, we have reported results showing that a given statistical problem may activate different strategies of solution. For example, Gonzalez and Chalvidal have shown that a given datum can elicit the construction of different sets of models, and that reasoners' answers are based on the elicited models. Stanovich and West (1998) recently reported some interesting results about the role of individual differences in statistical reasoning, which complement those reported in the present chapter. These authors showed that individuals who use $p(E|not\text{-}H)$ are also the most able reasoners in other domains. In particular, individuals who selected the $p(E|not\text{-}H)$ value as relevant for making a Bayesian inference, obtained significantly higher scores on verbal and mathematical Scholastic Aptitude Tests (SAT), and scored higher on syllogistic reasoning tasks, as well as on other statistical reasoning problems. According to Stanovich and West, these findings run counter to the typical criticisms in the standard literature on probabilistic reasoning. Indeed, many theorists have questioned the use of the probability calculus as an appropriate norm for assessing untutored people's performance in statistical reasoning tasks (for a relevant discussion, see Gigerenzer, 1996; Kahneman & Tversky, 1996; see also Cohen, 1981). Now, if these criticisms were correct, one should not expect to find any correlation between the responses to probability judgments tasks and various measures of cognitive capacity. In fact, Stanovich and West's results corroborated the idea that *"intelligent people [are] more likely to use the most effective reasoning strategies than [are] less intelligent people"* (Larrick, Nisbett, & Morgan, 1993, p. 333).

Even without accepting this conclusion (see also Stanovich, in press), the finding that there are significant individual differences in the use of statistical information can be considered as a piece of evidence in favor of the not-deterministic stance defended by the model theory.

In the domain of deductive reasoning, there are theories which posit the existence of only one strategy for solving different problems (see Rips, 1989). The model theory does not make the same deterministic assumption. Indeed, Johnson-Laird and Byrne (1990) showed that people use a variety of strategies in order to solve, for instance, a complex metadeductive task (see also Bucciarelli & Johnson-Laird, in press).

In the domain of statistical reasoning, early theories assumed that people use a single strategy when they have to solve, for example, a posterior probability problem (e.g., Edwards, 1968). More recently proposed theories have acknowledged the role of strategies. Some of them are based on the assumption that the activation of a given strategy essentially depends on the format in which information is presented (e.g., Cosmides & Tooby, 1996; Gigerenzer & Hoffrage, 1995). However, the reported evidence corroborates the model theory's assumptions, according to which people apply various strategies in tackling complex statistical problems, but their activation does not necessarily depend on the information format.

In conclusion, the model theory appears to be a plausible candidate for explaining both reasoning mechanisms and the way in which they are used in the application of strategic principles.

ACKNOWLEDGMENTS

We thank Phil Johnson-Laird and the editors of this volume for their helpful comments on a previous version of this chapter.

REFERENCES

Arkes, H. R., & Harkness, A. R. (1983). Estimates of contingency between two dichotomous variables. *Journal of Experimental Psychology: General, 112*, 117–135.

Bar-Hillel, M. (1980). The base-rate fallacy in probability judgement. *Acta Psychologica, 44*, 211–233.

Bar-Hillel, M., & Falk, R. (1982). Some teasers concerning conditional probabilities. *Cognition, 11*, 109–122.

Bertrand, J. (1889). *Calcul des probabilités* [Probability calculus]. Paris: Gauthier-Villars.

Bucciarelli, M., & Johnson-Laird, P. N. (in press). Strategies in syllogistic reasoning. *Cognitive Science*.

Chalvidal, A. (1998). *L'utilisation des représentations des possibles dans le raisonnement probabiliste* [Representing possible states of affairs in probabilistic reasoning]. Unpublished masters thesis. Université de Provence, Aix-en-Provence.

Cohen, L. J. (1981). Can human irrationality be experimentally demonstrated? *Behavioral and Brain Sciences, 4*, 317–381.

Cosmides, L., & Tooby, J. (1996). Are humans good intuitive statisticians after all? Rethinking some conclusions from the literature on judgement under uncertainty. *Cognition, 58*, 1–73.

Edwards, W. (1968). Conservatism in human information processing. In B. Kleinmuntz (Ed.), *Formal representation of human judgement*. New York: Wiley. Reprinted in D. Kahneman, P. Slovic, & A. Tversky (Eds.), *Judgement under uncertainty: Heuristics and biases* (pp. 159–169). New York: Cambridge University Press, 1982.

Evans, J. St. B. T., & Over, D. E. (1996). *Rationality and reasoning*. Hove, UK: Psychology Press.

Falk, R. (1992). A closer look at the notorious three prisoners problem. *Cognition, 43*, 197–223.

Gigerenzer, G. (1996). On narrow norms and vague heuristics: A reply to Kahneman and Tversky (1996). *Psychological Review, 103*, 592–596.

Gigerenzer, G., & Hoffrage, U. (1995). How to improve bayesian reasoning without instruction: Frequency format. *Psychological Review, 102*, 684–704.

Girotto, V., Evans, J. St. B. T., & Legrenzi, P. (1996, August). Relevance of information and consideration of alternatives: Pseudo-diagnosticity as a focussing phenomena. Paper presented at the *Third International Conference on Thinking*, University College, London.

Girotto, V., Mazzocco, A., & Tasso, A. (1997). The effect of premise order effect on conditional reasoning: A test of the model theory. *Cognition, 63,* 1–28.

Howson, C., & Urbach, P. (1993). *Scientific reasoning: The Bayesian approach.* Chicago: Open Court.

Johnson-Laird, P. N. (1994). Mental models and probabilistic thinking. *Cognition, 50,* 189–209.

Johnson-Laird, P. N., & Byrne, R. M. J. (1990). Meta-logical puzzles: Knights, knaves and Rips. *Cognition, 36,* 69–84.

Johnson-Laird, P. N., Legrenzi, P., Girotto, V., Sonino-Legrenzi, M., & Caverni, J. P. (in press). Naive probability: A model theory of extensional reasoning. *Psychological Review.*

Johnson-Laird, P. N., & Savary, F. (1996). Illusory inferences about probabilities. *Acta Psychologica, 93,* 69–90.

Kahneman, D., & Tversky, A. (1996). On the reality of cognitive illusions. *Psychological Review, 103,* 582–591.

Kleiter, G. D., Krebs, M., Doherty, M. E., Garavan, H., Chadwick, R., & Brake, G. (1997). Do subjects understand base rates? *Organizational Behavior and Human Decision Processes, 72,* 25–61.

Larrick, R. P., Nisbett, R. E., & Morgan, J. N. (1993). Who uses the cost-benefit rules of choice? Implications for the normative status of microeconomic theory. *Organizational Behavior and Human Decision Processes, 56,* 331–347.

Legrenzi, P., Girotto, V., & Johnson-Laird, P. N. (1993). Focussing in reasoning and decision-making. *Cognition, 49,* 37–66.

Macchi, L., & Girotto, V. (1994). Probabilistic reasoning with conditional probabilities: The three boxes paradox. Paper presented at the *Annual Meeting of the Society for Judgement and Decision Making,* St. Louis.

McKenzie, C. R. M. (1994). The accuracy of intuitive judgement strategies: Covariation assessment and Bayesian inference. *Cognitive Psychology, 26,* 209–239.

Mynatt, C. R., Doherty, M. E., & Dragan, W. (1993). Information relevance, working memory, and the consideration of alternatives. *Quarterly Journal of Experimental Psychology, 46A,* 759–798.

Nickerson, R. (1996). Ambiguities and unstated assumptions in probabilistic reasoning. *Psychological Bulletin, 120,* 410–433.

Rips, L. J. (1989). The psychology of knights and knaves. *Cognition, 31,* 85–116.

Selvin, S. (1975). On the Monty Hall problem. *American Statistician, 29,* 134.

Stanovich, K. E. (in press). *Variable rationality.* Mahwah, NJ: Lawrence Erlbaum Associates.

Stanovich, K. E., & West, R. F. (1998). Who uses base rates and P(D|-H)? An analysis of individual differences. *Memory and Cognition, 26,* 161–179.

Tversky, A., & Kahneman, D. (1982). Availability: A heuristic for judging frequency and probability. In D. Kahneman, P. Slovic, & A. Tversky (Eds.), *Judgement under uncertainty: Heuristics and biases* (pp. ....). New York: Cambridge University Press.

Wasserman, E. A., Dorner, W. W., & Kao, S. F. (1990). Contributions of specific cell information to judgements of interevent contingency. *Journal of Experimental Psychology: Learning, Memory and Cognition, 16,* 509–521.

14

Focusing Strategies in Reasoning About Games

Maria G. Devetag
Paolo Legrenzi
Massimo Warglien

Our experiments support the hypothesis of focusing phenomena in game playing. It consists in ignoringthe other player's motivations. This tendency depends upon the format of the game representation. Representations which are considered as equivalent in game theory are not equivalent in participants' minds, and lead to significant differences in choice behavior. When participants construct appropriate models of the game, they seem substantially able to debias their decisions. We try to extend the mental model theory from the domain of individual reasoning and choice to that of interactive, strategic decision making, supplying a unified account of focusing and defocusing strategies in naive game playing.

Traditionally, the study of thinking strategies in problem solving and decision making has concentrated on the analysis of a single person making a decision, where the normatively "right" solution can be found without considering the behavior of anyone else. Specifically designed tasks are presented to participants and strategies of thinking are singled out through the sequence of answers of each participant to the experimental situation. The experimental situations correspond to scenarios of everyday life where an individual is facing a problem or a difficulty which is impossible to bypass or to solve using a routine. However, our strategies often do not depend on a specific problem-solving scenario but on actions taken by other persons interacting with us. One of the most powerful analytical tools for describing interactive decision making is game theory (see, for an introduction, Osborne & Rubinstein, 1994). Game theory is a theory of interactive decision making. Like normative theories of individual decision making, its standard behavioral assumption is that individuals are rational, that is, they have well-defined preferences and maximize on the ground of such preferences. Furthermore, game theory specifies the normative thinking procedures individuals should follow to find the "solution" of the game. It is common to find in game theory a terminology that may be a source of ambiguity in this book, especially regarding the words *strategic* and *strategy*. A strategic interaction is a situation in which the outcome of an individual decision is conditional to decisions taken by others. A strategy is a complete plan specifying which action or sequence of actions an individual will take in a strategic interaction, given the rules of the game (including the timing of actions) and the moves the other players might play. Individual decision making can be considered as a special kind of game in which there is only one decision maker, interacting against "nature," whose "moves" specify in which state the player will find himself (e.g., in a gamble, nature draws the actual outcome of the lottery). When referring to strategy and strategic interaction, or to play against nature, we refer to the current use of such terms in game theory. On the converse, when we refer to reasoning strategies, we do it in the usual way psychologists do.

The use of game theory is now ubiquitous in economics and political science, but still rather rare in psychology. Game theoretic paradigms, such as the prisoner's dilemma, have been used by social psychologists in order to analyze the choices of collaboration versus competition in interactive situations. However, psychologists of reasoning and decision making have only recently used these problems to interpret games from the point of view of theories of reasoning such as the mental model theory of Johnson-Laird (for a review, see Legrenzi & Girotto, 1996).

In this chapter, we take into consideration people's underlying reasoning processes in general classes of games. We study the behavior of naive game players, that is, people without previous training in game theory. By concentrating on naive players we do not want to exclude all experience in strategic, interactive thinking. All of us had strategic interactions from childhood. But instead, we want to exclude from our sample participants whose behavior might be biased by their former academic training.

Traditionally, problems utilized by game theorists are presented as a tree or a matrix on a piece of paper or computer screen. But a player can have a matrix in front, and yet, as he or she thinks about what to do, operate on a representation of a very different form. In fact, teachers of economics, when they have to present the fundamentals of game theory to naive students, know by experience that learning to manipulate the basic game representations is not immediate and spontaneous. To understand the way in which the problem is represented and solved starting from a specific mental representation is a job for psychologists. The complication emerging in the case of game theory is that, even in the most simple problems, we have to consider the possibility that a player's representation includes representations of the other player. More precisely, if the first player acts independently from the possible actions of the other player, the representation is always incomplete and may not lead to the best solution of the problem. How players represent and, overall, fail to represent the other's representation is a question we try here to approach with the mental model theory.

In this chapter we use the mental model theory to explain some of the cognitive difficulties that participants experience in dealing with games. More precisely, in exploratory experiments we try to control the effects on game playing of a mechanism called "focusing effect" (Legrenzi, Girotto, & Johnson-Laird, 1993). The focusing effect refers to the tendency to concentrate on some aspects of a problem as a result of an incomplete representation of the problem itself, when some other aspects are left implicit according to the predictions of mental model theory. The mental model theory is a theory of how we build simplified representations of the inputs through the construction of models of them. In the case of decision making, this leads to a simplification and thus sometimes to systematically biased choices (see Johnson-Laird, Legrenzi, & Girotto, 1998, for a recent introduction to mental model theory). In this chapter we study how this simplification affects our representation of the strategic motivations of another player in the game. Focusing on our own possible moves and leaving implicit the motivations of the other player can transform a play against a person into a play against nature. It is a well-known fact that when thinking about a multiple persons scenario, we tend to build a model of it by making explicit our own actions (Legrenzi et al., 1993). Similarly, we tend to emphasize our point of view when analyzing the game. This is accentuated by the fact that we consider our actions under control, but the actions of the others out of our reach (Girotto, Legrenzi, & Rizzo, 1991; Mandel & Leman, 1996). The following three experiments show the effects of the tendency to focus on our model of the game, without taking into consideration the mental model of our partner. From this point of view, our exploratory studies can also be connected to the study of other minds, where it has been shown that the capacity to build a mental model of the content of other people's minds is not automatic, but is acquired at a certain level of intellectual maturity (Perner, 1991). We show that under certain circumstances, even adults can have severe problems in taking into account the other's mind.

EXPERIMENT 1: DO PEOPLE SEE DOMINANCE?

There are many kinds of games and many alternative ways to represent them (for a survey, see Osborne & Rubinstein, 1994). In this chapter we concentrate on the simplest kind of games—two-person games in matrix form, and on a peculiar reasoning process, that is, the elimination of dominated strategies. These are the very first games one usually meets in most introductions to game theory, and we think most people would agree they are basic to more complex games. In a way, these games are the prototypic means by which people learn how to reason in a game.

The simplest way to present a problem of interactive decision making is with the traditional payoff matrix, well known because of its use in the familiar Prisoner's Dilemma (PD). An example of a game in matrix form is the following:

Matrix 1:

		Paolo	
		A	B
Giovanna	A	6,1	4,3
	B	5,4	2,7

This payoff matrix describes completely the structure of the game, specifying the available actions and their consequences in terms of gains for both players. The numbers, usually, refer to monetary payoffs. In such a representation we have three main ingredients:

1. *two players, for example, Giovanna and Paolo*
2. *two actions, A and B, available to both players*
3. *four pairs of payoffs, specifying how much Giovanna and Paolo can win as a consequence of each combination of actions chosen*

We have four pairs of numbers. The first number of each pair refers to Giovanna's gain and the second to Paolo's gain. For example: When Giovanna chooses the *action A* and Paolo *action A*, Giovanna will win $6 and Paolo $1. For a naive player, this is a very complex structure, which needs a learning process in order to manipulate automatically the consequences of each choice. In absence of such a learning process, complexity may cause an overload on working memory.

The game of Matrix 1 can be solved by what game theory calls dominance. Formally, an action is dominated when there is at least one other action that *always* yields a higher payoff for a player, no matter what the other player does. A game is solved by dominance when participants, by deleting dominated actions, are left with only one action. The individual actions surviving the elimination process constitute the solution of the game. In the preceding case, one can see that for Giovanna *action A* yields a higher payoff than *B,* whatever action is chosen by Paolo (6 vs. 5 and 4 vs. 2). Conversely, for Paolo, *action B* will yield a higher payoff whatever action is chosen by Giovanna (3 vs. 1 and 7 vs. 4). Thus, (A,B) is the solution of the game by dominance.

The normative standing of dominance follows from the definition of preference (Kreps, 1990). This is why dominance appears to be an obvious principle to game theorists. However, the lesson of the psychology of reasoning is that we are not always good at seeing what seems obvious to experts (see Garnham & Oakhill, 1994). Thus, it is tempting to look at violations of dominance as good candidates for the understanding of naive deductive thinking in games. The concept of dominance is the weakest, and thus the most general, concept of rationality used in game theory. It implies only that one will avoid actions that are always less desirable than other ones available. Despite its appealing simplicity, the concept of dominance is not so easy to grasp as game theorists claim. A game matrix is a quite complex representation, within which dominance can be seen only if players adopt the right strategy. In order to see easily dominance relations, each player has to focus initially on the other's actions to infer the ordering of consequences for him or her. In order to understand the logic of such a reasoning strategy, let us assume (for the sake of expositional simplicity) that participants represent the matrix as a set of conditionals. For example, in order to see dominance, Giovanna has to build the following representation:

If Paolo chooses A then (I am better off playing A than playing B).
If Paolo chooses B then (I am better off playing A than playing B).

The inference that A is better in either case is now easy and immediate. However, the foregoing representation does not arise spontaneously in many participants. A player's spontaneous model specifies one's own actions and not those of his or her opponents. Thus, as the thinking-aloud protocols of many participants to our experiments have revealed, we tend to use our own actions as antecedents, and compare the implications of the other's moves in terms of our own benefit:

If I choose A then (I am better off if Paolo chooses A).
If I choose B then (I am better off if Paolo chooses A).

This representation hides the dominance relation, and doesn't suggest any self-evident choice. In a classical deductive reasoning experiment we might expect participants to state at this point that *"nothing follows,"* as, for example, when they are presented with a syllogism of the Modus Tollens form (Johnson-Laird & Byrne, 1991). But, in this case participants are facing a decision task, and they are forced to make a choice anyway. What happens then? We suggest that participants look for a representation with an unequivocal ordering of the outcomes. When they fail to do this by considering all elements of the game, they edit a simplified but incomplete representation of the game itself. Two simplifying strategies are usually employed. The first strategy simplifies the game by ignoring the other player's payoffs. The second one simplifies the game by deleting some cells of the matrix and considering only the psychologically most salient ones. In this chapter, we explore only the first of the two reasoning strategies, because it is related to focusing phenomena and can be explained by mental model theory (see Warglien, Devetag, & Legrenzi, 1998, for an analysis of the second strategy).

Our thinking-aloud protocols of participants playing dominance-solvable games reveal that they often "weigh" each conditional (the model of a single action) by using their own payoffs associated with each action—they make a sort of naive average. In this way, they transform a problem of strategic uncertainty (what will the other do?) into a problem of nonstrategic, naive uncertainty. By "deleting" the other's payoffs from their representation of the problem, they put themselves into a state of ignorance of the other's motivations. This ignorance naturally leads to treating each action of the other as equiprobable. In fact we know that individuals adopt a principle of equiprobability of the states of the world, unless they have knowledge or beliefs to the contrary (see Johnson-Laird, Legrenzi, Girotto, Sonino, & Caverni, in press, for the naive probability theory). In this way, naive people transform a strategic game into a game "against the nature," as the two possible actions of the other player are considered equiprobable (.50 probability each). In the earlier example, this implies that the "naive expected payoff" of the *action A* (= 6 x .50 + 4 x .50 = 5) is higher for Giovanna than the naive expected payoff of the *action B* (= 5 x .50 + 2 x .50 = 3,5). Thus Giovanna will play *A*, not because she sees dominance, but just because one action has a higher average payoff than the other. This has the drawback that it is hard to discriminate experimentally (except for thinking-aloud protocols) participants seeing dominance from participants calculating the naive expected payoff when both reasoning strategies lead to the same choice.

However, the difference can be immediately detected in games solvable by *iterated dominance*, that is, games where the elimination of dominated strategies has to be applied iteratively.

Consider the following game matrix:

Matrix 2:

		Player 2 (the other player)	
		U	*V*
	X	30,60	70,10
Player 1	*Y*	50,10	90,20
(you)	*Z*	55,10	75,20

Let us see how iterated dominance works in this case. Clearly, *action Y* dominates *action X* from your point of view (50 vs. 30 and 90 vs. 70). Thus, *X* should be deleted. Then we are left only with *actions Y,Z* and *U,V* (Matrix 2'):

Matrix 2':

		the other	
		U	*V*
you	*Y*	50,10	90,20
	Z	55,10	75,20

Facing Matrix 2', the other should never play *U* because it is dominated by *V* (20 vs. 10). But, if the other plays *V*, *Y* is better than *Z* for you (90 vs. 75). Thus, the solution is (*Y,V*).

We conducted a classroom experiment with hypothetical choices based on Matrix 2. It is necessary to make a methodological warning related to the tradition of research in experimental economics. In such tradition, it is common to make a distinction between hypothetical choices (where the payoffs are imaginary) and experiments involving real payoffs. The preference for the latter experiments is typical of economists, whereas experimental psychologists have a somehow more liberal (or skeptical) view of the role of monetary payoffs in experiments (see Camerer, 1995, for a balanced review of the controversy between economists and psychologists on incentive structures in experiments). We tried to use real payoffs where we felt it might make a significant difference in inducing participants' behavior (Experiments 2 and 3). Behaviors observed in hypothetical choice in Experiment 1 are however confirmed by behaviors observed in experiments with monetary payoffs in Experiments 2 and 3. Participants were undergraduate students of business of the Ca'Foscari University of Venezia. In one condition, participants were 108 undergraduate students of economics who had not yet studied game theory. Students were playing the "you" role facing Matrix 2, and had to choose an action (see Devetag, Legrenzi, & Warglien, 1998, for detailed instructions). The outcome of this condition of Experiment 1 is summarized in Table 14.1, Column 1.

With Matrix 2, it could seem as if a large majority of participants have captured the iterated dominance solution. Notice, however, that Y is also the action with the highest average payoff. What if we modify Matrix 2 so that the game solution doesn't change but another action has higher expected payoff? Consider the following game Matrix 3.

Matrix 3:

		the other	
		U	V
	X	30,60	70,10
you	Y	50,10	80,20
	Z	90,10	70,20

The game theoretic prediction is that there should be no changes in behavior, because Y is still the best action available to you by application of iterated dominance (as before: you prefer Y to X, the other V to U, and you prefer Y to Z: $80 > 70$). Our prediction, on the converse, is that most participants should now prefer *action Z*, since its average payoff is now higher than that one of *action Y*.

We conducted a second condition of Experiment 1 to test whether participants behave according to the game theoretic prediction or choose according to the highest average payoff rule.

Table 14.1 summarizes the outcome of the two conditions of Experiment 1. It is easy to see the reversal of preferences accorded to the Y and Z action. This result also sheds light on experiments in which people choose the dominant action in games solvable by simple dominance. For example, we suspect that many participants defecting in experiments on the prisoner's dilemma do not really see the dominance relation embedded in it (see Shafir & Tversky, 1992, for a somewhat similar conclusion).

Table 14.1.
Results of the two conditions of Experiment 1.

Action	Matrix 2	Matrix 3
X	5	3
Y	73	24
Z	30	89

EXPERIMENT 2: FOCUSING IN GAMES

Until now, we have claimed that people have problems in seeing dominance relations because they tend to "delete" the other player's payoffs in their (incomplete) mental model of the game. Consequently, alternative descriptions of the payoff matrix that are formally equivalent but make it more or less easy to represent the other's payoff, can be perceived as nonequivalent by naive participants and therefore affect their choices.

Consider the following matrix:

Matrix 4':

		the other		
		A	B	C
	A	4,4	3,0	5,3
you	B	0,3	8,8	1,9
	C	3,5	9,1	4,4

This matrix can be rewritten in a simplified form, exploiting the fact that both players have symmetrical payoff structures. One familiar way to simplify symmetrical payoff matrices is the following, where only the payoff of "you" of Matrix 4" are indicated:

Matrix 4"

		the other		
		A	B	C
	A	4	3	5
you	B	0	8	1
	C	3	9	4

This matrix indicates what an individual player gets from each combination of her or his action (row) and the other's action (column). Each player is informed that the other player is facing the same simplified payoff matrix.

From a game theoretic point of view, Matrices 4' and 4" are formally equivalent. In fact, one can generate the information on the other's payoffs by taking the transpose of the simplified matrix and obtaining the payoffs for the column player. For example, if you play C and the other plays B, you get 9 and he gets 1, because that's what you would get if you played B and the other C. Thus, for a game theorist, using one or the other presentation should not alter players' behavior—in fact, in some economics experiments the presentation format of 4" is used instead of that of 4' (e.g., Stahl & Wilson 1995). In particular, this game has a unique solution by iterated dominance: (A,A). For both players, B has to be eliminated because it is dominated by C (you: 9 vs. 8; the other: 9 vs. 8). If one restricts consideration to the actions A and C, A dominates C and has to be chosen by both players (you: 4 vs. 3; the other: 4 vs. 3). However, for both players C is the action presenting the highest average payoff. In fact, applying the equiprobability principle of the naive probability theory (see Johnson-Laird et al., in press), we have: 1/3 x 3 + 1/3 x 9 + 1/3 x 4 = 5.33.

Following our argument, the extent to which people accord privilege to C over A depends on how difficult it is to focus on the other's action as a premise in comparing alternatives. Clearly, Matrix 4" involves a higher cognitive load in order to make explicit the other's payoffs. Thus, we expect more people choosing C when Matrix 4" is presented instead of Matrix 4'.

In Experiment 2, there are three groups of participants. The first group is playing with Matrix 4', the second is playing with Matrix 4". Participants were randomly matched in each group to form players' dyads, and were paid according to the payoff actually realized. The outcome of Experiment 2 is summarized in Table 14.2 where the difference is shown between the presentations of Matrices 4' and 4" in terms of the respective choices of A and C.

We have suggested that when calculating a "naive expected value" of the actions, participants tend to transform strategic uncertainty into nonstrategic, naive uncertainty. They ignore the other's strategic motivations and treat her or his actions as equiprobable. Our point is that they do not simply average the payoffs of each action available to them, but instead greatly simplify their treatment of uncertainty. This implies that participants should still be reactive to factors affecting the perceived risk associated with each action. Thus, by manipulating the variance of each action's payoff without changing its average, one should expect shifts in players' choices.

Matrix 5 can be compared to Matrix 4". In these matrices, the average payoff associated with each action is the same, but the variance is changed. In particular, in Matrix 5 *action A* is riskless, while *action C* is much riskier (it has higher variance) than in Matrix 4".

Thus, our expectation is that if participants are risk averse, as they usually are in the domain of gains (Tversky & Kahneman, 1985), more people should prefer A in Matrix 5 as compared with Matrix 4".

Table 14.2.
Results of the three conditions of Experiment 2.

	Matrix 4'	Matrix 4"	Matrix 5
A	6	2	10
B	9	8	5
C	13	18	13

Matrix 5

		the other		
		A	B	C
	A	4	4	4
you	B	0	8	1
	C	1	12	3

The third condition of Experiment 2 was conducted with the same population of the previous conditions, and with similar procedures: This time, our participants were facing Matrix 5. Table 14.2 allows us to compare the results obtained presenting Matrix 4" and Matrix 5. In accordance with our hypothesis, the data show a significant shift in preferences in favor of A, according to the hypothesized risk aversion.

EXPERIMENT 3: DEFOCUSING IN GAMES

Following a preliminary pilot study devised by Devetag and Shafir (1997), we presented to 40 participants (Italian psychology students) the following game matrix. Participants were paid according to their choice.

A group of 20 participants received only the matrix form plus the usual explanatory information. The second group of 20 participants had the same information, plus an explicit invitation to consider before choosing what would be the most likely action to be taken by the other player.

Matrix 6:

		the other	
		X	Y
you	X	60,20	60,10
	Y	80,20	10,10

Matrix 6 presents another example of contrast between the "rational" action and the naive expected utility procedure. The "you" player should rationally choose Y, as the other is forced by dominance to choose X. However, "you" might be tempted to play X if you do not take in consideration the payoffs of the other. This makes salient the defocusing instruction.

Table 14.3.
Results of the two conditions of Experiment 3.

Action	No Defocusing Instructions	Defocusing Instructions
X	14	4
Y	6	16

Table 14.3 summarizes the results of Experiment 3. The defocusing device reverses once more participants' choices. It suggests that the inability to "see" the other players' motivations is, to use a classic distinction, a matter of performance rather than competence. When the procedure for constructing an appropriate mental model of the game is explicitly suggested to participants, they show the competence necessary for building such a model. At least in simple cases, straightforward "debiasing" procedures can thus help participants to take a less autistic view of the game. This corresponds to what was previously observed in the experimental research on focusing in individual decision making tasks (Legrenzi & Girotto, 1996).

In light of such a result, one might be tempted to consider that players' tendency to assume an egocentric perspective is only a laboratory construct, due to the participants' inexperience with objects like game matrices. The theory of mental models provides a different answer. It stresses that we can build a complete model, but our basic representation procedures tend to leave implicit information which is hidden by the way in which we have started building a model of the task (Johnson-Laird, 1983). When we start exploring a branch of a tree we don't see the other branches and we miss diagnostic information (Legrenzi et al., 1993). Similarly, if we start considering our actions we do not incorporate in our model of the game the other's people motivations.

The interesting question thus becomes: What cues of the game environment may help participants to think strategically? At this stage of our research, we can only suggest some possible factors affecting defocusing in games. We are currently exploring two research questions.

On the one hand, it appears that the content of the payoff cells in a matrix can affect the extent to which people tend to be "strategic," although sometimes in an incomplete way. For example, when there are strong elements of symmetry in the payoff cells, participants tend to incorporate the other's payoffs into their reasoning. An instance of such a process can be found also in our experiment with Matrix 4', where many participants are attracted by strategy B because of the salience of the central 8,8 payoff cell. Sometimes, this can generate peculiar types of interaction fallacies, like magical thinking (Shafir & Tversky, 1992). On the other hand, we also expect that representing a game in a tree (extensive) form may help in defocusing. At least, insofar as the temporal structure of the action, which is hidden in the matrix form, is made explicit in terms of a move sequence (Schotter, Weigelt, & Wilson, 1994; see Girotto & Legrenzi, 1989, for a similar result in a deductive reasoning task).

CONCLUSIONS

The results of our experiments seem to provide preliminary evidence supporting the hypothesis of focusing phenomena in game playing. We have shown that participants do not see even rather simple dominance relations, but instead tend to choose in ignorance of the other player's motivations. The tendency to do so seems to heavily depend on the format of the game representation. Representations that are considered as equivalent in game theory are not equivalent in participants' minds, and lead to significant differences in choice behavior. Finally, inducing participants to construct appropriate models of the game seems substantially to debias their decisions.

In conclusion, these exploratory results show it is possible to extend the mental model theory from the domain of individual reasoning and choice to that of interactive, strategic decision making. Moreover, they confirm that the mental model theory offers a unified account of focusing and defocusing strategies in naive game playing.

ACKNOWLEDGMENTS

We appreciate the useful comments from participants to the workshop on "Deductive reasoning and strategies," Brussels, March 1998. Jonathan Evans read a first version of the manuscript and provided insightful suggestions. Eldar Shafir was a relevant source of inspiration for our experiments. Marco Tecilla, Alessandro Narduzzo, and Alessandro Rossi provided invaluable help in preparing the experimental software and running the experiments. To all of them our warmest thanks. We were supported by grants from the CNR and the MURST.

REFERENCES

Camerer C. (1995). Individual decision making. In J. H. Kagel & A. E. Roth (Eds.), *Handbook of experimental economics* (pp. 598–704). Princeton, NJ: Princeton University Press.

Devetag, G., Legrenzi, P., & Warglien, M. (1998). *Focus strategies in reasoning about games*. Unpublished manuscript.

Devetag, G., & Shafir, E. (1997). *Experiments on naive game playing*. Unpublished manuscript, Princeton University Press.

Garnham, A., & Oakhill, J. (1994). *Thinking and reasoning*. Oxford: Blackwell.

Girotto, V., & Legrenzi, P. (1989). Mental representation and hypothetico-deductive reasoning: The case of the THOG problem. *Psychological Research, 51*, 129–135.

Girotto, V., Legrenzi, P., & Rizzo, A. (1991). Event controllability in counterfactual thinking. *Acta Psychologica, 78*, 111–136.

Legrenzi, P., & Girotto, V. (1996). Mental models in reasoning and decision making. In A. Garnham & J. Oakhill (Eds.), *Mental models in cognitive science* (pp. 95–118). Hove, UK: Psychology Press.

Legrenzi, P., Girotto, V., & Johnson-Laird, P. N. (1993). Focussing in reasoning and decision making. *Cognition, 49*, 37–66.

Johnson-Laird, P. N., & Byrne, R. (1991). *Deduction*. Hove, UK: Lawrence Erlbaum Associates.

Johnson-Laird, P. N., Legrenzi, P., & Girotto, (1998, August). *Mental models: A gentle guide for outsiders, Princeton*. Paper presented at the Conference on Mental Models in Games, Venice, Italy.

Johnson-Laird, P. N., Legrenzi, P., Girotto, V., Sonino, M., & Caverni, J.P. (in press). Naive probability: A model theory of extensional reasoning. *Psychological Review*.

Kreps, D. (1990). *Game theory and economic modelling*. New York: Oxford University Press.

Mandel, D. R., & Lehman, D. R. (1996). Counterfactual thinking and ascriptions of cause and preventability. *Journal of Personality and Social Psychology, 71*, 450–461.

Osborne, M. J., & Rubinstein, A. (1994). *A course in game theory*. Cambridge, MA: MIT Press.

Perner, J. (1991). *Understanding the representational mind*. Cambridge, MA: MIT Press/Bradford Books.

Schotter, A., Weigelt, K., & Wilson, C. (1994). A laboratory investigation of multiperson rationality and presentation effects. *Games and Economic Behavior, 6,* 445–468.

Shafir, E., & Tversky, A. (1992). Thinking through uncertainty: Nonconsequential reasoning and choice. *Cognitive Psychology, 24,* 449–474.

Stahl, D., & Wilson P. (1995). On players' models of other players: Theory and experimental evidence. *Games and Economic Behavior, 10,* 218–254.

Warglien, M., Devetag, M. G., & Legrenzi, P. (1998, August). *Mental models and naive game playing in strategic form games*. Paper presented to the Conference on Mental Models in Games, Venice, Italy.

15

Strategies and Tactics in Deductive Reasoning

Walter Schaeken
Gino De Vooght
André Vandierendonck
Géry d'Ydewalle

This book offers one of the first systematic attempts to discuss the role of strategies for deductive reasoning. After a review of the different proposals, we introduce an operational definition of strategies: A strategy is a set of explicit, systematic cognitive processes, which are used when solving a deduction problem in order to simplify the problem or to come as quickly/easily as possible to a conclusion. A strategy is composed of smaller steps, which we call tactics. These tactics are largely unconscious. With this definition, one can discuss much easier the different observations mentioned in the book. In the last part of the chapter, we discuss more extensively the relation between the mental model theory and strategies.

The title of the book is "Deductive reasoning and strategies." As you may have noticed, however, the term *deductive reasoning* is used very broadly. Theoretically, deductive reasoning has the following characteristics. It is goal-directed reasoning that begins with a definite starting point, that is, a set of premises. Furthermore, deductive inferences have conclusions that follow necessarily from the premises (based on the principles of logic). Consequently, a valid deduction yields a conclusion that must be true given that the premises are true. There are, of course, many other forms of reasoning, such as induction, reasoning by analogy, calculation, creation and so on. Nevertheless, deduction is a very important form of reasoning. It plays a crucial role in many aspects of our daily life and also in many psychological theories (e.g., about perception, text comprehension), or as Johnson-Laird and Byrne (1991) stated:

> A world without deduction would be a world without science, technology, laws, social conventions, and culture. And if you want to dispute this claim, we shall need to assess the validity of your arguments. (p. 5)

The chapters in the book correspond nicely to the main issues in the study of deduction, namely propositional reasoning (chaps. 3–7 and partly chap. 11), spatial reasoning (chaps. 8–10), and syllogistic reasoning (chaps. 11–12). In addition, chapters 1 and 2 present a theoretical analysis of deduction, related to the concept strategy. The book also presents two chapters, that are only loosely related to deduction: Chapter 13 deals with statistical inference, that is, reasoning about the probability of certain outcomes and chapter 14 discusses social reasoning, by offering a new analysis of behavior of participants in the prisoner's dilemma game. As these chapters convincingly show, however, techniques and ideas used in the study of deduction are indeed useful to understand the other kinds of reasoning. Moreover, these other kinds of reasoning are for a large part based on a deductive component.

Since 1970, the study of deductive reasoning has become more important. There was already some research on syllogistic reasoning in the early days of psychology (see Wilkins, 1928; Woodworth & Sells, 1935), but it was only after the pioneering work of Wason (1966; Wason & Johnson-Laird, 1972) that the study of deductive reasoning really flourished. After a while, three schools of study emerged. First, researchers, who follow closely the work of Wason and who can be called *bias* psychologists (e.g., Evans, 1989). Second, there are researchers that followed the footsteps of Piaget (see Beth & Piaget, 1966) and claimed that people were equipped with an internal logic (Braine & O'Brien, 1998; Rips, 1994). Third, there are researchers who claim that reasoning is based, not on syntactic derivations as the previous school proposes, but on manipulations of mental models, which represent situations (see Johnson-Laird, 1983; Johnson-Laird & Byrne, 1991; see also Polk & Newell, 1995). Between proponents of the latter two schools, there is considerable rivalry about the nature of the basic deductive machinery. Of course, the picture we presented here is an overgeneralization, and there are interesting theories that fall outside the scope of the three major schools (such as Oaksford & Chater, 1998).

STRATEGIES AND THEORIES OF DEDUCTIVE REASONING

Surprisingly, current theories of deductive reasoning have largely neglected the topic of strategies, unlike theories concerning other domains of reasoning. For example, in the field of problem solving and calculation, there has been much research and theorizing on strategies (see Newell & Simon, 1972; Siegler, Adolph, & Lemaire, 1996). One of the first and only times that proponents of the two main rival theories talked explicitly about strategies was while discussing *knight–knave puzzles*; that is, riddles in which there are *knights*, who always tell the truth, and *knaves*, who always lie. Rips (1989) proposed that reasoners rely on a single deterministic strategy (see also Rips, 1994) to solve such riddles. In reaction, Johnson-Laird and Byrne (1991; see also Byrne, Handley, & Johnson-Laird, 1995) claimed that reasoners used a variety of strategies.

What is the reason or what are the reasons for the neglect of strategies in the study of deductive reasoning? Roberts (chap. 2, this volume) offers a plausible explanation. Research of strategies is less glamorous than research concerned with other topics, especially with the deductive machinery. Roberts also points out two more practical problems: Individual differences research is hard to do well and there is no standard agreed nomenclature and taxonomy for methodology and phenomena. We believe that two other factors may also have contributed to the inattention. First, it seems obvious that there is some kind of deductive machinery that governs our solving of deduction problems. Furthermore, the solution for the problem of the nature of the deductive machinery appears to be easily found. In the past, philosophers thought it was formal logic, because formal logic gives us the correct answers to reasoning problems. Next, the solution was natural logic, a subset of (an adapted form of) formal logic, because reasoners have difficulties with certain types of problems, whereas other problems are easy to solve. And now, the solution lies apparently in the mental model approach, a semantic account of deduction. Empirical research has shown repeatedly, however, that the situation is much more complicated than originally thought. Although the mental model theory offers a plausible framework for deduction, there still are many important shortcomings/vaguenesses (see further). One of the complicating factors might be the existence of strategies.

It is the goal of this book to stimulate reasoning researchers to consider more carefully the role of strategies. In this chapter, we integrate the ideas presented in the book. Although it is impossible that all contributors will find their ideas in this chapter, nevertheless, our integration should cover much of their theorizing.

TOWARD AN OPERATIONAL DEFINITION

Let us begin with a question: What exactly is a strategy? Stanovich (1996) argued that, for science, it is not very important to produce an exact definition. He made the comparison with others disciplines, such as physics: Physicists don't know what gravity really is, what the underlying essence of it is. However, one has to develop an operational definition: One has to link a concept to observable events that can be measured. The different definitions of the concept *strategy* offered in this book are good examples of such operational definitions. Moreover, they resemble each other. Two aspects seem to be especially relevant and we outline these now.

The first aspect concerns the nature of strategies. Evans (chap. 1, this volume) uses the term strategy to refer to thought processes that are elaborated in time, systematic, goal directed, and under explicit conscious control. Furthermore, he assumes that strategic thinking is active and flexible. Johnson-Laird, Savary, and Bucciarelli (chap. 11, this volume) also make a distinction between an explicit–conscious part and an implicit, unconscious part. They claim that a strategy is the sequence of steps that an individual follows in solving, or attempting to solve, a problem. They refer to each step in a strategy as a tactic, whereby the mental processes underlying a tactic are seldom, if ever, available to consciousness. The overall strategy that reasoners use, however, is potentially available to introspection, and can be revealed by reasoners' verbal reports, especially if they have to think aloud as they tackle a problem. The same distinction can be found in chapter 3 by García Madruga, Moreno, Carriedo, and Gutiérrez. They make a distinction between implicit (language processing and linguistic) strategies and explicit (problem solving) strategies. In sum, it seems that we have to adhere to this important distinction between implicit and explicit processes. One can call, as Johnson-Laird et al. do, the explicit processes strategies and the implicit tactics, or one can, as Garcia Madruga et al. propose, add the adjective implicit or explicit before the term strategy. Whatever terms being preferred, one must acknowledge the important difference between the two kinds of processes. Ormerod (chap. 7, this volume) talks about strategies (which are used for exploration and constraining) and operators (which produce solution components). Although this distinction is not exactly the same as the one between strategies and tactics of Johnson-Laird et al., they are surely not incompatible.

The second aspect concerns the goal of a strategy. Garcia et al. argue that strategies can be considered as a set of actions aimed at satisfying a goal in the simplest, quickest, thus most economical way possible. Ormerod talks about mechanisms aimed at reducing the problem space. Remarkable about these two chapters is that they both link deductive reasoning with problem solving. Indeed, deductive reasoning can, for a large part, be rephrased in terms of problem solving: The representation and the manipulation of the premises is similar to the exploration and constraint of the problem space in problem solving. Other aspects of problem solving can easily be integrated in theories of deductive reasoning and vice versa (see Ormerod, chap. 7, this volume).

As a result of these thoughts, the following *operational definition* may be proposed: A strategy is a set of explicit, systematic cognitive processes, which are used when solving a deduction problem in order to simplify the problem or to come as quickly/easily as possible to a conclusion. A strategy is composed of smaller steps, which we call tactics. These tactics are largely unconscious.

EVIDENCE FOR THE EXISTENCE OF STRATEGIES

Now that we have an operational definition of strategies and tactics, we can take a closer look at strategies and tactics in deductive reasoning. Many chapters show that strategies and tactics are important. It is shown that both explicit strategical and implicit tactical processes have a profound influence on the outcome of the reasoning process, although the differences between strategical and tactical aspects is not always made. Johnson-Laird et al. offer a set of clearly explicit strategies that are used while solving sentential and syllogistic problems. García Madruga et al. offer examples of both explicit strategies and implicit tactics during propositional reasoning. Rauh (chap. 9, this volume) observed that at least two kinds of strategies govern the construction of initial/preferred mental models in spatial relational inference tasks: the equalizing of intervals when a relation and its inverse are used; and a strategy that conforms to the principles of regularization and linearization. With our definition of strategies and tactics, the observations of Rauh would be called tactics. Indeed, the processes seem to be implicit and, more important, common to most reasoners in his experiments. Rauh offers a plausible explanation for these tactics: They reduce the complexity of the representation of the mental model and the complexity of processes when there is new incoming information. Again, the link with the problem-solving literature can be made rather easily. Nevertheless, one may not ignore the findings presented in some of the chapters (see, e.g., Vandierendonck, De Vooght, Desimpelaere, & Dierckx, chap. 10, this volume) who didn't find evidence for strategical differences. Meaningful for such observations is the distinction between strategies and tactics. As García Madruga et al. (chap. 3, this volume) state, logical problems are most often linguistically formulated. Hence, language comprehension processes–tactics often have a large impact on the outcome, but are maybe not as easy to investigate or observe. Evans and also Johnson-Laird et al. argue for the use of thinking-aloud protocols to gather evidence for the existence of strategies. Hence, more care for such protocols is a prerequisite for more insight in the existence of strategies.

However, it is not enough to specify which strategies are used by the reasoners. As Lemaire and Siegler (1995) argue, there are four important dimensions. First, it is important to know which strategies are used. Second, one has to observe when each strategy is used, that is, one should know both the relative frequencies of each strategy and the types of problems on which the strategy is used, that is, what triggers a specific strategy. Third, it is useful to know how each strategy is executed. Developmental and individual differences can be very important with respect to this point. Fourth, one must know how strategies are chosen; that is, when one has multiple strategies for a certain problem, why one strategy is chosen over another. Johnson-Laird et al. stipulate another aspect that must be included in the study of strategies, which they call the "Holy Grail" for future research: the discovery of how logically-untrained individuals discover new strategies of reasoning. Roberts (chap. 2, this volume) describes two methods, that might help to unveil some of these dimensions. He argues that a developmental and cost–benefit analysis approach together can give an account not only of how new strategies are discovered, but also of how they are evaluated and chosen, and why individuals differ.

THE MENTAL MODEL THEORY, STRATEGIES, AND INDIVIDUAL DIFFERENCES

Striking is the observation that most contributors use the mental model theory as the framework in which they discuss their work. This is perhaps not so surprising, because most contributors (and the editors) favored the mental model theory. Anyhow, it is shown again how well this theory can explain observations made within different areas, not only in the purely deductive areas (propositional, spatial, and syllogistic reasoning), but also in related sorts of reasoning (such as statistical and social reasoning). Furthermore, the link between deductive reasoning on the one hand and problem solving on the other hand, which is made in two chapters, can be interpreted as further evidence for the mental model theory: Indeed, the construction and manipulation of mental models can be assimilated in theories of problem solving. Nevertheless, the different chapters also sketch some important shortcomings of the current version of the mental model theory. We review these shortcomings and relate them to the influence of strategies and individual differences.

Johnson-Laird et al. (chap. 11, this volume) show that in the domain of syllogistic reasoning the predictions of the model theory with respect to the interpretation of the mood of the premises and the representation of negation are falsified by the construction of external models. Take for example the fact that people were not always constant in the interpretation of the mood of the premises. Sometimes, reasoners constructed a model of the premise "*Some of the A are not C*" in which some of the *A* were *C*, and they sometimes constructed a model in which none of the *A* were *C*. Are these variations only chance-fluctuations or is there some kind of tactical process which leads to these different interpretations in different problems? Such questions are important for the further development of the model theory and for the study of deduction in general.

Byrne, Espino, and Santamaria (chap. 5, this volume) and Manktelow, Fairley, Kilpatrick, and Over (chap. 6, this volume) show that content has an important influence on the outcome of the reasoning process. Manktelow et al. argue that until now the model theory underestimated the role of pragmatics in practical reasoning. We agree with them that the mental model theory fails to give a principled account of the critical interpretative component involved in reasoning (see also Fillenbaum, 1993). Rule theories have clearly the same deficit.

Another neglected aspect is the role of individual differences. Dekeyser, Schroyens, Schaeken, Spittaels, and d'Ydewalle (chap. 4, this volume) show that psychological semantic informativeness is an important modulating factor in people's premise ordering behavior. Although there is a general tendency to start reasoning with the semantically most informative premise, there are also large individual differences. A large subset of participants selected the first premise as a function of its larger informativeness, where others select it as a function of its smaller informativeness. Handley, Dennis, Evans, and Capon (chap. 12, this volume) present strong evidence for individual differences in the search of counterexamples in syllogistic reasoning. Indeed, the tendency to search for alternative models varies across individuals.

Byrne et al. (chap. 5, this volume) show that people can benefit from counterexamples when they are given to them, and that the influence of counterexamples on the frequency of inferences that people make is profound. Hence, reasoners can represent and use counterexamples. However, both Evans and Ormerod suggest that a search for such counterexamples is not automatic. It is only one of the different strategies that reasoners can apply. Moreover, they both argue that it is only in very special circumstances (e.g., when absolute certainty is required) that the strategy of searching for counterexamples is invoked. This claim leads to an important reformulation of the original mental model theory, which we adhere. Indeed, although reasoners are in principle capable of searching for counterexamples (at least, within the boundaries set by the capacity of their working memory), in practice they are often satisfied with a plausible model of the situation.

The search for individual differences in reasoning is often successful, as chapters 4 and 12 by Dekeyser et al. and Handley et al. show. However, sometimes one cannot find such differences. Rauh (chap. 9, this volume) analyzed the preferred models reasoners build on the basis of spatial relational problems. He did not find any consistent patterns: No homogeneous subgroup of reasoners came up; all reasoners deviated from the mean to some degree. This lack of systematic individual differences is, nonetheless, a finding that has important implications for theory formation. Indeed, such uniformity in preference for certain initial models seems to reveal some universal tactical processes, which are applied when reasoners are confronted with the specific set of spatial problems.

This leads us to a last point. Roberts (chap. 2, this volume) claims correctly that individual differences have been neglected for a long time in the study of deductive reasoning, although the existence of these differences has crucial implications on theorizing in the domain. It is therefore promising that in the current book one chapter theorizes about the existence of individual differences (and the theoretical chapter of Evans also contains a discussion of individual differences) and that in at least three chapters there is an empirical search for the existence of these differences. Hence, in more than one third of the chapters (including this one) there is attention for this aspect. It is also interesting to note that Johnson-Laird et al. (chap. 11, this volume) discuss some of the points made by Ford (1995), who claims that when solving syllogisms, some reasoners use formal rules, whereas others use Euler circles. Johnson-Laird et al. argue that part of the verbal substitution strategy (Ford proposes a set of formal rules governing these substitutions) is perfectly explainable in terms of the model theory. Moreover, they also contest Ford's claim that because some of her participants drew Euler circles, it follows that these individuals were not using mental models.

So far, we have especially emphasized strategical and tactical differences between individuals. However, a complete account of human reasoning must also be able to explain strategical and tactical differences within an individual. Indeed, we must be capable of explaining why a certain individual sometimes uses these strategies or tactics, whereas in other circumstances the same reasoner uses other strategies or tactics. Systematic analyses of (possibly very small) differences between different tasks, together with an analysis of the potentials and capacities of the individual, might reveal solutions for this problem.

Robert's (chap. 2, this volume) definition of a strategy has some further implications. He calls a strategy a set of cognitive processes, which have been shown to be used for solving certain types of deductive reasoning tasks, but for which there is not sufficient evidence to assert that these processes themselves constitute all or part of the fundamental reasoning mechanism. According to our operational definition of strategies and tactics, the use of a strategy does not have to imply that the task was not solved by the fundamental reasoning mechanism. For example, Johnson-Laird et al. argue that the four strategies they discovered in propositional reasoning are all compatible with the use of models at the tactical level. Such exercises show clearly the possible strength of a theory. Nevertheless, such exercises are only possible if one considers the answers of reasoners in terms of tactics and strategies and if one takes into account the possibility of individual differences. This seems to us the most important outcome of this book and of the workshop from which the idea for this book arose.

ACKNOWLEDGMENTS

Walter Schaeken and Gino De Vooght are supported by the FWO-Flanders. André Vandierendonck and Géry d'Ydewalle are supported by the IUAP/PAI P4/19.

REFERENCES

Beth, E. W., & Piaget, J. (1966). *Mathematical epistemology and psychology.* Dordrecht, NL: Reidel.

Braine, M. D. S., & O'Brien, D. P. (Eds). (1998). *Mental logic.* Mahwah, NJ: Lawrence Erlbaum Associates.

Byrne, R. M. J., Handley, S. J., & Johnson-Laird, P. N. (1995). Reasoning with suppositions. *Quarterly Journal of Experimental Psychology, 48A,* 915–944.

Evans, J. St. B. T. (1989). *Bias in human reasoning: Causes and consequences.* Hove, UK: Lawrence Erlbaum Associates.

Fillenbaum, S. (1993). Deductive reasoning: What are taken to be the premises and how are they interpreted? *Behavioral and Brain Sciences, 16,* 348–349.

Ford, M. (1995). Two modes of mental representation and problem solution in syllogistic reasoning. *Cognition, 54,* 1–71.

Johnson-Laird, P. N. (1983). *Mental models: Towards a cognitive science of language, inference and consciousness.* New York: Cambridge University Press.

Johnson-Laird, P. N., & Byrne, R. M. J. (1990). Meta-logical problems: Knights, knaves, and Rips. *Cognition, 36,* 69–81.

Johnson-Laird, P. N., & Byrne, R. M. J. (1991). *Deduction.* Hillsdale, NJ: Lawrence Erlbaum Associates.

Lemaire, P., & Siegler, R. S. (1995). Four aspects of strategic change: Contributions to children's learning of multiplication. *Journal of Experimental Psychology, General, 124,* 83–97.

Newell, A., & Simon, H. A (1972). *Human problem solving.* Englewood Cliffs, NJ: Prentice-Hall.

Oaksford, M., & Chater, N. (1998). *Rationality in an uncertain world.* Hove, UK:

Psychology Press.

Polk, T. A., & Newell, A. (1995). Deduction as verbal reasoning. *Psychological Review, 102,* 533–566.

Rips, L. J. (1989). The psychology of knights and knaves. *Cognition, 31,* 85–116.

Rips, L. J. (1994). *The psychology of proof.* Cambridge, MA: MIT Press.

Siegler, R. S., Adolph, K. E., & Lemaire, P. (1996). Strategy choices across the life-span. In L. M. Reder (Ed.), *Implicit memory and metacognition* (pp. 79–121). Mahwah, NJ: Lawrence Erlbaum Associates.

Stanovich, K. E. (1996). *How to think straight about psychology?* New York: Harper Collins.

Wason, P. C. (1966). Reasoning. In B. Foss (Ed.), *New horizons in psychology* (pp. 106–137). Harmondsworth, UK: Penguin.

Wason, P. C., & Johnson-Laird, P. N. (1972). *The psychology of reasoning: Structure and content.* Cambridge, MA: Harvard University Press.

Wilkins, M. C. (1928). The effect of changed material on the ability to do formal syllogistic reasoning. *Archives of Psychology, 16,* No. 102.

Woodworth, R. S., & Sells, S. B. (1935). An atmosphere effect in syllogistic reasoning. *Journal of Experimental Psychology, 18,* 451–460.

AUTHOR INDEX

SUBJECT INDEX

A

Acquisition, 19, 45, 63, 169, 172
Affirmation of the consequent, 30, 100–104
Algorithms, 17, 74, 75, 77, 113, 130
Analogy, 148, 154, 173, 174, 301
Arguments, 3, 10, 11, 14, 23, 33, 34, 38, 49, 53, 55–58, 60, 61, 64, 65, 67–69, 84, 104, 108, 166, 241, 246, 264, 301
Artificial Intelligence, 75, 179
Atmosphere, 11, 20, 22, 27, 32, 36, 243, 265
Availability, 97, 102, 103, 105, 106, 127, 135

B

Bayes(ian), 267–269, 271, 274, 277, 278, 283
Biases, 4, 19, 21, 133, 134, 151, 178, 189, 243, 265, 284, 285
Biconditional, 53, 73, 83, 84, 87, 88, 91, 92, 98, 99–101, 107–109, 124, 127, 144, 212, 214, 216

C

Caution, 40, 141
Competence, 11, 12, 15, 17, 18, 21, 46, 48, 70, 73, 74, 227, 243, 297
Computational, 172, 183, 221, 222, 244, 251, 261,
Conditional, 5, 15, 49, 51–56, 59, 60, 63, 66, 67, 73, 75–78, 80, 83–85, 87, 88, 91, 92, 97–105, 107–109, 112–114, 116, 123, 125, 126, 131, 133–139, 143–146, 148
  and additional antecedents, 103–109
  and alternative antecedents, 102, 103–106, 109
  causal, 116, 122, 124–127, 144
  deontic, 116
  indicative, 126
  negated, 55, 56
  non-, 99, 101, 103–105, 109
  representation of, 54, 56
  reversed, 99, 101, 103, 105, 109
Conjunction, 49, 51–53, 55, 57, 58, 60, 61, 65–69, 73, 83–88, 91, 92, 94, 245, 275, 282
Conjunctive, 49, 50, 60, 61, 65, 66, 68, 69, 85, 216
Conscious, 1–3, 6, 8, 9, 11, 16–19, 24, 40, 49, 62, 63, 92, 97, 109, 252, 262, 303
Consciousness, 2, 4, 62, 189, 210, 239, 265, 304, 308
Construction task, 49, 57, 58, 60, 61
Content, 10, 24, 50, 58, 60, 67, 73, 80, 87, 106, 107, 109, 112, 113, 124, 131, 133, 136, 138, 141–151, 159, 162, 185, 188, 191, 204, 239, 240, 252, 268, 289, 297, 306
Context, 2, 24, 25, 106, 113, 116, 124, 133–135, 143, 146, 149, 155, 160, 162, 188, 241, 247
Counterexample, 12, 51, 62, 63, 74, 97–100, 102, 103, 105–110,